Digital Transactions in Asia

This book presents a comprehensive overview of transactional forms of the digital across Asia by studying the platforms and infrastructures that shape the digital experience. It provides a definitive account of the core features of the ways the digital economy in Asia is transforming everyday lives.

Transactional relations between digital media platforms and new forms of sociability are remediating social relationships for the digital age. In capturing the digital revolution through case studies from across the larger Asian region, the book offers a richly contextualised and comparative account that firmly situates the frontiers of the digital within the Asian experience.

The book will be a key reference point for scholars and students of Asian studies and media studies, and of particular value to the range of interdisciplinary courses now emerging on digital and social change with an international focus. The increasing internationalisation of debates on the digital will also make this book essential reading for researchers and students more widely in mass communications, development studies, business studies, sociology and economics.

Adrian Athique is an Associate Professor in cultural studies in the Institute for Advanced Studies in the Humanities, University of Queensland.

Emma Baulch is an Associate Professor of communication and media studies at Monash University Malaysia.

Routledge Research in Digital Media and Culture in Asia
Edited by Dal Yong Jin, Simon Fraser University

Chinese Social Media
Social, Cultural, and Political Implications
Edited by Mike Kent, Katie Ellis, and Jian Xu

Digital Media and Risk Culture in China's Financial Markets
Zhifei Mao

Mediatized Religion in Asia
Studies on Digital Media and Religion
Edited by Kerstin Radde-Antweiler and Xenia Zeiler

Digital Transactions in Asia
Economic, Informational, and Social Exchanges
Edited by Adrian Athique and Emma Baulch

Digital Transactions in Asia

Economic, Informational, and Social Exchanges

Edited by Adrian Athique and Emma Baulch

Routledge
Taylor & Francis Group
NEW YORK AND LONDON

First published 2019
by Routledge
52 Vanderbilt Avenue, New York, NY 10017

and by Routledge
2 Park Square, Milton Park, Abingdon, Oxon OX14 4RN

First issued in paperback 2020

Routledge is an imprint of the Taylor & Francis Group, an informa business

Library of Congress Cataloging-in-Publication Data
Names: Athique, Adrian, editor. | Baulch, Emma, 1968– editor.
Title: Digital transactions in Asia : economic, informational, and social exchanges / edited by Adrian Athique and Emma Baulch.
Description: New York, NY: Routledge, 2019. |
Series: Routledge research in digital media and culture in Asia |
Includes bibliographical references and index.
Identifiers: LCCN 2018058036 (print) |
LCCN 2018059936 (ebook)
Subjects: LCSH: Information society—Asia. | Digital media—Economic aspects—Asia. | Digital media—Social aspects—Asia. | Information technology—Economic aspects—Asia. | Information technology—Social aspects—Asia.
Classification: LCC HN655.2.I56 (ebook) |
LCC HN655.2.I56 D545 2019 (print) | DDC 302.23/1095—dc23
LC record available at https://lccn.loc.gov/2018058036

ISBN 13: 978-0-367-67161-7 (pbk)
ISBN 13: 978-1-138-35396-1 (hbk)

Typeset in Sabon
by codeMantra

Contents

Acknowledgements

This first collection on Digital Transactions in Asia emerges from a substantial collective effort, involving all our contributors here, along with many others who deserve acknowledgement for their support. Terry Flew, Jean Burgess and Mandy Thomas provided us with fantastic support for our first Digital Transactions event in Brisbane in August 2017. We would also like to thank our keynote and invited speakers at that event: Gerard Goggin, Yu Hong, Michael Keane, John Postill, Vibodh Parthasarathi, Cheryll Ruth R. Soriano and Ravi Sundaram. Thanks are also due to Shishir Jha and Vibodh, once again, for their academic insight, empirical expertise and logistical support for *Social Transactions in Digital India* held at IIT Bombay in December 2017. For our second Digital Transactions in Asia event at De La Salle Manila, which is taking place as this book goes to press, we would like to thank Professor Merlin Teodosia Suarez, Professor Raymond Tan, Professor Caridad Tarroja and Professor Jazmin Llana for institutional and intellectual contributions of great value. We would like to thank our keynote speakers in Manila: Rich Ling, Raul Pertierra and Jack Qiu. Across all three events so far, we would like to recognise the generosity and sheer effort of our organising teams, including Terry Flew, Shishir Jha, Luzhuo Nina Li, Sun Sun Lim, Jozon A. Lorenzana, Vibodh Parthasarathi and Cheryll Ruth R. Soriano. We would also like to thank Peter Harrison, Narelle Jones and Masako Suzoki at the University of Queensland for making a series of complex transactions in support of our collective efforts. Without the enthusiasm, academic expertise and collaborative spirit of all these people, initiatives like this don't happen. In terms of institutional support, we will remain very grateful to the Institute for Advanced Studies in the Humanities at the University of Queensland, the Digital Media Research Centre at Queensland University of Technology, the Shailash J. Mehta School of Management at IIT Bombay and the Social Development Research Centre and Department of Communication at De La Salle University.

1 Digital Transactions in Asia

Adrian Athique

Asia in the Digital Age

The number of internet users in Asia is now equivalent to those in the rest of the world combined (at two billion) (Internet World Stats 2017). Given their effective convergence over the past decade, the same dynamic carries over into the mobile domain, with phone subscribers in Asia marking more than half of the global total of 4.8 billion. There is more to come– just under half of the population of China, two thirds of India and a third of Indonesia and the Philippines are yet to come online (ITU 2018). Given that that uptake continues to increase and the majority of the global population lives in the Asian region, it is clear that we have passed the tipping point towards a digital system where Asia will be predominant. From where we are now, we can already discern some of the substantive changes that digital technologies have brought to the political, economic and social domains within, and between, the Asian states. In the global context, both the connections and disconnections of Digital Asia serve to demonstrate that the old binaries of the West-and-rest digital divide are being superseded by the dynamics of the region itself. Large-scale investments in digital infrastructure from North to South are reshaping the economic and social geography of Asia. After many decades of developing manufacturing chains and operating labour markets within the global digital economy, we now stand at a juncture where the regional potentials of these technologies have become paramount.

Critical mass in the scale of Digital Asia should not obscure the diversity, disparity and disjunctures across this vast region. User numbers alone do not explicate the deeper meanings that situate everyday usage and experience of the digital in and across Asian cultures. South Korea is an epicentre of the global digital economy, while North Korea is one of the few truly black spots in terms of both digital culture and infrastructure. Even as Singapore establishes its position as a warehouse and financial hub for the cloud economy, the digital infrastructure in Afghanistan is primarily a matrix for murder. India's digital agenda gives its primary emphasis to the infrastructure of e-governance and shortfalls in domestic capacity, even as China's vision of rejuvenation deploys its national champions as the logistical arm of an international trading empire. Thus, the geopolitics of information in a Digital Asia becomes apparent in many different ways (Aouragh and Chakravartty 2016). These differences are hardly surprising, given the spectrum of political regimes in Asia ranges from an iconic Stalinist regime to the world's largest democracy, with all the possible permutations in between. The disparate political configurations of the region find correspondence in the economic domain, which ranges from resolutely autarchic economies to the free trade hubs flourishing in historic port cities like Singapore and Hong Kong. Beyond their ideological differences, the economies of Asia also traverse a range of means from the world's richest economies to the very poorest.

Given that the digital revolution in Asia has emerged from very different development agendas played out in a variety of settings and circumstances, we can hardly be surprised that the mantra of 'ICT for Development' has produced multiple understandings and outcomes. In Japan and Malaysia, long-standing official programmes of digitization have always been closely tied to the economic domain and to a corporatist vision (Anchordoguy 2015). In China, the development of digital infrastructure has assumed the conformity of economic interests with cultural and political sovereignty (Hong 2017). In India, grandiose plans for infrastructure at the centre are diffused through uneven and unruly regional markets (Thomas 2019, forthcoming). In the Philippines, Thailand and Cambodia, digital technologies have been dispersed almost entirely through market forces and laissez-faire. Trading strategies also differ. Korea and China are the major players in the manufacturing domain, while India and the Philippines specialize in the provision of digital labour (Noronha and D'Cruz 2019, forthcoming). The economic and geopolitical value of these relationships has inflected the evolution of their respective digital domains. One useful example is the wide variety of relationships expressed in the ubiquity of the Facebook Basics programme in Vietnam and the Philippines (where this is effectively the Internet for most users), its visible absence in China and the paternalistic rejection of this rendering of Facebook 'for the poor' by India under the ambit of net neutrality clauses. It is abundantly clear that some parts of Asia are better placed to establish their own rules in the digital domain than others.

In everyday life, the capacity of individual citizens to gain digital access, to exercise digital rights and to influence the digital agenda is highly uneven. This is true within states as much as between them, and for wealthy states as well as for the poorer ones (see, for example, Dutta 2017; Lee and Chan 2018; Soriano 2012; Tapsell 2015). As such, we remain keenly aware of the black holes in Asia's digital fabric, and of the many challenges to equity, access, freedom and the areas of material and environmental want that will remain in play during Asia's digital age. Nonetheless, we also recognize that the coterminous expansion of mobile internet and economies in Asia as a consequence of cheap (largely digital) money has expanded public spheres and public participation in profound ways. Indeed, digital technologies have arguably played a key role in every substantial political movement and development from Indonesia's *reformasi* in 1998 to the virality of memes and massacres in contemporary Myanmar (Ibrahim 2018; Manning and Van Diemen 2000; Postill 2018). Since remediation is inherently a social process, the advent of digital cultures and societies in Asia inevitably constitutes a set of cultural as much as political transformations (see Lim and Soriano 2016). The cultural domain is of central importance, given that the diversity of languages, environments, philosophies and aesthetic traditions remains a defining feature of Asia. The popularity of supposedly universal internet platforms, and even the advent of Asian national champions such as WeChat, remains subject to significant cultural barriers beyond the logistical challenges of spanning geography and connecting populations that are variously dense and dispersed. Thus, in order to understand the sociotechnical interface that is shaping Asia's digital age, our focus in this volume encompasses the social, economic and informational processes that are determining the nature of digital transactions in Asia.

The Age of Transactions

Taken in the narrow definition of finance capital, the topic of digital transactions leads us to think of the trillion dollars reputedly moving outwards into the world from Hong Kong in 2016. Alternatively, we might think of the unprecedented interventions of the Indian government in trying to impose a cashless society through demonetization in that very same year (see Reddy 2017). Equally, we might also think of the conjoined economic and political transactions through which a number of Asia's political leaders became enveloped in the global financial flows and disclosures of the panama papers and the 1MDB affair (Case 2017). The intense mobility of digital money and the increasing interconnectivity of the region powerfully underline the importance of understanding the transformative effect of digital money exchanges. It is our contention, however, that we also need to think of informational exchanges and social interaction as taking on a transactional form in a much broader sense. Each and every encounter mediated by the digital carries with it a functional exchange, certainly, yet at the same time, each transaction implies certain 'relations of participation' that remediate social relationships for the digital age (Athique 2013). Thus, we can productively think of the practice of e-governance, for example, as recasting the everyday transactions between citizens and state. Equally, the emergence of political debates in digital forums evidences the transactional processes of the public sphere. When we consider the contours of popular culture and the conduct of interpersonal relationships, we begin to discern numerous ways in which digital platforms are enabling, commodifying and monetizing new forms of sociability.

In this larger sense, then, the unprecedented field of digitization in Asia today expresses the force of social change through a vast series of digital transactions. Both the technical and human capabilities underpinning this phenomenon have emerged through a series of developments around the potentials of the Internet that have evolved over three decades in both a material and a conceptual sense. In the early years of the World Wide Web, when bandwidth remained low and the medium was largely text-based, the Internet was commonly understood as an apparatus of communication. Heady predictions of a 'second media age' in academic papers did not substantially depart from this proposition of the Internet as telecommunication in its essence (Poster 1995). The sunrise players were Internet service providers and the main focus of debate was extending the 'information superhighway', in the American parlance. This was the era of Malaysia's Multimedia Super Corridor, inaugurated by Dr Mahathir Mohamed in 1996, and centred upon the hub of Cyber Jaya in Selangor state (Bunnell 2006). The centrality of dense communication capacity and Special Economic Zones to Malaysia's Development 2020 vision was paradigmatic of the 'ICT for Development' agenda championed through the UN and other global bodies (see Kaur et al. 2017). The premise was a technological leap whereby developing countries would make the shift from economies based upon the extraction of resources to economies based upon services, logistics and innovation, which would be fostered through Information Technology Enabled Services, or ITES, as they were classified in the Indian rendition (D'Costa and Sridharan 2004; Upadhya and Vasavi 2008).

By the end of the millennium, it was the role of the Internet as an apparatus of distribution that came to the fore. Expanding infrastructure, more efficient devices and compressed audiovisual formats enabled faster data transfers that saw the Internet become the major conduit for the circulation of intangible goods. The open architecture of the system, and its global ambit, thereby overturned existing market norms, positions and regulatory structures. In the USA, the ensuing battle over widespread filesharing and piracy pitched greedy libertarian consumers against the hegemonic cultural industries, culminating in the landmark Digital Millennium Copyright Act (Lessig 2004). Heated debates over digital goods in global trade forums saw much of Asia being characterized as a pirate zone, where the widespread usage of unlicensed software was playing a key role in economic modernization and the primary means by which Asian populations accessed digital content (Sundaram 2011). Conversely, the free flow of foreign media content via the World Wide Web provoked the People's Republic of China to inaugurate its 'Great Firewall' project in 1998 followed in 2003 by the 'Golden Shield' project (Zhang and Zheng 2009). Both of these programmes reflected the pursuit of a 'Chinese Information System' as a national and sovereign Internet. Nonetheless, the expanding flow of media content had a transformative effect upon popular culture across the region, not only from 'Western' material but also from Asian content producers such as South Korea (Yong Jin and Kwak 2018). The advent of the smartphone era, where Korea's Samsung played a key role in providing affordable hardware, extended the distributive capacity of the Internet down to the individual scale and, critically, beyond metropolitan districts (Goggin 2011).

Even as the dust was settling on the copyright wars, the next phase of Internet functionality was coming to the fore, with Internet 'Web 2.0' reconfigured as an apparatus of extraction. Over the past ten years, a range of Internet 'platforms' have enrolled billions of subscribers for the purposes of concentrating advertising revenues, aggregating data and creating virtual markets (Srnicek 2017). This was also the 'crash decade' following the global financial crisis of 2007–2008 in the West, one consequence of which was the creation of vast sums of purely digital money flowing through financial systems into developing economies. In the Asian case, the impact of outflows from the West was amplified by corresponding stimulus actions in China (Overholt 2010; Wong 2011). The exuberant growth arising from this cheap money made Asia the engine of economic growth in the global economy, giving rise to the notion of an 'Asian century' (as in Connors et al. 2017). In parallel, the vast accumulation of investment capital by 'technology' companies able to operate 'lean' businesses via the Internet allowed a handful of high traffic web portals to capture the vast bulk of the world's advertising revenues. This wealth allowed US companies to underwrite a large-scale expansion into rapidly growing Asian markets. It also encouraged technology companies to adopt strategic logics more akin to financial entities than device manufacturers or media retailers. In Asia, this trend is most evidently emulated in entities such as Japan's Softbank and China's Alibaba and Tencent. More fundamentally, the simultaneous monetization of data and datafication of money has encouraged the concentration of data and its propagation as a productive, and even magical, resource (see Appadurai 2013).

Platform as Transactional Systems

In each phase of the World Wide Web, it has been the commercial potentials of the system that have been paramount to the extension of the system, with each additional layer of functionality adding purposefully to the impetus towards commodification. Investments in Internet infrastructure have always been driven by the impulse to extract value in the form of profits and/or productivity gains. In the communication layer, value is extracted through the sale of hardware, software subscriptions, data packs and other forms of access rents. In the distribution layer, value is extracted through content subscriptions, pay-per-view offerings, user-generated content and the bulk of the world's advertising revenues. In the transactional layer, value is extracted from various forms of piece work, usertracking, data mining and the aggregation of commissions exercised over peer-to-peer exchanges. Each of these layers contributes to an integrated commodity form that subsumes production and consumption, along with the market economy and the social domain (Athique 2018). The sites of extraction continue to include material resources, such as rare earths, manufacturing plant and labour firmly located in the Asian region. Increasingly, however, investments have been directed towards 'high value' propositions fostered by the synchronization and automation of transactions via digital systems. As such, the affordances of the Internet – as a medium of record, as a medium of distribution and as a medium of transactions – have all been progressively developed towards the present nexus of micro-payments, data mining and peer-to-peer market platforms.

Consequently, any discussion of digital transactions in the contemporary setting must account for the emergence of 'platform economies' as the prevailing paradigm for digital commerce. Nick Srnicek has characterized the emergence of platform economies through the new affordances of 'platform capitalism' that they bring to light (2017). With these affordances in mind, Srnicek offers a basic typology of contemporary platforms, through which he identifies:

> *Advertising platforms*...which extract information on users, undertake a labour of analysis, and then use the products of that process to sell ad space...*Cloud platforms*...which own the hardware and software of digital-dependent businesses and are renting them out...*Industrial platforms*...which build the hardware and software necessary to transform traditional manufacturing intointernet-connected processes...*Product platforms*...that generate revenue by using other platforms to turn a traditional good into a service and by collecting rent...*Lean platforms*...which attempt to reduce their ownership of assets to a minimum and to profit by reducing costs.
>
> (Srnicek: 49–50)

As an exemplar, we could readily apply this model to the Indian case, whereby Google and the online editions of *The Hindu* could both be categorized as 'advertising platforms', TataSky could be positioned as a 'cloud platform', Infosys becomes a provider of 'industrial platforms', e-commerce operations like Flipkart and digital film companies such as UFO Moviez would all be 'product platforms', whereas labour-outsourcing operations such as Ola (taxis) and OYO (hotels) could be lumped together as 'lean platforms'. This sorting seems neat enough, being a typology based upon 'what does the firm do?' Srincek's typology thereby attempts to account both for different sources of profits and for the different products and services platforms offer to their users. In practice, however, this neatness is arbitrary, since these various categories do not constitute any definite series (Anderson 1998: 29–45). Consequently, as Srnicek himself notes, various platforms either operate across or simply fall into multiple categories and, equally critically, there is evidence to suggest that the various platforms are functionally and, often, financially dependent upon each other. It makes sense, therefore, to concentrate our attention upon the 'core architecture' and the governance of 'interaction possibilities' within platform systems. In doing so, it becomes clear that platforms primarily seek to enclose and systematize a series of social exchanges. The programmatic and proprietary logics of these forms of capture suggest that, somewhat unlike earlier media industries, the institutional logic of a platform is not the organization of any productive process per se, but rather the design and population of an automated market system.

From this perspective, platforms can only be partially understood as 'firms', 'brands', 'portals' or 'shopfront' businesses. These elements are primarily indicative of the ownership, functionality and retail interface of platforms, which tend to differ in each case. Rather, the commonality between what Srnicek categorizes as platforms is their formalization of peer-to-peer exchanges within a rules-based system. Thus, their primary characteristics are those of a marketplace, not a firm. These market forms are distinctive because of their capacity to furnish zero-level entry barriers. As part of this bargain, platforms outsource transactional costs to market participants, enforce arbitrary access conditions and enclose buyers and sellers within a proprietary system (Cohen 2017). Thus, by my account, platforms operate primarily within the transactional layer. Whereas early proponents of information technologies promised the reduction of transaction costs, the advent of platforms has deliberately inverted this logic, precisely because platforms make their money on each transaction. Their primary goal is to enhance and widen the number, depth and range of transactions in play (regardless of the overall 'efficiency' of this proliferation within the wider economy). Thus, platforms reflect the converging ethos of FinTech and Web 2.0, which is to ensure that every peer-to-peer exchange generates a commission that can be captured. It would be too narrow, therefore, to explicate platforms as data collection companies operating in the guise of service providers. There is a much higher order of integration in play, where each platform purposefully synchronizes multiple inputs and products in simultaneous transaction.

The Infrastructural Turn

Approaching platforms as a set of transactional markets rather than as types of firms thereby encourages some different thinking on the platform economy. Not least, it prompts us to reconsider the 'stack' of infrastructure as being, simultaneously, a stack of markets and a stack of technologies (Bratton 2015). In order to achieve the 'great integration' of financial, social and logistical systems that allows platforms to capture value within the transactional layer, the foundational layers of the stack must be in place. Consequently, the push towards 'virtual' business models has been accompanied by an equally substantive 'turn' towards the infrastructural requirements of the communication and distribution layers (see Parks and Starosielski 2015). This is where the prerequisites for platform businesses most clearly align with long-standing state interests in the development of information infrastructures. This common investment in the infrastructure for a transactional economy has been reflected in a wide range of public-private partnerships forming a central component of national innovation initiatives, including 'Digital India', 'Digital Korea' and China's 'Internet Plus'. Whereas the rise of the platform giants in the USA was predicated upon prior public investments in Internet infrastructure, the Asian scenario has been characterized by the simultaneous development of all three layers. The magnitude of this task and the huge scale of these initiatives require private interests large enough to operate across the stack. Given the centrality of these systems to macroeconomic strategy, the few domestic companies possessing this capacity have developed an intimate relationship with the state in question and, for their part, the Asian states have been required to develop close working relationships with the dominant global technology companies.

At the technical level, the critical infrastructure of the platform economy includes financial systems, mobile infrastructure, GPS technologies, data centres, supercomputers, manufacturing plant and a host of algorithms for data mining, analysis and securitization. Needless to say, only a handful of Asian economies have the means and propensity to develop a full suite of infrastructure. China's sheer size, closed Internet, vast cash reserves and its political and military ambitions have provided the means and imperatives to do so. Japan's early lead in the information age and its central role in electronics manufacturing supply chains have also underpinned an infrastructural advantage, accompanied by its extensive investments in information infrastructure and Internet platforms across Asia (including China's Alibaba and India's Paytm). India, despite its vast population and world-class skills base, has suffered from the concentration of its IT infrastructure into a small number of enclaves serving an export-led market (Mascarenhas 2012). In many of the ASEAN states, the lack of a comparable resource base has seen local information architectures relying upon infrastructure provided by Amazon Web Services, Facebook and Google. We can clearly see regional differentiation in autonomy and capacity at the level of infrastructure. This topography emerges from a number of considerations including geography, politics, history and language as much as it does from market size and wealth.

The pathways taken towards an information economy also reflect a different set of aims in each case. The 'cyber corridor' programme in the Philippines, for example, is primarily intended to develop the infrastructure concentrations necessary to link local labour pools into global information processing and service markets. In this domain, the Philippines has emerged both in competition and in partnership with the Indian companies who have become synonymous with the digital services sector. At the same time, India's Tata is a major operator of the undersea cables that carry Internet at the global scale (Thomas 2018). By contrast, China's digital payment systems and its BeiDou satellite navigation system are integral components of its world spanning Belt and Road Initiative, and clearly intended to provide an alternative to the existing US-dominated global information architecture (Keane and Fung 2018). Japan and Korea continue to direct investments towards high-tech manufacturing infrastructure, robotics and ICT patents (Hirakawa and Takahashi 2018). Singapore is seeking to become the leading data storage hub in the region, thereby commensurate with its role as a port city and financial centre (Rossiter 2017). In each case, infrastructure investments build upon established strengths and specializations in Asia's economic geography. We should also be attentive to the fact that investments in material infrastructure often require comparable investments in human infrastructure. Thus, we have seen a further tilt towards technical education, where Malaysia's concerted efforts to become an education hub reflect the uneven and insufficient infrastructure in much of the region.

A similar picture can be seen throughout the distribution layer. Whereas US President Donald Trump has accused Amazon's Jeff Bezos of building a commercial empire subsidized by the US postal service, most of Asia beyond Japan and Singapore lacks a comparable opportunity. E-commerce in the region has been held back by slow and low-capacity postal systems, thereby requiring companies to invest in their own courier and delivery systems. India's vast size and its notoriously underdeveloped distribution architecture (plagued as it is by poor storage, overloaded trucks, congestion and bad roads), require online retailers to build their own infrastructure. The situation in Indonesia and the Philippines is comparable, exacerbated by maritime geography and the concentration of wealth in Java and Metro Manila. Making provision for deficiencies in the physical distribution layer requires deep pockets, and once again it has been the major global companies that have been willing to occupy this space. Given the shortfalls in material capacity, the distribution of intangibles (such as content, social media and services) has expanded much more rapidly, despite being impeded by wireless traffic overload in the metros and intermittent electricity in most rural locations. In this domain, we need to consider the set of legal and regulatory norms required to formalize the distribution of digital content and platformization of services across Asia. That is, the mechanisms by which K-Pop producers are remunerated for their regional popularity and by which Malaysia's Grab, Japan's Viber and China's iQiyi platforms operate in other Asian states (Keane and Wu 2018; Zhao 2018). It makes sense to position intellectual property regimes, licensing systems, rights legislation, consumer support and digital exchange regulations as critical components of the transactional infrastructure.

Intellectually, an infrastructural turn reunites Marshall McLuhan with Harold Innis, but it also highlights the considerable transaction costs inherent to a ubiquitous digital architecture (Innis 1951; McLuhan 1964). Profits in the transactional layer are invariably predicated upon costs being borne in the communication and distribution layers. An economy of integrated and simultaneous transactions requires substantive infrastructural investments and maintenance costs that are 'off the books' of most platform businesses. Data centres are already consuming a significant portion of Singapore's electricity supply, while internet subscriptions are a real cost to many disadvantaged people in the region. In the digital economy, manufacturing and labour costs have tended to be offset globally, and this has formed a major component of Trans-Pacific economic relationships. Within the region itself, platform businesses seeking to operate in the transactional layer also rely upon outsourcing infrastructure costs to others, but the capacity to bear these costs varies considerably amongst states and citizens. Network effects and cross-subsidization (variously across products, between public and private interests and from global players) have made the evolution of this system possible. At the present time, all of the key actors in these domains are becoming attentive to the vulnerability of global supply chains to disruptive effects emerging from geopolitical tensions and protracted economic crisis at the global scale. Against this backdrop, the first part of this volume situates Asia's digital transactions within an unfolding story of platforms, infrastructure and regulation. By doing so, we are able to productively explore the emerging contours of a transactional infrastructure in and across different parts of Asia.

Financial Transactions

In the second part of this volume, we redirect our attention from the structural and macroeconomic frameworks of digital transactions towards the everyday experience of digital transactions across multiple locations and platforms. In each instance, these case studies demonstrate the interlacing of social, economic and informational exchanges in each set of transactions. While money may appear as an integer or unit in processes of accounting, its value is always activated within a set of social exchanges (as per Simmel 1907 [1978]). Despite its everyday naturalization, money is an extraordinary complex commodity, given it is used to price everything else but also trades as a commodity in its own right (as per Keynes 1936). The tenfold increase in currency trading over the millennial decade was testimony to both the attractions and the dangers of this duality. The rapid digitization of money over the crash decade has similarly enormous ramifications. At the onset of the global financial crisis, global markets largely consisted of lightning speed transactions of purely electronic money with no readily redeemable value outside of the bourses themselves (Ford 2009; Stiglitz 2010). This trend has since accelerated, becoming both cause and remedy of that crisis of complexity and connectivity (Schiller 2014). The conjuration of trillions of dollars of electronic cash by formerly 'prudent' central banks has been dramatic enough to bring to light the arbitrary value of the cash commodity amongst the general public (Kaul 2015). Consequently, widespread uncertainty about the security of banks and the value of money over the past ten years has prompted the 'everything bubble' in all the other asset classes.

This dynamic has inflated property markets across Asia, with the effects spilling out into 'safe haven' markets beyond the region (such as Australia, Canada and New Zealand). In a novel fashion, electronic money creation diverted inflation elsewhere due to the simple fact that it couldn't be readily accessed or spent in a fashion that impacted upon the 'real economy'. On the basis of this lesson, a new order has been suggested: a cashless society that will operate solely through electronic payments (and, conveniently, where no money can effectively leave the banking system). Clearly, both the technology and financial sectors have much to gain from the abolition of physical currencies, since any such system will make them custodians and rules setters for the global economy. China has been one of the most extensive adopters of digital payment platforms, becoming a world leader in the span of a few years. India's sudden and arbitrary push towards a 'cashless society' in 2016 was an economic debacle, but the commitment to digital money remains central to the planning of the Reserve Bank of India. Thus, state interests are also evident, as China becomes keen to constrain outward money flows and shadow finance and India seeks to clamp down on tax evasion and bring its notoriously large informal economy within a mechanism of legibility. Already, it seems, the establishment of electronic payment systems has inculcated an expectation that every transaction produces a record. A cashless world, by contrast, will ensure that each transaction exists *only* as a record.

The obvious extension of this logic is the deployment of blockchain technologies to mine cryptocurrencies such as Bitcoin. Here the securitization of transaction records has become a form of currency in its own right. Paradoxically, the debasement of fiat currencies and the 'everything bubble' caused by virtual money creation has prompted huge enthusiasm for cryptocurrencies in Asia. This exuberance has produced a rapid series of bubbles and corrections, with regional dynamics driving wild swings in their perceived worth during 2017. After two lost decades of deflation, cryptocurrencies have proved popular in Japan, despite a series of large-scale virtual 'heists' in 2017 and 2018 that saw more than half a billion dollars of digital currencies stolen in hacking operations. Korea has been similarly enthusiastic as a retail market. Singapore's central bank issued a warning on the risks of cryptocurrencies in 2017 after a tenfold increase in demand. The National Internet Association of China moved to ban trading in cryptocurrencies entirely in September 2017, on the basis of their contribution to cash outflows, drug trafficking and perceived risks to the integrity of the financial system. China nonetheless continues to produce the majority of the world's cryptocurrencies through extensive mining operations that consume a significant portion of its subsidized electricity. The Reserve Bank of India also issued a ban on cryptocurrencies in April 2018, accompanied by a statement that it was in discussion with other central banks on the launch of its own sovereign digital currency.

Nervousness around the volatility and supranational oversight of cryptocurrencies has not diminished the enthusiasm for the digitization of national currencies. A switch to digital money promises to reduce the significant transaction costs that go with providing material currency, bank branches and ATMs. However, since those savings are likely to be captured in the form of commissions by digital money system providers, the real gains lie in the visibility of digital transactions. This legibility promises to reduce losses induced by corruption, incorporate the large informal economies of the region and make taxation more efficient and effectively costless. A cynic might note that only digital systems could have provided for the questionable transactions that brought down the Prime Ministers of both Malaysia and Pakistan in 2017–2018. What is more significant, however, is the signal change in the culture of money in a region where cash has been king for a long time. Both Japan and India feature amongst the world's foremost cash economies, with the latter also consistently being the world's greatest consumer of gold. Rapid shifts towards digital money thereby imply changes not only in the systemic nature of money, but also in its everyday usage, its social aspects and the mores and manners that structure the rituals and sites of exchange. Very little consideration has been given to these dimensions of money by FinTech enthusiasts and government technocrats, but it is reasonable to expect profound changes in the social compacts that govern value and the sociality of economic relations (see Kaul 2013). We must remain aware that money is a social object.

Social Transactions

In turning our attention towards the social dimensions of transactional economies, we have to account for the fact that this has indisputably been the decade of social media in Asia. Free use mobile platforms such as Facebook, Skype and Whatsapp have transformed interpersonal communication and the public sphere in most of Asia. China has, of course, developed its own comparable systems with WeChat, Weibo and QQ. There is no doubt that the rapid expansion of connectivity has brought substantial benefits to users, notably for the regions' many labour migrants and their families in, often, provincial settings (Madianou and Miller 2012). Nonetheless, through the popularity of these platforms, everyday interactions with family, friends and strangers have been intensely commodified through a complex of handsets, datapacks, datapoints, advertising and the intense personalization of consumption. At the very least, the social media ecologydemonstrates the profusion of implicit market exchanges across the social domain. The larger implication is that, within a platform economy, all communicative actions be regarded as social transactions. That is, the integration of various forms of user data into digital business models infers the simultaneous integration of platform logics within the nooks and corners of everyday speech and action. It is this orchestrated commercialization of sociability itself that constitutes the signal achievement: an expansive marketization that establishes a new tidemark for the commodification process. Thus, the present phenomenon of 'Instagram influencers' as a category of users seeking to strategize and monetize personal popularity for subsequent on-sale is indicative both of the final collapse of boundaries between personal and public communication and of the massification of identity performances as a symbolic commodity (Marwick 2015).

Users become aware of, and internalize this commodity form, as they seek to 'prosume' themselves across the discernable spectrum of personal opportunity (Kinports 2017). Across Asia, this phenomenon is manifested amidst a burgeoning economy of celebrity endorsements, of faith-based consumerism, and in self-branding of local artists and entrepreneurs (Abidin 2017). The competitive pursuit of personal publics is quantified in fine detail by a panoply of page views, click trails, followers, recommendations and likes, all of which have emerged as effective currencies of social capital in the digital domain. These currencies are clearly not money, but their accumulation can be effectively exchanged for income through various means, and is therefore strategically pursued as a means of livelihood. As a new form of work, social media production fits neatly into a regional labour market long characterized by piecework, mobility and precarity. It is also significant that this is a highly gendered domain where the monetization of self-performance is predominantly (although not exclusively) a female profession. More broadly, the uptake of mobile communication is providing a major expansion of in-the-home piecework in various forms, thereby enabling a dispersed variant of the digital labour through which hundreds of thousands of Asian workers undertake content moderation for Facebook and data analysis tasks for Google (Qiu 2017). A further prosaic echo, perhaps, is the piecework of virtual girlfriends catering to China's vast pool of unmarried and surplus males. Thus, while labour relations have always constituted both economic and social transactions, the nature and content of tasks in the digital economy are increasingly devolved from social interaction itself.

In the context of rapid growth, inflation and a large pool of precarious and surplus labour, the mobile phone has become an essential tool for discovering income opportunities and maintaining the survival networks that mitigate intermittent employment (Lorenzana 2017). Despite significant deficiencies in the distribution layer, Asia's platform economy has expanded precisely because labour is incredibly cheap. It is nearly always cheaper than any reliable form of automation. This fact alone undermines a central rationale for platform economies in the West. In Asia, the major opportunities for platforms lie not simply in outsourcing labour costs, but in capturing large sectors of economic activity that previously operated in the informal economy (see Athique and Parthasarathi 2019, forthcoming). Guest houses, street food, rickshaws, housemaids, drivers and guards – these were all previously cash-based sectors. Their aggregation within platforms thereby simultaneously formalizes these markets and brings them within the ambit of transactional records. In Bangalore, where domestic security guards are often Santhalis, personal recommendations fostered a labour network dominated by specific ethnic groups. With 'platformization', we have seen the emergence of online platforms, where you can browse CVs and select your Santhali. This also appears to be the case for 'non-economic' social transactions, especially those centred around romantic partnerships. Across Asia, the popularity of matrimonial and dating sites has formalized the reciprocities of sexual relationships as a platform economy (Parthasarathi 2018). Thus, in various ways, all these examples imply the dis-embedding of social economies and their re-embedding in new transactional forms.

The profusion of social transactions in the digital era requires us to think substantively beyond monetary systems and into the domain of economic sociology. Polanyi, in his seminal work, *The Great Transformation*, emphasized the historical novelty of the market society (1944). He argued that prior to the emergence of capitalism in the modern era, human societies were typically organized around distinctively 'non-market' principles. In particular, he noted exchange systems based upon reciprocity, where the gift of a good or service was undertaken with the understanding of an obligation in return from the receiver, whether in that moment or subsequently. He also noted extensive systems of redistribution, where surpluses were collected and then distributed by central authorities through systems of patronage. Polanyi regarded these systems as distinct from, and superseded by, the logics of the market. I will strike a point of difference here by contesting both the obsolescence and the periodization of these forms of exchange. Rather, I argue that the functioning of markets through money, which I characterize here as 'remuneration', is always dependent upon the simultaneous operation of reciprocity and redistribution in the economy as a whole. Conversely, the economics of the family unit are determined by reciprocity and redistribution, but they also entail the use of money. When it comes to surplus, wage labour markets are the most far-reaching and classic mode of redistribution, along with government patronage through subsidies, taxation and welfare. In the era of social media, social credit and virtual currencies, it is evident that reciprocity, redistribution and remuneration are inextricably enmeshed within an expansive series of social transactions.

Political Transactions

Taken within the larger interaction of the 'three Rs', it is also evident that a digital transfer of $681million from a Saudi prince comes laden with reciprocity. Other reciprocities that have perpetuated capital interests in Malaysia have operated in tandem with the redistributive politics that sustained UMNO (United Malays National Organisation) for half a century. Similarly, multiple reciprocities govern the relationship between Baidu and the Communist Party in China (and the relationships between Silicon Valley and US government for that matter). The heavy sunk costs necessary to underwrite digital transformation at this scale necessarily require the largest capital interests and an accommodating policy regime. Thus, in the present context of 'Digital India', the administration of Narendra Modi has become firmly enmeshed in the logistical procurement inherent to this vision, with the state itself becoming a transactional player in an era of 'public-private partnerships' (Thomas 2019, forthcoming). The common interests of state and capital in economic modernization are closely networked with their international counterparts, allowing them to broker expansion into overseas markets as well as transacting domestic market access and technology transfers. Needless to say, any transaction at this apex level is necessarily a political transaction, and this is true for China and Vietnam's socialist market economies, India and Malaysia's mixed economies and the 'free market' economies of Thailand and Singapore. The fact that companies such as Google negotiate directly with Asian governments is an indication not only of the importance of Asian markets, and of their market power, but also of the political reciprocities that operate in apex markets.

At the grassroots, the rapid expansion of social transactions inevitably carries over into the political domain. In the last Cambodian election, social media commentators alleged that Hun Sen's campaign had paid directly for the generation of Facebook likes to bolster his popularity and used the platform to intimidate his opponents. This can scarcely be verified, even if the purchase of 10,000 'genuine likes' for approximately $2,000 is a well-advertised service. The consequent revelations of the Cambridge Analytica scandal (where India's major political parties were on the customer roll) have focused Western public attention upon the orchestrated manipulation of democratic opinion via social media. Even before that, the strategic manipulation of social media as a political battlefield was clearly evident in the stand offs between red and yellow shirt movements in Thailand and Malaysia in 2013–2015 (Nyblade et al. 2015; Sinpeng 2014). In the day-to-day conduct of the political process, protagonists across Asia now compete for attention and bandwidth through interventions in digital forums. Political and social movements use social media platforms as their primary means to mobilize support. In response, government 'cybertroopers' in Malaysia have been deployed to monitor and talk down dissent (Hopkins 2014, Tapsell 2013). At the village level, Indian police have been similarly compelled to pursue virtual crowd control as memes on Whatsapp provoked lynchings of minorities and passing strangers (Sundaram 2017). An orchestrated campaign of incitement against Muslim minorities in Sri Lanka and Myanmar since 2015 has engendered large-scale bloodshed, staining the image of both countries and their closely linked Theravada Buddhist clergies (Wade 2017).

Much of this political turmoil has been an unintended consequence of the platformization of sociability, where the circulation of political 'clickbait' has been an explicit tendency in Asia as much as it has been elsewhere. The extension of media access and the channelling of publics into social media feeds have significantly displaced the political function of newspapers and broadcast television in the democratic process. Thus, in the Philippines, we have witnessed the eclipse of newspapers aligned with political dynasties reaching back to the Commonwealth period in favour of populist campaigns waged in Facebook feeds. This dynamic can be seen as central to the Rodrigo Duterte presidency and sustaining support for his anti-establishment and hard-line politics (Curato 2017; Miller 2018). What we have also witnessed is a breakdown in the compact between governments and their 'authorized' critics in universities, non-governmental organizations and religious institutions. Having constituted the voice of civil society for much of the postcolonial period, these entities are now contending not only with official repression, but also with an orchestrated campaign of intimidation via social media forums. Thus, in India, the actions of 'troll armies' in cyberspace signify not just the rise of populism but also the application of insidious and systematic political violence (Chaturvedi 2016). There is no doubt that the social media era has allowed for the democratization of social communication and for the unprecedented flow of events and ideas, but the era of red and yellow shirts has also been the era of the brown shirts. Thus, there is clearly a pressing need to reconfigure norms and mechanisms in the domain of human rights.

The era of digital transactions has equally significant geopolitical dimensions. The expansion of Chinese platforms across the region, along with the acquisition and facilitation of digital infrastructure in Asia and the Pacific, has raised security concerns in various countries across the region (including Australia, Papua New Guinea and India). In 2017, the feedback of user data from Chinese-made handsets to Beijing was a much publicized component of the wider tussle with the USA over the operations of Chinese manufacturer ZTE. It was never clearly explained why the transfer of user data to the Chinese government in this instance was more sinister than the transfer of the same by US manufacturers to Washington. Nonetheless, the more critical point is that digital infrastructure has been firmly positioned as a national security domain, by China as much as by her neighbours or rivals (although Japan's considerable and comparable regional investments in digital assets have yet to prove similarly contentious). At the present time, few other Asian states have the capacity to develop and deliver the infrastructure through which digital development goals can be realized. Thus, regional leaders like Rodrigo Duterte must walk a tightrope between the political and economic interests of both China and the USA. The commercial fortunes of South Korea have been similarly subjected to fluctuations in its relationships with China and Japan, even as the cultural transactions fostered by its music and fashion have played a prominent role in its evolving relationship with North Korea and the wider region. For all these reasons, Asia's age of digital transactions requires a political economy in the fullest sense of the term.

Transacting Asia

To talk merely of payment systems, securitization and transfer protocols will likely tell us as much about digital transactions as a discussion of inks and armoured vans would reveal about the social and cultural significance of money. It is evident that Asia is passing through a period of substantive social, economic and political change and that transactional systems operate at the centre of these processes. The pursuit of economic modernization by digital means is clearly both a functional and symbolic component of the competitive futurism that infuses development ambitions. At the same time, the density of connectivity, both within societies and between states, is increasing exponentially. The sheer complexity of this transactional system, technically and economically, creates interdependencies whereby the logics of competition become counterproductive. As such, there can be no doubt that this is a story of the region and one that cannot be captured within the narrative of any single state. The age of digital transactions thereby promises to bring the entire concept of Asia to light in new ways. As a tentative starting point, this volume attempts to situate a broad series of financial, social and cultural transactions in the context of this larger whole.

References

Abidin, Crystal (2017) 'Influencer Extravaganza: A Decade of Commercial 'Lifestyle' Microcelebrities in Singapore', in Hjorth, Larissaand Horst, Heather etal. (eds) *Routledge Companion to Digital Ethnography*, London: Routledge, pp. 158–168.

Anchordoguy, Marie (2015) *Reprogramming Japan: The High Tech Crisis under Communitarian Capitalism*, Ithaca, NY: Cornell University Press.

Anderson, Benedict (1998) *The Spectre of Comparisons: South East Asia and the World*, London: Verso.

Aouragh, Miriam and Chakravartty, Paula (2016) 'Infrastructures of Empire: Towards a Critical Geopolitics of Media and Information Studies', *Media, Culture & Society*,38(4): 559–575.

Appadurai, Arjun (2013) *The Future as Cultural Fact: Essays on the Global Condition*, London: Verso.

Athique, Adrian (2013) *Digital Media and Society: An Introduction*, Cambridge: Polity Press.

Athique, Adrian (2018) 'Integrated Commodities in the Digital Economy', unpublished paper.

Athique, Adrian and Parthasarathi, Vibodh (eds.) (2019, forthcoming) *Platform Capitalism in India*, Basingstoke: Palgrave.

Bratton, Benjamin H. (2015) *The Stack: On Software and Sovereignty*, Cambridge, MIT Press.

Bunnell, Tim (2006) *Malaysia, Modernity and the Multimedia Super Corridor: A Critical Geography of Intelligent Landscapes*, Abingdon: Routledge.

Case, William (2017) 'Stress Testing Leadership in Malaysia: The 1MDB Scandal and Najib Tun Razak', *The Pacific Review*, 30(5): 633–654.

Chaturvedi, Swati (2016) *I Am a Troll: Inside the Secret World of the BJP's Digital Army*, New Delhi: Juggernaut.

Cohen, Julie E. (2017) 'Law for the Platform Economy', *U.C. Davis Law Review*, 51: 133.

Connors, Michael K., Davison, Rémy and Dosch, Jörn (eds.) (2017) *The New Global Politics of the Asia-Pacific: Conflict and Cooperation in the Asian Century*, Abingdon: Routledge.

Curato, Nicole (ed.) (2017) *A Duterte Reader: Critical Essays on Rodrigo Duterte's Early Presidency*, Ithaca, NY: Cornell University Press.

D'Costa, Anthony and Sridharan, Eswaran (eds.) (2004) *India in the Global Software Industry*, New Delhi: MacMillan India.

Dutta, Dilip (2017) *Development under Dualism and Digital Divide in Twenty-First Century India*, Singapore: Springer.

Ford, Martin (2009) *The Lights in the Tunnel: Automation, Accelerating Technology and the Economy of the Future*, Wayne, PA: Acculent Publishing.

Goggin, Gerard (2011) *Global Mobile Media*, London and New York: Routledge.

Hirakawa, Hitoshi and Takahashi, Nobuhiro (2018) *Innovative ICT Industrial Architecture in East Asia: Offshoring of Japanese Firms and Challenges Faced by East Asian Economies*, Singapore: Springer.

Hong, Yu (2017) *Networking China: The Digital Transformation of the Chinese Economy*, Urbana: University of Illinois Press.

Hopkins, Julian (2014) 'Cybertroopers and Tea Parties: Government Use of the Internet in Malaysia', *Asian Journal of Communication*, 24(1): 5–24.

Ibrahim, Azeem (2018) *The Rohingyas: Inside Myanmar's Hidden Genocide*, London: C. Hurst and Co.

Innis, Harold (1951) *The Bias of Communication*, Toronto, ON: University of Toronto Press.

International Telecommunications Union (2018) *Measuring the Information Society Report 2017.* Available:www.itu.int/en/ITU-D/Statistics/Pages/publications/default.aspx, accessed 4 March 2018.

Internet World Stats (2017) 'Internet Usage in Asia'. Available: www.internetworldstats.com/stats3.htm, accessed: 4 March 2018.

Kaul, Vivek (2013) *Easy Money: Evolution of Money from Robison Crusoe to the First World War*, New Delhi: Sage.

Kaul, Vivek (2015) *Easy Money: The Greatest Ponzi Scheme Ever and How It Is Set to Destroy the Global Financial System*, New Delhi: Sage.

Kaur, Harleen, Lechman, Ewa and Marszk, Adam (eds.) (2017) *Catalyzing Development Through ICT Adoption: The Developing World Experience*, Cham: Springer.

Keane, Michael and Fung, Anthony Y.H. (2018) 'Digital Platforms: Exerting China's New Cultural Power in the Asia-Pacific', *Media Industries*, 5(1): 47–50. doi:10.3998/mij.15031809.0005.103.

Keane, Michael and Wu, Huan (2018) 'Lofty Ambitions, New Territories, and Turf Battles: China's Platforms "Go Out"', *Media Industries*, 5(1): 51–68. doi:10.3998/mij.15031809.0005.104.

Keynes, John Maynard (1936) *The General Theory of Employment, Interest and Money*, Cambridge: Cambridge University Press.

Kinports, Nicholas (2017) *Becoming an Instagram Influencer: How I Make a Six-Figure Income by Partnering with Brands*, New York: Notice Agency.

Lee, Francis L.F. and Chan, Joseph M. (2018) *Media and Protest Logics in the Digital Era: The Umbrella Movement in Hong Kong*, New York: Oxford University Press.

Lessig, Lawrence (2004) *Free Culture: How Big Media Uses Technology and the Law to Lockdown Culture and Control Creativity*, New York: Penguin.

Lim, Sun Sun and Soriano, Cheryll Ruth (eds.) (2016) *Asian Perspectives on Digital Culture: Emerging Phenomena, Enduring Concepts*, New York: Routledge.

Lorenzana, Jozon (2017) 'Social Media and Precarious Intimacy in Metro Manila', unpublished paper.

Madianou, Mirca and Miller, Daniel (2012) *Migration and New Media: Transnational Families and Poly-Media*, London: Routledge.

Manning, Chris and Van Diemen, Peter (eds.) (2000) *Indonesia in Transition: Social Aspects of Reformasi and Crisis*, Singapore: Institute of Southeast Asian Studies.

Marwick, Alice (2015) 'Instafame: Luxury Selfies in the Attention Economy', *Public Culture*, 27 (1, 75): 137–160.

Mascarenhas, R.C. (2012) *India's Silicon Plateau: Development of Information and Communication Technology in Bangalore*, Hyderabad: Orient BlackSwan.

McLuhan, Marshall (1964) *Understanding Media: The Extensions of Man*, New York: McGraw Hill.

Miller, Jonathan (2018) *Duterte Harry: Fire and Fury in the Philippines*, Melbourne, VIC: Scribe.

Noronha, Ernesto and D'Cruz, Premilla (eds.) (2019, forthcoming) *Critical Perspectives on Work and Employment in Globalizing India*, Singapore: Springer.

Nyblade, Benjamin, O'Mahony, Angela and Sinpeng, Aim (2015) 'Social Media Data and the Dynamics of Thai Protests', *Asian Journal of Social Science*, 43(5): 545–566.

Overholt, William H. (2010) 'China in the Global Financial Crisis: Rising Influence, Rising Challenges', *The Washington Quarterly*, 33(1): 21–34.

Parthasarathi, Vibodh (2018) 'Platformisation and the Governance of Trust', Paper presented at *Digital Emporiums: Platform Capitalism in India*, University of Queensland, 13 August 2018.

Parks, Lisa and Starosielski, Nicole (eds.) (2015) *Signal Traffic: Critical Studies of Media Infrastructures*, Urbana: University of Illinois Press.

Polanyi, Karl (1944) *The Great Transformation: Political and Economic Origins of Our Time*, Boston, MA: Beacon Press.

Poster, Mark (1995) *The Second Media Age*, Cambridge, MA: PolityPress.

Postill, John (2018) *The Rise of Nerd Politics: Digital Activism and Political Change*, London: Pluto Press.

Qiu, Jack Linchuan (2017) *Goodbye iSlave: A Manifesto for Digital Abolition*, Urbana: University of Illinois Press.

Rossiter, Ned (2017) 'Imperial Infrastructures and Asia beyond Asia: Data Centres, State Formation and the Territoriality of Logistical Media', *The Fibreculture Journal*, 29. Available: http://twentynine.fibreculturejournal.org/fcj-220-imperial-infrastructures-and-asia-beyond-asia-data-centres-state-formation-and-the-territoriality-of-logistical-media/, accessed: 8 June 2018.

Schiller, Dan (2014) *Digital Depression: Information Technology and Economic Crisis*, Urbana: University of Illinois Press.

Simmel, Georg (1907) [1978] *The Philosophy of Money*, London: Routledge.

Sinpeng, Aim (2014) 'The Cyber Coup', *Cultural Anthropology*, 23 September 2014. Available: https://culanth.org/fieldsights/568-the-cyber-coup, accessed: 9 March 2018.

Soriano, Cheryll Ruth (2012) 'The Arts of Indigenous Online Dissent: Negotiating Technology, Indigeneity, and Activism in the Cordillera', *Telematics and Informatics*, 29(1): 33–44.

Srnicek, Nick (2017) *Platform Capitalism*, Cambridge, MA: Polity Press.

Stiglitz, Joseph (2010) *Freefall: Free Markets and the Sinking of the Global Economy*, London: Penguin.

Sundaram, Ravi (2011) *Pirate Modernity: Delhi's Media Urbanism*, London and New York: Routledge.
Sundaram, Ravi (2017) 'Circulation Takes Command? The Sensory Infrastructure of the Mobile Phone', Paper presented at *Digital Transactions in Asia*, Queensland University of Technology, 8–10 August 2017.
Tapsell, Ross (2013) 'The Media Freedom Movement in Malaysia and the Electoral Authoritarian Regime', *Journal of Contemporary Asia*, 43(4): 613–635.
Tapsell, Ross (2015) 'The Media and Subnational Authoritarianism in Papua', *South East Asia Research*, 23(3): 319–334.
Thomas, Pradip (2018) *Empire and Post-Empire Telecommunications in India: A History*, New Delhi: Oxford University Press.
Thomas, Pradip (2019, forthcoming) *The Politics of Digital India*, New Delhi: Oxford University Press.
Upadhya, Carol and Vasavi, Aninhalli Rame (eds.) (2008) *In an Outpost of the Global Economy: Work and Workers in India's Information Technology Industry*, New Delhi: Routledge.
Wade, Francis (2017) *Myanmar's Enemy Within: Buddhist Violence and the Making of a Muslim 'Other'*, London: Zed Books.
Wong, Christine (2011) 'The Fiscal Stimulus Programme and Public Governance Issues in China', *OECD Journal on Budgeting*, 11(3): 1–22.
Yong Jin, Dal and Kwak, Nojin (eds.) (2018) *Communication, Digital Media, and Popular Culture in Korea*, Lanham, MD: Lexington Books.
Zhang, Xiaoling and Zheng, Yongnian (eds.) (2009) *China's Information and Communications Technology Revolution: Social Changes and State Responses*, London and New York: Routledge.
Zhao, Elaine Jing (2018) 'Negotiating State and Copyright Territorialities in Overseas Expansion: The Case of China's Online Video Streaming Platforms', *Media Industries*, 5(1). doi:10.3998/mij.15031809.0005.107.

Part 1

Platforms, Infrastructure and Regulation

2 Zhejiang's Digital Dream

Michael Keane and Huan Wu

> ...so far as China's peaceful rise is concerned, it is only a cherished 'Chinese dream' based on China's national condition and it aims at solving China's own problems, but certainly not any other dream.
>
> (Zheng Bijian, Senior Policy Advisor, Beijing, 25 November 2005; in Zheng 2011)

Many nations have had dreams of greatness; many have experienced periods of great prosperity and influence. China, now increasingly prosperous, is dreaming of becoming a 'strong power' (*qiangguo*). China's dream was unveiled by President Xi Jinping shortly after he assumed office in 2012. While the dream is essentially one of national rejuvenation, part of it entails the expansion of China's influence in East Asia and throughout the Asia-Pacific and Eurasia (Ellis 2015; Frankopan 2015; Maçães 2018). To date, considerable attention has been focused on the massive infrastructural investments involved in modernizing these territories, bridges, roads, ports, railways. Equally important, however, is the role of Chinese communication companies. This chapter considers how digital transactions are transforming the fortunes of a province in China, well known for its manufacturing expertise. Zhejiang, situated in eastern China between Jiangsu, Anhui, Fujian and Jiangxi, is considered by many observers to be China's most entrepreneurial province. The chapter looks at three cities in Zhejiang that collectively provide the infrastructure to connect China's businesses to the Belt and Road Initiative (hereafter BRI) nation states throughout Eurasia. The three cities are Hangzhou, Ningbo and Yiwu. The common node is Alibaba.com, one of China's three internet giants. The chapter argues that e-commerce, now a driver of China's economic transformation, is central to Zhejiang's 'digital dream'.

The aim of this chapter is to show how digital transactions are relevant to the modernization of commerce in China, and in particular how China's e-commerce platforms are targeting territories along the BRI. The nomenclature, sometimes referred to as the One Belt One Road, describes the overland corridors that connect Western China with Europe via Central and South Asia, known as the Silk Road Economic Belt—and the maritime routes that are intended to link China's southern provinces to South East Asia and beyond, encapsulated by the concept of the 21st Century Maritime Silk Road (Cai 2017: 2). Our focus, however, is not Xi'an, traditionally regarded as the Chinese gateway to the overland Silk Road Economic Belt, or Quanzhou in Fujian province, once an entry point to what is now the Maritime Silk Road, but three linked hubs in Zhejiang province: the metropolis Hangzhou, the port city Ningbo and the county level city Yiwu. This is a story of Zhejiang's digital dream: how the province has moved from basic manufacturing to value-added services. While many provinces in China now claim a stake in the BRI project, we will argue that Zhejiang is uniquely positioned as a digitally enabled province. It is home to China's largest internet telecommunication company, Alibaba, whose data assets, logistics, and internet finance services are the model for the next stage of the Chinese economy, one in which online consumption is driving growth.

Alibaba's success in recognizing the immense value of the digital economy, both globally and domestically, has impacted on its neighbour cities in Zhejiang, and on its neighbour provinces Jiangsu, Jiangxi, Fujian and Anhui. For some critics Alibaba is a clone of eBay, the US e-commerce multinational founded in 1995 at the height of the dot.com bubble. Alibaba made its move into e-commerce just four years later. Its growth into a global communications empire, now complemented with content (online video and motion pictures), has drawn valuable human capital to Hangzhou. Indeed, the e-commerce model championed by Alibaba has lifted the national economy, moving China from a manufacturing model towards a modern services economy. In the second decade of the 21st-century Zhejiang's competitive advantage is primarily its strength in the digital economy, underpinned by considerable infrastructural logistics. These elements are particularly evident in the spectacular rise of its capital Hangzhou, but also in the transformation of Ningbo and Yiwu. We argue that the expansion of Zhejiang-based enterprises into territories outside the mainland, thanks to the entrepreneurial troika, Hangzhou-Ningbo-Yiwu, serves the Chinese government's soft power strategy. More consumption of Chinese products and services, along with Chinese-led infrastructure projects, adds up to greater influence, which in the new global strategy called 'going out' (*zou chuqu*) contributes to national rejuvenation. Baogang He argues that such rejuvenation, and the BRI, encapsulates Xi's vision of 'new Sino-empire building'. In other words, the rejuvenation of the Chinese nation is extending 'globally' (2018).

The first section discusses how the efficacy of digital transactions is understood according to platformization terminologies, namely 'digital economy', 'platform economy' and 'platform capitalism'. Platform capitalism, now widely used in academic studies, explains the rapid rise of platforms in the global economy. Platforms represent a new kind of firm—an 'intermediary' that brings together different users 'customers, advertisers, service providers, producers, suppliers, and even physical objects' (Srnicek 2017). In regard to digitally enhanced communicative practices, the platform constitutes an industrial manifestation of social network sites and their transformation in 'programmable systems' (Helmond 2015); the argument presented here is that digital platforms 'reformat the web' around the affordances of social media. In mainland China 'digital economy' and 'platform economy' are widely used in academic and industry discourse. In particular, due to the massive expansion of internet infrastructure in China, the platform economy (*pingtai jingji*) has entered the *lingua franca* of development. In 2018, there were 772 million registered users, or 'netizens' as they are sometimes described in China (Pandaily 2018). The section therefore considers some Chinese uses of the term 'platform economy'. The discussion then focuses on the relation between physical infrastructure and digital platforms, emphasizing the need to reconsider the role of logistics.

The second section, Made in China, links the outsourcing of the global economy in the 1980s and 1990s to the subsequent economic rise of low-cost production regions, what the economist Richard Baldwin calls 'the great convergence' (Baldwin 2016). Market openings provided by China's World Trade Organisation accession in 2001 led to China gaining significant advantages in the upgrading of its technological infrastructure, coinciding with two key policy initiatives 'innovative nation' (*chuangxin xing guojia*) and 'indigenous innovation' (*zizhu chuangxin*). The section discusses two strategic initiatives that followed in 2015 and 2016, Internet+ and Made in China 2025, respectively, and how they are bound up with the rise of Alibaba. The next section considers the positioning of the three axes that are enabling digital transactions—Hangzhou, the digital city; Ningbo, the deep-water port which connects to the Maritime Silk Road; and Yiwu, the centre of small goods production and the node for the overland rail system (traversing the old Silk Road)—and how the platform economy, the Internet of things (IoT), the Cloud and smart manufacturing are changing the economy of Zhejiang. Finally, in the discussion we return to the BRI and the Digital Silk Road.

Transactions: Platforms and the Digital Economy

A transaction generally refers to a negotiated agreement or settlement, or in a more specific sense it refers to a commercial transaction. A digital transaction utilizes electronic finance of some sort, for instance online banking payments. In relation to e-commerce, it is important to note that a digital transaction is the sale or purchase of goods or services conducted over computer-mediated networks via a third party, which in the case of Taobao, Alibaba's dominant e-commerce platform, is its popular escrow service called Alipay (*zhifu bao*). As Ming Cheung details, sellers and buyers conduct transactions via Alipay.

> Once a buyer has confirmed an order with the seller, he or she remits payment for the goods to Alipay, which then notifies the seller that payment has been received. After the buyer has accepted the goods and confirmed that they are satisfactory, the third party then remits the payment to the seller.
>
> (Cheung 2016: 419)

A similar system operates with eBay, the third party in this case being PayPal.

The range of players in the digital field has expanded rapidly, to include e-commerce companies, IT companies and mobile operators. Internet finance has advanced in industries where products can be digitized: for instance, journalism, publishing, television and music (Xie et al. 2016). In particular internet finance facilitates e-commerce. The rise of the 'digital economy' according to Melecki and Morriset (2008: 36) is made possible by fast, cheap computing capacity, data storage, standardized software platforms and a worldwide, integrated digital network. Atkinson and McKay say that the digital economy 'represents the pervasive use of IT (hardware, software, applications, and telecommunications) in all aspects of the economy' (2007, cited in Malecki and Moriset 2008: 4). Applying this broad ranging definition to China, we note the transformation of economic activity over the past two decades due to rapid computerization, the availability of cheap personal computers (Lenovo) and smartphones (Xiaomi, Oppo), and digital affordances (WeChat), together with the ascendency of large state-owned telecommunication carriers (China Mobile, China Netcom), fast broadband connectivity and, of course, massive numbers of people spending time online. It is an understatement to say that the digital economy has transformed many aspects of Chinese society, allowing communication companies like Baidu, Alibaba and Tencent, known colloquially as BAT, to use their powerful data harvesting capabilities to become 'digital champions' (Keane and Chen 2017; Keane and Wu 2018).

The government has made it clear in recent policy statements that China is on track to become an 'innovative nation', thanks to the application of advanced technologies such as artificial intelligence, internet finance and sophisticated logistics. The uptake of smartphones in China has precipitated a spike in M-commerce (Liang 2017). As early as 2009, the World Bank had declared mobile telephony to be the 'world's largest distribution platform' (World Bank 2009). Advanced in internet finance, linking payment systems to mobile apps has transformed the speed and scale of transactions, and led to new players offering financial services that are more convenient than those offered by banks.

Whereas visitors to China a decade ago encountered a society in which vendors accumulated large reserves of paper money, nowadays the same vendors are advocates of the digital economy and the cashless society. In most retail sectors in China, the digitization trend is accelerating. However, while goods may be purchased online, their creation, production and delivery are often offline; in addition, various tasks are conducted by agents in different locations. Depending on the kind of product, for instance, electronic goods, production tasks are frequently separated, a process referred to as 'unbundling' (Baldwin 2016). When it comes to sales, the online provider is required to engage in price negotiation, billing, delivery, tracking and sometimes after sales service and product returns. The services necessary to coordinate these tasks might include express parcel delivery, air cargo and customs clearance. In China parcel delivery drivers are omnipresent. Most significantly, in contrast to a decade ago, goods are digitized and are available for consumption instantaneously once a transaction is complete, for instance e-books, audio books, streaming music and video. Chinese internet users are avid downloaders and streamers.

In Chinese academic parlance, the term 'platform economy' is now widespread. Economy is a more neutral and time-honoured description than capitalism and is therefore more amenable to political support in the context of the commercial expansion of Chinese platforms. One of the most prominent academic discussion of the platform economy comes from Xu, who says:

> The platform is a kind of space or place that can exist in the real world and the virtual network space. It guides or promotes transactions between two or more customers. It manages to attract parties of the transaction to use the space or place through charging appropriate fees, and in the end it pursues the maximization of profits.
>
> (2013, translated from Chinese)

Other Chinese sources offer a positive spin on the platform economy, a way to allow the logic of the former planned economy to transfer into a consumer-driven society, the so-called 'new normal': whereby the potential market demand hidden in the long tail can be exploited; for instance Wang and Li contend: 'Under the new normal of the Chinese economy, imitative large-scale consumption has ended, and personalized and diversified consumption has come' (2017: 149). While diversified consumption and consumer choice is now made possible, production, marketing, transaction and distribution facilities have modernized accordingly. The competitive advantage of platform companies according to Johannes Koponen is the ability to 'continuously and exponentially improve, personalize and position their offerings via machine learning' (2017).

While scholars contend that people are living in a globalizing platform society, Koponen believes that the era of platform dominance may be declining, especially as some platforms are now investing in material assets, thereby opening up space for competition in niches that emerge (Van Dijck et al. 2018). In China, Alibaba is now investing in shopping centres. More importantly, the longevity of the dominance of China's big three internet players, Baidu, Alibaba and Tencent (BAT), increasingly depends on their capacity to integrate their virtual services and the logistics of production and distribution. For this to happen they need to manage physical networks and have human capital to deliver products and services. Such a trend, however, doesn't necessarily determine the demise of the platform economy, but it shows how it is integrating even more with material culture. Accordingly, it is worth reconsidering the priority given to the digital platforms as an economic model, their rise to prominence and their latest phase of development. We could therefore think of the platform as constituting two levels of structural organization: digital and physical (or infrastructural).

The digital layer is more often associated with the online traffic, user-generated content, social media and video sharing, and instant messaging, while the physical layer is required to distribute products and services, to manage data storage (the Cloud) and to facilitate the supply chain (e.g. the IoT). The physical layer extends to logistics, what Rossiter (2014: 53) calls 'logistical worlds'. He says, 'Shipping container yards and warehouses coordinate the movement of people and things through technologies of remote control. Wharf-side loading and unloading of cargo becomes increasingly automated, with labour displaced by algorithmic tracking devices and human oversight of machine-operations'. In her account of the power of infrastructure space, Kelly Easterling writes, 'Microwaves bounce between billions of cell phones. Computers synchronize. Shipping containers stack, lock, and calibrate the global transportation and production of goods' (2014: 1). The transformation of tasks is made possible by technological progress. Adam Greenfield writes of such radical technologies: 'truly transformative circumstances will arise not from any one technology standing alone, but from multiple technical capabilities woven together in combination' (Greenfield 2017, Kindle Locations 4408-4409). For China's leaders, such technologies are central to realizing the dream of national rejuvenation.

Made in China

The transformation we describe represents more than the upgrading for China's economy. Richard Baldwin describes how outsourcing destinations, for instance 'Factory Asia' and 'Factory Africa', have become more competitive globally by taking know-how and IP from more developed economies. According to Zhu, 17.8% of China's total population work in manufacturing or manufacturing-related jobs, compared to 3.8% in the USA (2015: 4). China however has been gradually moving away from the kind of capital-intensive and low-margin activities associated with outsourcing. While the outsourcing of manufacturing tasks to China has provided jobs, and allowed the transfer of expertise, it has polluted much of the country. Companies such as Alibaba.com offer great hope for the modernization of production, and in particular the policy vision known as Made in China 2025. Made in China 2025 refers to China's ambitious, and in some policy circles, contentious plan to upgrade its manufacturing industries through the use of emerging technologies such as artificial intelligence, cloud computing and the IoT. To understand the thinking behind Made in China 2025, it is important to consider the moment in 2006 when President Hu Jintao announced at a national science and technology conference held at Beijing's Tsinghua University that China would become an 'innovative nation' by 2020. The slogan escaped the attention of many foreign observers in the tech community, typically more concerned with finding ways to navigate the complexity of market access in China and protect their intellectual property. Nonetheless, the document was mandatory reading for provincial, municipal, and district leaders.

Essentially, 'innovative nation' announced that China would move from its dependence on low-cost manufacturing, particularly outsourcing for foreigners and develop its own technologies and standards, hence an emphasis on 'indigenous innovation' (*zizhu chuangxin*: see Jacobson 2007; Zhu 2015). The 12th Five-Year Plan (2011–2016) emphasized the role of information and communication technologies in China's development plan, a recognition that played into the hands of a new class of industry leader, the CEOs of China's internet technology companies. In particular Jack Ma (Alibaba), Ma Huateng (Tencent) and Robin Li (Baidu) soon became prophets of innovation (Leong 2018), turning their thoughts into books and DVDs. In late 2013, Ma Huateng, also known as Pony Ma, unveiled an idea called 'internet thinking', essentially a business strategy for his company. Impressed by the logic of internet thinking, China's state think tanks transformed this into Internet+, a forward-thinking blueprint for enhancing China's economy in the digital age. Internet+ was announced in March 2015. The objectives were:

> to integrate mobile Internet, cloud computing big data, and the Internet of things with modern manufacturing, to encourage the healthy development of e-commerce, industrial networks, and Internet banking, and to get Internet-based companies to increase their presence in the international market.
>
> (*China Daily* 2015)

The technological frontier includes next-generation information networks, core electronics, high-end software and new information services. In June 2015, the State Council issued further instructions in a document entitled 'China boosts mass entrepreneurship and innovation' (State Council 2017). Among the eight recommendations were a range of policies and fiscal incentives to maximize the development of an 'entrepreneurial ecosystem'. To say that Made in China 2025 is contentious is an understatement. The idea is a direct sinicization of Germany's Industrie 4.0, (or I40) which was adopted by the German Federal Government in 2010. It is described as follows:

> The I40 strategy aims to ensure an industry fit for future manufacturing in Germany. It supports the integration of cyber physical systems (CPS) and Internet of Things and Services (IoTS) with an eye to enhance productivity, efficiency and flexibility of production processes and thus economic growth.
>
> (Digital Transformation Monitor 2017)

The embrace of this idea was more than serendipitous, as mentioned above China had been moving rapidly since the early 2000s towards making technology part of its development plans. The emergence of dominant internet communications companies with links to global financial institutions was further proof of China's embrace of 'digital capitalism' (Hong 2017). China was no longer on the margins as evidenced by the World Internet Conference, an annual event held in Wuzhen, a small city in eastern Zhejiang province. It now draws CEOs from international companies including the likes of eBay and Apple. In December 2017, the organizers convened a special forum on day two entitled, 'International Cooperation Along the Digital Silk Road'. Opening the event, Lin Nanxiu, representing the National Development and Reform Commission of China, noted: 'Digital is the new driving force of the Chinese economy and growth. It is a great opportunity for countries to work together with a new ecological development mentality' (Fishwick 2017). In the USA, Made in China has come under fire from the Trump administration because Chinese companies have reportedly appropriated US trade secrets and intellectual property (Hopewell n.d.).

Positioning Zhejiang: Hangzhou, Ningbo and Yiwu

Geographically located in the middle of China adjacent to the coast, Zhejiang is bounded by the East China Sea to the east, by the provinces of Fujian to the south, Jiangxi to the south-east, Anhui to the west and Jiangsu to the north. It is also proximate to the booming metropolis of Shanghai (less than an hour by fast train). Whereas the north-western inland city

Table 2.1 GDP of leading cities in Zhejiang (Ningbo Municipal Statistics Bureau Portal, 2018).

The GDP of each city in Zhejiang province (100 million RMB)	*Quarters 1–4 in 2017*	*Year-on-year growth (%)*
Zhejiang province	51768.26	7.8
Hangzhou city	12556.16	8.0
Ningbo city	9846.94	7.8
Wenzhou city	5453.17	8.4
Shaoxing city	5108.04	7.1
Jinhua city (including Yiwu)	3870.22	6.5

of Xi'an is usually identified with the ancient Silk Road, Zhejiang's positioning has allowed it to become a node linking the western (land) corridor and the southern (maritime) corridor. It now functions as a strategic province with respect to China's opening to the outside world, reviving its history of foreign contacts since ancient times. Natives from East Zhejiang known as 'Guyue' clansmen made a great contribution in the exploration of 'Maritime Silk Road', especially in what was termed the East Asian Mediterranean (China, Japan and South Korea) route in the Han dynasty (206 BCE–220 CE) as well as in the development of the southern maritime route. In the prosperous periods of the Maritime Silk Road, and the Tang, Song, Yuan and Ming dynasties, three cities—Hangzhou, Ningbo and Wenzhou—were prominent in the trade of silk, porcelain and tea. Trade engendered cultural exchange between Chinese and foreign cultures and the formation of 'golden link' of Buddhism throughout China, Japan and South Korea, as well as the consolidation of 'Confucian culture' in East Asia.

In the early 2000s the term 'Zhejiang model' was bandied about by Chinese economists to illustrate how low-tech manufacturing had lifted productivity and GDP. It was a model fit to be emulated by the rest of the nation—at the time. Zhejiang epitomized the factory of the world; its legions of low-skilled workers churned out zippers, buttons, kitchen utensils, toys, tents and cigarette lighters (Keane 2007: 146). Zhejiang's locational advantage was enhanced in the economic reform era beginning in 1978. It is now the most prosperous province in China, measured by the density of home-grown private enterprises. While Guangdong province has more private enterprises, much of these are foreign invested companies. The so-called 'Zhejiang model' had come to refer to the proliferation of self-reliant small-scale enterprises. Since the economic reforms of the 1980s, thousands of factories have been engaged in basic manufacturing, as well as in providing low-end components for new economy industries. The key cities in the Digital Silk Road are now Hangzhou, Ningbo, Wenzhou, Shaoxing and Jinhua (including Yiwu) (see Table 2.1).

Whereas in the 1980s and 1990s Zhejiang region was characterized by small-size enterprises, often working together to produce complementary goods without the need for high technology, for instance Wenzhou and Shaoxing (garments), things have now changed as Zhejiang finds itself the key player in the 'Digital Silk Road', largely thanks to the emergence of Alibaba, whose headquarters are found in Hangzhou.

Hangzhou

Over many centuries Hangzhou has earned a reputation for both commerce and culture, profiting in particular from the region's renowned silk and tea trade. Hangzhou grew in political importance during the Southern Song Dynasty (1127–1179 AD). The imperial court's patronage boosted the city's importance as a commercial hub, attracting scholars, artists and poets to the city. Marco Polo visited Hangzhou on several occasions, writing that 'it is without a doubt the finest and most splendid city in the world' (Bartleby.com n.d.). Hangzhou is a renowned tourist destination with two listed World Heritage sites, West Lake and the Grand Canal. The 1,776 km Grand Canal, China's first 'commons', was the longest canal or artificial river in the world. The canal linked Hangzhou to Beijing, the capital from the Yuan dynasty onwards, and to ocean trade routes to Japan, Korea, South East Asia and the Middle East. Today Hangzhou is a city of both attraction (tourism) and transaction (e-commerce). In regard to the latter Hangzhou is the largest mobile payment city in the world, advertising its strengths as digitally enabled convenience. The convenience brought about by its internet finance platform Alipay is exported nationally and beyond, to the world. Chinese tourists in particular are able to use Alipay when they shop overseas without need for international credit cards. As early as the city's Ninth Five-Year Plan (1996–2000), Hangzhou harboured aspirations to build a 'Silicon Valley in Paradise' (*tiantang guigu*). Arguably this is now a reality: Hangzhou has transformed into a financial centre enabled by digital technology. The city's economic transformation from secondary industries to new information service industries was a combination of government planning and 'people-managed' (*minban*) firms.

By 1999, the city had set its course to be an 'informatization city test point'. Kathleen Hartford notes how Hangzhou sought to distinguish itself from other contenders in this regard: first, by adopting the Silicon Valley in Paradise theme; second, by exploiting the municipality's position as a tourist centre and the role of informatization in tourism; and, third, through an emphasis on 'informationized communities' and 'informationized households' (Hartford 2003). Hangzhou is now home to many of the world's largest high-tech corporations, including 39 businesses in the Fortune 1000 and thousands of start-up companies. It demonstrates that small cities can have strong output capacity.

San Jose (the largest city of Silicon Valley) Metropolitan Area has the third highest GDP per capita in the world (after Zurich, Switzerland and Oslo, Norway), according to the Brookings Institution (Hall 2015). Whereas the centre of the industrial age was London, and of the financial age New York, the centre of the information age is undoubtedly Silicon Valley. According to information provided by Hangzhou Statistical Information Net, Hangzhou's GDP at the end of 2017 was 1255.6 billion RMB. It had a population of 7.539 million (household registration population) (Hangzhou Statistics Information Net 2018a). In 2017, the total revenue of foreign trade import and export was 508.51 billion RMB. The report claims that 104.9 billion RMB worth of trade, more than 25%, was transacted between Hangzhou and BRI countries (Hangzhou Statistics Information Net 2018b).

Leading the development of Hangzhou's innovation programme is Alibaba.com. In fact, an often-cited article refers to the Hangzhou's 'Ten Year Dream', a miniature version of the Chinese Dream (Jiang 2017). Founded by Jack Ma, in Hong Kong in October 1999, Alibaba drew on the professional expertise of foreigners, that is, people already ensconced in the Silicon Valley ethos. Its first website was in English, Alibaba.com, a global wholesale B2B marketplace; this was followed by the C2C online shopping website Taobao in May 2003. A year later Aliwangwang, a personal computer-based instant messaging tool, was launched along with the key innovation being Alipay, a third-party online payment platform. Alibaba subsequently used its competitive advantages to create related online services: Alimama, an online marketing technology platform; Tmall.com, a dedicated platform for third-party brands and retailers; and AliExpress, the company's global platform. In addition to its e-commerce assets, Alibaba has positioned itself in the cultural and creative industries, establishing a new cultural and entertainment group in 2016. The group includes Alibaba Pictures, Youku-Tudou, web browser UCWeb and Alibaba music. The venture into culture is strategic for the company, appealing to a broader demographic than its e-commerce communities.

Alibaba, along with Baidu and Tencent, is leading the charge into the knowledge economy, echoing the rhetoric of the fourth industrial revolution. Alibaba e-commerce and logistics focuses on big data, Cloud and Internet+ applications. It established the Cainiao Network together with a consortium of logistics companies in May 2013. In the new era celebrating 'mass entrepreneurship, mass innovation' (*dazhong chuangye, wanzhong chuangxin*), Hangzhou is staking its claim as a digital hub populated by thousands of start-up communities. Leading companies and universities are playing a key role in providing 'open innovation resources' to small and medium enterprises, and entrepreneurial start-ups. Cloud Town, situated in the Xihu (West Lake) District, offers a picture of China's latent capabilities. The key project here is the transformation of the former production-oriented industrial base known as Zhuan Tang Technology and Economic Park into a service-oriented centre. Initially named the Hangzhou Cloud Computing Industrial Park in 2011, it was rebranded Cloud Town (*yunqi xiaozhen*) in 2013 and is now jointly managed by the Hangzhou Economics and Information Committee and the West Lake District (Keane and Chen 2017). In April 2013 Cloud Town developed a partnership with the Alibaba Cloud Computing Company to build the Aliyun Entrepreneurship and Innovation Base. The relationship with Alibaba includes benefits for registered enterprises including promoting and selling Cloud products and services on the Aliyun website without a commission fee for three years. Enterprises can apply to Aliyun for subsidies when work contributes to Aliyun's cloud computing ecosystem.

Ningbo

The port city of Ningbo is most famous as being one of the so-called 'Treaty Ports'. Five designated ports (Ningbo, Canton (now Guangzhou), Shanghai, Fuzhou and Xiamen) were opened to foreign trade after the First Opium War between China and foreign powers concluded in 1842. Ningbo, however, has an even longer legacy connection to the Silk Road, dating more than a thousand years. During the Tang dynasty period (618–907 CE), the Five Dynasties period (907–960 CE) and Song dynasties period (960–1297 CE), Ningbo, then known as Mingzhou, was frequented first by Arab traders and then the Portuguese. In recent times under the policies of Made in China 2025 Ningbo has been reimagined as a gateway for modern manufacturing. In fact, Ningbo is described as a 'pilot city' for Made in China 2025. A policy called the '3511 (the numbers here represent different types of industries) industrial system' outlines how Ningbo will transform in the digital age:

> Encourage the development and application of large data. Support the manufacturing enterprises to join the cloud, encourage and promote enterprises to rely on cloud computing, large data, the Internet of things platform, the implementation of intelligent manufacturing, collaborative manufacturing and service manufacturing and other new manufacturing models.
>
> (Ningbo Municipal Government Portal 2017)

The extent of Ningbo's digital transformation encompasses smart retailing, combined with e-commerce. Having the largest deep-water port in Zhejiang, Ningbo sends shiploads of commodities sold on Amazon's Taobao platform to foreign destinations including those along the BRI. Ningbo's Made in China 2025 upgrading includes artificial intelligence and use of virtual reality technologies. From original equipment manufacturer (OEM) production, located at the bottom of the value chain, to the design and manufacture, Ningbo's manufacturing industry is gradually ascending to the high end of the industrial chain. An online sweater customization platform, Ningbo Cixing Co. Ltd, is popular among customers. The customization process works as follows: take a few photos of yourself on your smartphone, send them to the factory and after a few days receive a unique custom-made sweater. According to data, M-commerce comprised 75% of the total amount of online transactions in Ningbo in 2016 (Department of Commerce of Zhejiang Province 2016).

Yiwu

In many advertisements found in air terminals Yiwu announces itself to business as the small household goods capital of the world. In fact, Yiwu is the centre of the 'Made in China' model that pre-existed the digitally enabled Made in China 2025 policy. Chances are that much of what turns up in the budget marts in the developed world are products made in Zhejiang and distributed through Yiwu's rail terminal. Mechanical and electrical products and labour-intensive products are still the main export commodities. Paralleling Richard Florida's (Florida 2002) argument about creative environments acting as attracters for business, Yiwu's so-called 'small dog cluster economy' attracted the Zipper Industry Association of China to relocate from Shanghai in 2005. The top ten export commodities of Yiwu in the first quarter of 2018 were: mechanical and electrical products, apparel and clothing accessories, cultural products, plastic products, textile yarn, fabric products, toys, shoes, suitcases and bags, glass products and ceramic products. Yiwu has the highest density of domestic trade e-commerce merchants and the second highest density of foreign trade e-commerce merchants in China. It has been ranking first in the top 100 Chinese e-commerce counties for four consecutive years since 2013. Moreover, Yiwu is the only county-level city to be approved as a National E-commerce Demonstration City and National County E-commerce Big Data Application Statistics Pilot. In 2017, the turnover of e-commerce transactions in Yiwu was 222 billion yuan, and the total number of postal and courier services reached 1.9 billion (Zeng 2018).

Alibaba's 'spillover' effect into Yiwu is further reflected in the number of Taobao villages—113. Taobao village operations take place in rural areas and have an annual turnover of e-commerce of over RMB 10 million with the number of active online shops in the village more than 100, or the number of active online stores reaching more than 10% of the total local households. When a town/village/street has three or more administrative villages which meet the above standards, it can be classified as a 'Taobao village'. The top ten Taobao village clusters in China in 2015 saw Yiwu ranked first: other in the top ten included Wenling and Zhuji (both in Zhejiang), Cao County (Shandong), Jinjiang (Fujian province), Puning (Guangdong), Shuyang and Suining, (Jiangsu), Baiyun district (Guangzhou), Chaonan district (Shantou). In 2017, Yiwu's annual GDP reached 115.8 billion yuan (Yiwu Municipality Website 2017). In the first quarter of 2018, it exported RMB 30.01 billion worth of products to the countries along the BRI, accounting for 53.1% of its total export value. The top five destinations were India, Iraq, Iran, the USA and the Philippines (Yiwu Municipality Website 2018).

The BRI and Digital Silk Road

A 21st-century composite of the traditional Silk Road through Eurasia and the Maritime Silk Road through the Malacca Straits, the BRI was unveiled during Xi Jinping's state visit to Kazakhstan in 2013, leading many observers to speculate about its relationship to the previous year's 'Chinese dream' proclamation. The initiative took the world by surprise; its subsequent articulation in China's outward-bound trajectory, known as 'going out' (*zou chuqu*), has irrevocably altered the geopolitical landscape. The BRI aims to connect Asia, Europe and Africa along five routes. The Silk Road Economic Belt focuses on linking China to Europe through Central Asia and Russia, connecting China with the Middle East through Central Asia, and bringing together China and South East Asia, South Asia and the Indian Ocean. The 21st Century Maritime Silk Road, meanwhile, focuses on using Chinese coastal ports to link China with Europe through the South China Sea and Indian Ocean, and connect China with the South Pacific Ocean through the South China Sea. The ultimate objective of the BRI for China is to establish infrastructure linkages and use these to develop trading points along this route and into Europe (Ellis 2015).

For many observers the term 'Silk Road' retains an orientalist character; it was reportedly coined by a German traveller in the 1800s to describe the transportation of goods overland via camel. The journey would take months and the Silk Road was littered with caravanserai, places where travellers would stop. One of the key facilitators of connectivity in the modern age is China's fast train technology. The launch of a rail freight service from the Chongqing through Central Asia to Europe in March 2011 signalled a new era for rail freight as an alternative to shipping by sea or air. With the launch of the Yiwu-London line in January 2017, the trans-Eurasian network was extended to 15 cities in 10 European countries. The so-called 'China Railway Express' service or the 'Belt and Road on rail' is helping boost connectivity between China and the rest of Eurasia. In addition to offering freight transport solutions, the new infrastructure contributes to flows of global investment, resources, technology and skilled personnel, and facilitates global cross-sector collaboration.

Table 2.2 The strategic position of the five provinces in 'One Road' (Wang 2015).

Province	*Functional positioning*	*Cities*
Fujian	Core area in 'One Road'	Fuzhou, Xiamen, Quanzhou, Pingtan
Guangdong	Bridgehead in 'One Road'	Guangzhou, Shenzhen, Huizhou
Jiangsu	Intersection node of 'One Road'	Xuzhou, Lianyungang
Zhejiang	Pioneer in strategic economic and trade cooperation, test area of the Digital Silk Road, hub of trade and logistics	Hangzhou, Ningbo, Wenzhou
Hainan	Strategic fulcrum of 'One Road' portal	Haikou, Sanya

Nations in the central Asian region are anticipating much needed infrastructural projects to come to fruition with Chinese help. China and Pakistan have mapped out a provisional long-term plan for building highways, railways, oil and natural gas pipelines and optic fibre networks stretching from Kashgar to Gwadar Port. Much of the fibre optic infrastructure is provided by Chinese firms Huawei and ZTE.

How then does the Digital Silk Road work to connect China and the countries on the BRI, and how is Zhejiang positioned? As depicted in Table 2.2, Zhejiang is officially classified as a 'Test area of the Digital Silk Road, Hub of trade and logistics'. In this sense 'digital Zhejiang' encapsulates three layers of the digital economic system: the communication layer (Alibaba.com), the distribution layer (air, rail and sea freight) and the transaction layer (the digitally enabled online payment system, in this instance Alipay).

Transactions and Rejuvenation

This chapter has illustrated the rising technological capacity of Zhejiang, from low-tech factories employing predominantly unskilled workers towards state-of-the-art technology precincts deploying artificial intelligence and attracting some of the best talent in China as well as from abroad. The driver of much of this growth has been Alibaba.com, based in Hangzhou, but now with branch offices globally. As noted in the introduction, the term Digital Silk Road has been used to describe the potential riches on offer as e-commerce extends beyond China into new territories. The role of Ningbo and Yiwu is central to Zhejiang's positioning in this grand plan. Alibaba is undoubtedly key to the rise of Zhejiang, already a powerful economic entity. With the rapid development of e-commerce platforms and escrow financial services, trade between China and the world has entered a new stage. Moreover, the transformation of ordinary Chinese people, those living outside the tier-one cities of Beijing, Shanghai and Shenzhen, into online entrepreneurs, and the rise of Taobao villages, has changed the industrial landscape. Within this new digital transaction ecosystem Alibaba is emblematic of the Internet Plus blueprint, central to the strategic initiatives of the government's 13th Five-Year Plan (2016–2020), which is moving China closer to becoming an innovative nation. Connecting to the BRI is an incentive to build up Alibaba's business profile, while keeping the company in step with the government's ambitions, that is, the BRI offers a conduit for Chinese goods, technology, ideas and culture. The three cities Hangzhou, Ningbo and Wuxi constitute a combination of digital superhighway and logistical infrastructure, supplementing the existing transport links to the BRI and foreign territories that have been established by state-owned enterprises. An ancient region reinvested with political significance; the BRI forms a central component of China's dream of rejuvenation.

References

Atkinson, Robert D. and McKay, Andrew S. (2007) *Digital Prosperity: Understanding the Economic Benefits of the Information Technology Revolution*, Washington, DC: Information Technology and Innovation Foundation.

Baldwin, Richard (2016) *The Great Convergence: Information Technology and the New Globalization*, Cambridge, MA: Harvard University Press.

Bartleby.com (n.d.) 'Marco Polo. An Explanatory Essay'. Available: www.bartleby.com/essay/Marco-Polo-An-Exploratory-Essay-P3JNXHFZTJ, accessed: 27 February 2017.

Cai, Peter (2017) *Understanding China's Belt and Road Initiative*, Sydney, NSW: Lowy Institute.

Cheung, Ming (2016) 'The E-commerce Revolution: Ensuring Trust and Consumer Rights', in Keane, Michael (ed) *The Handbook of the Cultural and Creative Industries in China*, Cheltenham: Edward Elgar, pp. 412–430.

China Daily (2015) 'Report of the Work of the Government', Third Session of the 12th National People's Congress on 5 March 2015. Available: www.chinadaily.com.cn/china/2015twosession/2015-03/05/content_19729663.htm, accessed: 17 February 2017.

Department of Commerce of Zhejiang Province (2016) 'Mobile E-Commerce Lights Up the Public's New Life'. Available: http://zhejiang.mofcom.gov.cn/article/sjdixiansw/201608/20160801379709.shtml, accessed: 15 August 2016.

Digital Transformation Monitor (2017) 'Germany Industrie 4.0'. Available: https://ec.europa.eu/growth/tools-databases/dem/monitor/sites/default/files/DTM_Industrie%204.0.pdf, accessed: 8 January 2019.

Easterling, Kelly (2014) *Extrastatecraft: The Power of Infrastructure Space*, London: Verso.
Ellis, Chris Devonshire (2015) *China's New Economic Silk Road: The Great Eurasian Game and the String of Pearls*, Hong Kong: Asia Briefing.
Fishwick, Owen (2017) 'China in the Fast Lane on Digital Silk Road', *China Daily Online*, 4 December 2017. Available: www.chinadaily.com.cn/business/4thwic/2017-12/04/content_35201648.htm, accessed: 15 August 2018.
Florida, Richard (2002) *The Rise of the Creative Class and How It's Transforming Work, Leisure, Community and Everyday Life*, New York: Basic Books.
Frankopan, Peter (2015) *The Silk Roads: A New History of the World*, London: Bloomsbury.
Greenfield, Adam (2017) *Radical Technologies: The Design of Everyday Life*, London: Verso.
Hall, Gina (2015) 'San Jose Area Has World's Third-Highest GDP Per Capita', *Silicon Valley Business Journal*, 24 January 2015. Available: www.bizjournals.com/sanjose/news/2015/01/23/san-jose-has-worlds-third-highest-gdp-per-capita.html, accessed: 18 August 2018.
Hangzhou Statistics Information Net (2018a) 'Main Comprehensive Economic Indicators (of Hangzhou in 2017)'. Available: http://tjj.hangzhou.gov.cn/content-getOuterNewsDetail.action?newsMainSearch.id=88010484-6229-11e8-97a6-d89d676397bf, accessed: 31 January 2018.
Hangzhou Statistics Information Net (2018b) 'Foreign Trade, Investment Promotion of Hangzhou in 2017'. Available: http://tjj.hangzhou.gov.cn/content-getOuterNewsDetail.action?newsMainSearch.id=8800f4e1-6229-11e8-97a6-d89d676397bf, accessed: 31 January 2018.
Hartford, Kathleen (2003) 'West Lake Wired: Shaping Hangzhou's Information Age', in Lee, Chin-Chuan (ed) *Chinese Media, Global Contexts*, London: Routledge, pp. 177–195.
He, Baogang (2018) 'The Domestic Politics of the Belt and Road Initiative and Its Implications', *Journal of Contemporary China*. doi:10.1080/10670564.2018.1511391.
Helmond, Anne (2015) 'The Platformization of the Web: Making Web Data Platform Ready', *Social Media and Society*, 1(2): 1–11. doi:10.1177/2056305115603080.
Hong, Yu (2017) *Networking China: The Digital Transformation of the Chinese Economy*, Urbana: University of Illinois Press.
Hopewell, Kristen (n.d.) 'What Is 'Made in China 2025' — and Why Is It a Threat to Trump's Trade Goals?' *Washington Post*. Available: www.washingtonpost.com/news/monkey-cage/wp/2018/05/03/what-is-made-in-china-2025-and-why-is-it-a-threat-to-trumps-trade-goals/?noredirect=on&utm_term=.3d788a803bae, accessed: 18 August 2018.
Jacobson, Linda (ed.) (2007) *Innovation with Chinese Characteristics: High-Tech Research in China*, Basingstoke: Palgrave Macmillan.
Jiang, Daqiao (2017) 'Hangzhou's Ten Year Dream'. Available: www.kunlunce.com/ssjj/guojipinglun/2017-07-24/117722.html, accessed: 24 July 2017.
Keane, Michael (2007) *Created in China: the Great New Leap Forward*, London: Routledge.

Keane, Michael and Chen, Ying (2017) 'Entrepreneurial Solutionism, Characteristic Cultural Industries and the Chinese Dream', *International Journal of Cultural Policy*. doi:10.1080/10286632.2017.1374382.

Keane, Michael and Wu, Huan (2018) 'Lofty Ambitions: New Territories, and Turf Battles: China's Platforms 'go out'', *Media Industry Journal*, 5(1): 51–68.

Koponen, Johannes (2017) 'Rise and Fall of the Platform Business', *DemosHelsinki*. Available: www.demoshelsinki.fi/en/2018/03/26/rise-and-fall-of-the-platform-business/, accessed: 25 May 2018.

Leong, Susan (2018) 'Prophets of Mass Innovation: The Gospel According to BAT', *Media Industry Journal*, 5(1). doi:10.3998/mij.15031809.0005.105.

Liang, Ophenia (2017) 'Why M-commerce Is Taking China by Storm', *Digital Crew*, 5 September 2017. Available: www.digitalcrew.com.au/m-commerce-taking-china-storm/, accessed: 18 August 2018.

Maçães, Bruno (2018) *The Dawn of Eurasia: On the Trail of the New World Order*, London: Penguin.

Malecki, Edward J. and Moriset, Bruno (2008) *The Digital Economy: Business Organization, Production Processes and Regional Developments*, London and New York: Routledge.

Ningbo Municipal Government Portal (2017) 'Opinions of Ningbo Government on the Construction of Ningbo as the "Made in China 2025" Pilot Demonstration City'. Available: http://gtog.ningbo.gov.cn/art/2017/3/28/art_1617_797691.html, accessed: 28 March 2017.

Ningbo Municipal Statistics Bureau Website (2018) '2017 Indicators of Zhejiang Province (1): GDP & Fixed Assets Investment'. Available: http://tjj.ningbo.gov.cn/read/20180412/30656.aspx, accessed: 18 August 2018.

Pandaily (2018) 'China's Internet Use Counts 772 Million'. Available: https://pandaily.com/chinese-internet-user-count-hits-772-million-90-percent-mobile/, accessed: 18 August 2018.

Rossiter, Ned (2014) 'Logistical Worlds', *Cultural Studies Review*, 20(1): 53–76.

Srnicek, Nick (2017) *Platform Capitalism*, Cambridge: Polity Press.

State Council (2017) 'China Boosts Mass Entrepreneurship and Innovation'. Available: http://english.gov.cn/policies/latest_releases/2015/06/16/content_281475128473681.htm, accessed: 28 March 2017.

The World Bank (2009) *Extending Reach and Increasing Impact: Information and Communications for Development*, Washington, DC: The World Bank.

Van Dijck, Jose, Thomas, Poell and Mattijin, de Waal (2018) *The Platform Society*, Cambridge: Oxford University Press.

Wang, Yiwei (2015) *One Belt One Road: Opportunities and Challenges*, Beijing: People's Publishing Housebusiness.linkedin.com/content/dam/members/regional/zh_CN/site/events/2016/nov/one-belt-and-one-road/%E4%B8%80%E5%B8%A6%E4%B8%80%E8%B7%AF1101_1.0.pdf, accessed: 23 April 2018.

Wang, Binbin and Li, Xiaoyan (2017) 'Big Data, Platform Economy and Market Competition: A Preliminary Construction of Plan-Oriented Market Economy System in the Information Era', *World Review of Political Economy*, 8(2): 138–161.

Xie, Ping, Zou, Chuanwei and Liu, Haier (2016) *Internet Finance in China: Introduction and Practical Approaches*, London: Routledge.

Xu, Jin (2013) *Platform Economics (2nd Edition)* (*pintai jinjixue*), Shanghai: Shanghai Jiaotong University Press. Available: www.aliresearch.com/blog/article/detail/id/20947.html, accessed: 15 March 2018.

Yiwu Municipality Website (2017) 'Main Features of Economic and Social Development in Our City'. Available: www.yw.gov.cn/zjyw/jjfz/zhsl/201803/t20180315_1391346.shtml, accessed: 15 March 2018.

Yiwu Municipality Website (2018) 'Yiwu's Foreign Trade Exports Reached 56.53 Billion Yuan in the First Quarter of 2018, Increase 16.6% Compared with Last Year'. Available: www.yw.gov.cn/zjyw/jjfz/zhsl/201804/t20180424_1408742.shtml, accessed: 24 April 2018.

Zeng, Yihua (2018) 'Zhejiang Yiwu Building a "Model" for Internet Economic Innovation', *China Today*. Available: www.chinatoday.com.cn/zw2018/sh_4980/201804/t20180418_800127409.html, accessed: 18April 2018.

Zheng, Bijian (2011) 'China's Rise Is a Peaceful Rise. The Rejuvenation of the Chinese Nation Is the Rejuvenation of Its Civilization', Speech at the Beijing Regional Conference of the Asia-Pacific Working Group of the 'Trilateral Commission' in 25 November, 2005, reprinted in *China's Road to Peaceful Rise*. Translated by Peter Nolan, London: Routledge, chap. 30.

Zhu, Jinzy (2014) *China Cloud Rising: China's Journey toward Technological Supremacy*, Heidelberg: Springer.

3 Infrastructure and Platform Anxieties in India

Pradip Thomas

Digital India and State Power

I would like in this chapter to try and explore some aspects and anxieties related to the pursuit of a transactional economy in India by highlighting what appear to be consolidations in the e-commerce economy and increasing cartographic anxieties related to Google Maps. Before exploring these examples, I will situate them within the broader context of the nationwide Digital India programme initiated by the Government of India (GOI). Digital India is an ambitious and vast, US$17 billion exercise designed to usher the whole of India into the knowledge economy era. It is based on a vision of seamless flows and of multilevel transactions becoming the basis for commerce, socialities and citizen engagement with public services. In this respect, Digital India has been exemplified by *Aadhaar*, a biometrics-based unique identity card that was ostensibly devised to establish a fool-proof framework for welfare payments (notwithstanding its evidently substantive implications for the biopolitical control of citizens). Extending a digital trace to every citizen is regarded as a foundational aspect of the larger project that entails major public-private investments in infrastructure building, national connectivity, e-governance, e-commerce and smart cities. At the heart of all these projects are a variety of 'core' transactions between the state and a variety of users – private citizens, industry, the public and private sectors – that are based on investments in expanding technical functionalities to create network effects. Thus, Digital India is explicitly an aspirational project closely linked to the government's central ambitions to mainstream the transactional economy and to become a recognized global power.

Launched in 2015, under the aegis of the Ministry of Electronics and Information Technology, Digital India is based on nine programme pillars including IT manufacturing and IT job creation along with the areas mentioned above. An explicit aim of Digital India is to integrate public IT services and to bridge the rural-urban digital divide through extending digital empowerment projects via e-banking, e-health, e-education and e-agriculture, extending digital access initiatives via

Common Service Centres and the Post Office and expanding the electronic delivery of services and, by extension, the transactional economy. The State via Digital India initiatives is involved in expanding its transactional imprint via digitized payments, applications and registrations, and a range of digital services. Digital India is being built on both pre-existing and new conduits and layers; there are 33 organizations including peak bodies such as the National Association of Software and Services Companies, various research and development centres of ministerial departments such as the Centre for Development of Advanced Computing, cybersecurity units such as the Indian Computer Emergency Response Team (ICERT), the National Centre of Geo-Informatics, the National Informatics Centre that provides the network backbone for e-government and the Unique Identification Authority of India that is responsible for a nationwide 'smart' identity project, among a number of other organizations and digital initiatives.

The backbone of this network, the National Information Infrastructure, is built on an integration of existing networks inclusive of the State Wide Area Network, National Knowledge Network, National Optical Fibre Network, Government User Network and the MeghRaj Cloud. The digitization of projects under the e-Kranti e-governance initiative is based on 44 Mission Mode Projects covering the digitization of land records to banking, e-courts and rural development. Digital India also has provisions for the sharing of open data with its citizens under the MyGov initiative, an ambitious net zero import policy for certain electronic products by 2020, ICT training and capacity building especially in North East India along with a variety of short-term projects including the provisioning of public WiFi hotspots throughout the country, weather/disaster information monitoring and a national portal for missing/lost children among other initiatives. There is a specific focus on the informational development of North East India and its seven states that have been systematically neglected by successive governments in India. This region has primarily functioned as a buffer region between India on the one hand and China, Myanmar and Bangladesh on the other. The long-standing invisibility and neglect of this region has fostered insurrections against the Indian state, and China's claims on this territory are probably the key reason of State to 'develop' this region through securitization. More broadly, while the vision of Digital India is ambitious, its roll out has been patchy everywhere. To date, it would seem that impulses of governmentality have, at least for the moment, trumped other projected goals that were part of the vision (including nationwide connectivity and smart cities).

Given India's open policy towards multinational internet platforms, the further issue of whether or not to regulate platforms and their many services such as the messaging-based Whatsapp has come to the fore in the context of the use of such services by Hindu extremists and their circulations of lynchings of mainly Muslim traders of cattle and suspect child kidnappers. While the Telecom Regulatory Authority of India (TRAI) has issued a consultation paper on the regulation of OTTs (Over the Top) primarily in response to licensed telecom operators that have cited unfair advantages accruing to OTT operators (see Consultation Paper on Regulatory Framework for Over the Top Services 2015), TRAI is yet to issue a more comprehensive paper inclusive of the need to curb messaging-services-based mobilizations to carry out hate acts and the circulation of videos and images of acts of violence and murder in closed online groups. In spite of investments in projects geared towards the expansion of the digital footprint in India across many levels, it is clear that the State is not in a position to control or curb disruptive socialities on platforms that thrive on connectivities and socialities such as Whatsapp and Facebook. Such anxieties are arguably overshadowed and compounded by India's lack of preparedness and inability to compete with the impact of these global platforms and/or build capacities in artificial intelligence that are key to the shaping of the knowledge economy across multiple sectors (Singh 2018).

Beginning with a theory-informed exploration of infrastructure and platforms, this chapter highlights the relationship between digital infrastructures, platforms and politics in India by highlighting two instances of platform dynamics and their corresponding anxieties when it comes to the regulation of infrastructures and platforms. These are Amazon and the politics of platform-based e-commerce, and Google maps and the politics of national security and cartographic anxiety.

The Geopolitics of Digital Infrastructures

Recent studies on information and media infrastructures and platforms have attempted to highlight both their unique and overlapping characteristics, their centrality to modern-day information empires and their absolutely critical roles in shaping the global distribution, production and consumption of goods and services (Dourish and Bell 2011; Gillespie 2010; Parks and Starosielski 2015; Plantin et al. 2016). While distinctions can be made between infrastructures and the algorithmically driven nature of platforms, it would seem that the correspondences between the two are increasing and one consequence of the privatization of the internet has been the infrastructuralization of platforms and growth reliant on network effects exemplified by the enormous reach and shaping powers of the big three – Amazon, Google and Facebook– enhanced by their algorithmic dominion over cultures, the idea of the social, political practices, economic futures, and their investments in and control over cloud computing. In other words, and arguably, there has been a steady colonization of the internet by the big three through their capture of storage, distribution, search, sociality and to a lesser extent devices.

Platforms as we well know engage with markets through many gradations of mediation and transactional processes that contribute to democratic, user-led innovations (Arab Spring) while paradoxically also reinforcing infrastructural control. So there is a case to be made for both the affordances of platformization in the reinforcement of the local and the strengthening of social networking, social processes and democracy along with 'platform imperialism' based on algorithmic control over the rules that govern its architecture and codes (Schwarz 2017).

It is clear that the dominant platforms today are more than just involved in the commercial opportunities offered by search and sociality. While the market capitalization of the big three exceeds a trillion US dollars, the sustainability of 'pure-play' data-driven empires is not assured; hence, Amazon's foray into bricks and mortar is highlighted by its purchase of the Whole Foods Empire for $13.7 billion on 16 June 2017 and its ownership of media, retail, data and entertainment. Its CEO, Jeffrey Bezo, owns the *Washington Post* (Bhattaria 2017). Rather unsurprisingly, its chief competitor in the groceries market in the USA, Walmart, has begun to buy into online companies. And this would seem to be pattern today with companies striving to own both online and offline enterprises. With such purchases it would seem that these platform companies are becoming like the conglomerates of old although unlike these old companies, these new companies are 'affectively' closer to their consumers through their algorithmically driven production cultures. While the ubiquity of such infrastructures and platforms is undeniable, it would seem the case that the jostling for global dominance by the big three has been eventful with successes accompanied by failure of Facebook's Free Basics initiative in India, the emergence of global competition such as Alibaba and local firms such as Flipkart in India along with national and international efforts to regulate platforms and platform practices particularly on the issue of national security. This would suggest that sooner rather than later, supranational and national regulatory regimes will emerge to curb the total domination fantasies of platform imperialists.

As is clear from the many anxieties that have been publicly expressed by many governments that have been subject to terrorist attacks, most recently in the UK, platform inclusivities, encrypted data and secure information flows can be used and abused with critical consequences for both infrastructure and lives. Issues related to cybersecurity have become of particular importance to governments throughout the world in the context of the rise of terrorism and social media platforms such as Facebook have been forced to respond to the fact that platforms facilitate many constructions of reality and have become spaces where identities are created, practices and performances valorized and pathways to actionings experienced and explored – highlighted by Facebook's Online Civil Courage Initiative that has been launched to tackle online extremism in Germany, France and the UK (Ruddick 2017). Infrastructure and platform anxieties are experienced by most if not all governments not least because of the disruptive consequences that stem from the creation of value, their potential to be deployed in anti-state activities, the repositioning and rescheduling of work and their consequences for traditional industries. The regulatory implications of such disruptions for governments constitute a major challenge, perhaps best illustrated by the fact that the innovative in-betweenness of the major platforms has enabled them to largely bypass the rules and regulations that pertain to ordinary manufacturers and purveyors of goods and services. This manufactured and constructed self-identity is also under question across the world. Against this backdrop, I will seek to explore the GOI's evolving approach towards platforms and regulated infrastructure.

The Nature of Infrastructure

How to think through the meaning of infrastructure is a challenge precisely because we take it for granted most of the time. The fascination of infrastructuralism as John Durham Peters (2015: 33) observes '…is for the basic, the boring, the mundane…'. Infrastructure is most often invisible and in the background and only claims our attention when things fail – when there is an electricity 'trip' or when the roads are consistently congested. In other words there is a strong relational element in our engagements with infrastructure and we make sense of it through the many ways in which we engage and connect with its many functionalities and the occasional (dis)functionalities of infrastructure. While we are embedded in multiple infrastructures, each of these infrastructures such as roads for example is embedded in material and immaterial realities – technology, planning, finances, policy, supply chains of material, resources and so on that most of us taken for granted. And this is also true of what one can call information infrastructures given that most of us take for granted the protocols that enable our computer to work, access our Facebook page and buy things online unless there is a breakdown in connectivity and access. One of the better definitions of infrastructure is that by Susan Star in which she highlights nine properties that are fundamental to its understanding (1999: 381–382). These include its embeddedness in 'technologies, arrangements and social structures' and its largely invisible transparency, its reach or scope and the fact that it is always learned as part of membership meaning, its links with and shapings by conventions of practice, as embodiments of standards reflected through standardization of protocols, and its building on an installed base (meaning that its architectures radiate from existing foundations such as optical fibres that run along railway lines, pre-existing ducts, canals and roads).

Infrastructures typically become visible on breakdown and when fixed in modular increments. This is especially the case with the internet as infrastructure. 'Infrastructure', as Ribes and Finholt have observed,

> stretches across multiple fields of action: (i) It is a technological venture, seeking to deploy durable resources, to support work, automate tedious tasks, and enable collaboration; (ii) It is matter of human work, organization and maintenance...and (iii) It is an institutional venture, seeking to provide stable and accessible services to communities at national and international levels.
>
> (2009: 377–378)

Parks and Starosielski highlight the need for infrastructure studies to deal with issues of scale, relationality, difference and unevenness, labour/repair/maintenance, natural resources/environment, affect and innovative methodologies (2016: 11–17). They highlight the need to study affect: 'A phenomenology of affect might begin by excavating the various dispositions, feelings, moods, or sensations people experience during encounters with infrastructural objects, sites and processes' (ibid: 15). One can also add aspects of a political economy of infrastructure to this list including its governance, its objectives, whether it is in the public or private interest, its resourcing, the befuddling and invisibility of power concentrations and economic and social interests, its control over all manner of data flows, its exclusions and so on. In other words, it is important that we include in our definition of infrastructure both the relative invisibility of its architecture and the ways in which political and economic decisions and interests enable and shape the consumption of such infrastructure through a multiplicity of everyday practices. In the words of Graham and Marvin, 'Infrastructure networks are...involved in sustaining what we might call 'sociotechnical geometries of power' (2001: 11).

The complexity of infrastructure requires heavy sunk costs, and public-private partnerships are central to delivery of the Digital India initiative. Along with the 33 government bodies and organizations involved in the project, the programme relies upon the contributions of numerous private sector firms involved in telecommunications, data and internet infrastructure, along with a variety of digital platforms that have assumed both national and international provenance. Private sector infrastructural investments in Digital India include those made by Reliance Industries in wireless broadband, cloud computing and data centres ($37billion); Bharti Airtel in 4G connectivity, e-health and e-education ($16 billion); Sterlite Technologies Limited in fibre and cable manufacturing ($3.7 billion); Aditya Birla Group in network roll-out, broadband network and WiFi deployment ($7 billion); Cisco in early stage and growth stage companies ($1 billion)and Qualcom in digital and innovation start-ups ($15 billion) (Digital India2017). While e-governance will account for a number of initiatives under Digital India, these are bound to facilitate a multiplicity of cultures of consumption over a typology of access and use from open to closed. Arguably, open data and public sector software initiatives are reflective of open systems while surveillance via the Unique Identity scheme and other types of profiling are indicative of closed systems. Given the involvement of private, and often proprietary technology companies, the role of open as opposed to closed information infrastructure systems remains an area of contestation in India today.

The Nature of Platforms

If the meaning of infrastructure is multilayered and involves a reckoning with technology, relationalities, policy, the material and the immaterial, that of platform is as complex given that it is made up of many meanings and etymologies. While there is definitely a case to study how individuals relate to infrastructure, arguably, the central power of platforms is inherently linked to their creation of a monetized, marketing strategy linked to the mining, nurturing, shaping and selling of individual affect. Gillespie has focused on the computational, architectural, figurative and political meanings of platform (2010: 349–350). So when we typically speak of online platforms it refers to computational, programmed interfaces whose realization is based on a proliferation of relatively closed or open interactivities. Srnicek refers to five types of platforms – advertising platforms such as Google and Facebook, cloud platforms such as Microsoft that rent out hardware and software, industrial platforms such Siemens that supply traditional manufacturing with platform capacities, product platforms such as Spotify that generate revenue through using other platforms to transform traditional goods into service and lean platforms such as Uber that are based on a minimum ownership of assets (2017: 49–50). The word 'platform' also connotes a raised surface that is readied for dialogue, a neutral place for all those who want to use it, a space that is access-heavy and control-lite.

> 'The more conceptual use of 'platform' leans on all of the term's connotations: computational, something to build upon and innovate from; political, place from which to speak and be heard; figurative, in that the opportunity is an abstract promise as much as a practical one; and architectural, in that YouTube is designed as an open-armed, egalitarian facilitation of expression, not an elitist gatekeeper with normative and technical restrictions. This multisided definition fits in neatly with the long-standing rhetoric about the democratizing potential of the internet, and with the more recent enthusiasm for user-generated content (UGC), amateur

> expertise, popular creativity, peer-level social networking and robust online commentary'
>
> (Gillespie 2010: 352).

However, the apparently agnostic meaning of the word 'platform' conceals more than it reveals given that platforms such as Facebook and Google are involved in mining and selling algorithmic-driven, increasingly finely tuned profiles of the consumption habits of individuals to advertisers, even subtly shaping their consumer preferences thereby adding value to those who profit from such profiling. One of the ways in which they have exerted control over our socialities and consumer behaviour is by positioning themselves as cultural intermediaries involved in merely facilitating information exchange and sharing thereby excusing themselves from being identified as content providers and therefore outside the purview of regulation that old media companies fall under. However, as the major platform providers have grown into content providers with Amazon Studio and Amazon Video and Facebook Live that is based on original, long form video content that can be watched through 'Facebook mobile apps and the company's Apple TV and Samsung Smart TV apps', there is pressure on these platforms to fall under the regulatory purview of traditional content and carriage media (Alba 2017). However, platforms such as Facebook claim to be user-neutral, meaning that it can be used by all manner of groups from terrorists and hate speech advocates to social movement collectives to enact agency. At the very same time and as Plantin et al. have observed, 'social media platforms bind pre-defined communicative acts to an economic logic' (2016: 5).

Platforms demand academic investigation precisely because their approach to their customers is through exploring and experimenting with a plethora of interactive socialities that are based on an increasingly finely tuned understanding of affective behaviours. Carah has worked on the nature of algorithmic branding used by brands such as Coca-Cola, Virgin and Smirnoff at music festivals in Australia through social media platforms and mobile devices (2017: 398). His research details the role played by brands in continually experimenting with 'consumer creativity and participation' and branding as a cultural form 'that works to make the human capacity to give and gain attention available to the decision-making logic and learning sequences of algorithmic media'. Arguably this close attention to consumer behaviour offers insights into the shaping of such behaviours and it is not surprising therefore that the relationship between social media and politics has become such a newsworthy issue especially in the light of Trump and alt news in the USA and Twitter and trolls in India in the context of Narendra Modi's and his party the BJP's strategic investments in social media platforms. Dourish points to the need to study algorithms not as much as a topic for conceptual study but as an 'object of professional practice' for software engineers and computer scientists although the question that he proposes 'What power does the notion of 'algorithm' have within their conversations and collaborations, and in what way are algorithms invoked, identified, traded, performed, produced, boasted of, denigrated, elided?' can also be posed to those involved in the implementations of algorithmic power including cybersecurity experts and politicians (2016: 9).

Digital Anxieties and the GOI

While the blurrings between infrastructure and platform need to be acknowledged, for all practical purposes the GOI's approach to infrastructure is very different from their approach to platforms. The availability and access to nationwide infrastructures – railways, electricity, roads, public hospitals, education – have featured in the promise of development supported by successive governments and arguably both the experience of infrastructure and the infrastructure of experience have been dimensions of the engagement with infrastructures in India. Dourish and Bell explain these two dimensions:

> By the experience of infrastructure, we point to the ways in which infrastructure, rather than being hidden from view, becomes visible through our increasing dependence on it for the practices of everyday life (2011: 98). By the infrastructure of experience, we draw attention to the ways in which, in turn, the embedding of a range of infrastructures into everyday space shapes our experience of that space even as it provides a framework through which our encounters with space take on meaning.

The provisionings of infrastructure remains one reason for government and it necessarily includes policy, regulatory and fiscal dimensions along with ministerial oversight. In recent years and in the context of cyber and other attacks, the GOI has identified critical infrastructure that includes agriculture and food, banking and finance, telecommunications, critical manufacturing industries, defence industrial base, emergency services, energy, healthcare, information technology, national icons and monuments, postal and shipping, transportation and water supply. This identification of critical infrastructure has been accompanied by attempts to secure online infrastructures through regulatory means such as the Information Technology Act (2000) and the National Cyber Security Policy along with institutional responses such as the ICERT (Singh et al. 2014).

The GOI has essentially continued with a top-down approach to governance as the preferred model although this has been muddied by multi-stakeholder approaches especially in the context of the governance of the internet where the model for the peak body Internet Assigned

Names and Numbers Agency (ICANN) is a consensual approach (although this model of multi-stakeholderism too has its own limitations). The Indian government's position has veered from a multilateral stance to a multi-stakeholder one, positions that are also reflected in civil society that has only episodically been involved in matters related to internet governance. The private sector too has had limited involvement in matters related to internet governance (Alwadhi 2016). While large countries like India and China do want to have a more substantive role at ICANN especially in the light of the apparent ceding of control over ICANN by US-based entities in 2016, India's 'schizophrenic' approach to internet governance is illustrated by its support, at one time or the other for four different models of internet governance highlighted by Subramaniam:

> The ITU (International Telecommunications Union)-based inter-governmental model; the IGF (Internet Governance Forum)-based inter-governmental + equal multi-stakeholder model; the UN-CIRP (Committee on Internet-related Policies) (based inter-governmental + limited stake-holder model; and the fully participatory model where the ICANN becomes a completely independent body without any supervision from any government or UN Agency.
>
> (2013: 12)

India, in other words, has not been able to successfully bring internet infrastructure under its control. A further complication stems from the fact that information infrastructures can be collectively developed outside of the oversight of any government, as with open-source and free software-based infrastructures that are socially, collectively produced, that are based on networked interdependencies that resist government moves to centralize and control information infrastructures (Constantinides 2012). Collective, multilayered weavings of information infrastructures by a range of communities in India outside of government control contest the domination of government over information infrastructures.

Amazon, Walmart and the Politics of Platform-Based E-Commerce

The entry of Amazon.com into the Indian online retail market completely changed prospects for dominant domestic players such as Flipkart and Snapdeal. Amazon's venture in India was based on a purchase by them and Catamaram Private Services in August 2014 of Prione Business Services Pvt. Ltd floated by the billionaire software czar Narayana Murthy of Infosys. In September 2014 Prione acquired a company called Cloudtail that was liberally funded by Amazon and it was able to use the cover of an 'Indian-owned' company to make downstream investments that was not counted as foreign direct investments (FDIs) (Choudhary 2010). However, Amazon's ambitions to control the online retail market have been placed on hold following their inability to outbid Walmart from purchasing a 77% stake in Flipkart for US$16 billion in May 2018 thus acquiring 34.3% of the e-commerce market (see Molla and Rey 2018). Another player keen on getting a slice of the US$38.5 billion e-commerce market is Google that plans to launch its own e-commerce services in India in late 2018. It plans leverage its Gmail subscriber base and its large 12,000-strong Internet Saathi (digital literacy) base (Dan 2018). While the general euphoria over online retail has declined in the context of a very slow growth in online shoppers (between 35 and 40 million in 2015) and slowing revenues (see Delayed Delivery2017), there have been major lobbying efforts by the domestic players to restrict the entry of a non-Indian company Amazon, although the financial bases of local companies have themselves been based on investments from venture capitalists from the USA and elsewhere.

Interestingly enough, the main political challenge to FDIs in multi-brand retail and the grocery business has come from the Rashtriya Swayamsevak Sangh (RSS), via its economic advocacy unit, the Swadeshi Jagran Manch (SJM), that is vociferously opposed to the major e-commerce vendors including the now foreign-funded Indian company Flipkart and the impact of such vendors on the offline retail market (see Mathew 2015). A brainchild of the RSS chief Balasaheb Deoras, the SJM, was formed to counter the liberalization policies adopted by the Narasimha Rao government in 1991. Embarrassingly enough for the RSS, the SJM has continued to oppose the globalization policies adopted by the Vajpayee government through organizing *Chetna Yatras* throughout the country. Earlier this year, the SJM launched a campaign against Paytm (financially supported by Alibaba), a reflection of its growing anti-China stance, following the standoff between India and China in Doklam (PTI 2017). It waged a campaign against the government regulator's (Genetic Engineering Appraisal Committee, or GEAC) support for GM mustard and the pro-pharma policies adopted by Niti (National Institute for Transforming India), Aayog (the successor to the Planning Commission) and the Public Health Foundation of India (an NGO supported by funds from the Bill and Melinda Gates Foundation). It did so due to their links with big pharma companies and their influence on health policy in India. Retail associations such as the All India Footwear Manufacturers and Retailers Association and the Retail Association of India have also filed lawsuits in the Delhi High Court against e-commerce companies and their breaking of investment rules in India (Kazmin 2015).

With Alibaba entering the market through its investments in Paytm and Snapdeal and Softbank's investments in Flipkart, it is clear that 'Made in India' is proving to be a difficult proposition. The Indian government's granting of 100%FDI in electronic marketplaces in 2016 enabled Amazon to invest close to $5 billion in its services in India including $500million in the brick and mortar grocery business. The Indian government had previously only allowed e-commerce vendors to follow the business-to-business model or marketplace model where the portals were only allowed to facilitate transactions between buyers and sellers (who held control over their inventories). This tradition was followed by a number of e-commerce companies, although companies such as Flipkart and Amazon were accused of selling their own products directly to consumers. The new inventory model is based on direct e-commerce rather than its facilitation. Although the BJP in opposition were against FDI in the retail market, they have since become its champions. They have abolished the 25-year-old Foreign Investment Promotion Board that was the inter-ministerial body involved in providing single window clearances for FDIs (Arun 2017). While giving individual ministries oversight on FDI clearance may speed up processes, there is no guarantees of a common framework in support and and/or regulation of inward investments. Already friction between ministries has been illustrated, with the case of the Department of Telecommunications that is keen on global e-commerce players locating their servers in India, while the Ministry of Electronics and Information Technology is opposed (Mishra 2017). Platform capitalism is global and platforms in India are fundamentally involved in the economic globalization of India, much to the chagrin of nationalists who now find themselves fundamentally incapable of altering or curbing flows of international capital.

Google Maps, National Security and Cartographic Anxiety

While the embrace of online infrastructures and platforms is a central plank of the Indian government's development policy best highlighted in their ambitious Digital India initiative, the risks associated with contentious citizen's actions online, platform complicities in anti-Indian postings, and data access to devices and platforms have led to an infrastructural approach to online national security that includes legal means, the establishment of monitoring institutions and the constant airing of the need for governmental oversight over online data flows. The Indian government's bid to get access to encrypted data over Blackberry devices is just one example of their attempts to control the flow of online information. Between July 2016 and December 2016, Facebook in their *Government Requests Report* (2016) restricted 719 items.

> We restricted access to content in India in response to legal requests from law enforcement agencies from various states and the India Computer Emergency Response Team within the Ministry of Communications and Information Technology. The majority of content

> restricted was alleged to violate local laws against anti-religious speech, hate speech, and disrespect of national symbols.
>
> (ibid)

India has consistently been among the leading countries involved in the censoring of Facebook, Google and other platforms (Facebook took down 30,126 posts in 2015 in India alone (Mehta 2016)). In the context of unrest in Kashmir, both mainstream media and close to 22 online platforms have been banned and Facebook has been involved in blocking/deleting accounts (as, for example, that of the Kashmir Solidarity Group) (Lakshmi 2016).

A report by the International Federation of Journalists highlights that

> The order issued by Principal Secretary (Home) R K Goyal under the Indian Telegraph Act 1885 asked all the ISPs to immediately stop transmission of Facebook, Twitter, WhatsApp, QQ, We Chat, Qzone, Tumbir, Google, Baidu, Skype, Viber, Line, Snapchat, Pinterest, Telegram, Reddit, Snapfish, You Tube (upload), Vine, Xanga, Buzznet and Flickr for one month or until further notice.
>
> (2017)

A range of laws regulating the internet have been used to censor freedom of expression and a number of sections in laws have been used to control dissent. These include: Sedition (Section 12A of the Indian Penal Code (IPC)), Criminal Defamation (Sections 499 and 500 of the IPC), Hurting Religious Sentiments (Section 295c of the IPC), Hate Speech (Section 153A of the IPC), Criminal Intimidation (Section 503 of the IPC), Public Tranquility (Section 505 (1)(b) of the IPC), Official Secrets Act, Contempt of Courts Act (Subsection (2)(i)), Information Technology Act and 'Blocking Rules' (Section 66A), the Scheduled Castes and the Scheduled Tribes (Prevention of Atrocities) Amendment Act (Section 3 (1)) (see Mukherjee 2016). Apart from general concerns related to cybersecurity and cyberespionage, both platforms and media infrastructures have been implicated in 'cartographic' violations against the state. Media outlets such as *The Economist* and Al Jazeera and applications such as Google Earth and Google Maps and Facebook posts have earned censure from the GOI for carrying disputed geo-spatial information on borders, especially in Kashmir with Pakistan and in North East India with China. The fact that terrorists who attacked Mumbai in 2008 and Pathankot in 2016 had used Google Earth to locate sites for attacks highlighted the changes that have occurred in access to and use of geo-spatial tools for high-resolution imaging, hitherto a domain of governments, and the difficulties that GOI had to address this issue with Google Earth.

There is however an additional issue, as Lisa Parks reminds us, is that 'Google Earth functions…as a property development engine' given that the company exerts IP over any data produced on its platforms (2013: 298). Sangeet Kumarhas drawn attention to the tussles between Google that champions the free flow of information and nation states such as India that are now on the backfoot trying to reassert their sovereignty in a context in which universal access to such imaging has highlighted the messiness of disputed borders, territories and representations (2010). Such writings point to an emerging interest in understanding imperceptible, invisible infrastructures from satellite footprints to undersea fibre optic cables that are critical to the global network society (see Starosielski 2015). These wireless and wired networks are resolutely material and represent infrastructural and geopolitical interests (see Parks 2009). Satellite-based valuations of both territory and resources in any given country highlight the power of these institutions and it is therefore unsurprising that a country like India with its own geospatial ambitions has taken umbrage at mapping and imagery generated by Google and other platforms. Among other effects, such mapping exposes the limits to banal forms of nationalism since it exposes the contested, imprecise nature of territory since mapping always tells a story and there are always multiple stories of the same map. In order to regulate this sector, the GOI was involved in 2016 in drawing up a draft National Geospatial Bill that is meant to regulate the 'acquisition, dissemination, publication and distribution of geospatial information in India which is likely to affect the security, sovereignty and integrity of India…'. If this Bill had been legislated, its contraventions would have invited million dollar fines along with imprisonment (Bearak 2016). Platforms such as Google, Uber and others would have had to apply for special licences to carry out their work in India.

While the Bill's intent included the streamlining and centralization of the acquisition and depiction of such information by organizations under the National Spatial Data Infrastructure inclusive of the Survey of India, the Indian Space Research Organisation (ISRO), National Remote Sensing Centre, the Census of Indiaand the National Atlas and Thematic Mapping Organisation, among other agencies (see Singh 2009), it was also directed at controlling mapping activities and information gathering by external applications such as Google Maps. An article in *The Mint* on this Bill by Saikia and Doval (2016)refers to a blogpost hosted by Geospatial World, in which Arup R writes: 'the definition is so wide it includes everything from satellite imagery to atlases, books, car navigation system, GPS enabled devices like cameras, smartphones and tablets'. From car manufacturers to publishers to ordinary users, the act might end up bringing everyone under its purview'. The Bill was shelved earlier this year after representations from the $2 billion geospatial industry to the Home Ministry. The Bill would have led to mapping becoming a highly bureaucratized operation with implications for universities, research centres and researchers in India (Rajuand Alam 2016). It therefore brings into relief the impossibility of attaining 'accuracy' in the collection of data, for example, on topography. Water sheds, for example, are ever-changing. There are also inherent difficulties in curbing external, remote sensing of data (be it for cartographic, economic or geopolitical reasons). Any such legislation also has to contend with the availability of open-source mapping technologies and, perhaps most problematically, the ubiquity of mobile technologies such as smartphones that rely on a variety of geo-mapping apps.

The GOI has tried to counter Google Maps and Google Earth through not giving permission to Google Street View (The Indian Express 2017). It has launched its own geospatial mapping platform Bhuvna, a derivative of Google Earth, and made a case for 'authenticated' local mapping technologies, such as that produced by the Survey of India. It is clear that at the heart of this struggle is the entrenched belief that only the GOI can generate accurate information on borders and topography, an attitude that merely reinforces the 'control' paradigm. ISRO's launch of the remote sensing satellite, Cartosat-2E, is also meant to reduce dependency on the import of high-resolution imagery although the sub-metre images will only be available to government agencies and the defence establishment (Madhumathi 2017). These are technical responses of fundamental political and psychological concerns. Sankaran Krishna argued long ago that India's 'cartographic anxiety' is much more than a mapping of the country, since it comprises of myriad representational practices that define belonging, insider and outsider, nation and neighbour, national and anti-national through multiple media and mediations. Krishna highlights the big picture of India as an imagined country made real through multiple cartographies that have, in modern times, been reinforced by the project of Hindu nationalism and visions of Greater India. Thus, as he puts it:

> Cartographic anxiety may be described, then, as one symptom, among many, of a postcolonial condition. This preoccupation with national space and with borders reveals an obsession to approximate a historical original that never existed, except as the telos of the narrative of modernity: a pure, unambiguous community called the home-land.
>
> (1994: 517)

Opportunities and Risks

Infrastructure and platform anxieties are inherent to contemporary 'risk' societies. The inability of government to exert sovereignty and control over digital information flows is one of the major challenges facing nation states throughout the world. The availability of and access to digital mapping platforms along with the largely unregulated nature of the three platform giants – Google, Facebook and Amazon – in India has already led to platform domination on an unprecedented scale. These examples highlight the multifaceted response to platforms and infrastructure, and the nature of anxieties felt by GOI in spheres which it has tightly controlled in the past. With the exception of TRAI's involvement in Facebook's failed ambitions to dominate mobile access to the internet through the Free Basics initiative, the GOI has largely been unable and for that matter unwilling to resist the disruptive consequences of the big three. At least partly, this is because it has used these platforms for the advancement of its own electoral politics and heavily invested in its commitment to Digital India as a means of shaping a transactional economy. India's political parties use platforms actively for sectarian political purposes and, as a consequence, government's attempts to regulate platform content have tended to be reactive and partisan. As the digital domain expands rapidly, how governments in India respond to the challenges posed by digital disruptions will be of critical importance to India's ambitions to become a transactional economy. Clearly, there is a need to balance participation, equity, regulation, sovereignty and control. As it is, the instrumentalist nature of the Digital India programme and the multiple divides across Indian society suggest that the platforms and infrastructures of a transactional economy will develop unevenly across the nation.

References

Abraham, Sunil (2016) 'Facebook's Fall from Grace: Arab Spring to Indian Winter', *Tech*, 2, 19 February 2016. Available: file:///Users/uqpthom4/Desktop/Facebook's%20fall%20from%20grace:%20Arab%20Spring%20to%20Indian%20winter%20–%20Tech2.webarchive, accessed: 8 June 2017.

Alba, Davey (2017) 'Facebook's Officially a Media Company. Time to Act Like One', *Wired*, 3 June. Available: www.wired.com/2017/03/facebooks-officially-media-company-time-act-like-one/, accessed: 10 June 2017.

Arun, S. (2017) 'Govt. Approves Phasing Out of 25-year Old Foreign Investment Promotion Board', *The Hindu Online*, 24 May 2017. Available: www.thehindu.com/business/Economy/cabinet-approves-abolition-of-fipb/article18561815.ece, accessed: 8 June 2017.

Bearak, Max (2016) 'Cartographers Beware: India Warns of $15 Million Fine for Maps It Doesn't Like', *The Washington Post*, 6 May 2016. Available: www.washingtonpost.com/news/worldviews/wp/2016/05/06/cartographers-beware-india-warns-of-15-million-fine-for-maps-it-doesnt-like/?utm_term=.fd871d0a6205, accessed: 7 May 2017.

Bhattaria, Abha (2017) 'Amazon to Buy Whole Foods Market in Deal Valued at $13.7 Billion', *The Washington Post*, 16 June 2017. Available: www.washingtonpost.com/news/business/wp/2017/06/16/amazon-to-buy-whole-foods-market-in-deal-valued-at-13-7-billion-2/?utm_term=.107a4267a7f49, accessed: 11 June 2017.

Carah, Nic (2017) 'Algorithmic Brands: A Decade of Brand Experiments with Mobile and Social Media', *New Media and Society*, 19(3): 384–400.

Choudhary, Rahul Nath (2010) 'India's FDI Policy on e-commerce: Some Observations'. Available: http://111.93.232.162/pdf/DN1503.pdf, accessed: 7 June 2017.

Constantinides, Panos (2012) 'The Development and Consequences of New Information Infrastructures: The Case of Mashup Platforms', *Media, Culture and Society* 34(5): 606–622.

Dan (2018) 'Google Looking to Expand in e-commerce: Amazon, Flipkart Dominating India Is First Up', *MySmartPrice*, 27 May 2018. Available:www.mysmartprice.com/gear/2018/06/27/google-looking-expand-e-commerce-amazon-flipkart-dominating-india-first/, accessed: 9 June 2017.

Digital India (2017) 'Agencies Enabling DI Initiatives'. Available: www.digitalindia.gov.in/ecosystem/Agencies-Enabling-DI-Initiatives, accessed: 9 June 2017.

Dourish, Paul (2016) 'Algorithms and Their Others: Algorithmic Culture in Context', *Big Data and Society*, 3(2): 1–11.

Dourish, Paul and Bell, Genevieve (2011) *Divining a Digital Future: Mess and Mythology in Ubiquitous Computing*, Cambridge, MA and London: MIT Press.

Gillespie, Tarelton (2010) 'The Politics of 'Platforms'', *New Media and Society*, 12(3): 347–364.

Government of India (2016) *The Geospatial Information Regulation Bill, 2016*. Available: www.prsindia.org/uploads/media/draft/Draft%20Geospatial%20Bill,%202016.pdf, accessed: 8 June 2017.

Graham, Stephen and Marvin, Simon (2001) *Splintering Urbanism: Networked Infrastructures, Technological Mobilities and the Urban Condition*, London and New York: Routledge.

The Indian Express (2017) 'Google Street View Denied Permission in India: Here's the Reason Why', 10 June 2017. Available: http://indianexpress.com/article/technology/tech-news-technology/googles-street-view-turned-down-by-india-2843618/, accessed: 12 June 2017.

International Federation of Journalists (2017) 'Kashmir Crackdown: Twenty Two Social Media Channels Blocked', 27 April 2017. Available: www.ifj.org/nc/news-single-view/backpid/30/category/events-1/article/kashmir-crack-down-twenty-two-social-media-channels-blocked/, accessed: 5 May 2017.

Krishna, Sankaran (1994) 'Cartographic Anxiety: Mapping the Body-Politic in India', *Alternatives*, 19: 507–521.

Kumar, Sangeet (2010)'Google Earth and the Nation State: Sovereignty in the Age of New Media', *Global Media and Communication*, 6(2): 154–176.

Lakshmi, Rama (2016) 'Facebook Is Censoring Some Posts on Indian Kashmir', *The Washington Post Online*, 26 July 2016. Available: www.washingtonpost.com/news/worldviews/wp/2016/07/27/facebook-is-censoring-posts-on-indian-kashmir-some-say/?utm_term=.f798e8552d3d, accessed: 21 June 2017.

Madhumathi, D.S. (2017) 'India Gets a Sharper Eye in the Sky', *The Hindu Online*, 29 June 2017. Available: www.thehindu.com/sci-tech/science/india-gets-a-sharper-eye-in-the-sky/article19180628.ece?homepage=true, accessed: 29 June 2017.

Mathew, Liz (2015) 'An RSS Reminder: Ban e-tail like Amazon, FlipKart', *The Indian Express*, 18 January 2015. Available: http://indianexpress.com/article/india/india-others/meanwhile-an-rss-reminder-ban-e-tail-like-amazon-flipkart/, accessed: 9 June 2017.

Mishra, Asit Ranjan(2017) 'India not Keen to Put e-commerce Under FTA with Russia-led Group', *Live Mint*, 29 May 2017. Available: www.livemint.com/Politics/OUXyKIwZHpnoJPhj6mfuyK/India-not-keen-to-put-ecommerce-under-FTA-with-Russialed-g.html, accessed: 4 June 2017.

Molla, Rani and Rey, Jason Del (2018) 'WhyWalmart Bought Flipkart in Five Charts', *Recode*, 11 May 2018. Available: www.recode.net/2018/5/11/17335708/walmart-flipkart-india-ecommerce-charts, accessed: 23 June 2018.

Parks, Lisa (2009) 'Signals and Oil: Satellite Footprints and Post-communist Territories in Central Asia', *European Journal of Cultural Studies*, 12(2): 7–156.

Parks, Lisa (2013) 'Earth Observation and Signal Territories: Studying U.S. Broadcast Infrastructure Through Historical Network Maps, Google Earth, and Fieldwork', *Canadian Journal of Communication*, 38: 285–307.

Parks, Lisa and Starosieslki, Nick (eds) (2015) *Signal Traffic: Critical Studies of Media Infrastructures*, Urbana: University of Illinois Press.

Peters, John Durham (2015) *The Marvelous Clouds: Towards a Philosophy of Elemental Media*, Chicago, IL and London: University of Chicago Press.

Plantin, Jean-Christophe, Lagoze, Carl, Edwards, Paul N. and Sandvig, Christian (2016) 'Infrastructure Studies Meet Platform Studies in the Age of Google and Facebook', *New Media and Society*, 20(1): 293–310. doi:10.1177/1461444816661553.

Raju, K.N. Prudhvi and Alam, Sarfaraz (2016) 'The Geospatial Information Regulation Bill', *Economic and Political Weekly*, L1(31): 22–24.

Ribes, David and Finholt, Thomas Albert (2009) 'The Long Now of Technology Infrastructure: Articulating Tensions in Development', *Journal of the Association for Information Systems* 10(5): 375–398.

Ruddick, Graham (2017) 'Facebook Launches Drive in UK to Tackle Online Extremist Material', *The Guardian*, 23 June 2017. Available: www.theguardian.com/technology/2017/jun/23/facebook-launches-drive-in-uk-to-tackle-online-extremist-material, accessed: 26 June 2017.

Saikia, Arunabh and Doval, Nikita (2016) 'Govt Seeks to Make Google, Others Toe the Cartographical Line', *The Mint*, 10 May 2016. Available: www.livemint.com/Politics/wLDSG2y2RiwMhsMDY1M0PJ/Govt-seeks-to-make-Google-others-toe-the-cartographical-lin.html, accessed: 9 June 2017.

Schwarz, Jonas Andersson (2017) 'Platform Logic: An Interdisciplinary Approach to the Platform-based Economy', *Policy and Internet*, 9(4): 374–394. doi:10.1002/poi3.159.

Singh, Abhisek Narain, Gupta, M.P. and Ojha, Amitabh (2014) 'Identifying Critical Infrastructure Sectors and Their Dependencies: An Indian Scenario', *International Journal of Critical Infrastructure Protection*, 7: 71–85.

Singh, Parminder Jeet (2018) 'AI Superpower of Client Nation?', *The Hindu*, 27 July 2018. Available: www.thehindu.com/opinion/op-ed/ai-superpower-or-client-nation/article24523017.ece?homepage=true, accessed: 14 August 2017.

Singh, Pramod Kumar (2009) 'Spatial Data Infrastructure in India: Status, Governance, Challenges, and Strategies for Effective Functioning', *International Journal of Spatial Data Infrastructures Research*, 4: 359–388.

Srnicek, Nick (2017) *Platform Capitalism*, Cambridge and Malden, MA: Polity Press.

Star, Susan Leigh (1999) 'The Ethnography of Infrastructure', *American Behavioral Scientist*, 43(3): 377–391.

Starosielski, Nicole (2015) *The Undersea Network*, Durham, NC: Duke University Press.

Subramaniam, Ramesh (2013)'Internet Governance: A Developing Country Perspective', *Communications of the IIMA (International Information Management Association)*, 13(4): 1–16.

Telecom Regulatory Authority of India (2015) *Consultation Paper on Regulatory Framework for Over the Top Services*. Available: https://trai.gov.in/sites/default/files/OTT-CP-27032015.pdf, accessed: 9 June 2017.

4 Recalibrating China in a Time of Platforms

Tom O'Regan and Luzhou Li

In China, as in other countries, the terms under which public communication are taking place are rapidly changing. With the impact of social media and other online media, the press is shifting to become the 'platform press' (Bell and Owen 2017). Subscription video and audio on-demand services and advertiser-supported online video and audio services are recalibrating television and radio services into portal services (Lotz 2017). The smartphone is seamlessly connecting users and their interpersonal networks to media content, including content specifically generated for mobile. Online media and services' singular capacity to generate market information on media use and transactions and then to use that information in data-driven systems of algorithmic selection is transforming the production, marketing, advertising and distribution of goods and services more generally. In this process what is being reshaped is not only access to media product but the very basic infrastructures for modern—social, political, economic and cultural—life as media and communication services are being more tightly woven into broader economic, social, governmental and political worlds. At the centre of these transformations are mostly American and Chinese technology companies whose principal products are platforms and the processes of platformization they drive. Platforms typically mix communication, media and the delivery of other goods and services in new combinations for digital contexts. They create distinct marketplaces in which both the platform provider and third parties contribute to products and services.

Platforms and Platformization

At the centre of these platforms is their focus on the user/audience and their interactions with the platform. This audience and user focus has enabled platforms not only to create and control market information regimes of great value to themselves and third parties but also to develop powerful user recommendation regimes valued by its users/audiences (Webster 2010). In each of these cases their centrality in market information provision is based on the large amounts of data that these platforms are able to control, collect, coordinate, apply and strategically share with third parties. What they are offering is more than the distribution of audio, video and print online or through physical networks but the tracking, facilitating, coordinating and controlling of digital interactions generally across an increasingly digitalized economy. As Keane and Wu neatly put it, 'platforms transcend internet companies or tech companies—they operate wherever digital interaction takes place' (2018). Platforms are best seen, pace Cohen, as multisided in that 'they serve buyers, the sellers seeking to reach them, and often advertisers seeking the buyers' attention' and they are multi-levelled servicing different parts of the same ecosystem they create. In this way everyday transactions of all kinds are being enabled and shaped by a handful of dominant global platforms (2017: 146).

The platforms in question here are the handful of mega American and Chinese corporations (sometimes called technology companies) that have emerged over the past 20 years. These include the US 'big six' of Alphabet (Google's company), Facebook, Apple, Microsoft, Amazon and Netflix and the Chinese BAT of Baidu, Alibaba and Tencent Holdings. Together with a number of other global companies including taxi services Uber and Didi Chuxing, and e-commerce platforms like China's JD.Com, these online companies sit in a pivotal position in a growing digital economy reliant upon their potent mix of information technology, data and online services (Clark 2016: 243–244; Srnicek 2017; Zhigang 2016). Many of these platform companies now number among the largest companies by market capitalization in the world. Through their related companies, whether Baidu's iQiyi (dubbed 'China's Netflix') or Alphabet's YouTube and Alibaba's Youku (compared to both YouTube and Netflix), these companies' reach is now spread across a number of distinct online services in social media, messaging, streaming, search, gaming and traditional media businesses. This chapter specifically examines the ways platforms have developed and taken shape in China. We will consider aspects of the general processes of platformization such as these platforms' market formation capacities, their infrastructural dimensions, their role as simultaneously conduit for third parties and providers in their own right, their extension of media's provenance, their creation of new metrics, their reshaping of the terms of interpersonal communication concluding with a consideration of the continuing role played by language and culture in platformization, the consequences of having distinct Chinese and American platforms for media and market formation and transformation more generally, and the national policy and government contexts that have shaped Chinese platforms. Throughout we will be considering what these Chinese platforms share and do not share with their American counterparts and broader Western platformization logics.

Social and Economic Infrastructures

Globally, platform companies have not only become conduits for others' content and goods but also become traditional media providers: witness Alibaba's acquisition of a Hong Kong film studio, its investment in films such as *Mission Impossible—Rogue Nation* (2015) and its 2015 takeover of the Hong Kong *South China Morning Post* (Clark 2016: 259–264). These moves parallel Amazon's involvement in Amazon Prime and its 2013 acquisition of *The Washington Post* (Farhi 2013). With the growth of these 'technology companies'—now increasingly and more accurately described as platforms—the traditional media of the press, magazines, radio and television are losing control over their content, audiences and advertising. Traditional media now need to not only translate themselves through such platforms—whether to have their content carried on online platforms or to attempt to reshape their operations to be more like the platforms themselves—but they also need to go head to head with these platform competitors as competing media content providers in their own right with the need to continue extending their reach and depth. Likewise, the traditional independent market research and statistical services industry represented by audience measurement and consumer panels and other market information services is losing its control of market information provision. This is because these same platforms command rich data generated by their social media, search, streaming and other online services. Consequently independent market research and statistical service providers are being displaced by media platforms that generate, coordinate, market and control rich data sets collected in the very processes of online distribution and service provision.

The processes marking this potent mix of media, mediated interpersonal communication, market information provision and transactions have significantly extended media's provenance leading to the forging of as new market and user metrics. In China and the rest of the world, these privately operated platforms are seeking and successfully becoming critical and indispensable *social and economic infrastructures* whose reach extends well beyond social communication, the buying and selling of audiences and the trading of cultural content (see Tse 2016; Woetzel et al. 2017). Constantly innovating their form and function, these platforms are transforming the terms under which our respective media markets, public speech and information, retail transactions and markets, governance and economic life are operating. With reach and immense global power these platforms blur the lines marking media from non-media. Just as the gap between media and (interpersonal) communication has narrowed with social media's advent, so too the gap between media's marketing and advertising functions and retail has been transformed as online services increasingly stitch together media and retail through e-commerce. This is affecting not only media institutions but also other political, social and economic institutions. All need to accommodate media platforms and wider processes of platformization, which interconnect these institutions in new ways. Around the world, media platforms are increasingly central to public communication and draw their power from being more than media content providers. They carry not only 'mass media' but also social media; they not only provide market information and user recommendation services to guide and shape consumer uptake of goods and services, but also transact business through their e-commerce vehicles. One of the reasons these platform providers are identified as 'technology companies' is that their online services being computer based are 'programmable', they 'make accessible data and logic through application programming interfaces', they are characteristically built on particular technological 'affordances and constraints' and they connect up various sorts of 'heterogeneous actors' allowing them to leverage their 'programmability and interconnection to achieve control' (Plantin et al. 2018: 194, 307).

Platforms function here as particular kinds of publicly available resources that are akin to infrastructures for everyday life in that they are 'widely shared, widely accessible, and essential' (Plantin et al. 2018: 294). In each case technology companies—whether Google or Baidu, YouTube or Youku, Netflix or iYiQu, Twitter or Weibo, Amazon or Alibaba and JD.Com, Facebook, WhatsApp, Skype, Instagram, Tinder and WeChat (Ho 2016)—have developed online services which have become widely shared platforms. Just as our public communication is increasingly organized through these platforms, these are the same platforms that are reorganizing our shopping, retail, finance, logistics and supply chains. Increasingly then these platforms have become building blocks shaping public interaction, markets for goods and services and the logistics of supply chains. In this way as Plantin et al. (2018: 293) observe 'platform-based services acquire characteristics of *infrastructure*' (our emphasis). That is to say various platforms are becoming basic building blocks in the way that 20 years ago Microsoft Word, Microsoft Excel and Adobe PDFs became the 'basic' grammar or infrastructure for calculation, document creation and circulation in offices and workplaces, or in the way that in an earlier period telephone networks emerged as 'common carriers' and public infrastructures funded or closely regulated by government in light of the important public interest purposes they served. Plantin et al. usefully identify this process as an 'infrastructuralisation of platforms' (2018: 295). While there are large differences in approach between China and Western countries on many issues, the problem common to each remains one of domesticating, mitigating and managing these fundamental and far-reaching processes where private platforms have become indispensable public infrastructures. These infrastructural dimensions to platforms and platformization raise important shared regulatory and competition policy issues as to how public interests and public accountability can be secured.

Platforms Rework and Reorganize Markets

Platforms increasingly organize the marketing, buying, selling and payment systems for goods as well as recalibrating logistical services for these goods and services. This combination makes for new corporate business models and new, more interconnected models for media firms. Platforms are social technologies connecting people. They are generators, manipulators and vendors of data not only on users and audiences, but also on the transactions, sales volumes and logistical operations themselves. They are e-commerce platforms. They are also players in the logistical space whether as in JD.Com's case through establishing its own logistical services for delivering its products purchased through its e-commerce platforms or as in Alibaba's case working closely with a number of logistic companies to deliver third-party products through its e-commerce platforms. Much more than media companies such platforms are becoming as Cohen aptly put it, a 'core organizational form of the emerging informational economy' (2017: 133). For Cohen the critical point is not that these platforms are doing more than entering into and expanding markets but that they are supplanting, reworking and reorganizing the markets themselves on their terms (Cohen 2017: 145–148). In response to these platforms' success and cannibalization of their target markets, broadband and internet service providers and television networks are each seeking to reorganize themselves in platform-like ways, adopting many of the same processes. They are seeking to use their coverage and data sets of customer information to position themselves not merely as neutral conduits and service providers but as platforms offering a comprehensive and ever-expanding array of services. In this way leading technology, telcos and internet providers are each becoming more platform like, while established media companies are seeking to become platform providers.

Consider some examples: a report by the McKinsey Global Institute observed that e-commerce and mobile payments in China had created new markets and reconstructed supply chains and retail, making '"made in China" digital business models' and 'solutions' into 'a leading global force in the digital economy' (Woetzel et al. 2017: vi). The capacity of platform media to rework markets is greatly facilitated by their reach extending as they do across a variety of industries well beyond that of the traditional media industries of radio, press and television, to transport, finance, retail, hospitality, health, government operations and tourism. This diversification can be seen in Tencent's case with some 600 companies now in its portfolio (Cotterill and Lucas 2018). A platform's market-making power can be seen with Alibaba's shopping website Taobao which has facilitated the development of some 1,000 'Taobao villages' in rural areas of China by turning 'farmers into online vendors'

(W. Ma 2017). To qualify as a 'Taobao Village' a community must have more than 10% of households running online stores and its e-commerce revenues must exceed 10 million RMB (roughly $1.6 million) per year (W. Ma 2017). The platform here is literally market making, powerfully connecting online to offline as dispersed rural businesses connect through a central online e-commerce service which not only organizes the market place and undertakes the transaction between buyers and sellers but also coordinates the logistics of distribution and delivery of the goods and services. This is leading to a division of labour within platform companies. In terms of financial intermediaries, Alipay is used for close everyday transactions, while its Ant Check Later (MayiHuabei) is a consumer lending and credit payment service.

Platforms Are Conduits and Providers

Media platforms are not only conduits through which other provider's goods and services pass, but increasingly 'providers' themselves of competing goods and services. Amazon, JD.Com and WeChat not only become the platform to sell other vendors' goods and services but become, increasingly, a vehicle to provide their own goods and services. These Chinese platforms in creating their own services and home brands are in a position to use their control over distribution to organize and subordinate other actors; in this they are like the cable TV companies of the 1980s and 1990s and the 'national' grocery chains of the 2000s like America's Walmart, Germany's Aldi and the Australian Coles and Woolworths. The need to balance the relation between platforms as simultaneously conduits and providers with enormous market power will increasingly occupy regulators and policymakers in China as well as elsewhere. Do regulators serve or check monopoly market power and its exercise? Is monopoly power a problem if its exercise is managed for broader societal benefit? With these platforms becoming so large (Facebook with its two billion users, WeChat with its one billion users), their market capitalization becomes so large, these corporations now have the capacity to wield enormous power on and over governments. Already these platforms are practising forms of diplomacy we associate with sovereign states. In Western countries, American platforms have been at the centre of negotiations but increasingly in East, South East and South Asia these are just as likely to be Chinese platforms negotiating with governments. One indication of this is the 2017 move by the Indonesian government to appoint Alibaba's Jack Ma as its e-commerce advisor to help it 'come to grips with the growing e-commerce and service market'. Indonesia's Minister of Communications and Information Technology, Rudiantara, was asking Ma to 'develop the ecosystem so micro-, small and medium enterprises – people living in suburban areas and villages – can get additional economic value by using technological development' (quoted in Delia 2017).

Here Alibaba's record of connecting small- to medium-sized business to platforms and transforming supply chains and creaky logistics in China was what was important to the Indonesian state. This constituted its political and economic edge over its American rivals. Of course, by then Alibaba had also made significant investments in South-East Asian e-commerce including its acquisition of Indonesia's two leading e-commerce platforms, Lazada and Tokopedia (Deila 2017). This makes the point that the circumstances in which and for which they were invented may make Chinese platform a better fit in many parts of the world than their American competitors. Currently the domestic market in which Chinese platforms operate dwarfs in scale and size that of their presence in any other country, with 19% of the world's population and with Chinese speakers numbering the largest group of native language speakers—sitting at 1.2 billion native speakers globally and overwhelmingly centred in China and compared to English's 378 million native English speakers spread across several countries (Statista 2018). This China market focus has, as Keane and Fung point out, considerable further room to grow given its current 771 million internet users on 2017 figures (2018). As Chinese platforms expand globally from their strong Chinese base, these platforms will increasingly encounter some of the same issues as have their American counterparts. The Chinese market will always be their central concern, but their expanding interests will link them into international and, especially, regional markets. As they expand, they will increasingly encounter governments, private corporations and consumers that are better placed to pick and choose providers—and discipline foreign platforms for breaches—on the basis of their national interest and the attraction of competing international services.

Platforms Extend Media's Provenance

As 'technology companies' become 'media companies' they expand our sense of media's provenance. We are used to telling this story with reference to the American companies like Apple, Amazon and Netflix and Telcos, whether in the USA, Canada, the UK and Europe, or Australia, and New Zealand as they buy into the media and create their own media content. But this is equally a Chinese story. China's search engine giant Baidu, for example, set up online video streaming in 2010. For years, it leveraged its strength as a search portal to divert traffic to its online video subsidiary which successfully launched an initial public offering on NASDAQ in 2018. Similarly, another Chinese internet giant, Tencent, has begun to dominate in music streaming and downloading in China via its application Tencent Music and others, and is expanding its influence in South East Asia. Tencent Music has benefited from the parent company's octopus-like business including its app store *Yingyong Bao* (Tencent MyApp), its well-known messaging app WeChat, its video streaming service Tencent Video and its karaoke appQuanmin K Ge (WeSing for the English version). Beyond it, Tencent has also gained advantages from the political economy of the device and system software in China where most smartphones manufactured in China are using the Android operating system. Furthermore, Google's forced decision to withdraw from the Chinese market in 2010 has created ample space for local players building on top of the Android operating system to flourish. These circumstances walled off both Apple Music and Spotify, which at the time had limited presence in the Android system. With media now extending to user-generated content, these platforms are transforming what we mean by media itself as previously separate activities and functions become dynamically related in Tencent's ecosystem.

Platforms Reshape Mediated Interpersonal Communication

In two major studies establishing communication as a field in the 1940s and 1950s, Paul Lazarsfeld and his collaborators emphasized the central importance of interpersonal communication, personal networks and opinion leaders to the uptake of media (Lazarsfeld et al. 1968; Lazarsfeld and Katz 1955). Personal influence, they argued, was critical to the success or otherwise of all kinds of marketing campaigns whether for elections, movies, fashion or advertisements for goods and services. To get at the dimensions of personal influence they approached it as if it were a medium in its own right. The 'media metaphor' allowed personal influence to be recognized as the most important medium. Seventy years later, interpersonal communication, with its influential opinion leaders and 'influencers' became, through social media, a medium in its own right. While mediated communication has long been a feature of interpersonal and organizational communication—through letters, phone calls, faxes, emails—the advent of social media in its various forms 'mediatized' previously one-to-one and one-to-group networks facilitating the significant extension of these interpersonal networks. Indeed we could say that social media achieved its extraordinary penetration owing to its efficient 'mediatizing' of 'interpersonal' communication which effectively reconstituted the previous sharp distinction between mediated interpersonal and mass communication into a more graduate continuum. Social media, then, is not just a new media content platform consisting of user-generated content used to sell audience attention to advertisers, but it is also, through 'word of mouth', a central vehicle in managing the uptake of goods and services and political messaging alike (Carah 2017).

Social media and search also provide invaluable market information about audiences at a significant scale and depth. Furthermore, through its recommendations and likes, it offers effective information regimes of great value to users in 'cutting through' a fragmented media landscape. Social media here is shaping and influencing the uptake of other 'media' whether through 'news stories', feature films, documentary films, television drama series and other television programmes (Webster 2010). A prominent example of this in the Chinese context is the posts on social media platforms such as WeChat, which are increasingly dominated by professional content providers and embedded with advertisements of various products including blockbusters, hit television series and entertainment shows. This mediatizing of interpersonal communication into an identifiable advertiser-supported medium—social media—inevitably drew advertising and marketing dollars away from established media providers. When coupled with search and e-commerce, 'social media' became a portal for a huge range of transactions. Just as Amazon can now assemble comprehensive data sets—tying together the consumer survey and the media survey, matching media purchases of books, movies, TV series with the buyers' location and his/her purchase of particular kinds of clothes, food, electrical goods, etc.—so too its Chinese counterparts, Alibaba and JD.com, are likewise able to tie together these same elements: with the particular configuration taken by Chinese e-commerce bearing a family resemblance to that undertaken by Amazon in that they resemble each other in some respects but are different in others (for example, Alibaba and WeChat's innovation in online payments have made them core players in China's financial system). These major market, social and medial shifts are reorganizing social, political and market information provision globally as platforms become basic infrastructures for our modern life.

Platform Ecology in China

The media platforms in China are, as we noted above, not those operating elsewhere and for which much contemporary scholarship covers with notable exceptions (see Hong 2017; Keane and Wu 2018; Leong 2018; Zhao 2018). The hardware, the interface, the software, the terms of online infrastructure provision and access, governmental expectations of these platforms and the ways media, particularly mobile media, are used are different in sometimes small and sometimes larger ways. So while the applications and the platforms in which they operate bear a broad family resemblance to non-Chinese and principally American platforms, they have been improvised for different political, organizational, market and financial contexts. The Chinese market configuration for apps and their technical character are informed by distinct Chinese versions of technology and media, cultural design preferences, networking infrastructure and market circumstances. The ways in which users co-shape platforms with platform developers, user practices and cultures can differ significantly from those in other parts of the worlds (Poell et al. 2014). They are, to all intents and purposes, different inventions.

China's platforms were developed for its own market context characterized initially by significant regionalization, infrastructural deficits, an underdeveloped bricks and mortar retail sector and poorly developed logistics and supply chains coupled with a less developed personal computing and laptop penetration and lower levels of discretionary income than in the West. This paved the way for the more rapid and extensive uptake of smartphone-based services in China than in Western countries. Mobile allowed the 'leapfrogging of PC terminals' (Keane and Fung 2018). Moreover, these Chinese platform companies developed under the strong support of the government leading to a kind of platform nationalization (Hong 2017). The centrality of this government involvement to platform shape can be seen in Tencent's Open Platform initiative, which attracted millions of start-up entrepreneurs. It is an entrepreneurship incubation project involving various levels of local governments, high-tech industrial zones, financial agencies and venture capital investors. These platform ecologies are also succeeding in managing urban spaces and population in distinct ways. By contrast platform uptake in countries like Australia occurred in the context of well-established national markets for goods and services, significant transportation and logistical infrastructure, developed bricks and mortar retail sector that had much to lose from e-commerce and a transitions to online through the PC and laptop to the mobile phone. There was little expectation of the state's significant involvement. These market characteristics made Australia a ready environment for the uptake of American platforms given their similarly constituted starting points. While the differences between Chinese and Western markets in income and other measures are lessening, the differences in physical infrastructure, retailing, media marketplaces and market leaders will persist because all platform markets have their own internal logics of development and path dependencies.

Platform Opportunities Outside China

China has developed its own set of bespoke connected media—in social media, search, e-commerce, and online platforms and associated hardware—which it is now exporting. China, as a recent *New York Times* article put it, is achieving parity with the USA in the internet and has emerged 'as the one true rival in scale, value and technology'. The article singled out its smartphone-based innovations in e-commerce platforms such as WeChat and Alipay as being especially notable in this regard (Mozur 2017). As an innovator, China faces many of the same problems the Japanese faced with its industrialization from the 1950s (and the USA faced with its earlier global expansion). In becoming global, China will need to become local in the territories it enters, territories marked by linguistic and cultural differences. It will need to manage the relation between its own relatively isolated and distinct linguistic and cultural sphere and that of the worlds within which it enters. The contrast with other countries into which Chinese platforms enter is instructive. These countries, apart from the USA and China itself, tend to be mostly importers of these platforms and media devices. Where they differ is in where each country is up to with this importing and their general market development. Such market characteristics mean that China is largely dealing in its platform export markets with markets that have been formed as adaptors not innovators. They are therefore less in the platform development business as in the platform *adjustment* design and *recalibration* business. Take Australia as an example. It has long been used first by the USA, then by Japan and now by China as an out-of-the-way place to perfect a marketplace innovation developing bridgeheads for later export to English language markets.

Some countries, indeed many Western countries, are firmly oriented to the North American-derived, formats and platforms of Apple, Alphabet (Google), Facebook, Microsoft, Amazon and now Netflix. However, other countries in South East Asia and South Asia (such as Indonesia and India) have market characteristics which may predispose at least large sections of their markets to Chinese media platforms and services, developed as they initially were for people with less disposable income (Leong 2018). In the former case, China will need to find ways around American market dominance, while in the latter case China's proximity advantage provides an opportunity to reshape these markets in its image and in relation to these characteristics. The problem that China inevitably faces, after securing its domestic market dominance, is one of gaining access to markets that have generally been built for different operating conditions and market formations and which already have media platform market leaders with bridgehead 'infrastructure' positions. Understanding this, Chinese platform companies have targeted opportunities in undeveloped markets for which China's transition to a digital economy represents a proven development path, whether in South East Asia and South Asia, along the One Belt, One Road central Asian states and Africa (Keane and Wu 2018). They have also sought to recognize and work with the pull towards the Chinese platforms from its Chinese diaspora for Chinese language online service provision among the sizeable minority populations in East and South East Asia, the Americas and Australasia (Leong 2018). They collaborate with the three Chinese markets beyond the mainland (Hong Kong, Taiwan and Singapore) and the culturally proximate South Korean and Japanese partners that can be culturally drawn into extensive and deep cooperation and collaboration in certain defined areas (Keane et al. 2018; Leong 2018).

Platforms, Language and Culture

While the international uptake of media platforms is pushing many countries towards the removal of institutional restrictions and more exposure to freely circulating information flows, China stands out as something of an anomaly. This is sometimes posed as a contrast between an American libertarian view and a more statist, controlling, centralized and directed Chinese view intent on geo-blocking and censoring speech through the Great Firewall of China (Hong 2017). But language and culture are also important as a way of thinking about the uptake of the Chinese internet and Chinese platforms globally. Analysing the patterns of overlap among the world's 1,000 most popular websites in two related articles, Wu and Taneja show that language and geography remain important predictors of audience overlap (Taneja and Wu 2014; Wu and Taneja 2016). In their cluster analysis, the sheer scale of the Chinese internet becomes evident as befitting the world's largest country, second largest economy and biggest online community. But also evident in their analysis is China's continuing separation from the rest of the 'Internet' world, replicating a pattern of separation they also find for Japanese, Russian and Korean internets. China dominates the Chinese language(s) world and consequently a number of Chinese regional websites start to show up in these data as websites of global significance. When considering whether these results for China are related to the system of firewalls and filters that have enabled China to censor and control the internet for people in China, Taneja and Wu argue that cultural proximity rather than access blockage best explains the patterns of user online behaviour they observe (2014: 306–307). China, Japan and to a much lesser extent Korea are each unusual in that they are large, linguistically bound countries, in which local programming, local news sources and local entertainment typically trump imports and substitute for them. In this they are like the USA.

China dominates the Chinese language markets. Its content markets, like those of the USA and Japan, are overwhelmingly for local product. Its popular vernacular programming consists largely of its own programming. Its local companies dominate the internet and the ownership of media platforms is in Chinese hands. The problem China confronts in exporting 'content' and some aspects of its platforms stems from some of the same cultural dynamics that protected it when developing its platforms. Cultural markets are simultaneously language markets. Not only do these markets have their own vernacular media programming—within English language countries like Australia, New Zealand and English Canada, the programming is American and British—but the uptake, management of media platforms and the content recommended, liked and reworked are undertaken largely through these language spheres in particular path dependent ways. Countries have extensive, deep and long-standing connections with other countries in same and adjacent language markets. Countries sharing the same language often also share market organization, regulation and policymaking which can facilitate and inhibit particular kinds of uptake not only of content but of associated services shaping media devices. Smaller countries also take as a given, for instance, that cultural market leadership resides in the dominant nodes of the world languages with which they are affiliated. Such developments make the point that while media platforms have been able to spread across languages globally what has facilitated this spread is less 'content' than the platforms for delivering, finding and paying for content. This means that platforms as they travel need to negotiate cultural configurations based in language. The strength of social media and search has been their capacity to command the geographically 'local' advertising and marketing by providing a distant infrastructure that facilitates local area service provision. But to do so processes of platformization for Alibaba, Facebook or Google need to be calibrated to the management and staging of cultural difference.

National Policy and Government Contexts

Yu Hong stresses the important role that Chinese government initiatives and national policy frameworks have played in enabling the transformation of the Chinese economy and ensuring the emergence of 'born in China' platforms (2017). She sees the respective Chinese and American platforms as products of their different national online models and policy frameworks. On the one hand, there is China's state-led model of digital capitalism that she charts over her book and, on the other hand, the USA's 'system of global digital capitalism' (Hong 2017: 147). Both have served their respective media platforms well in that they each provided propitious circumstances for platform media to develop. Yu Hong charts how Chinese government policy and political leaders strove to modernize China's 'network infrastructure', to make their ICT sector 'more competitive', to 'corporatize' their 'media-and-entertainment institutions' and to use 'ICT as a crosscutting catalyst for innovation, industrial modernization, and export upgrades' (2017: 4). They did so not only to transform China into a 'global ICT leader' but also to end their 'dependence upon foreign corporations'. Further assisting the capacity of the Chinese state to effect change is that as a development state it has had many more levers available to it to accomplish these policy ends than do other nations where the state plays a less central and guiding role. The Chinese state in short wanted its own Silicon Valley, but one that was under its control and was developed on its terms (see Clark 2016: 133). However, the Chinese platforms are not straightforwardly creatures of either singular macro-level governmental logics.

For a start, these Chinese policies are not new. In one shape or another these very prescriptions have been, in their broad outlines, policies pursued in any number of countries with varied success over the past 20–30 years. Many countries have sought to develop their own Silicon Valleys, create circumstances for their own national technology start-ups and champions to emerge, and sought to ensure some measure of national control over their respective digital economies to ensure what was developed met long-standing economic, social and cultural objectives—national interests. As Keane and Wu observe what made these policies different was China's combination of industry protection and national security considerations with which these policies were tightly coupled ensuring close collaboration among 'government, communications companies in China, and transnational corporate interests' (2018). This combination had the advantage, as Clark neatly put it, of allowing the Chinese state to have a 'thriving internet culture, while maintaining control' and ensuring emergent Chinese platforms clear air in which to develop their command of the Chinese domestic market from which they could project internationally (2016: 134). While many countries wanted to also see homegrown digital champions emerge, they did not have the carrot of China's huge domestic market and rapidly growing internet and smartphone base to ensure that foreign investment and particularly American and Japanese venture capital investment would not be turned away by the Chinese state's central role. Indeed, the development of these Chinese platforms is not wholly a Chinese story (see Jia and Winseck 2018; Keane and Wu 2018). Clark's account of Alibaba's development provides an illustration of this joint development with international partners and expertise gained in America's top universities (2016). The company was supported by both Japanese and American SoftBank and Goldman Sachs – in its critical early stages and then later by Yahoo. For a time it had a Silicon Valley arm as its R&D centre (Clark 2016: 128–129). While founder Jack Ma was wholly Chinese-educated, his long-term partner Joe Tsai is Taiwanese with an American high school and Yale University education first in economics and East Asian Studies and then the Yale Law School (Clark 2016: 97–98). In Tencent's case the South African media company, Naspers, made a $32 million investment in Tencent in 2001 but unlike Goldman Sachs retained its holding making it Africa's largest company by market capitalization (Cotterill and Lucas 2018).

Market Constraints and Platform Innovation

There is a somewhat mixed record of missteps by the global American platforms with their Chinese forays. For an account of this aspect of Chinese platform media development, we need to turn business biographies such as those of Jack Ma and Richard Li of JD.Com (Clark 2016;

Zhigang 2016). In his business biography, *Alibaba: The House That Jack Ma Built*, Clark chronicles the decisions made by Yahoo, eBay and even Goldman Sachs that enabled Ma's Alibaba to become a dominant platform player in China (2016). He also points to how Baidu's Robin Liu took the step of creating his own 'branded service' after being a 'third party supplier of Chinese language search engines' taking the step because 'the portals did not want to pay for it' (Clark 2016: 192). Likewise the head-to-head conflict between Uber and Didi Chuxing over 2015 for the leadership of ride-sharing in China which began with Uber's 2013 entry to China would see Uber blink first after both sides had spent up to $2 billion each seeking control of the critical Chinese market (Crabtree 2018). The Chinese ride share provider, now dominant in China, makes an average of 25 million fares a day from its 400 million registered users in over 400 Chinese cities. This is, as Crabtree points out, 'roughly twice as many as Uber and all the other global sharing apps combined' (Crabtree 2018).

Chinese media providers have often started in different market and cultural circumstances than have their American counterparts with this having path dependent consequences for their platform development. Tencent with its roots in telecommunication services, messaging and games provision ensured it charted a different route for its platforms than did Google or Facebook. Console games and devices were often beyond the reach of Chinese publics. Subscription was not initially a particularly viable model, and bandwidth was initially a problem. Similarly, the bells and whistles features of the Apple iPhone and its competitors were out of reach for ordinary Chinese consumers. This scenario encouraged Tencent, very early on, to join up in compelling ways with advertiser-supported and content payment systems that enabled games to be supported and the WeChat platform to morph into becoming the 'app for everything'.

For its part, Alibaba began by creating business-to-business web pages to connect and make visible Chinese manufacturers to interested international parties, then moving to create e-commerce websites in a substantially undeveloped national market for goods and services with limited logistical capabilities and finally connecting dispersed global brands with Chinese consumers. While Alibaba is often seen as China's Amazon, Alibaba grew out of a different logic and set of commitments to small- and medium-sized businesses as well as large businesses which it coupled with an Amazon like attention to the three elements of logistics, finance and e-commerce (Clark 2016: 1–21). Alibaba was making a market where there was none, whereas Amazon was cannibalizing already-established national markets and building its network on top of pre-existing national supply chains. So while, the Great Firewall of China and the national Chinese policy environment have helped Chinese platforms by providing regulatory barriers to entry and the setting of limits on the operation of non-Chinese firms in China, too much can be made of these national policy settings. They are part of but not the whole story. Focusing on them can turn attention away from the specific entrepreneurial and inventive experiments in platformization so evident in the trajectories of these Chinese platforms as with their American counterparts.

Platforms and China's Transactional Economy

As media platforms have become central to public communication, their influence and power now stretch well beyond the historic staples of media and interpersonal communication into transactional systems coupling recommendation and discovery functions with the buying and selling of goods and services. In the process, Chinese companies have become critical players in the notable and extensive development of media and technology platforms within the Chinese economy, including financial instruments such as banking and loans. Tencent Research Institute claims that by 2016 the digital economy in China made up 31% of the country's GDP (P. Ma 2017; Shicong 2018). The McKinsey Institute in its report *Digital China: Empowering the Economy to Global Competitiveness* claimed that China was already, by 2016, responsible for 42% of global e-commerce with mobile payments then 11 times bigger than in the USA (Woetzel et al. 2017). China hosts one in three of the world's privately owned start-ups which captured an impressive 43% of the global value of start-ups (ibid). Like their counterparts dominating the US economy, China's Alibaba, Tencent, Baidu and JD.Com dominate their local digital economy. They also own an expanding array of related platforms and applications that are shaping, managing and controlling the future of such platforms. Indeed as *The Economist* observed the fact that these three Chinese companies between them accounted for nearly half of all domestic Chinese venture-capital investment in the tech sector ensured that they would be in a good position to shape the 'future' of rival platforms (2018: 11). As with the dominant American platforms these Chinese platforms started off with just the one or two online media businesses, but subsequently became umbrella companies for an increasingly diversified portfolio reaching well beyond their original moorings in media and mediated interpersonal communication services.

As transactional conduits, they now utilize an expanding array of ways of paying for their media and social media. Their reach stretches well beyond both the marketing and guide media functions of traditional media. Their market information provision now extends to all areas of the economy including transport, finance and banking, retail, hospitality, manufacturing and tourism. Their control of data and data technology stitches together otherwise separated media, services and sectors into connected wholes linking e-commerce, logistics and finance to create new synergies among them (Clark 2016: 1–22; Lucas 2017). They are consequently rewriting ideas about what kinds of business go with what kinds of other businesses as the boundaries between businesses, especially between media and non-media, are entirely disrupted. In becoming the primary vehicles for connecting offline to online in China, Chinese platforms have become the drivers of e-commerce, mobile payments, financial services, population management and the digital transformation of logistics and infrastructures. They are now at the centre of organizing business-to-business and business-to-consumer interfaces through their role as intermediaries linking commercial operations to personal, social and media communication within the Chinese language and beyond. In their reworking of markets, and redefining of the infrastructures of the everyday, these Chinese platform media have been with their American counterparts at the forefront in reimagining transactional spaces in ever tightly interconnected ways (see Greenfield 2018). Not only have these Chinese platforms built an ever-widening array of transactions on their digital platforms such as WeChat, T-mart and JD.Com but the data technologies, particularly algorithms that drive them, have become critical to stitching together e-commerce, logistics and finance and payments in new seamless and more friction-free ways.

These moves have enabled them to multiply the social and economic transactions they capture as they pursue both greater connectivity and greater volumes of exchange to create new models of growth in a more intensively mediated economy in which their control of data and therefore market information is central. In the process these Chinese media platforms have rapidly commercialized and reorganized the sphere of social communication and economic exchange in globally significant ways. Given the signal importance of the Chinese market globally—not merely as the second largest economy but also as the largest country by population—we can expect that what has been through the 2000s and 2010s largely an internal Chinese story of platform market development and digital economy formation will become a more global story as the platforms—and the processes and lessons gained from Chinese experience—are rolled out in other countries, as we are now seeing in Indonesia. As we move into the 2020s, Chinese and American platforms are increasingly likely to 'coset' standards globally in the digital economy (Hong 2017: 153). We can expect that the already deep connections and cross-shareholding among Chinese and American platform providers and their quite extensive cooperation to continue. We can also assume that competition and collaboration between US and Chinese platforms will continue to grow, becoming more pointed and at times fractious. We will increasingly seeing pointers to the future of the digital economy not only in American but also increasingly in Chinese platforms. But we can equally expect that China's platform media will be increasingly competitive particularly in the area of new applications based on artificial intelligence and machine-learning against American platform media in high-income countries. We can certainly expect that aspects of the Chinese platform system, designed as it has been for lower wage, limited income circumstance, will prove relevant and accessible not only in middle- and lower-income countries but also among the increasingly precarious consumers of high-income countries.

Acknowledgements

We are especially grateful to Adrian Athique for his comments on earlier drafts of this chapter and to Vibodh Parthasarathi, Andrew Ventimiglia, Allison Fish, Angela Wu, Nicholas Carah and Dan Angus for our discussions on platform media. The work described in this chapter was supported by a grant from the Australian Research Council, 'Media Transformation in Its Australian and International Contexts: Analysis and Theory-Building', DP130101455.

References

Bell, Emily and Owen, Taylor (2017) *The Platform Press: How Silicon Valley Reengineered Journalism*, New York: Tow Center for Digital Journalism.

Carah, Nicholas (2017) 'Algorithmic Brands: A Decade of Brand Experiments with Mobile and Social Media', *New Media and Society*, 19(3): 384–400.

Clark, Duncan (2016) *Alibaba: The House That Jack Ma Built*, New York: Harper-Collins.

Cohen, Julie E. (2017) 'Law for the Platform Economy,' *U.C. Davis Law Review*, 51: 131–204.

Cotterill, Joseph and Lucas, Louise (2018) 'Naspers Trims Tencent Stake with $10bn Share Sale', *Financial Times*, 23 March 2018.

Crabtree, James (2018) 'Didi Chuxing Took on Uber and Won. Now It's Taking on the World', *Wired*, 9 February 2018. Available: www.wired.co.uk/article/didi-chuxing-china-startups-uber, accessed: 9 February 2018.

Deila, Tabita (2017) 'Alibaba Founder Jack Ma Agrees to Advice Indonesia on E-Commerce', *JakartaGlobe*, 23 August 2017. Available: http://jakartaglobe.id/business/alibaba-founder-jack-ma-agrees-to-advise-indonesia-on-e-commerce/, accessed: 9 February 2018.

The Economist (2018) 'Peak Valley', *The Economist*, 1 September 2018, p. 11.

Farhi, Paul (2013) 'Washington Post Closes Sale to Amazon Founder Jeff Bezos', *Washington Post*, 1 October 2013. Available: www.washingtonpost.com/business/economy/washington-post-closes-sale-to-amazon-founder-jeff-bezos/2013/10/01/fca3b16a-2acf-11e3-97a3-ff2758228523_story.html?noredirect=on&utm_term=.5febb10a47aa, accessed: 10 January 2018.

Greenfield, Adam (2018) *Radical Technologies: The Design of Everyday Life*, London: Verso.

Ho, Sheji (2017) 'The Four Horsemen in SouthEast Asia: Why the Region Is the Next Proxy War for Chinese Internet Companies', *ecommerce*, 5 May 2017. Available: https://ecommerceiq.asia/four-horsemen-southeast-asia, accessed: 30 September 2018.

Hong, Yu (2017) *Networking China: The Digital Transformation of the Chinese Economy*, Urbana: University of Illinois Press.

Jia, Lianrui, and Winseck, Dwayne (2018) 'The Political Economy of Chinese Internet Companies: Financialization, Concentration, and Capitalization', *The International Communication Gazette*, 80(1): 30–59. doi:10.1177/1748048517742783.

Keane, Michael and Fung, Anthony (2018) 'Digital Platforms: Exerting China's New Cultural Power in the Asia-Pacific', *Media Industries*, 5(1): 47–50. Available: doi:10.3998/mij.15031809.0005.103, accessed: 30 September 2018.

Keane, Michael and Wu, Huan (2018) 'Lofty Ambitions, New Territories, and Turf Battles: China's Platforms 'Go Out'', *Media Industries*, 1(5): 51–68. Available: doi:10.3998/mij.15031809.0005.104, accessed: 30 September 2018.

Keane, Michael, Yecies, Brian and Flew, Terry (eds.) (2018) *Willing Collaborators: Foreign Partners in Chinese Media*, London: Rowman and Littlefield International.

Lazarsfeld, Paul, Berelson, Bernard and Gaudet, Hazel (1968) *The People's Choice: How the Voter Makes Up His Mind in a Presidential Campaign*, New York: Columbia University Press.

Lazarsfeld, Paul and Katz, Elihu (1955) *Personal Influence: The Part Played by People in the Flow of Mass Communication*, New York: Free Press of Glencoe. Leong, Susan (2018) 'Prophets of Mass Innovation: The Gospel According to BAT', *Media Industries*, 5(1). doi:10.3998/mij.15031809.0005.105, accessed: 30 September 2018.

Lotz, Amanda D. (2017) *Portals: A Treatise on Internet-Distributed Television*, Ann Arbor, MI: University of Michigan Library.

Lucas, Louise (2017) 'Alibaba Taps User Data to Drive Growth Spurt', *Financial Times*, 22 June 2017.

Ma, Pony (2017) 'What They Say: Pony Ma, Chairman and CEO of Tencent Holdings Ltd', *Guizhou China Official Website*. Available: www.eguizhou.gov.cn/2017-05/31/content_29557422.htm, accessed: 30 September 2018.

Ma, Winston Wenyan (2017) 'China's Mobile Economy, Explained', *World Economic Forum*, 26 June 2017. Available: weforum.org/agenda/2017/06/china-mobile-economy-explained, accessed: 14 September 2018.

Mozur, Paul (2017) 'The World's Biggest Tech Companies Are No Longer Just American', *New York Times*, 17 August 2017.

Plantin, Jean-Christophe, Lagoze, Carl, Edwards, Paul N. and Sandvig, Christian (2018) 'Infrastructure Studies Meet Platform Studies in the Age of Google and Facebook', *New Media and Society*, 20(1): 293–310. doi:10.1177/1461444816661553.

Poell, Thomas, de Kloet, Jeroen and Zeng, Guohua (2014) 'Will the Real Weibo Please Stand Up? Chinese Online Contention and Actor-Network Theory', *Chinese Journal of Communication*, 7(1): 1–18. doi:10.1080/17544750.2013.816753.

Shicong, Dou (2018) 'China's Digital Economy Accounted for Nearly One-Third of GDP Last Year, Says Tencent Research', *YiCaiGlobal*, 13 April 2018. Available: www.yicaiglobal.com/news/china%E2%80%99s-digital-economy-accounted-nearly-one-third-gdp-last-year-says-tencent-research, accessed: 14 September 2018.
Srnicek, Nick (2017) *Platform Captialism*, Cambridge: Polity.
Statista (2018) 'Most Spoken Languages Worldwide (Figures in Millions)', *Statistica: The Statistics Portal*. Available: www.statista.com/statistics/266808/the-most-spoken-languages-worldwide/, accessed: 18 September 2018.
Taneja, Harsh and Wu, Angela Xiao (2014) 'Does the Great Firewall Really Isolate the Chinese? Integrating Access Blockage with Cultural Factors', *The Information Society*, 30(5): 297–309.
Tse, Edward (2016) *China's Disruptors: How Alibaba, Xiaomi, Tencent, and Other Companies are Changing the Rules of Business*, London: Penguin.
Webster, James (2010), 'User Information Regimes: How Social Media Shape Patterns of Consumption', *North Western University Law Review*, 104: 593–612.
Webster, James G. (2011) 'The Duality of Media: A Structurational Theory of Public Attention', *Communication Theory*, 21(1): 43–66. doi:10.1111/j.1468-2885.2010.01375.x.
Woetzel, Jonathan, Seong, Jeongmin, Wang, Kevin Wei, Manvika, James, Chui, Michael and Wong, Wendy (2017) *Digital China: Powering the Economy to Global Competitiveness*, McKinsey Global Institute. Available: www.mckinsey.com/featured-insights/china/digital-china-powering-the-economy-to-global-competitiveness, accessed: 14 September 2018.
Wu, Angela Xiao and Taneja, Harsh (2016) 'Reimagining Internet Geographies: A User-centric Ethnological Mapping of the World Wide Web', *Journal of Computer-Mediated Communication*, 21: 230–246. doi:10.1111/jcc4.12157.
Zhao, Elaine Jing (2018) 'Negotiating State and Copyright Territorialities in Overseas Expansion: The Case of China's Online Video Streaming Platforms', *Media Industries*, 5(1). doi:10.3998/mij.15031809.0005.107.
Zhigang, Li (2016) *JD.Com Story: An E-commerce Phenomenon*, London: LID Publishing.

5 Demonetization

India's Year of Living Digitally

Adrian Athique

On 8 November 2016, I transited through Kuala Lumpur on my way to sign contracts and hand over manuscripts in New Delhi. As I flew across the Bay of Bengal, the Prime Minister of India was addressing the nation with one of the most dramatic statements heard since the days of Emergency in the 1970s. Offline and oblivious to one of the most extraordinary events in modern monetary history, I cheerfully arrived at Indira Gandhi International Airport. The often slow and surly money-changers could not switch my dollars for rupees quickly enough. Indeed, they pressed me to change more. Having saved a good 15 minutes on the usual process, I grabbed a taxi chit and made the always-terrifying journey along Delhi's airport highway I arrived at my hotel close to midnight. This is where the new reality began to kick in. First of all, the taxi driver didn't want to take my money, just offering many shakes of his head. In the end, I handed over a 1,000 Rupee note and stomped off into the hotel. I wasn't sure what his problem was, but it's well known these guys never have any change available and I was too tired to argue. By the time I checked into a room, it was midnight exactly. As soon as I sat down on the bed, a piece of paper was slid under the door. It informed me, apologetically, that as per the Prime Minister's announcement a few hours previously, all 500 and 1,000 Rupee notes would cease to be legal tender at midnight. I was on my feet and back down at reception with my wad of useless currency pretty quickly, as you might imagine.

Having confirmed that this money was now worthless, I tried to change some remaining $100 bills for smaller notes. Regrettably, their supply had run out some hours previously, and no one had any idea where and when a hundred dollars' worth of 100 Rupee notes could be procured. Well, at least the room was prepaid. Come the morning, newspapers arrived, carrying their endorsement of the Government's bold strategy to cut out the 'black money' in India's economy. Wrapped around every edition were full page advertisements for Paytm and other mobile wallet providers who had set up shop in India. So I sat over breakfast with my newspaper, reflecting on the consequences of this move for a country where half the population has no bank account and where 90% of daily transactions are in cash. At the next table, a well-to-do Indian lady was explaining to a visiting American businessman that black money was a scourge and he enthusiastically agreed that this move was vital in eliminating the corruption holding back the Indian economy. For my part, I held back on intervening with the observation that digital money was the central mechanism behind the offshore scandal that had unfolded in the so-called Panama papers in 2016, including the subsection that read like a virtual 'who's who' of India (Sarin et al. 2016). Introspectively, I recalled the last time I was penniless in Delhi some 25 years previously when, having been robbed by unscrupulous tourists, I ended up eking out three weeks on 20 Rupees a day and an earnest promise of eventual payment to a student hostel.

Now, at the other end of the 'liberalization' era, I sat in privilege in a business hotel, with a credit card, among a class of people who now rarely touched money at all. Nonetheless, I knew full well that out in the city there were millions of people, daily labourers, vendors, maids, drivers and others who would be going hungry along with their families. Further announcements were being made throughout the day: banks would be shut for three days to make preparations for receiving new currency notes to replace the old currency stock. Special arrangements were in place for tourists to change up to 5,000 Rupees at airports, while Indian railways would still accept the old notes for advance bookings and petrol stations would take the old notes for a further three days. Borrowing someone else's driver, a friend managed to cross the city to meet me, and we discussed the unfolding panic. Gold shops had been open through the night. ATMs had already run out of money, petrol was running out across the city and it seemed the Rajdhani express had been booked well beyond its operating lifespan. Vegetable sellers sat dejectedly in neighbourhoods where no one dared to part with any of the small notes they still had (BBC 2016a). Rickshaws sat idle on every corner. Private hospitals that took only cash payments were turning away patients, especially those from rural districts who had come into the city clutching their life savings and their loved ones (Al Jazeera 2016; BBC 2016b; Financial Express 2016). Unable to sustain themselves, migrant labourers and street vendors had begun an exodus out of the city. Domestic workers took their wages in foodstuffs. Beggars starved. Food rotted. Tourists went home. Cinemas were emptied (Dubey 2016; Hebbar 2016). Traffic police lost most of their income. Sex workers vanished (Safi and Brown 2016). For all but the rich, trade in non-essentials ceased.

Inside the business hotels and the bungalow zone of South Delhi, the first week of demonetization was a talking point. For the middle classes of Delhi, it was a further exercise in ingenuity, as they conspired, characteristically, to carry on about their business in the absence of a functioning system. Unable to receive cash, the city's *Kirana* stores provided provisions on account to millions of people. Out in the countryside, it was planting season, but somehow many farmers arranged the credit that would allow them to sow crops. The wedding season was a little more problematic, given that relatives tapping a credit card on the head of the bride and groom has yet to be incorporated into customary practice. In a notoriously 'leaky' system, the capacity to keep secret the preparations for such a large-scale and radical economic intervention was unprecedented. Rumours began to circulate, regarding who had been in the know and who hadn't, and who would profit from the chaos (Abraham 2016; The Hindu 2016). Despite official assurances, it was immediately obvious that the impact and import of these events would be protracted. For me at least, things were more simple. In order to close the publishing deal, I had to reach the plush Imperial Hotel in Janpath, which meant shaking out the small change from a university department for the auto fare. Given that the airport train link was still accepting the old notes, and giving change, there was no shortage of people wanting to come and see me off. At the terminal itself, the provision for departing passengers to change old notes had produced a melee. Given that 5,000 Rupees is not a lot of money, I returned to Australia with a good collection of these now historic banknotes.

Intervention and Its Rationale

An anecdotal account has limited value, but it serves to illustrate something of the scale of this policy intervention, which paralyzed the Indian economy at a scale comparable to the 9/11 attacks on the USA in 2001. Despite the frantic scenes around the transactional firestorm that exploded in the first hours of the crisis, the remarkable stoicism of the population reflected their long experience of financial crises. For the most part, these have occurred due to the chronic balance of payments issues inherent to a large country that has to import almost all its energy supplies. The 'liberalization' of India's command economy opened with just such a crisis in 1991, but a monetary shock of this magnitude was unprecedented. To be fair, this wasn't India's first experiment with demonetization as a mechanism to flush out cash hoards. However, the previous occurrence, in 1978 under the Morarji Desai government, targeted 1,000, 5,000 and 10,000 Rupee notes that, by the standards of the day, were unquestionably stores of value rather than transactional notes. In 1978, a meal could be had for less than ten Rupees and these 'high value' notes made up less than 1% of the money supply (Ghosh et al. 2017: 11). By contrast, after 38 years of inflation, the 500 and 1,000 Rupee notes removed in 2016 were the most commonly used notes, constituting 86% of the total cash supply. This was the first time in modern economic history that a country growing at a very respectable 7.7% per annum, and regarded as an emerging engine of the global economy, has elected to dismantle its currency and to do so within a matter of hours, rather than weeks and months. To understand the rationale for this shock treatment upon an apparently healthy patient, we are obliged to trace the official account of the demonetization exercise.

In doing so, I will draw upon the analysis of C. Rammanohar Reddy as well as Jayati Ghosh, C.P. Chandrasekhar and Prabhat Patnaik from the respected Centre for Economic Studies and Planning at Delhi's Jawaharlal Nehru University (Ghosh et al. 2017). Ghosh et al. emphasize how the justification and purported aims of demonetization evolved rapidly over the period from 8 November to 31 December 2016. It began with the 'black money' story, where demonetization was a 'surgical strike' at the hoards of cash held by criminals, terrorist and tax avoiders, who created economic distortions that brought suffering to the general population. Thus, Prime Minister Modi's national address emphasized the need to deal, once and for all, with the scourge of 'black money' (see Reddy 2017: 213–219). He posited demonetization as a means of 'purifying our country' of criminality and corruption. Black money was a significant electoral platform for the BJP in 2014, with the Panama papers scandal eliciting a promise to repatriate black money stashed in Swiss bank accounts. While the phrase itself confers a notion of illicit profits and shadowy transactions, the classification of black money is broad. Much of it is untaxed wealth from the informal sector, which employs 85% of the workforce. Thus, tax avoidance at this scale is somewhat correspondent to the institutionalized tax avoidance provided for Indian businesses via offshore subsidiaries, transfer pricing, participatory notes and other legal instruments (Hill and Athique 2018). However, a larger part of the whole is simply the cash earnings of India's working poor, who are in any case well below the threshold of the income tax regime, and of those living in rural districts without banking facilities and electricity. Some black money, certainly, is derived from criminal activities, but how large this proportion is remains a point of contention (see Reddy 2017: 14–33).

As Kaushik Basu, formerly chief economist at the World Bank, observed prior to demonetization, the scale of the informal economy was such that it effectively shielded India's economy and banking sector from the repercussions of the 2007–2008 global financial crisis and subsequent global recession (BBC 2016c). Thus, the Government of India confidently predicted in November 2016 that demonetization would destroy up to a third of the monetary wealth held outside of the banking system. To ensure this outcome, limits were placed on the size of cash deposits of the old notes, initially 4,000 Rupees per person could be exchanged for new notes. Once the end of year deadline had passed, anyone holding the remaining notes would be criminalized. This was later arbitrarily brought forward to 25 November. Although businesses could pay, and forward pay, their tax liabilities using their cash reserves, individuals with basic bank accounts could only make banking deposits to an upper limit of 50,000 Rupees with strictly rationed withdrawals. Even so, the flood of money into the banking sector by the end of year was so vast that it is estimated that 95–97% of the old currency stock was fed back into the banking sector. The massive scale of these deposits was remarkable given that 500 million people in India had either inactive bank accounts or no bank accounts at all. For the last two months of 2016, queues into bank branches snaked around every conurbation in India. It became widely assumed that many depositors were being paid a commission, both as a queuing fee and for the service of offering their bank accounts to launder the holdings of others. It also came to light that, since 80% of Indian women had no personal account, a large proportion of them held secret stores of cash at home which they were now obliged to transfer into the banking system (Doshi 2016).

In many ways, the entire proposition of black money in cash holdings ran counter to the White Paper on black money published in 2012, which noted that most black money was created by accounting scams rather than through the cash economy, and that most illicit holdings were held in real estate, jewellery, *benami* (proxy) bank accounts and similarly anonymous investments and holdings in companies (Ministry of Finance 2012). Cash, after all, is a poor option as a store of wealth in an inflationary economic system. Further, the rationale of capitalist accumulation is to create profits through money circulation, not through hoarding. To seize hoarded wealth, the government would have needed to ban and seize gold, hardly a tenable proposition in the country dubbed by the gold-averse Keynes as 'the world's sink of precious metals' (see Reddy 2017: 173–181). In any case, according to Ghosh et al., the narrative had begun to shift within two weeks of demonetization towards the need to combat the rising threat of counterfeit paper currency introduced by Pakistan and supporting terrorism. However, it soon transpired that the proportion of counterfeit currency detected through demonetization was more or less the same as it had always been, a measly 0.0018% of the paper money supply (Ghosh et al. 2017: 19). To make matters worse, the replacement 500 and 2,000 Rupee notes were no better securitized than the old ones and didn't fit in the ATM machines, thus further extending the cash supply crisis. Notwithstanding the illogic of destroying high value banknotes to replace them with higher value banknotes, the mints were flat out producing these new notes. Thus, they couldn't simultaneously produce enough new smaller denomination notes (beyond 14% that escaped demonetization) to guarantee the change necessary to make the larger new notes an effective transactional currency. Thus, India went into a protracted 'less cash' scenario, which the government then adopted as a virtue.

The purported benefits of replacing just half of the previous amount of paper currency by mid-2017, and that disproportionately in high-value notes, was to reduce money circulation in the economy. This inevitably had a deflationary effect on prices, as spending power was curtailed. Falling inflation allowed for a reduction in interest rates and was therefore declared as delivering a welcome boon to borrowers. Thus, according to Ghosh et al., demonetization by the end of December 2016 (that is a period of seven weeks) became framed in terms of the fortuitous capitalization of banks, falling inflation and lower interest rates (2017: 21–22). By mid-2017, the reduction in cash supply had pricked the real estate bubble, given that properties were often bought for one price, officially, with the remainder paid in cash. Inevitably, all of these factors impacted upon GDP and the growth rate, which sank to 5.6% by mid-2017. As Ghosh et al. point out, even on its own terms the monetarist argument about the benefits of deflation doesn't really hold water. The Reserve Bank of India could have altered interest rates without demonetization, the banking sector had no reserves crisis to start with and the uptake of cheaper credit was held back by the fact that 85% of the population receiving their wages in cash, or trying to, were in no position to take out loans (2017: 69–75). The 'less cash' argument was closely linked to a 'cashless' argument by which an enforced shift to digital transaction systems was an unqualified good in itself, taking us back to those fortuitous Paytm advertisements on day zero. The question, therefore, is whether this cashless agenda was a fig leaf for demonetization as a failed disciplinary measure or whether this was the central aim of the exercise all along.

The International Interest

In India, there is always a strong autarchic tendency in public debate, through which political and economic developments are narrated in a wholly domestic context. Demonetization was no exception to this general rule. Nonetheless, in the context of India's growing importance to the global economy, there was substantial international interest in Narendra Modi's dramatic intervention. To begin with, the international press was wrong-footed. A BBC journalist, Jack Simon, who was in Delhi to report on the UK Prime Minister's trade mission, wrote:

> The news channels are trying hard to interpret the news for viewers who are worried that they will not be able to get a cab, buy milk, or even have their life savings in cash. It feels they are scrambling right now…I'm not sure how I'm going to get back to the airport.
>
> (BBC 2016d)

Over the following days, more expert voices were carried in BBC reports, from Raghuram Rajan (former Reserve Bank of India Chairman), Kaushik Basu (former World Bank Chief Economist) and other well-respected Indian economists such as Prabhat Patnaik and Vivek Kaul. They all agreed that: (1) the initiative would have no lasting impact on stocks of black money, (2) it would lead to a substantial slowdown in the economy, and (3) the pain caused by the initiative would fall disproportionately upon the poorer segments of the population (that is, some 500 million people) (BBC 2016e). The UK *Guardian* also followed this line in a series of reports, concluding by 17 November that: 'Mr Modi's scheme has more in common with the failed experiments of dictatorships which led to runaway inflation, currency collapse and mass protests' (*The Guardian* 2016).

There was marked difference in tone from the USA, the *New York Times*, that began neutrally on 10 November: 'The plan, kept top secret until Mr. Modi's announcement, was hailed by financial analysts as bold and, potentially, transformational for India. It is also a high-stakes experiment' (New York Times 2016a). Opinion was offered on 17 November:

> Cash is king in India. It is used in an estimated 78 percent of transactions, compared with 20 percent to 25 percent in industrialized countries like Britain and the United States...Paper currency makes it easy for people to avoid taxes and engage in corruption.
>
> (New York Times 2016b)

On 27 November, they ran an article from Kaushik Basu, who repeated his criticism of demonetization as a way to tackling black money, but nonetheless ventured that:

> it would do better to move India toward becoming a more cashless society. About 53 percent of adult Indians have a bank account, but many signed up at the government's initiative and so quite a few of the accounts are dormant. On the other hand, more than one billion people in India have a cell phone, and this could be tapped to encourage more active banking, in the form of mobile banking...India's push to issue a unique I.D. number to all Indians based on their biometric information is a major step in the right direction.
>
> (Basu 2016)

The Washington Post observed that: 'Prime Minister Narendra Modi has long made fighting black money a priority — as the country moves to legitimize its shadow economy, change an age-old culture of corruption and attract foreign investment', while *The Wall Street Journal* advised that: 'Indian government bonds, a favourite among emerging-market investors, have rallied since the announcement. That may be a bet the reforms will work. But it could also be a bet that India's economy is about to slow. It could take Mr. Modi's plan a while to come together' (Wall Street Journal 2016). Overall, the financial press and financial institutions more generally were either effusive in their praise or positioned demonetization as a qualified good. A week prior to its comments on 'failed experiments', even *The Guardian* (on 11 November) had included commentary from Societe Generale claiming: 'This demonetisation step reinforces Modi's reformist and anti-corruption credentials and raises the prospect of higher long term growth potential', and from Ashburton Investments:

> This initiative will likely hurt growth in the very short term, but will yield significant benefits in the medium to long term as corruption is cut and the ease of doing business improves, as more of the economy moves into the formal sector.
>
> (Doshi and Allen 2016)

By far the most interesting and illuminating overseas commentary, however, came from *Forbes*, in a series of articles from 17 November to 30 December. The lead writer was Tim Worstall, who wrote:

> large deposits are going to be subject to tax scrutiny, rather the point of the exercise in fact. But what is interesting is that the flood of cash being deposited is such that it's actually bringing interest rates down. This is an interesting and welcome macroeconomic effect: Lower interest rates should, all else being equal, produce a stimulus to the economy...This entire extinguished or disappeared black money will be profit to the RBI, and will be transferred to the central government as dividend...Reducing the base money supply will lower inflation. At least some of that money will indeed be taxed and it would not have been taxed without the demonetization program. This means that the budget deficit will be smaller than it otherwise would have been...All in all then a rather interesting set of effects. A lower budget deficit, lower interest rates and also lower inflation. Not bad for the one simple plan, is it?
>
> (Worstall 2016a)

As reports began to spread of the economic chaos unfolding in India, Worstall followed up with a much more interesting piece on 22 November, that is worthy of a long excerpt:

> Larry Summers, the former US Treasury Secretary, has announced that he thinks that the demonetisation of India's Rs 500 and Rs 1,000 notes is a bad idea. I think that the interplay of economic efficiency and freedom and liberty needs to be carefully considered and where I'd come down on the side of a bit more economic inefficiency in return for a bit more freedom and liberty...One of us (Larry) has long advocated the abolition of the $100 note in the US context and the 500 euro note (aka the Bin Laden) in the European context...I disagree with both propositions

there, both that the high value notes in the US and euro system should go and that the Rs 500 and RS 1,000 notes should not have gone.

Of course, the existence of high value notes aids in black money and tax evasion (as well as properly illegal activity like drug smuggling etc). These are not, in and of themselves, good things. There is the minor point that the issuing governments make good profits out of this. However, we've also got that freedom and liberty thing to think about. Yes, obviously, people shouldn't break the law and all that but given the legal burdens and restrictions we all do labour under there has to be a certain amount of ignoring some of those laws. No one would really want, say, jaywalking to be turned into a strict liability offence and then strictly and comprehensively enforced. We do want the murder laws to be strictly enforced—and in between we'd like a bit of give and take. Cash allows that, produces that give and take in economic arrangements. A cashless society, one in which the government could track each and every detail of every transaction, would not be a free, liberal nor happy one.

So, cash might be inefficient in governmental terms, might at the margin even be inefficient in economic terms. But it has a value still, in that it gives us, the people, more freedom of action. Which should mean, of course, that the other proposition, that India should not have demonetised, is also true. And yet I don't think so...That some people occasionally pay their window cleaners with untaxed cash seems to me a reasonable price to pay to keep government out of every nook and cranny of our lives. That darn near all the decent houses in nice areas of the country have been bought at least partially with black money is going too far. There is a spectrum of behaviour which good governance should turn a blind eye to and some extremes of that spectrum which it should crack down upon. And my argument is that India was at that extreme end and the US, UK and so on are largely not.

(Worstall 2016b)

Thus, there is an interesting admission here that India's demonetization was closely linked to wider macroeconomic debates about the future of cash, along with a clear recognition that the advent of a cashless society threatened economic totalitarianism, or perhaps totalitarianism more generally. He concludes that it would be fundamentally anti-democratic to pursue such a course in the USA, but completely acceptable to do so in India, where everyone was corrupt. This mix of too much exceptionalism at home and too much totalitarianism abroad is generally consistent with American attitudes towards developing countries. Nonetheless, *Forbes* also ran an alternative voice on 2 December, from

Frank Holmes who proclaimed that demonetization was a 'cure worse than the disease in India' (Holmes 2016). Once again, he linked it to a wider scenario:

> I've previously written about the possible ramifications of the "war on cash," which is strengthening all over the globe...Electronic payment systems are convenient, fast and easy, but when a government imposes this decision on you, your economic liberty is debased. In a purely electronic system, every financial transaction is not only charged a fee but can also be tracked and monitored. Taxes can't be levied on emergency cash that's buried in the backyard. Central banks could drop rates below zero, essentially forcing you to spend your money or else watch it rapidly lose value.
>
> (ibid)

On 30 December, Worstall returned to defend demonetization. He began by dismissing a story in *The LA Times* of a farmer's daughter who died when the hospital refused to take cash as payment for her treatment, saying:

> It is of course possible that this specific death can and even should be blamed upon demonetization. But that a poor rural Indian dies for lack of heart surgery is not such a rare occurrence that we can confidently blame it upon demonetization.
>
> (Worstall 2016c)

He then goes on to say: 'the real background issue is really all about Adam Smith...The specific effectiveness of the demonetization campaign itself isn't all that important. It's the psychological effect in general which is' (ibid). Notwithstanding its predispositions, the *Forbes* coverage was able to situate India's demonetization, and monetary transformation in general, in terms of a bigger picture. At the same time, it has to be noted that *Forbes* gave its 'Business of the Year' Award in 2016 to Paytm, the leading digital payments business in India. Paytm is backed by investments from Alibaba, Taiwan's Meditek, US Berkshire Hathaway and Japan's Softbank. Paytm banking services are interlinked with the Government of India's eTaal tax payments system and were inaugurated by Finance Minister Arun Jaitley. Like *Forbes*, Paytm was clearly not a disinterested party in demonetization.

The Cashless Agenda

If, following the *Forbes* line, we broadly situate India's cashless agenda within the context of an international 'war on cash', we have to consider a larger multinational agenda that has emerged as a consequence of the opening calamities of the 21st century: the 'War on Terror', the 'Global

Financial Crisis' and the 'Great Recession' of the past decade. If it has an ideological voice, the most likely candidate would be the Harvard Economics Professor, Kenneth Rogoff, who has developed an argument for obliterating cash over the past 20 years, recently expressed in his book, *The Curse of Cash* (2016). It was Roggoff who first awarded the 500 EURO bill the status of being an almost entirely criminal instrument (1998). Going on to develop a similar argument against the $100 bill, the underlying macro-economic argument is that stores of cash not only underwrite criminality and create transaction costs, but also distort economic activity and thereby undermine the aims and benefits of monetarist economics as expounded by the likes of Milton Friedman (1962). Rogoff is prominently cited in Rhagbendra Jha's laudatory report on India's demonetization for the Australian Institute of International Affairs (2016). Rogoff's aversion to paper money is as instinctive and sincere as John Maynard Keynes fierce opposition to the gold standard (1936). Rogoff is not, by any means, a lone voice in debates on economic policy. To try and summarize the most commonly heard arguments for a cashless society in equally pragmatic terms, I shall posit them under a set of four predominant interests: law enforcement, revenue departments, financial industries and technology companies.

In the first instance, the argument generally prevails that cash is the primary means for funding international terrorism and organized criminality, with *Hawala* systems of cash distribution, such as found in India, being singled out in particular for their links to terrorist financing. Cash as anonymous or 'dumb' money facilitates vice crimes such as drug dealing and prostitution and, obviously, provides the primary motivation for all scales of cash robbery (and thereby a significant proportion of violent crime) as well as corruption in government and law enforcement itself. Under the aegis of combating international terrorism, restrictions on international movements of cash and cash deposits were put in place soon after 2001, and subsequently extended after 2008. An increasingly common line taken by leaders in law enforcement is that cash be replaced entirely by digital payment systems that leave a clear trail of transactions, by which questionable money exchanges can be identified, investigated and proven.

In the second instance, a leading argument for going cashless revolves around the desire of governments to collect tax revenues and reduce their transactional costs. As we all know, one consequence of the 2007–2008 global financial crisis was that government accounts were forced to shoulder the inextricable and unredeemable debts of the global financial industry. By undertaking this socialization of losses, Western governments were plunged into a recessionary crisis which required them to devalue their currencies, cut spending and impose austerity programmes that contracted their economies and raised welfare costs. This protracted crisis in government revenues can only be resolved through taxation and spending cuts. Thus, previously unthinkable scrutiny of offshore tax havens was pushed heavily by the Obama administration in the USA. For many governments, digitization and automation of public services was seen as a means of reducing delivery costs and eliminating fraud. Increasingly, there is also a drive to clamp down on petty 'off the books' cash transactions. As the notion has become entrenched that cash holdings must *de facto* be a matter of tax avoidance, the logics of eGovernance advocate the abolition of cash and full transactional visibility through digital systems.

In the third instance, the argument is that a cashless system will provide cheaper credit. The global financial crisis left the world with the institutional legacy of 'zombie banks', kept alive through quantitative easing, near-zero interest rates and interventions in bond markets. As the bail outs proceeded, a spate of banking regulations required banks to simultaneously build up capital reserves, while maintaining their lending. Beyond the imposition of stress tests, a significant series of 'bail in' transferred the liabilities of bank debts from bond holders to customers. In this context, a shift towards cashless economies has numerous implications. For one, the inability of customers to withdraw their money from the banking system means that there can never be another run on the banks in general. For the same reason, there will be no need to resume paying above-inflation interest rates to attract customer capital. Further, in the absence of tangible monetary wealth, banks can impose both negative interest rates on depositors and transaction charges on the everyday use of money, as an alternative source of profits from lending to over-extended customers. Full digitization also means huge reductions in workforces and premises, and the considerable transactional costs of managing paper money will disappear. Greater bank profits are assumed to expand credit, with both considered as an unqualified good.

In the fourth instance, the arguments of technology companies for cashless economies are, as ever, efficiency, convenience and seamless integration with their other products. The world's largest technology companies have an evident interest in the implementation of a cashless economy. The proposition itself rests entirely upon the back-end infrastructure of the World Wide Web to deliver the capacity, coverage and reliability to make universal mobile payments a reality. Cashless economies will therefore require, and subsequently underwrite, the expansion of digital infrastructure across the world. In a virtuous combination, the compulsion towards digital transactions will compel the remainder of the world's population to get online and to maintain mobile connectivity. Providers of software, support and devices will all profit from the acceleration of their market expansion, especially in emerging markets, but the real winners will be the large technology companies who will manage the integrity of the system itself. Thus, if Lehman Brothers was considered 'too big to fail' in 2008, then Android will become such at an infinitely larger scale. Technology companies will become as central to the everyday economy as they have already become in the money markets, thereby enshrining FinTech as the controlling interest in the world economy.

Evidently, all of these arguments appeared in various forms in the pronouncements and commentaries that accompanied India's demonetization experiment. This, then, has to be understood not simply as a national impulse, but as part of a global experiment in monetary reform. In countries such as Denmark and Sweden, the use of cash has dwindled to scarcely 10% of transactions. The Netherlands is well down this path, with many shops refusing to take cash payment and commissions already being collected on the use of digital money. Australia has made a series of moves to reduce the use of cash, while South Korea has committed to becoming entirely cashless by 2020. Clearly, a digital switchover in developed economies with good infrastructure and small populations is an entirely different proposition from a Cashless India. Having said that, the popularity of digital payments in countries like Kenya has been driven precisely by a lack of banking infrastructure and China, while being far from cashless, is already the leader in digital transactions in numerical terms. When India's Prime Minister finally gave an interview on 29 December 2016, he said:

> Experts across the world have advocated demonetisation over the years. In 1980, James Henry, the former chief economist of McKinsey, had recommended that high-value currency in the United States be suddenly demonetised...This has also been said by Prof. Kenneth Rogoff, author of the book *The Curse of Cash*. Prof. Larry Summers has called for demonetising the $100 note. In a Harvard University paper in February 2016, the former CEO of Standard Chartered Bank mentioned the role played by high denomination notes in illegal activities throughout the world and called for their elimination... Digital transactions should not be viewed only as a short-term substitute to help through the period of cash shortage. That is not my objective. Many have forgotten that this push to digital has been on for quite some time. As early as February 2016, the cabinet had decided to give a major thrust to digital transactions...Digital transactions deliver multiple benefits. They facilitate proper accounting and sizing of the formal economy. They provide greater ease and security in handling of money, especially for small businesses and ordinary people. They ensure the building of financial records, which enables access to the formal financial system, including loans. They also deliver greater tax compliance...Therefore, I see digital payments as a method of cleaning up our economy in the long run.
>
> (Modi 2016)

Thus, as Mukesh Butani observed in the midst of the chaos in November 2016: 'Demonetisation can hardly be viewed as an isolated action', given that 'In September 2015, India joined the United Nations' "Better Than

Cash Alliance", an implementing partner for G20 Global Partnership for Financial Inclusion' (Butani 2016). Also, less than a month before demonetization: 'USAID announced the establishment of 'Catalyst: Inclusive Cashless Payment Partnership' with the Indian Ministry of Finance, with the goal of effecting a quantum leap in cashless payment in India' (Ghosh et al. 2017: 92).

The Year of Living Digitally

Usha Rodrigues has also traced the evolving rationale of demonetization in the context of Narendra Modi's rolling political campaign via Twitter which, in this instance, began 'with #Indiadefeatsblackmoney, and moved on to solution-focused messages of a cashless society #ipaydigitally, a utopia where most Indians used digital technology to pay for their monetary transactions' (2017). The Prime Minister's Twitter strategies are a core component of his cultivated image as a tech-savvy economic modernizer. As such, we have to situate the events of 2016–2017 within the larger context of Narendra Modi's flagship 'Digital India' programme launched in July 2015. The programme has nine 'pillars': Broadband Highways, Universal Mobile Access, Public Internet Access, eGovernance, Electronic Service and Education delivery, IT Manufacturing, IT Job Creation and 'Early Harvest' (which is linked to the Aadhaar biometrics programme, welfare securitization and monitoring of government employees). The various pillars are grouped into three core areas: 'digital infrastructures', 'governance service' and 'digital empowerment' (Digital India 2017). Within this larger vision, the drive for a 'Cashless India' has emerged as a core component of the programme. In this domain: 'Faceless, Paperless, Cashless is one the professed role of Digital India. As part of promoting cashless transactions and converting India into a less-cash society' (Cashless India 2017). This drive is promoted across a range of functionalities, including: debit cards, Unstructured Supplementary Service Data (SMS payments), Aadhaar Enabled Payment System, Unified Payments Interface, mobile wallets, bank prepaid cards, point of sale, Internet banking, mobile banking and micro ATMs.

From 8 December 2016, in the midst of demonetization, the Government of India began to issue a series of incentives via the Cashless India programme encouraging businesses and individuals to switch to digital transactions (ibid). Digital India Payments Ltd (incorporated on 13 November 2016), however, is a private-sector company providing many of these services (Digital India Payments 2017). Paytm and Reliance Jio are two other private sector players identified by Ghosh et al. as the 'disproportionate beneficiaries' of demonetization (2017: 91). Thus, as with all facets of the Digital India programme, the Government of India has a close working relationship with commercial providers (see Thomas 2019). The Aadhaar programme is intended to provide the foundation for a robust digital transactions system. In 2017, the delivery of government services, including welfare and work guarantees, became dependent upon enrolment in Aadhaar. The government's institution of bank accounts for all, under the Jan Dhan Yojana scheme, also became linked to the Jan Dhan-Aadhaar-Mobile (JAM) payment pathway as the preferred infrastructure for welfare payments (Ranade 2017). Although India's Supreme Court has ruled that Aadhaar enrolment cannot be mandatory, possession of an Aadhaar card was commonly a prerequisite for exchanging banknotes during demonetization, and Aadhaar numbers have since been linked to the provision of banking and mobile services across the private sector (Aiyar 2017). Thus, the high rhetoric of 'Digital India' dovetails with the intrusive reality of the Aadhaar platform, the world largest and most ambitious 'mechanism of legibility' (Ramanathan 2010, Shukla 2010). In return, the creation of a digital transactional infrastructure becomes critical to the fortunes of the unified GST introduced in July 2017, through which the government seeks to realize its long-held ambition to switch from an income- to a consumption-based tax regime.

This close cohabitation between government and the digital and financial sectors, both at home and abroad, raises obvious questions around the state's role as the watchdog and arbiter of the transactional economy. The critical issue, in this respect, is that the governance of transactional platforms is not easily separated from the platformization of government transactions (and indeed, governance itself). While government claims of 90% public support for demonetization and digital transactions in 2016 were dismissed even by *Forbes*, a target for 2017–2018 of 25 billion digital transactions was nonetheless set by the Ministry of Finance. One year on, there was a clear consensus that the quantum of digital transactions had increased substantially, although not at a much faster rate than they were expanding prior to demonetization (D'Souza 2018; Reddy 2017). Nonetheless, in the year of living digitally, it became possible to take the debate out of economic theory and situate policy and into the domain of lived experience. In doing so, Vivek et al. investigated the delivery of work payments in Andhra Pradesh under the auspices of the Rural Employment Guarantee scheme (2018). They sought to establish whether the use of digital transactions was achieving its goals of (1) removing intermediaries, (2) guaranteeing instantaneous payments and (3) reducing corruption. They found that, owing to the lack of banking infrastructure, Internet connectivity and access to both in the villages, a three-tier system of private contractors had been instituted for collecting the digital payments and delivering them to workers.

It was found that there were often considerable gaps between the electronic disbursement of funds by government and actual payments to workers by these agents. The average delay between government payment and payment by agencies was 15.5 days, as-yet-unpaid workers had waited an average of 43.6 days and 13% of payments never reached the intended recipients (Vivek et al. 2018: 61). Further evidence was found of tampering with point-of-sale (POS) machines, taking of illegal commissions and diversion of payments. They concluded therefore that, even in a state with comparatively good digital infrastructure, the digital payments system was reproducing all the features of corruption found in the predigital rendition of the scheme. Intermediaries benefited from holding money in transit and opaque reporting regimes made it easy to divert and delay payments (ibid: 63). In an ethnographic study of migrant workers in Punjab and Bihar, Anand and Ajmal found that all sectors of the economy were badly hit by demonetization in the rural districts, with the loss of opportunities and business continuing through 2017. Most respondents lost their livelihoods and many were ultimately forced to return to their villages, with the number of workers still down a year later, and damaged harvests in the fields. Their respondents also claimed that a black market charging up to 40% commission for paper notes had preyed upon the middle classes, while corrupt bank managers had taken care of the needs of the wealthy. Distrust of the banks was widely expressed, with demonetization being regarded as wholesale theft (Anand and Ajmal 2017).

For subsistence workers, almost their total monetary income is used in everyday transactions for meeting their basic needs. They have little savings and are not considered creditworthy. As such, they have very little to gain from entering the banking system. For them, digital payments impose device and connectivity costs that they are generally unable to bear. To a lesser degree, when it comes to small businesses in the informal economy, Renita D'Souza, writing for a think tank supported by India's Reliance Industries, noted that: 'Those operating in the unorganised retail are not profiteers; rather their businesses are survivalist or marginal activities. Going digital adds significantly to their business costs and affects the viability of their business' (2018: 11). Drawing our attention to the imposition of transaction costs chimes with Ghosh et al.'s observation that

> The shift to e-money would make all Indians pay for all transactions, as compared to transactions in cash that do not involve any costs for those engaging in it. This point was glossed over by those pushing for this change, as it would have drawn attention to the transfer of income from all consumers and producers to a few banks and 'fintech' companies involved in e-commerce and mobile wallet services.
>
> (2017: 91)

Thus, although digital transaction rates have increased, unreliable connectivity, lack of POS machines and the means to support personal devices all impede progress towards universal coverage. Further, it is by no means evident that the majority of Indians have been persuaded of the benefits of digital payments, or why they should bear the costs involved.

The Consequences of Cashing Out

By the end of 2017, commentators on demonetization were in broad agreement that it did not destroy any significant amount of black money, nor prevent its future creation. It did not address any significant counterfeiting crisis nor eliminate corruption in government services. It did contribute to a spike in gold prices and demand for US dollars and Bitcoins. It did reduce the rate of economic growth for some 18 months and contribute to deflation, to lower interest rates and, arguably, to the ongoing devaluation of the Rupee. As an accidental bystander, I think that the two-step process of Demonetization and Cashless India reflects the genuine faith of Narendra Modi in digital technologies, India's broad cooperation with G20 institutions and a sincere desire to modernize, formalize and purify India's economic system. Perhaps India's demonetization is best seen as an attempt to apply First World solutions to First World problems in a developing country with entirely different problems. India became a test site for a radical monetary experiment in introducing the cashless agenda to a major world economy by fiat. Now that the smoke is clearing from Bikini Atoll, and various macroeconomic indicators become available, economists will be debating the merits and demerits of the exercise for many years to come.

I am not an economist, but the entire episode brings home the importance of understanding the medium of money and the expansion of transactional systems in any credible account of digital culture and communication. Conversely, more economists might take account of medium theory when considering the practicalities of digital transactions. Fintech companies, without any doubt, need to consider the social and cultural anthropology of money much more carefully before they invoke monetary revolutions. Outside of academic and banking circles, it is clear that everybody should give some thought to the utility and implications of a cashless future. The transfer of the risks and costs of the monetary system onto citizens is much more than an infrastructural concern. The acquisition of taxation powers by Fintech companies and the end of independent value outside the banking sector is an unprecedented shift in the contract between citizens and the state. So, as much as this is an Indian story, it is also an international story and one that is becoming central to the evolution of digital society and to the future of democracy itself.

References

Abraham, Bobins (2016) 'PM's Friends Were Given Advance Information on Demonetization, It Is a Surgical Strike on Common People Says Kejriwal', *India Times*, 12 November 2016. Available: www.indiatimes.com/news/india/pm-s-friends-were-given-advance-information-on-demonetization-it-is-a-surgical-strike-on-common-people-says-kejriwal-265342.html, accessed: 9 January 2017.

Aiyar, Shankar (2017) *Aadhaar: The Biometric History of India's 12-digit Revolution*, Delhi: Westland.

Al Jazeera (2016) 'India Demonetisation: Chaos as ATMs Run Dry', 9 November 2016. Available: www.aljazeera.com/news/2016/11/india-demonetisation-chaos-atms-run-dry-161109061403011.html, accessed: 4 January 2017.

Anand, Atul and Ajmal, Zaheeb (2017) 'Demonetization and Digital India: Experiences of Migrant Workers in Punjab and Bihar', Paper presented at *Social Transactions in Digital India*, IIT Bombay, 6–7 December 2017.

Basu, Kaushik (2016) 'In India, Black Money Makes for Bad Policy', *The New York Times*, 27 November 2016. Available: www.nytimes.com/2016/11/27/opinion/in-india-black-money-makes-for-bad-policy.html, accessed: 27 November 2016.

BBC (2016a) "No Customers': Indians React to Currency Ban', 10 November 2016. Available: www.bbc.com/news/world-asia-india-37921672, accessed: 10 November 2016.

BBC (2016b) 'How India's Currency Ban Is Hurting the Poor', 12 November 2016. Available: www.bbc.com/news/world-asia-india-37947029, accessed: 12 November 2016.

BBC (2016c) 'How Black Money Saved the Indian Economy', 22 February 2016. available: www.bbc.com/news/world-asia-india-35610332, accessed: 22 February 2016.

BBC (2016d) 'India Currency Bombshell', 8 November 2016. Available: http://www.bbc.com/news/business-37915359, accessed: 8 November 2016.

BBC (2016e) 'Indian Rupee Ban: Currency Move Is 'Bad Economics'', 14 November 2016. Available: www.bbc.com/news/world-asia-india-37970965, accessed: 14 November 2016.

Butani, Mukesh (2016) 'Demonetisation Decoded: Time to Embrace a Cashless Economy: Global Trend Moving That Way', *Financial Express*, 30 November 2016. Available: www.financialexpress.com/opinion/demonetisation-decoded-time-to-embrace-a-cashless-economy-global-trend-moving-that-way-demonetisation-gdp-cashless-economy-indian-economy/459780/, accessed: 30 November 2016.

Cashless India (2017) 'Digital Payment Methods'. Available: cashlessindia.gov.in/, accessed: 8 August 2017.

Digital India (2017) 'Digital India', Ministry of Electronics and Information Technology, Government of India, http://www.digitalindia.gov.in/, accessed: 8 August 2017.

Digital Payments India (2017) 'Domestic Money Transfer'. Available: http://www.digitalindiapayments.com/, accessed 22 May 2017.

Doshi, Vidhi (2016) 'Women Bear the Brunt as Finances and Families Are Undone by India's Cash Crisis', *The Guardian*, 22 December 2016. Available: www.theguardian.com/global-development/2016/dec/22/india-cash-crisis-women-bear-brunt-finances-families-undone, accessed: 6 January 2017.

Doshi, Vidhi and Allen, Katie (2016) 'Your Money's No Good: Rupee Note Cancellation Plunges India into Panic', *The Guardian*, 11 November 2016. Available:www.theguardian.com/world/2016/nov/10/rupee-note-cancellation-panic-in-india-banks-500-1000, accessed: 4 January 2017.

D'Souza, Renita (2018) *Cashless India: Getting Incentives Right*, ORF Occasional Paper, Mumbai: Observer Research Foundation.

Dubey, Rachana (2016) 'Box Office Grapples with Demonetisation', *Times of India*, 2December 2016. Available: http://timesofindia.indiatimes.com/entertainment/hindi/bollywood/news/Box-office-grapples-with-demonetisation/articleshow/55725486.cms, accessed 9 January 2017.

Financial Express (2016) 'Demonetisation Crisis: 25 people Dead in a Week Already', 15 November 2016. Available: www.financialexpress.com/india-news/demonetisation-row-many-lives-lost-for-crores-of-unaccounted-money-in-only-5-days/445560/, accessed: 9 January 2017.

Friedman, Milton (1962) *Capitalism and Freedom*, Chicago, IL: University of Chicago Press.

Ghosh, Jayati, Chandrasekhar, C.P. and Patnaik, Prabhat (2017) *Demonetisation Decoded: A Critique of India's Demonetisation Experiment*, New Delhi: Routledge India.

The Guardian (2016) 'The Guardian View on India's Demonetisation: Modi Has Brought Havoc to India', *The Guardian*, 17 November 2016. Available: www.theguardian.com/commentisfree/2016/nov/17/the-guardian-view-on-indias-demonetisation-modi-has-brought-havoc-to-india, accessed: 6 January 2017.

Hebbar, Prajakta (2016) 'Demonetisation Hits the Indian Film Industry', *The Huffington Post India*, 11 November 2016. Available: www.huffingtonpost.in/2016/11/11/demonetisation-hits-the-indian-film-industry/, accessed: 11 November 2016.

Hill, Douglas and Athique, Adrian (2018) 'The Role of Offshore Financial Centres in Indian Telecoms', in Athique, Adrian, Parthasarathi, Vibodh and Srinivas, S.V. (eds) *The Indian Media Economy Vol. 1: Industrial Dynamics and Cultural Adaptation*, New Delhi: Oxford University Press.

The Hindu (2016) 'Move Was in the Pipeline for Months', *The Hindu*, 9 November 2016. Available: www.thehindu.com/news/national/Move-was-in-the-pipeline-for-months/article16440793.ece, accessed: 9 January 2017.

Holmes, Frank (2016) 'Modi's Demonetisation Is a Cure Worse Than the Disease For India', *Forbes*, 2 December 2016. Available: www.forbes.com/sites/greatspeculations/2016/12/02/modis-demonetization-is-a-cure-worse-than-the-disease-for-india/#4757c9d55c58, accessed: 6 January 2017.

Jha, Raghbendra (2016) 'India's Demonetisation in Practice', *Australian Institute of International Affairs*, 21 December 2016. Available: www.internationalaffairs.org.au/australian_outlook/indias-demonetisation-in-practice/, accessed: 4 January 2017.

Keynes, John Maynard (1936) *The General Theory of Employment, Interest and Money*, Cambridge: Cambridge University Press.

Ministry of Finance (2012) *White Paper on Black Money*, New Delhi: Government of India.

Modi, Narendra (2016) 'Interview of the Year: PM Narendra Modi Exclusive, His First Since Demonetisation', *India Today*, 29 December 2016. Available: http://indiatoday.intoday.in/story/narendra-modi-black-money-demonetisation-opposition/1/845224.html, accessed: 31 December 2016.

New York Times (2016a) 'Crowds Line Up at India's Banks to Exchange Banned Rupee Notes', *New York Times*, 10 November 2016. Available: www.nytimes.com/2016/11/11/world/asia/india-rupee-ban-narendra-modi.html, accessed: 11 November 2016.
New York Times (2016b) 'India's Strange Cash Problem', *New York Times*, 17 November 2016. Available: www.nytimes.com/2016/11/18/opinion/indias-strange-cash-problem.html, accessed: 4 January 2017.
Ramanathan, Usha (2010) 'A Unique Identity Bill', *Economic and Political Weekly*, VXV(30): 10–14.
Ranade, Ajit (2017) 'Role of 'Fintech' in Financial Inclusion and New Business Models', *Economic and Political Weekly*, LII(12). Available: https://www.epw.in/journal/2017/12/money-banking-and-finance/role-%E2%80%98fintech%E2%80%99-financial-inclusion-and-new-business-models, accessed: 6 April 2017.
Reddy, C. Rammanohar (2017) *Demonetisation and Black Money*, Hyderabad: Orient Blackswan.
Rodrigues, Usha (2017) 'Hashtag Modi and Demonetisation', *The Hoot*, 12 January 2017. Available: www.thehoot.org/story_popup/hashtag-modi-and-demonetisation-9897, accessed: 12 January 2017.
Roggof, Kenneth (1998) 'Blessing or Curse? Foreign and Underground Demand for Euro Notes', *Economic Policy*, 13(26): 262–303.
Roggof, Kenneth (2016) *The Curse of Cash: How Large-Denomination Bills Aid Crime and Tax Evasion and Constrain Monetary Policy*, Princeton, NJ: Princeton University Press.
Safi, Michael and Brown, William (2016) 'India Currency Note Ban Sparks 'Dramatic Fall' in Sex Trafficking', *The Guardian*, 22 December 2016. Available: www.theguardian.com/global-development/2016/dec/22/india-currency-note-ban-sparks-dramatic-fall-sex-trafficking, accessed: 6 January 2017.
Sarin,Ritu, Iyer, P. Vaidyanathan and Mazoomdaar, Jay (2016) 'Indians in #PanamaPapers List: Aishwarya Rai, Amitabh Bachchan, KP Singh, Iqbal Mirchi, Adani Elder Brother', *Indian Express*, 5 April 2016. Available: https://indianexpress.com/article/india/india-news-india/panama-papers-list-amitabh-bachchan-kp-singh-aishwarya-rai-iqbal-mirchi-adani-brother/, accessed: 5 April 2016.
Shukla, Ravi (2010) 'Reimagining Citizenship: Debating India's Unique Identification Scheme', *Economic and Political Weekly*, XLV(2): 31–36.
Thomas, Pradip (2019) *The Politics of Digital India*, New Delhi: Oxford University Press.
Vivek, Srinivasan, Narayanan, Rajendran, Chakraborty, Dipanjan, Veeraraghavan, Rajesh and Vardhan, Vibhore (2018) 'Are Technology-enabled Cash Transfers Really 'Direct'?', *Economic and Political Weekly*, LIII(30): 58–64.
Wall Street Journal (2016) 'India's Black-Money Experiment Shines Bright for Bonds: Indian Bonds Appear to Be the Big Winner in the Cash-Draining Move', *Wall Street Journal*, 14 November 2016. Available: www.wsj.com/articles/indias-black-money-experiment-shines-bright-for-bonds-1479124524, accessed: 22 November 2016.
Worstall, Tim (2016a) 'India's Rs 500 and 1,000 Demonetization Is Lowering Interest Rates and also Inflation', *Forbes*, 17 November 2016. Available: www.forbes.com/sites/timworstall/2016/11/17/indias-rs-500-and-1000-

demonetisation-is-lowering-interest-rates-and-also-inflation/#2b1744422edf, accessed: 4 January 2017.

Worstall, Tim (2016b) 'India's Demonetisation – Larry Summers Thinks It's a Bad Idea', *Forbes*, 22 November, 2016. Available: www.forbes.com/sites/timworstall/2016/11/22/indias-demonetisation-larry-summers-thinks-its-a-bad-idea/#4921bc041a78, accessed: 4 January 2017.

Worstall, Tim (2016c) 'India's Demonetization 50 Days In – Not Perfect But Moving in the Right Direction', *Forbes*, 30 December 2016. Available: www.forbes.com/sites/timworstall/2016/12/30/indias-demonetisation-50-days-in-not-perfect-but-moving-in-the-right-direction/#2f60475d52bd, accessed: 4 January 2017.

6 Another Dimension of Digital

3D Printing and Intellectual Property in Asia

Angela Daly, Jiajie Lu and Luke Heemsbergen

3D printing has emerged onto the global stage as a new and potentially highly disruptive manufacturing technology, with an impact predicted by some to be as revolutionary as the Internet. However, much of the existing research from humanities, arts and social sciences disciplines concerns 3D printing in North America and Western Europe, with limited literature on 3D printing's trajectory in other parts of the world, including Asia. In this chapter, the relationship between 3D printing and other digital technologies will be considered from a western perspective, before we focus specifically on Asian developments, taking 3D printing in India and China as case studies. We will look at the approaches in these countries to innovation and intellectual property in general, how the relationship is playing out in the 3D printing space and the extent to which the regional – and global – experience is converging or diverging.

Additive Manufacturing

Additive manufacturing, better known as '3D printing', is an innovative, advanced manufacturing technique which has entered the mainstream in the last decade. 3D printing has an older history, dating back at least until the first patents over the technology were issued in the 1980s. Yet a combination of factors including some of those patents expiring, technological advancements and price reductions has pushed 3D printing to manifesting as a more widespread technology in society. Cheap 3D printers, which use plastics as raw material, currently retail for under US$200, placing them within the purchasing power of consumers in developed economies, and increasingly also consumers in developing economies. The emergence of cheap 3D printers in the retail shelves of bricks-and-mortar stores, and in online e-commerce sites, has been accompanied by a significant degree of hype about 3D printing's transformative nature. In a technical sense, 3D printing is indeed revolutionary and transformative but significant questions remain about the extent to which 3D printing is transformative and disruptive from other perspectives – social, political, economic, cultural and legal. Succinctly, lowering economic barriers to 3D printers has encouraged new types of 3D printing, shifting manufacturing practices from intra-firm prototyping to inter-firm commerce as well as peer-to-peer consumer activities that are creating new sociotechnical cultures linked to making (Fordyce et al. 2016).

One important aspect of how 3D printing has emerged, and how it has been used to date, is its interaction with the Internet and digital technologies. Many 3D printing machines themselves have Internet connectivity and could be said to form part of the Internet of Things. Even those machines which are not connected to the Internet are still reliant on digital data in the form of 3D printing design or 'CAD' files, which are the design plans from which the eventual 3D object is created. These files can be obtained from a number of sources, but often they are downloaded from online file platforms such as Thingiverse, where creators upload the files they have created and permit others to download them for no cost but with certain restrictions depending on the Creative Commons or free software licence chosen (see Moilanen et al. 2015). While Thingiverse is a free site, and ostensibly does not make money for its owner, 3D printing machine vendor MakerBot (itself owned by 3D printing conglomerate Stratasys), there are other sites which inhabit more of an 'e-commerce' character and adopt a different business model. Prominent among these is Shapeways, a 3D printing marketplace and print-on-demand service. Users upload 3D printing design files to Shapeways' site, and can order Shapeways to print out the object in that file in a number of different materials, for a fee. In addition, other consumers can browse Shapeways' marketplace and pay for someone else's design to be printed out for them in the material of their choice.

These are different ways in which the 3D printing ecosystem, which includes a commercial market but also a significant amount of non-profit or amateur activity, exhibits digital transactions. However, the physicality or materiality of 3D printing adds a further 'dimension' to discussions on the digital. While recent work in infrastructure studies foregrounds the fact that the digital always has a tangible, material aspect (e.g. Kitchin & Dodge 2011; Pickren 2018), this aspect is clearly exhibited with the very processes by which 3D printing functions. Yet the nature of the 'digital transactions' making up 3D printing has received little attention, and in particular there is very little scholarship on the topic relating to 3D printing developments outside of the west. Here, we will outline western views of 3D printing present in the literature, before moving to consider some Asian developments, in the form of two case studies of 3D printing in India and China. We will look at the approaches in these countries to innovation and intellectual property in general, how the relationship is playing out in the 3D printing space and the extent to which the regional – and global – experience is converging or diverging.

Western Views of 3D Printing

Much of the research and subsequent literature on 3D printing and its social, cultural and economic implications pertain to 3D printing ecosystem/industry in the west, loosely defined as North America and Western Europe. Indeed, much of the 3D printing industry globally remains geographically concentrated in the west (Gress and Kalafsky 2015). Prominent arguments made in this literature, especially in sociolegal texts, in the last decade have concerned the idea that 3D printing would bring about a reduction of scarcity and a reduction of effective (government) control over the technology.

> By democratizing the precision creation of physical objects, 3D printing may make the creation of physical objects nearly as widespread as the creation of [digitised] copyright-protectable works.
>
> (Weinberg 2010)

> [T]hree disruptive technologies—file sharing, 3D printing, and distributed digital currency—have severely undermined the legal and regulatory capacity of the state, resulting in an anarchic environment where actors' behavior is determined primarily by factors other than legislation or governmental authority.
>
> (Michael 2013b)

In previous research, Daly focused on 3D printing and legal frameworks in some major western countries, namely the United States of America (USA), the United Kingdom (UK), European Union (EU) and Australia (2016). It seems that there had not been a significant take-up of 3D printing among western/northern consumers and prosumers, which is limiting the 'disruptive' effect that 3D printing is having on society and the economy. It cannot be discounted that there may be more widespread take-up of 3D printing due to better, cheaper machines in the future. However, the current picture appears to be that 3D printing is not bringing us to a post-control, post-scarcity world just yet. However, there has been some acknowledgement that this 3D printing scenario may not hold for other parts of the world. For instance, Birtchnell and Hoyle (2014) have posited that 3D printing may have more impact in emerging economies including the BRICS nations (Brazil, Russia, India, China, South Africa). In addition, the World Intellectual Property

Organization (WIPO), in its 2015 report, pointed to a potentially different trajectory for 3D printing in developing economies and remote areas. In order to examine the extent to which this may be true, we examine the trajectory of 3D printing in case studies on China and India in the following section.

3D Printing Developments in China and India

China and India, as the two 'fully' Asian BRICS countries and the world's two most populous countries, where digital media, in particular through mobile devices, has been strongly embraced, are the focus for our overview of 3D printing developments comprising Asian digital transactions. Overall 3D printing is more mature and widespread in China, although its breakthrough moment in India may not be far off. There is significantly more literature and knowledge about the dynamic of 3D printing's digital transactions in China, with a very limited amount on India, which makes understanding the nature of current – and potential future – digital transactions there challenging. Given the potential for 3D printing in India, this is an area which requires more research.

3D Printing in China

In recent decades, China has emerged as the world's dominant manufacturing nation (Li 2018). Some Western countries, especially the USA, have instituted policies around 3D printing and other forms of 'making', in part as an attempt to wrestle manufacturing away from China and its mass production as a form of 'insourcing' rather than 'outsourcing' (Garrett 2014; Jackson 2017; Stein 2017). Yet 3D printing is also present in China itself, and China has been investing in the technology since the 1990s (Ford 2014). Moreover, particularly in the Chinese context, 3D printing and conventional forms of mass production cannot be separated, given China's capacity for mass manufacturing is also utilised to create actual 3D printing machines, which are then used within the country and transported to other locations globally, including the west. The Chinese government also has policies which involve or affect 3D printing. Most specifically on the topic of 3D printing, the Chinese government issued a National Additive Manufacturing Industry Development Plan in 2015, which raised 3D printing techniques to the 'national strategic level' (Huang and Wang 2016). In 2017, eight national-level policies had been launched by 23 departments of the Chinese government to support the 3D printing industry, covering manufacture, research and education sectors (Xincailiao 2018). Among these policies,

The 13th Five-Year Plan for Scientific and Technological Innovation in the Field of Advanced Manufacturing Technology, formulated by the Ministry of Science and Technology, is a particularly significant one. It highlights five dimensions of additive manufacturing process: the fundamental science of additive material formation; the technology of optimising structural design; the production of special additive material; the design and production technology of core equipment; and the evaluation system and standards for 3D printing manufacture.

Additionally, the Ministry of Education launched *The Guideline of Comprehensive Practical Activity Curriculum in Primary and Middle Schools* on 25 September 2017. This guideline encourages schools to procure 3D printers for students from Grades 7 to 9 to learn the principles of 3D printing technology, model building and the human-machine interaction in the process of design. These policies promote a comprehensive system of 3D printing manufacture, from material research to product standards, along with the education of a skilled workforce. These actions indicate that the Chinese government does not adopt 3D printing technology merely for the purpose of industrial production and upgrading manufacturing. In a broader context, 3D printing technology is considered as one of the gateways to the next-generation social system, accompanied by artificial intelligence, big data, mobile Internet and the Internet of things. Indeed, another major policy is Internet+ which has various aims, including to 'digitise' manufacturing and integrate it into the Internet of Things (Keane 2016). 3D printing, as a form of digital manufacturing, may be included within this policy, although its scope is evidently broader, encompassing other forms of manufacturing and their digitisation, including 'traditional' manufacturing techniques. A further major Chinese government policy is 'Made in China 2025', which has been compared to Germany's 'Industry 4.0' policy, and 'signals China's intention to launch an industrial transformation from labor intensive production to knowledge intensive manufacturing' (Li 2017). To do this, Li points to the main features of Made in China 2025:

> The plan focuses on improving the quality of products made in China, creating China's own brands, building a solid manufacturing capability by developing cutting-edge advanced technologies, researching new materials, and producing key parts and components of major products.
>
> (Li 2017)

The digitised manufacturing features of Internet+ overlap with Made in China 2025. Both policies foresee the increased use of robots and automation in manufacturing (Brown 2017). 3D printing is also included in the Made in China 2025 policy, given one of the policy's goals is 'building a solid manufacturing capability via developing cutting-edge advanced technologies' (Huang and Wang 2016; Li 2017). Other aspects of Made in China 2025 which may pertain to 3D printing and associated activities are the desire for the design part of the manufacturing process also to take place in China or be 'Designed in China', in comparison to the previous scenario where product design occurred in developed economies, and then those products were manufactured in China (Li 2017). Promoting homegrown design may entail the need for customised products, and also the need to create prototypes for products that may be mass-produced in the end, both of which may be achieved through 3D printing.

In the last decade China has seen the creation of makerspaces, the first being XinCheJian in Shanghai, and many more have been set up since the Made in China 2025 policy was released, notably in Shenzhen (Shea and Gu 2018). China has also seen the emergence of new and innovative 3D printing design service companies such as Xuberance in Shanghai, established in 2014 (Ma 2017), which would seem to be a prime example of the kind of innovative design digital manufacturing company Made in China 2025 aims to create and foster. Nevertheless, similarly to 3D printing in developed countries, there are various barriers to uptake in China and challenges to be overcome, particularly around the cost of production, and expediency as compared to traditional techniques when a large quantity of a product is required (Chan et al. 2017). Another aspect of the Made in China 2025 policy associated with more design, innovation and manufacture in China is the stimulus to increase intellectual property accumulation, in particular through patent applications and the creation of well-known brands (Li 2017). For 3D printing, China seems to be on course to achieving this goal. According to WIPO (2015), it is the only middle-income country coming close to advanced industrialised nations as regards its number of patent filings in the 3D printing space, many of which have been filed by public institutions such as universities. This picture may be surprising to some in the west, given China's reputation as a user (and often an illegitimate one) of the IP created by (western) others (Liu 2015; Mehta 2007). However, there have been significant reforms to China's IP system in recent years, although enforcement remains a challenge (Beebe 2014; Cao 2014; Holland 2017; Liu 2015).

In terms of the digital transactions present in the Chinese 3D printing ecosystem, there are some differences from the globalised/western system. There are different online service providers operating in China to Thingiverse, which is the most popular 3D printing file platform globally and in the west (Moilanen et al. 2015). In China, however, there is no exact equivalent of Thingiverse, and instead prominent online 3D printing services include Simpneed (a start-up incubated in Hangzhou's 'Dream Village') and Mohou (which also now offers English-language services) more closely resemble Shapeways' print-on-demand service (Table 6.1).

Table 6.1 Comparison of online 3D print-on-demand services

	Simpneed	*Mohou*	*Shapeways*
Establishment	2013 in the USA Moved to Hangzhou in 2014	2013 in Beijing	2007 in New York
Services	Scanning, printing, products, prototype downloading, printers, hardware solution, consumable material	Scanning, printing, products, prototype downloading, printers, education, monitoring solution, small batch manufacturing	Printing, product development, small batch manufacturing, open a store, hire a designer, events, join a crew
Metaphor	Industrial vanguard	Individual user educator	A marketplace

Thus, in China, the shape of digital transactions in the 3D printing space is somewhat different to that of digital transactions in the western/globalised ecosystem. The lack of Thingiverse analogue is a major point of departure. 3D printing digital transactions seem to take place more through print-on-demand for-payment services than through the open and not-for-payment sharing of digital design files (and thus also a sharing of IP) on a dedicated online platform. IP sharing in Chinese 3D printing activities, however, takes place in different ways to Thingiverse in the West. According to Lindtner and Li the ethic of 'shanzhai' characterises Chinese maker culture (2010). This term has previously been used to describe the 'copycat' or counterfeit products made in Shenzhen, but more recently has come to represent an alternative, self-reliant open innovation vision for novel and remixed products 'created in China', including more recently through 3D printing in Chinese makerspaces (Lindtner and Li 2010). IP sharing involving 3D printing and 3D printed products may occur through shanzhai practices, which may be legitimate or may infringe IP rights. In light of this, Lindtner argues that 'China's culture of making can neither be understood based on Western principles of copyright and intellectual property nor on Western histories of hacking' (2015: 21).

However, in what may be a departure from the shanzhai ethic, Shanghai 3D printing design company Xuberance has developed 'an online and offline platform for digital copyright trading' in the form of digital models, which, it argues, demonstrates the 'different' business model for 3D printing in China compared to western countries (Ma 2017). One of Xuberance's digital models, of a lamp, was traded to a Chinese company for 3.2 billion yuan (about US$480 million), constituting 'the first case in the world of a 3D-printed product being traded with such a high value' (Ma 2017). Aside from the very large amount of money spent on this product, it is unclear precisely how this IP-based business model differs from western companies inasmuch as Xuberance was the holder of the IP, and traded it in an ostensibly legitimate fashion. In fact, without further information, this seems to be closer to 'conventional' (western) IP transfer than, for instance, shanzhai exchanges. Chinese 3D printing actors are also participating in digital transactions in the global economy, and may facilitate access to shanzhai activities – and thus potentially less conventional, and at times illegitimate forms of IP usage – for those outside of China. For instance, Lindtner has pointed to prominent Chinese open hardware companies Seeed Studio and DFRobot structuring their businesses:

> around enabling (mostly foreign) makers to move from prototying (of one thing) into production (of thousands of things). They provide services such as in-house agile manufacturing, sourcing of components, and assembly. In doing so, they provide makers access to China's intricate social world of manufacturing and a culture of production that has evolved in the South of China over the last thirty years: *Shanzhai*.
>
> (2015: 14)

Furthermore, as of 2018 Mohou now offers services in the English language, as mentioned above (Mohou 2017). It has an online 'shop front' in English which seems to be aimed at potential customers outside of China, offering a range of 3D printing services: scanning, printing, designing and small batch as well as mass production manufacturing. If Mohou is successful in attracting foreign customers to its digital 3D printing services, then it may represent a 'success story' for China's 'Going Out Strategy' through globalising Chinese Internet and digital manufacturing services (Keane 2016).

3D Printing in India

While more attention regarding 3D printing in Asia has been paid to developments in China, India is emerging as another site of 3D printing activity as well as other digital and manufacturing developments. Lema et al. (2015) have pointed to India accumulating significant innovation capabilities as well as production capabilities in recent years. Furthermore, other recent 'disruptive' digital technologies have had significant impact in India, in particular the profound societal and economic ramifications of the enormous take-up of mobile phones in India (Doron and

Jeffrey 2013). Indeed, Michael speculates that 'India has the most to gain from the additive manufacturing revolution, while China will lose': due to the possible threat from 3D printing to China's low-cost manufacturing base, and India's current industrial underdevelopment and logistical challenges making it well placed to implement small-scale 3D printing (2013a: 2). So far, though, while 3D printing is present in India, it seems to be less prevalent, with Indian 3D printing to date having less impact on domestic and international commerce than has been the case with China and the west. Yet various commentators consider that there is significant potential for 3D printing in India, which may be realised in the coming years (e.g. Arora 2018; Singh and Nafis 2015).

Forerunner sectors in India which have used or integrated 3D printing are information and communication technology start-ups, university engineering students and software companies (Birtchnell and Hoyle 2014). There is some manufacturing of 3D printing machines in India, along with resellers of premium western-branded machines, 3D printing service sellers and partnerships between Indian entrepreneurs and foreign collaborators to sell 3D printing technology in India (Camdir 2016). Billed as India's oldest 3D printing company, Makemendel has manufactured 3D printers (including entry-level models based on the open hardware RepRap) and provided 3D printing services and accessories (Gress and Kalafsky 2015; Grunewald 2014). Makerspaces exist in India, especially in university environments and libraries, although there seem to be far fewer of them than, for instance, in China (Ahmad et al. 2017; Hussain and Nisha 2017). Yet, institutionalising pockets of 'start-up culture' in, for example, Indian Institutes of Technology, offers new platforms to increase not only the technical expertise, but the social and cultural expertise needed to stimulate 3D printing innovations in India. Such approaches may be starting to pay dividends as Indian scholars are starting to share – and publish – their own technical advancements (see Wimpenny et al. 2017) and contextual product applications (for example, Rao et al. 2017; Sahoo et al. 2017) with each other more widely than during the previous decade.

There have been various applications of 3D printing to date in India. The environmentally sustainable and entrepreneurial prospects of 3D printing have been realised to some extent in India whereby plastic 3D printing filament has been made from recycled plastic materials provided by waste-pickers who have been paid a fair amount for them (Ishengoma and Mtaho 2014). More recent developments include the emergence of Mumbai-based Imaginarium, an Indian 3D printing and prototyping company which is providing services, including print-on-demand, to various industries including creative industries and healthcare (Arora 2018). The most in-depth study of 3D printing in India so far has been conducted by Dwivedi et al. in the Indian automotive sector – an industry identified by the Indian government as key to the

Make in India policy (2017). They found that the technology is 'mainly used for rapid prototyping' and its use is not yet 'widespread' due to certain barriers that they identify, principally production technology capabilities and government support, with intellectual property rights also identified among other barriers of lesser importance. Despite the Indian government policies mentioned below, Dwivedi et al. found that the government needed to take more measures to promote 3D printing in the automotive sector, including through tax rebates/subsidies, more R&D programmes, education and the introduction of 'stricter IPR laws' (2017: 986).

The Indian government has been active in issuing policies which may impact on 3D printing. One such policy is 2015's Digital India, whose 'vision is to turn India into a digitally empowered society and knowledge economy', by improving digital infrastructure, instituting more e-government services and empowering citizens digitally. The Indian government is beginning to invest in 3D printing facilities, and has also issued policies which encompass 3D printing, notably the National Manufacturing Policy's Advanced Manufacturing Technologies programme and Make in India. Make in India is a government policy which aims to make India a global manufacturing hub by encouraging more manufacturing to take place in India, including design manufacturing (Selvam 2016). Together these policies may foster an environment in which digitised advanced manufacturing techniques such as 3D printing may thrive in India. Such a result might reflect more macro-trends in consumer and commercial technology adoption and development in India, which seem to show both lag compared to national neighbours and explosive growth hinged on important enablers of technical know-how of entrepreneurs and government policies (Gupta and Barua 2016).

Unlike China, India does not feature among WIPO's top countries internationally for patent filings on 3D printing (2015). It has been reported that the Indian Patent Office has received a number of applications for patents on 3D printing topics, but it is not clear whether the applicants are from India or elsewhere (Selvam & Selvam 2015). In contrast to China, there is almost no research already carried on what kinds of 'digital transactions' are being conducted in India with 3D printing and intellectual property, such as the extent and uses (both legitimate and illegitimate) of 3D printing in India, the extent to which it is complementary to, or supersedes, existing forms of manufacturing and the extent to which western/globalised platforms such as Thingiverse and Shapeways are widely utilised among those involved with 3D printing. However, Singh and Nafis consider that there is a potential for IP infringement brought by increased low-cost consumer-oriented 3D printing (2015). India is already considered by some commentators not to provide a high level of IP protection (and in fact a lower level than China) in practice by curtailing the IP rights of others (especially western actors) including through utilising exceptions to infringement, and through underenforcement (for example, Shapiro and Mathur 2014). However, without further research it is not clear whether such IP infringement is occurring, and will occur, in India with 3D printing, particularly since similar claims made about 3D printing in other parts of the world have largely not eventuated in practice. Furthermore, it is not clear that stricter IP laws and enforcement would lead to more use and take-up of 3D printing in India.

3D Printing and Global Digital Transactions?

The preceding discussion has examined some developments in China and India to provide the basis for an analysis of the extent to which there are globalised digital transactions in 3D printing, intellectual property and innovation. There is a truly globalised aspect of 3D printing, with western firms operating across different regions of the world, and Chinese-made 3D printing machines being distributed internationally. There is also the potential for the globalisation of at least part of China's own homegrown 3D printing service sector, with Mohou's launch of English-language services. However, China's own 3D printing industry and maker culture demonstrates a different pathway, and different shapes of digital transactions in this field, to the west. India appears to have a less mature 3D printing industry and less developed applications of 3D printing compared to China and the west, with its own 3D printing services not yet globalised, although this may change in time. Another commonality among the different regions is government policies aimed at stimulating advanced manufacturing. There is a level of intellectual property harmonisation internationally, but differences in implementation and enforcement remain, especially as regards India.

There is very little information about the shape of digital transactions in the 3D printing field in India, such as the extent to which platforms such as Thingiverse are used, the vitality of sneaker-net sharing, and the existence and prevalence of homegrown platforms: for instance, the extent to which Shapeways is used when Indian print-on-demand services such as Imaginarium are now present. Given the potential, till now seemingly mostly unrealised, for 3D printing in India, and the general lack of scholarship on this topic, developments in India warrant much more attention and scholarly research. This study has been limited to analysing developments in India and China; 3D printing may take other forms, and implicate other kinds of digital transactions, in other countries and regions outside the west which also have not received much attention and consideration. The extent to which we will see a level of harmonisation internationally regarding 3D printing – and its relationship with innovation and intellectual property – or something more akin to the diversity of Goggin's 'Global Internets' – driven by differences in infrastructure, policy, market, language and cultures – remains to be seen (2012).

Acknowledgement

This research was funded by the United Kingdom Intellectual Property Office grant '3D Printing and Intellectual Property Futures' 2016–2018. We acknowledge our collaborators Thomas Birtchnell, Thierry Rayna and Ludmila Striukova.

References

Ahmad, Tameem, Ahmad, Shamim, Jamshed, Mohammed, Khan Sherwani, Faizan, Ali, Rashid, Khan, Waseem, Nomani, Abuzar and Qaisar, Tajdar Mohammad (2017) 'An ISM Approach for Analysing the Enablers in India's Makerspace platforms', *Proceedings of 2017 Learning and Technology Conference (L&T) – The MakerSpace: from Imagining to Making!*, pp. 14–22.

Arora, Nishant (2018) 'From Healthcare to Manufacturing, 3D Printing Set to Grow Big in India. YourStory'. Available: https://yourstory.com/2018/01/healthcare-3d-printing-india/, accessed: 15 September 2018.

Beebe, Barton (2014) 'Shanzhai, Sumptuary Law, and Intellectual Property Law in Contemporary China', *University of California Davis Law Review*, 47(3): 849.

Birtchnell, Thomas and Hoyle, William (2014) *3D Printing for Development in the Global South: The 3D4D Challenge*, London: Palgrave Macmillan.

Brown, Ronald (2017) 'Made in China 2025: Implications of Robotization and Digitalization on MNC Labor Supply Chains and Workers' Labor Rights in China', *Tsinghua China Law Review*, 9(2): 186.

Camdir, John (2016) *3D Printing Industry in India: The Current Scenario. 3D Printing Industry.* Available: https://3dprintingindustry.com/news/3d-printing-industry-in-india-the-current-scenario-79537/, accessed: 13 September 2018.

Cao, Qing (2014) 'Insight into Weak Enforcement of Intellectual Property Rights in China', *Technology in Society*, 38: 40–47.

Chan, H.K. Griffin, J., Lim, J.J., Zeng, F. and Chiu, A.S.F. (2017) 'Impact of 3D Printing Technology on Supply Chain in China', *Proceedings of 24th International Conference on Production Research*, 30 July–3 August 2017, Poznan, Poland, pp. 492–495.

Daly, Angela (2016) *Socio-Legal Aspects of the 3D Printing Revolution*, London: Palgrave Macmillan.

Digital India. Available: http://digitalindia.gov.in/, accessed: 14 August 2017.

Dwivedi, Gourav, Srivastava, Samir K. and Srivastava, Rajiv K. (2017) 'Analysis of Barriers to Implement Additive Manufacturing Technology in the Indian Automotive Sector', *International Journal of Physical Distribution & Logistics Management*, 47(10): 972–991.

Doron, Assa and Jeffrey, Robin (2013) *The Great Indian Phone Book: How the Cheap Cell Phone Changes Business, Politics and Daily Life*, Cambridge, MA: Harvard University Press.

Ford, Sharon (2014) 'Additive Manufacturing Technology: Potential Implications for U.S. Manufacturing Competitiveness', *Journal of International Commerce and Economics*, 6: 40–74.

Fordyce, Robbie, Heemsbergen, Luke, Apperley, Thomas, Arnold, Michael, Birtchnell, Thomas, Luo, Michael and Nansen, Bjorn (2016) 'Things, Tags, Topics: Thingiverse's Object-centred Network', *Communication Research and Practice*, 2(1): 63–78.

Garrett, Banning (2014) '3D Printing: New Economic Paradigms and Strategic Shifts', *Global Policy*, 5(1): 70–75.

Goggin, Gerard (2012) 'Global Internets: Media Research in the New World', in Volkmer, Ingrid (ed) *The Handbook of Global Media Research*, Chichester: Wiley-Blackwell, pp. 352–364.

Gress, Douglas and Kalafsky, Ronald (2015) 'Geographies of Production in 3D: Theoretical and Research Implications Stemming from Additive Manufacturing', *Geoforum*, 60: 43–52.

Grunewald, Scott (2014) *India's Oldest 3D Printer Company Makemendel Offers More Than Just 3D Printers. 3D Printing Industry*. Available: https://3dprintingindustry.com/news/indias-oldest-3d-printer-company-makemendel-offers-just-3d-printers-31277/#, accessed: 12 August 2017.

Gupta, Himanshu and Barua, Mukesh Kumar (2016) 'Identifying Enablers of Technological Innovation for Indian MSMEs Using Best–Worst Multi criteria Decision Making Method', *Technological Forecasting and Social Change*, 107: 69–79.

Hussain, Akhtar and Nisha, Faizul (2017) 'Awareness and Use of Library Makerspaces among Library Professionals in India: A Study', *Journal of Library & Information Technology*, 37(2): 84–90.

Holland, Jacob (2017) 'Intellectual Property Rights in China: Patents and Economic Development', *Nnamdi Azikiwe University Journal of International Law and Jurisprudence*, 8(1): 40–45.

Huang, Hao and Wang, Guohong (2016) 'Comparison Study on the Industrial Policies of Additive Manufacturing in U.S. and China', *International Conference on Industrial Economics System and Industrial Security Engineering (IEIS)*, pp. 1–6.

Ishengoma, Frederick and Mtaho, Adam (2014) '3D Printing: Developing Countries Perspectives', *International Journal of Computer Applications*, 104(11): 30–34.

Jackson, Beau (2017) 'Barack Obama on 3D Printing and America's Manufacturing Industry. 3D Printing Industry'. Available: https://3dprintingindustry.com/news/barack-obama-3d-printing-americas-manufacturing-industry-103802/, accessed: 15 September 2018.

Keane, Michael (2016) 'Internet+ China: Unleashing the Innovative Nation Strategy', *International Journal of Cultural and Creative Industries*, 3(2): 68–74.

Kitchin, Rob, and Dodge, Martin (2011) *Code/Space: Software and Everyday Life*, Cambridge: MIT Press.

Lema, Rasmus, Quadros, Ruy and Schmitz, Hubert (2015) 'Reorganising Global Value Chains and Building Innovation Capabilities in Brazil and India', *Research Policy*, 44: 1376–1386.

Li, Ling (2018) 'China's Manufacturing Locus in 2025: With a Comparison of "Made-in-China 2025" and "Industry 4.0"', *Technological Forecasting and Social Change*, 135: 66–74.

Lindtner, Silvia (2015) 'Hacking with Chinese Characteristics: The Promises of the Maker Movement Against China's Manufacturing Culture', *Science, Technology, & Human Values*, 40(5): 854–879.

Lindtner, Silvia and Li, David (2010) 'Created in China: The Makings of China's Hackerspace Community', *Interactions*, 19(6): 18–22.

Liu, Haiyan (2015) 'Consequences of Legal Transplantation: The Unique Justifications and Roles of Enforcement of Intellectual Property Rights in China', *Journal of Law, Technology and Public Policy*, 1(3): 377.

Ma, Steven (2017) 'Mass Customisation: Designed in China, Produced Globally', *Architectural Design*, 87(6): 58–63.

Make in India (2017) Available: www.makeinindia.com/home, accessed: 15 September 2018.

Mehta, Andrew (2007) *The Politics of Piracy: Intellectual Property in Contemporary China*. Ithaca, NY: Cornell University Press.

Michael, Bryane (2013a) 'Bringing Manufacturing Home: Implications for Emerging Markets of the Reindustrialisation of the Core OECD', *SKOLKOVO Business School - Ernst & Young Institute for Emerging Market Studies* (IEMS), 13–06.

Michael, Gabriel J. (2013b) Anarchy and Property Rights in the Virtual World: How Disruptive Technologies Undermine the State and Ensure that the Virtual World Remains a 'Wild West'. SSRN Working Paper. Available: http://papers.ssrn.com/sol3/papers.cfm?abstract_id=2233374, accessed: 15 September 2018.

Moilanen, Jarkko, Daly, Angela, Lobato, Ramon and Allen, Darcy (2015) 'Cultures of Sharing in 3D Printing: What Can We Learn from the Licence Choices of Thingiverse Users?', *Journal of Peer Production*, (6) Disruption and the Law.

Pickren, Graham (2018) 'The global assemblage of digital flow': Critical data studies and the infrastructures of computing', *Progress in Human Geography*, 42(2): 225–243.

Rao, G.K., Shah, T., Shetty, V.D. and Ravi, B. (2017) 'Custom Design & Fabrication of 3D Printed Cast for Ankle Immobilisation', *KnE Engineering*, 2(2): 98–103.

Sahoo, Aparajita, Wahi, Akshat and Patel, Sonali (2017) 'A Novel Clip-on for Smartphone Dermoscopy in India', *IEEE Healthcare Innovations and Point of Care Technologies (HI-POCT) Conference*,6–8 November 2017, Bethesda, MD, USA, pp. 101–104.

Selvam, V. (2016) 'Make in India a Manufacturing Hub: The Real Opportunities and Challenges: A Literature Review', *Current Research*, 8(8): 36493–36497.

Selvam & Selvam (2015) '3D Printing and Intellectual Property'. Available: https://selvams.com/blog/3d-printing-and-intellectual-property/, accessed: 15 September 2018.

Shapiro, Robert and Mathur, Aparna (2014) 'How India Can Attract More Foreign Direct Investment, Create Jobs, and Increase GDP: The Benefits of Respecting the Intellectual Property Rights of Foreign Pharmaceutical Producers', *Georgetown McDonough School of Business Research Paper*, No. 2540591.

Singh, Manisha and Nafis, Zoya (2015) 'Intellectual Property and 3D Printing: A Clash in the Rising', *China Business Law Journal*, 136–137.

Stein, Jesse Adams (2017) 'The Political Imaginaries of 3D Printing: Prompting Mainstream Awareness of Design and Making', *Design and Culture*, 9(1): 3–27.

Weinberg, Michael (2010) *It Will Be Awesome If They Don't Screw It Up*, Public Knowledge White Paper.

Wimpenny, David, Pandey, Pulak and Kumar, L. Jyothish (eds.) (2017) *Advances in 3D Printing and Additive Manufacturing Technologies*, Singapore: Springer.

WIPO (2015) *World Intellectual Property Report: Breakthrough Innovation and Economic Growth*. Available: www.wipo.int/edocs/pubdocs/en/wipo_pub_944_2015.pdf, accessed: 15 September 2018.

Xincailiao (2018) Available: http://xincailiao.com/news/news_detail.aspx?id=123548, accessed: 12 July 2018.

7 Digital Rights in Asia

Rethinking Regional and International Agendas

Gerard Goggin, Michele Ford, Fiona Martin, Adele Webb, Ariadne Vromen, and Kimberlee Weatherall

After successive waves of digital technology-associated changes in Asia, and several national moves to regulate Internet communications and content, there is a renewed sense of the need to interrogate the new sets of transactions and arrangements being established across many arenas under the name of the 'digital'. An emphasis on digital technologies as a driver of economic efficiencies and innovations is engendering substantive changes in commerce, government, and social and cultural arenas. In the commercial domain, the emergence of a platform model for digital transactions centred on virtual marketplaces is implicated in the wide-ranging changes to the nature of work, consumption, and everyday exchange. In the domain of governance, the digitization of services, security, compliance, and enforcement processes is reconfiguring everyday transactions between citizens and the state. The expansion of the digital as the locus of social communication, largely through mobile technologies, has furbished a new set of dynamics in democratic politics, popular culture, personal interaction, and public speech.

These wide-reaching developments touch upon almost every aspect of life, and necessarily transform the social, economic, and cultural transactions that take place in private and public exchanges. In aggregation, the combination of technological affordances, new information alliances and relationships, and strategic, networked agency brings about novel concerns, challenges, and debates regarding the social contracts, explicit and implicit, upon which emerging digital societies are being organized. In the West, these debates have focused, for example, around the Facebook/Cambridge Analytica scandal, and the banning of alt-right commentator Alex Jones from social media platforms. Yet despite the range, gravity, and importance of these issues and the sheer effort of innovation and analysis being given to the digital sector, it is not clear that the intrinsic challenges presented by digital transformations to the moral principles of society and human life are receiving the attention that they merit (Horst and Foster 2018). Certainly they require reconception in the Asian context, with the rapid growth in mobile and broadband connections in India, South East Asia, and China underpinning significant changes in markets, governments, and societies.

While one issue, symptomatic risk, or another may give rise to set of public concerns that play out in digital forums, the foundational principles of human rights are yet to exert sufficiently coherent influence upon the general and global conceptions of digital rights. It is fair to say that the rights agenda has been largely reactive, following the evolution of sociotechnical interfaces as and when issues arise, for example in India around the Aadhaar biometric identification programme or Whatsapp mobilized political violence. The advent of concerns such as privacy, subsistence, and public safety should not, however, be considered as arising merely from the affordances of digital technologies. It is also important to recognize that the new transactional relationships emerging in the digital domain come into being as a consequence of deliberate intent in design and execution, as well as unintended effects shaped by use and abuse.

Across Asia, the digital turn is being pressed into service in and across various countries in order to gather together and mark regional, national, and subnational projects, such as *Digital India* and China's *Internet Plus*, to mention just two of the biggest and most prominent instances (Athique et al. 2018; Hong 2017; Kar et al. 2018; Shi 2018). These initiatives are also shaped by advent of global commercial plays (such as Facebook's Free Basics or Internet.org project). Consequently, national and international 'digital agendas' are unfolding across the backdrop of the complex evolution of social, mobile, locative, and other digital media platforms, technologies, and cultures, deeply yet unevenly underpinning everyday lives in the region (Digital Asia Hub 2016; Hjorth and Khoo 2016; Jin 2017; Jurriëns and Tapsell 2017; Neilsen et al. 2018; Niranjana and Xiaoming 2015). In the context of such overarching political and economic visions, it is evident that we need to conceive of a similarly comprehensive agenda for the role and rights of citizens.

In the past few years, we have already witnessed an expanding set of issues concerning the nature, needs, and demands for digital rights across different Asian locations. At the risk of overstating their internal coherence, we can group these debates under three areas: first, as they pertain to the role and responsibilities of the state in digital spaces (Sinpeng 2013). Over the past two decades, international human rights debates have focused on the implications of national and cross-border security, cybersecurity, information warfare, and terrorism in various forms and settings (Chatfield et al. 2015; Digital Rights Foundation 2018; Shah 2007). Meanwhile, the extension of digital modes of governance in other domains, and largely within states, has led to the creation of new systems of social control and governmentality via Internet, social media, algorithms and automation, ranking, rating, and enumeration of citizens. These developments raise critical questions regarding democracy and equality in digital policy agendas (Gurumurthy et al. 2016; Shah 2013). Intervention in these domains, in turn, requires us to consider fundamental questions of justice and rights in systems of digital media (Qiu 2009, 2016). Commonly, engagements in these debates, albeit often uneven and unsatisfactory, are between institutions of state (both national and international) and a broad range of non-governmental organizations (NGOs) involved in the advocacy of digital rights conceived across the evolution of the Internet era.

This civil society mobilization has traditionally centred upon a second set of issues. The central discourses tend to regard digital media as core to the maintenance of a public sphere and/or commons, which subsequently serves as a guiding principle in a variety of approaches to net neutrality, freedom of speech and expression, citizen participation, access to information, and, at the present moment, towards data privacy and human rights (Greenleaf 2014). Within the public sphere, such debates also encompass mediated interactions between citizens. Critical rights issues have emerged around the profusion of hate speech, abuse, harassment, and other violence online, and the use of digital networks by both state and non-state actors to organize and incite physical attacks for political purposes (George 2015; Stecklow 2018). Our attention has also been drawn to the different gendered implications of emerging sociotechnical digital systems, especially, for example, in relation to censorship, surveillance, and security (Jensen 2012). These civil society concerns with public safety and well-being also increasingly triangulate with a third area of debates arising from the emerging centrality of digital technologies to accessing economic opportunities and, more broadly, from the expansive power and agency of technology corporations to determine the forms of our social and economic transactions. Here, the pursuit of social and economic innovation via the digital necessitates a debate on our economic rights, to consider challenges for equality, fairness, and participation in digital economy (Azali 2017; Gray and Suri 2019, forthcoming). Currently, our attention is given to the nature and conditions of new forms of digital work and labour (such as the 'gig economy') and to the underlying power relations and governance of digital platforms within and across national borders (Ford and Honan 2017; Jin 2015; Lee 2012).

In this chapter, we seek to reflect upon the complex demands of providing a coherent response to challenges across these three domains. We do so in order to open up and encourage consideration of the appropriate conception and agenda for digital rights and associated governance in Asia. Also, we do so from the perspective of an Australian location in the Asian region (Daly 2016a), and are informed by our interdisciplinary research on digital rights (Goggin et al. 2017). Our starting point is a dissatisfaction with the framing, assumptions, and norms of digital rights globally (Karppinen 2017a, 2017b). At the risk of simplification, we will argue that the dominant ways of framing digital rights and governance continue to be modelled on a limited repertoire of Western experiences and concepts of digital technology, rights, and freedom (cf. Kelly and Reid 1998; Lim and Soriano 2016; McLelland et al. 2018). We see such dominant accounts underpinning global reference points such as the widely utilized *Freedom on the Net* annual report by the US-based NGO Freedom House, which in its 2017 sorted the world's Internet population into 23% free, 28% partly free, and 36% not free (leaving aside the 13% globally it was not able to assess) (Freedom House 2017, but see also the fuller, better contextualized account in UNESCO 2018b). Of the Asian countries evaluated for the 2017 report only three were rated as 'free': the Philippines, Japan, and Australia (Freedom House 2017: 23). In the context of this chapter, an immediate question is the extent to which these notions of freedoms correspond with the principles and exercise of rights.

Digital Rights in Asia

Clearly, rights must be established in order that they can be freely exercised and cannot be imposed under purely external suppositions. A further, necessary, consideration is where certain freedoms impinge upon the rights of others, prompting us to bear in mind whose freedoms are being defined and privileged and whose perspective is determining the nature of that evaluation. In an international context, Asian digital rights debates are often cast in the negative, featuring as dystopian, 'worst' or 'limit' cases, where Internet rights are being breached and Internet freedoms trampled upon. Against this backdrop we draw attention to the narrow and stereotypical representations of Asian digital rights as these 'imaginaries' circulate in global discussions of digital technology transformations and digital citizenship (Hintz et al. 2018; McCosker et al. 2017). As we outline, study of Asian digital rights has considerable potential to inform a full understanding of the development and dynamics of digital technology use in the region, and to be a rich resource for conceptualizing digital rights, justice, and freedom struggles internationally.

The Asia context demonstrates a complex set of debates of social, economic, political, and geopolitical rights, all of which are now becoming interlaced with the rapid expansion of the digital across the region, thereby converging these various concerns in important ways. As noted by Adrian Athique in Chapter 1, there is a new geography to the digital unfolding across the sheer scale and diversity of Asian locations and interregional dynamics (Athique 2019, forthcoming). Enormous economic and cultural investments in digital infrastructures across Asia underpin global as well as regional economies and societies. At the same time, how these new platforms, markets, and capabilities unfold pivots on the ways that users, households, workers, governmental and civil society actors, business people, scientists, and technology actors imagine and shape these technical and social forms. Thus the emergence of digital rights concepts, practices, and struggles engages complex dynamics across the disparity of political systems, languages, cultures, religions, and local traditions in the region.

Consider some elements of Asian societies that bear decisively on rights. The 'Asian values' discourse accents notions of individualism versus collective identity in a way that is often rather homogenizing in terms of differences when it comes to rights (Avonius and Kingsbury 2008; Lim and Soriano 2016; Price and Stremlau 2018; Visweswaran 2010). Consider, for instance, the centrality of religious beliefs to rights in South and South East Asia, as opposed to their absence in Northeast Asia. Alongside such claims to the primacy of collective identities, underpinned by recourse to cultural specificity and particularity, we need also acknowledge the real internal diversity of most Asian polities (Goh 2011). We see a strong manifestation of the principle of self-determination remaining marked by intense cultural diversity within communities. In a number of countries, intense economic growth brings pressures in addressing the huge social disparities, characterized by uneven development leaving large numbers of people below the poverty line. In legal and political terms, there are different forms of constitutionalism conceived within the dawning of the United Nations (UN) and heyday of the principles of the Universal Declaration of Human Rights (UDHR) and ensuing six or so decades of development of human rights instruments, now being reconfigured, displaced, or shunted aside in the wake of political and media change (Sen and Lee 2008). We see, moreover, an emerging set of intra-regional relationships alongside broader international linkages, with many Asian actors contesting questions of rights within international systems and bodies. This further complicates matters, adding more layers to a history of constraints of free expression despite constitutional provisions in most cases.

In order to address this larger set of regional and local dynamics, there is a need to develop much more sophisticated frameworks on rights and governance in Asia, which comprehend and engage with the complex, specific contexts of evolution of digital technologies across various countries and settings (as well as appreciating intra-regional, cross-regional, and international transactions) (Erni and Chua 2005; Goggin and McLelland 2009; Goggin et al. 2017). This is consistent with international efforts to offer a new framework for putting media and communications struggles, justice, and rights at the heart of social progress (Couldry et al. 2018). In particular, we wish to highlight the importance of unpacking, analysing, and engaging with the various conceptions, movements, and arena of digital rights across the full diversity of Asian locations, and especially perspectives, practices, and meanings from citizen and user perspectives. This also entails taking account of the inter-Asian transactions and borrowings across digital and cultural histories and models of rights and governance (Wang and Liu 2018).

The Global Emergence of Digital Rights

The notion of rights has a long, complex, and rich set of histories, based in politics, law, philosophy, and ethics. Following the 70th anniversary of the UN UDHR, it is evident that the very idea of rights is still strongly contested from a wide range of perspectives (Moyn 2018). Acknowledging these heritages and debates, we do believe that rights remain important. We take a broad, pluralistic approach to investigating digital rights that encompasses: rights explicitly set out or recognized in law, policy, and regulation; rights ideas and practices developed and asserted by a wide range of movements, organizations, and individuals (Erni 2011). These are rights that extend beyond traditional frameworks of states, national, regional, and international communities of countries. Nonetheless, the recognition of certain rights and not others is shaped by cultural, social, political, and linguistic dynamics, as well as particular contexts and events (Eckel and Moyn 2014; Gregg 2012; Hunt 2007; Moyn 2010). Markets, technology design and implementation, social innovation and option, outcomes for consumers, citizens, civil society, business, and institutions are often highly influenced by the kinds of rights set out in international frameworks, and shaped and policed (or not) by institutions, such as the UN, the World Trade Organization, and the World Intellectual Property Organization, as well as domestic law, courts, and regulation. In relation to digital technologies and platforms, we also see the emergence of non-state-based governance and regulation arrangements, which hinge on either self- or co-regulatory codes of practice, or the policies of large corporate or organization actors, to implicitly define, moderate, and manage particular behaviours (Cole et al. 2017, Gillespie 2018; Tusikov 2017). These arrangements have occasioned wide-ranging debates about the appropriate legal concepts and frameworks to frame such dynamic and emerging governance and regulatory institutions, settings, efforts, and work—such as the project of 'digital constitutionalism' (Suzor 2018).

Over the last three decades the emergence of digital, networked technologies into this rights scenario has generated new rights scenarios and propositions. Consider, for instance, the expansion of copyright in the digital domain and net neutrality (Daly 2016b). Consider new claims such as the right to be forgotten and the right to inclusive design (Bates et al. 2016; Boys 2014; Brock 2016; Postigo 2012). Consider demands such as the right to transparency in the operation of algorithms, artificial intelligence (AI), the Internet of Things, and smart or connected cities, as well as ways to mitigate automated inequality and to ensure data justice (AHRC 2018; Bunz and Meikle 2017; Dencik et al. 2016; Eubanks 2017; Pasquale 2015). These new agendas underscore the point that the scope and nature of digital rights is in pressing need of clarification (Karppinen 2017a, 2017b). As digital rights are being reshaped, there is an opportunity to position them front and centre in contemporary human rights agenda. This is important given that conventional human rights groups and institutions have been relatively slow to pay sufficient attention to the imperative for rights struggles and concepts that digital technologies represent. Broadly speaking, we see the present conjuncture being one in which digital rights can be brought into the fold of human and others' rights debates and struggles, and that the challenges and implications of digital rights are grappled with by the full range of rights institutions and actors.

Institutional recognition of, and support for, such digital rights has tended to come first from organizations focusing on digital technology governance issues, such as the Internet Society and its various regional chapters, or the long-running Association for Progressive Communications (APC). Subsequently, there has been marked growth in new advocacy organizations, enabled by digital platforms. Forerunner groups include: the US-based Electronic Frontiers Foundation, various activists, grassroots-based movements, including Free, Libre, and Open Source Software (FLOSS), CryptoParties, Pirate Parties, Creative Commons and digital commons groups, community informatics and community technology movements, and research organizations. Organizations with an explicit digital rights focus and identity include the leading international group, Access Now, established in 2009.

In the Asian region, digital rights groups are flourishing. So we find a wide range of national groups such as Pakistan's Digital Rights Foundation, Thai Netizen Network, or Australia's Digital Rights Watch (2018). There are journalists and bloggers in the vanguard of freedom of expression struggles (stretching back to at least the heyday of online news pioneer *Malaysiakini*); long-term players' online community networks, the Internet, and capability building such as the APC; civil society groups engaged with, or premised upon, digital platforms, including Internet Democracy Project (based in New Delhi); activist groups such as Australian-based GetUp!; Internet and society research centres and think tanks (often affiliated with the Global Network of Internet and Society Research Centers), such as the long-running Centre for Internet & Society in Bangalore or the more recent Hong Kong-based Digital Asia Hub; community development and social justice NGOs such as IT for Change (also based in Banglore); and new civil society-corporate alliances such as the Australian Digital Inclusion Alliance, established in 2017. Across Asia, a wide range of other rights and justice organizations have also embraced digital rights issues, including the strong press freedom groups such as Southeast Asian Press Alliance (SEPA) and Southeast Asia Freedom of Expression Network, based in Indonesia. A sign of the times was the October 2017 COCONET (Connecting Communities and Networks): Southeast Asia Digital Rights Camp, organized by Engage Media, APC, SEPA, and others (Wolf 2017). Given the number and significance of organizations active in the field, the question of the relative role of international or Western groups versus Asian counterparts in advocacy for digital rights in Asia is a very interesting one. Fair to say, however, that the ferment in the field in Asian digital rights deserves further attention and support from the wider global community, as we shall now discuss.

Imaginaries of Asian Digital Rights

This thumbnail sketch of the emergence of digital rights helps set the scene for a discussion of Asian digital rights. Clearly Asian actors and organizations have figured prominently in the creation of digital rights, as this brief account reveals. Yet this involvement belies two key issues: (1) digital rights, it can be argued, are still imagined and configured according to a narrow set of social experiences and identities, and particular histories, as well as particular policy and legal concepts and frameworks; something revealed by the strong emphasis given to 'net neutrality' and 'Internet freedom', both concepts originating from and deeply coloured by the US normative contexts; (2) insufficient attention is still paid to Asian digital practices, rights conceptions and movements, and institutional settings and frameworks.

Consider, for instance, that the reflex frameworks concerning digital technology internationally, but especially it seems in the Asia Pacific region, have to do with three main issues in particular: trade and markets; security and cybersecurity; and antiterrorism and related issues of cyber safety or e-safety (on trade and markets, see Velut et al. 2017). These are areas, we would suggest, where governments are putting significant resources into consolidating frameworks for regional cooperation and action, and where industry, and other actors, are being encouraged to join in partnerships. In contrast, issues of access and inclusion is one where regional frameworks have been weak, despite international efforts from governments, industry, and civil society, to drive better connectivity and access—for instance, in the follow-up work from World Summit on the Information Society, the Sustainable Development Goals, or the UNESCO Internet Indicators project (Servaes 2017; UNESCO 2018). In terms of digital rights, the situation is worse still, and there appears to be a real gap in regional frameworks and action from governments (Aaronson 2018). At a workshop of civil society actors and researchers on Asian digital rights convened by the authors in April 2018, there were deep concerns expressed about the equity, justice, and transparency of rolling out large-scale government data gathering and monitoring programmes (Sydney Ideas 2018). Concrete instances entailed India's Aadhaar and also China's social credit system—the 'beta-testing' of intrusive technologies as one participant put it, in the absence of rights frameworks and with information asymmetries and other power inequalities making citizen protest or pushback difficult. Participants noted such programmes, including the integration of predictive technologies for social control, could be tied to aid and development goals and to significant private/public partnerships, which introduce political-economic pressures to move on them regardless of their social impacts.

If we start with the regional level, it could be suggested that the lag in initiatives on digital rights by Asia Pacific governments is not surprising, given the stakes it represents. Like elsewhere in the world, most countries in Asia have seen ongoing conflicts between citizens asserting aspects of digital rights, especially freedom of expression, as key to political and social participation, versus governments regulating to foreclose or curtail exercise of such rights (Berenshot et al. 2017). The stakes become higher, for these governments as well as the governed, with the positioning of digital technology policy at the centre of whole-of-society, economy, and polity plans and futures. Across Asian governments, there has also been significant if varying levels of interest in digital innovation agendas—yet it is clear that these require society-wide participation premised upon trust and, in turn, adequate and feasible rights (Greenleaf 2014; Stagars 2016). If we are to pursue this line of thought further, we think it leads to a much deeper challenge—the urgent need to reorient global digital rights discussions via a much more extensive and systematic engagement with Asian digital rights (cf. Chen 2010).

Reorienting Digital Rights in/from Asia

A wide range of Asian countries have consistently been in the vanguard of the development of technology, from telecommunications and Internet through to mobile, locative media, social media, and digital platforms. In South East Asia, for instance, we might recall: Indonesian plans for national development, telecommunications, and television, in the form of the Palapa satellite (Kitley 2000; Thomas 2005; Triastuti 2017); Singapore's *Vision of an Intelligent Island IT 2000* (Chun 1997; NCB 1992); and Malaysia's *Multimedia Super Corridor* and the new centre Cyberjaya (Bunnell 2004; Kobie 2016). In East Asia, pioneering efforts also go back various decades, with celebrated cases being Japan's 1972 *Plan for the Information Society* and Korea's broadband development (Lee 2012). At the present time across Asia, as this volume bears out, there is significant capital, social, and political investment being put into AI, algorithms, and data, and the various associated and influential social imaginaries of technology. Against this backdrop, we still find particular kinds of global imaginaries of Asia in relation to digital technologies, rights, and governance (Wang 2007).

There are long, tangled histories of specific sociotechnical developments being circulated globally in particular ways. Consider, for instance, the way Singapore's intelligent island figured as a dystopian panoticon (BBC 1990; Sandfort 1993). Or the manner in which the rise and rise of China's Internet was closely associated with the accounts of the 'Great Firewall', Internet filtering, and the ground zero of the extirpation of Internet freedom.

More recently, we see global imaginaries of digital China featuring particular representations of the highly problematic social credit system as, for instance, 'Big Data Meets Big Brother' often compared to the 'Nosedive' episode of the TV show *Black Mirror* (Botsman 2017; Locker 2018). As well as the fact that such updated 'techno-orientalist' imaginaries greatly simplify the complex and exceedingly worrying new relations between state, technology corporations, and society, such visions crowd out the bandwidth for other accounts and futures of digital rights (Jefferson 2018). What is rarely foregrounded, for instance, are imaginaries generated by the rich and influential body of work by Asian activists, social movements, policymakers, media and technology actors, and scholars on communication, information, media, and, more recently, digital rights (Thomas 2011, 2012). Two resonant examples here come from the Indian context, in the work of the Delhi Sarai group, especially on commons and publics, and from various NGOs and think tanks on Internet governance, not least in the *Delhi Declaration for a Just and Equitable Internet*—not as celebrated or developed perhaps as the Brazilian *Marco Civil* but also an important moment in the social conceptualization of digital rights (Just Net Coalition 2014).

The lack of recognition of, and attention paid to, Asian digital rights is despite efforts to broaden and internationalize evident in 'international' digital rights campaigns. An excellent example of this is found in the wide international extension, coverage, and staffing of US-headquartered digital rights organization *Access Now*, well known for its high-profile work globally including various Asian countries (for instance, it held its premier event *RightsCon* in 2015, as discussed in Postill 2018). John Postill's *Nerd Politics,* and his earlier work on the localization of the Internet, is a key exemplar in theorizing digital politics and activism in situated, contextualized ways, especially drawing upon Asian locations and cultures of digital rights (2018). Postill reminds us that the 'global digital rights space is more heterogeneous, dynamic and messy', and cannot simply be understood via the dominant liberal versus radical narratives (Postill 2018: 91). He argues that 'we should still take seriously the cultural heterogeneity of the digital rights space; that is, the divergent histories, ideologies and institutions found in different political cultures' (Postill 2018: 92). For Postill this cues us to attend to the creative and canny ways in which 'nerds' (digital rights actors) 'translate or "modulate' ... key digital issues in culturally specific ways', so comprehending the 'local distinctions' that enable us to 'understand the global movement in all its unity and diversity' (Postill 2018: 92).

Transaction Rights

In the spirit of this volume, it is important to posit digital rights as a rich and consequential area for digital transactions in Asia. This is especially important if it is the case, as we have contended in this chapter, digital rights are often left off the agenda in the discussion of digital transformations, especially the highly visible, mainstream, official, and authorized discussions. Such theoretical, empirical, comparative, and cross-sectoral work is urgently needed, not least because questions of digital rights and governance are moving beyond earlier, if still pressing, issues of freedom of expression to a wider range of privacy, data justice, labour rights, communication rights, governance, and democratization issues, posed by the new platforms (such as sharing and caring economy). Not only are such new Asian and inter-Asia theorizations and practices of rights and governance important in this region (especially for countries such as Australia), but they stand to help us rethink and confront the impasses and political and conceptual problems with dominant global digital rights thinking. In turn, this project of reimagining and mainstreaming digital rights conceptions, practices, and norms makes a powerful contribution to advancing key issues and challenges arising in contemporary Asia. The expansion of digital transactions across Asia requires more comprehensive and considered rights frameworks to guarantee social justice, citizenship, and political participation, as well the economic benefits of the many initiatives underway. Otherwise the danger is that digital transformations can hinder rather than advance social progress.

Acknowledgement

Our thanks to Adrian Athique for his helpful and suggestive comments. This chapter is an output of the *Digital Rights and Governance in Australia and Asia* project, funded by the University of Sydney's Sydney Research Excellence Initiative (SREI) 2017–2018.

References

Aaronson, Susan Ariel (2018) 'The Turn to Trade Policies to Regulate the Internet' in Velut, Jean-Baptiste, Dalingwater, Louise, Boullet, Vanessa and Peyronel, Valérie (eds) *Understanding Mega Free Trade Agreements: The Political and Economic Governance of New Cross-Regionalism*, London and New York: Routledge, pp. 191–220.

Athique, Adrian (in press) 'Digital Transactions in Asia' in Athique, Adrian and Baulch, Emma (eds) *Digital Transactions in Asia: Economic, Informational, and Social Exchanges*, London and New York: Routledge.

Athique, Adrian, Parthasarathi, Vibodh and Srinivas, S.V. (eds.) (2018) *The India Media Economy*, 2 vols., New Delhi: Oxford University Press.

Australian Human Rights Commission (AHRC) (2018) *Human Rights and Technology Issues Paper*, Sydney, NSW: AHRC. Available: https://tech.humanrights.gov.au/, accessed: 2 October 2018.

Avonius, Leena and Kingsbury, Damien (eds.) (2008) *Human Rights in Asia: A Reassessment of the Asia Values Debate*, New York: Palgrave.

Azali, Kathleen (2017) *Indonesia's Divided Digital Economy. Essay for ISEAS Perspectives*, Singapore: ISEAS Yusof Ishak Institute, No. 70. Available: https://think-asia.org/handle/11540/7458, accessed: 2 October 2018.

Bates, Charlotte, Imrie, Rob, and Kullman, Kim (eds.) (2016) *Care and Design: Bodies, Building, Cities*, New York: Wiley-Blackwell.

Berenshot, Ward, Nordholt, Henk Schulte and Bakker, Laurens (eds.) (2017) *Citizenship and Democratization in Southeast Asia*, Leiden: Brill.

Berry, Chris, Martin, Fran and Yue, Audrey (eds.) (2003) *Mobile Cultures: New media in Queer Asia*, Durham, NC: Duke University Press.

Botsman, Rachel (2017) 'Big Data Meets Big Brother as China Moves to Rates Its Citizens', *Wired*, 21 October. Available: www.wired.co.uk/article/chinese-government-social-credit-score-privacy-invasion, accessed: 2 October 2018.

Boys, Jos (2014) *Doing Design Differently: An Alternative Handbook on Architecture, Dis/ability, and Designing for Everyday Life*, London and New York: Routledge.

Brock, George (2016) *The Right to be Forgotten: Privacy and the Media in the Digital Age*, London: I.B. Tauris.

Bunnell, Tim (2004) *Malaysia, Modernity, and the Multimedia Super Corridor: A Critical Geography of Intelligent Landscapes*, London: Routledge.

Bunz, Mercedes and Meikle, Graham (2017) *The Internet of Things*. Cambridge: Polity Press.

Chatfield, Akemi Takeoka, Reddick, Christopher G. and Brajawidagda, Uuf (2015) 'Government Surveillance Disclosures, Bilateral Trust and Indonesia–Australia Cross-Border Security Cooperation: Social Network Analysis of Twitter Data', *Government Information Quarterly*, 32: 118–128.

Chen, Kuan-Hsing (2010) *Asia as Method: Towards Deimperialization*. Durham, NC: Duke University Press.

Chun, Wei Choo (1997) 'IT2000: Singapore's Vision of an Intelligent Island', in Droeger, Peter (ed) *Intelligent Environments: Spatial Aspects of the Information Revolution*, Amsterdam: Elsevier, pp. 49–65.

Cohen, Julie E. (2012) *Configuring the Networked Self: Law, Code, and the Play of Everyday Practice*, New Haven, CT: Yale University Press.

Cole, David D., Fabbrini, Federico and Schulhofer, Stephen (eds.) (2017) *Surveillance, Privacy, and Transatlantic Relations*, Oxford and London: Bloomsbury; Portland, OR: Hart.

Couldry, Nick, et al. (2018) 'Media and Communications', in International Panel on Social Progress (IPSP) (ed) *Rethinking Society for the 21st Century: Report of the International Panel on Social Progress*, Cambridge: Cambridge University Press, Vol. 2, pp. 523–562.

Daly, Angela (2016a) 'Digital Rights in Australia's Asian Century: A Good Neighbour?', in Digital Asia Hub (ed), *The Good Life in Asia's Digital 21st Century*, Hong Kong: Digital Asia Hub, pp. 128–136. Available: https://www.digitalasiahub.org/thegoodlife/, accessed: 2 October 2018.

Daly, Angela (2016b) 'Net Neutrality in Australia: The Debate Continues, But No Policy in Sight', in Belli, Luca and De Filippi, Primavera (eds) *Net Neutrality Compendium: Human Rights, Free Competition and the Future of the Internet*, Heidelberg: Springer, pp. 141–156.

Dencik, Lina, Hintz, Arne and Cable, Jonathan (2016) 'Towards Data Justice: The Ambiguity of Anti-Surveillance Resistance in Political Activism', *Big Data & Society*. doi:10.1177/2053951716679678.

Digital Asia Hub (ed.) (2016) *The Good Life in Asia's Digital 21st Century*, Hong Kong: Digital Asia Hub. Available: www.digitalasiahub.org/thegoodlife, accessed: 2 October 2018.

Digital Rights Foundation (2018) 'Content Regulation in Pakistan's Digital Spaces', Civil Society Submission to June 2018 Human Rights Council Report. https://digitalrightsfoundation.pk/wp-content/uploads/2017/12/DigitalRightsFoundationSubmissionSpecialRapporteurFreedomofExpression.pdf.

Digital Rights Watch (2018) *State of Digital Rights*. Sydney, NSW: Digital Rights Watch. https://digitalrightswatch.org.au/wp-content/uploads/2018/05/State-of-Digital-Rights-Media.pdf.

Eckstein, Lars and Schwarz, Anja (eds.) (2014) *Postcolonial Piracy: Media Distribution and Cultural Production in the Global South*, London: Bloomsbury.

Eckel, Jan and Moyn, Samuel (eds.) (2014) *The Breakthrough: Human Rights in the 1970s*, Pittsburgh: University of Pennsylvania Press.

Erni, John (ed.) (2011) *Cultural Studies of Rights: Critical Articulations*, New York and London: Routledge.

Erni, John (2019, forthcoming) *Law and Cultural Studies: A Critical Rearticulation of Human Rights*, London and New York: Routledge.

Erni, John, and Chua, Siew Keng (eds.) (2005) *Asian Media Studies: Politics of Subjectivities*, Malden, MA, and Oxford: Wiley-Blackwell

Eubanks, Virginia (2017) *Automating Inequality: How High-Tech Tools Profile, Police, and Punish the Poor*, New York: St. Martin's Press.

Ford, Michele and Honan, Vivian (2017) 'The Go-Jek Effect', in Jurriens, Edwin and Tapsell, Ross (eds) *Digital Indonesia: Connectivity and Divergence*, Singapore: ISEAS Publishing (Institute of Southeast Asian Studies), pp. 275–288.

Fredriksson, Martin and Arvanitakis, James (eds.) (2014) *Piracy: Leakages from Modernity*, Sacramento, CA: Litwin Books.

Freedom House (2017) *Freedom on the Net*, Washington, DC: Freedom House. Available: https://freedomhouse.org/sites/default/files/FOTN_2017_Final.pdf, accessed: 2 October 2018.

George, Cherian (2015) 'Managing the Dangers of Online Hate Speech in South Asia', *Media Asia*, 42(3–4): 144–156.

Gillespie, Tarleton (2018) *Custodians of the Internet*, New Haven, CT: Yale University Press.

Goggin, Gerard and McLelland, Mark (eds.) (2009) *Internationalizing Internet Studies: Beyond Anglophone Paradigms*, New York: Routledge.

Goggin, Gerard, Vromen, Ariadne, Weatherall, Kimberlee, Martin, Fiona, Webb, Adele, Sunman, Lucy and Bailo, Francesco (2017) *Digital Rights in Australia*, Sydney, NSW: Department of Media and Communications. Available: http://hdl.handle.net/2123/17587, accessed: 2 October 2018.

Goh, Beng Lan (ed.) (2011) *Decentring and Diversifying Southeast Asian Studies: Perspectives from the Region*, Singapore: ISEAS.

Gray, Mary L. and Suri, Siddarth (2019, forthcoming) *Ghost Work: How to Stop Silicon Valley from Building a New Global Underclass*. Boston: Eamon Dolan/Houghton Mifflin Harcourt.

Greenleaf, Graham (2014) *Asian Data Privacy Laws: Trade and Human Rights Perspectives*, Oxford: Oxford University Press.

Gurumurthy, Anita, Nandini, Chami and Thomas, Sanjana (2016) 'Unpacking Digital India: A Feminist Commentary on Policy Agendas in the Digital Moment', *Journal of Information Policy*, 6: 371–402.

Hallin, Daniel C. and Mancini, Paolo. (2004) *Comparing Media Systems: Three Models of Media and Politics*, Cambridge and New York: Cambridge University Press.

Hintz, Arne, Dencik, Lina and Wahl-Jorgensen, Karin (2018) *Digital Citizenship in a Datafied Society*, Cambridge: Polity Press.

Hjorth, Larissa and Khoo, Olivia (eds.) (2016) *Routledge Handbook of New Media in Asia*, New York: Routledge.

Hong, Yu (2017) *Networking China: The Digital Transformation of the Chinese Economy*, Urbana: University of Illinois Press.

Horst, Heather A. and Foster, Robert J. (eds.) (2018) *The Moral Economy of Mobile Phones: Pacific Island Perspectives*, Canberra, ACT: ANU Press.

Hunt, Lynn (2007) *Inventing Human Rights: A History*, New York: W.W. Norton.

Jefferson, Ed (2018) 'No, China Isn't *Black Mirror*— Social Credit Scores Are More Complex and Sinister Than That', *New Statesman*, 27 April 2018. Available: www.newstatesman.com/world/asia/2018/04/no-china-isn-t-black-mirror-social-credit-scores-are-more-complex-and-sinister.

Jensen, Heike (2012) 'Women and Virtual Citizenship? Gendered Experiences of Censorship and Surveillance', Think Piece for *IT for Change*, Bengaluru, India. www.gender-is-citizenship.net/sites/default/files/citigen/uploads/Heike_TP_final.pdf.

Jin, Dal Yong (2015) *Digital Platforms, Imperialism and Political Culture*, New York: Routledge.

Jin, Dal Yong (ed.) (2017) *Mobile Gaming in Asia: Politics, Culture and Emerging Technologies*, Dordrecht: Springer.

Jurriëns, Edwin and Tapsell, Ross (eds.) (2017) *Digital Indonesia: Connectivity and Divergence*, Singapore: ISEAS—Yusof Ishak Institute.

Just Net Coalition (2014) *Delhi Declaration for a Just and Equitable Internet*. https://justnetcoalition.org/delhi-declaration.

Kar, Kumar Arpan, Sinha, Shuchi and Gupta, M.P. (eds.) (2018) *Digital India: Reflections and Practice*, Cham: Springer.

Karppinen, Kari (2017a) 'Deconstructing Digital Rights: Promises and Problems of Rights-Based Politics', Paper presented at the *Nordmedia 2017 Conference, Political communication division Tampere*, 17–19 August 2017. Available: www.researchgate.net/publication/319877470_Deconstructing_Digital_Rights_Promises_and_Problems_of_Rights-Based_Politics.

Karppinen, Kari (2017b) 'Human Rights and the Digital', in Tumber, Howard and Waisbord, Silvio (eds) *Routledge Companion to Media and Human Rights*, New York: Routledge, pp. 95–104.

Kelly, David and Reid, Anthony (eds.) (1998) *Asian Freedoms: The Idea of Freedom in East and Southeast Asia*, Cambridge: Cambridge University Press.

Kitley, Philip (2000) *Television Nation and Culture in Indonesia*, Ohio RIS Southeast Asia Series, No. 104, Athens: Ohio University Press.

Kobie, Nicole (2016) 'Inside Cyberjaya, Malaysia's Failed Silicon Valley', *Wired* (UK), 5 April. Available: www.wired.co.uk/article/malaysia-cyberjaya-silicon-valley-smart-cities.

Leach, James and Wilson, Lee (2014) *Subversion, Conversion, Development: Cross-Cultural Knowledge Encounter and the Politics of Design*, Cambridge: MIT Press.

Lee, Kwangsuk (2012) *IT Development in Korea: A Broadband Nirvana?* London and New York: Routledge.

Lim, Merlyna (2013) 'Many Clicks But Little Sticks: Social Media Activism in Indonesia', *Journal of Contemporary Asia*, 43(4): 636–657.

Lim, Merlyna (2017) 'Freedom to Hate: Social Media, Algorithmic Enclaves, and the Rise of Tribal Nationalism in Indonesia', *Critical Asian Studies*, 49(3): 411–427.

Lim, Merlyna (2018) 'Roots, Routes, Routers: Communications and Media of Contemporary Social Movements', *Journalism & Communication Monographs*, 20(2): 92–136.

Lim, Sun Sun and Soriano, Cheryll (eds.) (2016) *Asian Perspectives on Digital Culture: Emerging Phenomena, Enduring Concepts*, New York: Routledge, pp. 191–198.

Locker, Melissa (2018) 'China's Terrifying "Social Credit" Surveillance System is Expanding', *Fast Company*, 24 April. Available: www.fastcompany.com/40563225/chinas-terrifying-social-credit-surveillance-system-is-expanding.

Mandal, Purnendu and Yong, John (eds.) (2016) *Smart Technologies for Smart Nations: Perspectives from the Asia-Pacific Region*, Singapore: Springer.

Maslin, Nigel (1990) *The Intelligent Island*, London: British Broadcasting Corporation (BBC).

McCosker, Anthony, Vivienne, Sonja and Johns, Amelia (2016) (eds.) *Negotiating Digital Citizenship: Control, Contest, Culture*, London: Rowman & Littefield.

McLelland, Mark, Yu, Haiqing and Goggin, Gerard (2018) 'Alternative Social Media Histories in Japan and China', in Burgess, Jean, Marwick, Alice E. and Poell, Thomas (eds) *The SAGE Handbook of Social Media*, London and Thousand Oaks, CA: Sage, pp. 53–68.

Moyn, Samuel (2010) *The Last Utopia: Human Rights in History*, Cambridge, MA: Harvard University Press.

Moyn, Samuel (2018) *Not Enough: Human Rights in an Unequal World*, Cambridge, MA: Harvard University Press.

National Computer Board (NCB) (1992) *A Vision of an Intelligent Island: The IT2000 Report*, Singapore: SNP Publishers.

Neilsen, Brett, Rossiter, Ned, and Samaddar, Ranabir (2018) *Logistical Asia: The Labour of Making a World Region*, Singapore: Springer/Palgrave.

Neves, Joshua and Sarkar, Bhaskar (eds.) (2017) *Asian Video Cultures: In the Penumbra of the Global*, Durham, NC: Duke University Press.

Niranjana, Tejaswini and Xiaoming, Wang (eds.) (2015) *Genealogies of the Asian Present: Situating Inter-Asia Cultural Studies*, Hyderabad: Orient BlackSwan.

Pasquale, Frank (2015) *Blackbox Society: The Secret Algorithms that Control Money and Information*, Cambridge, MA: Harvard University Press.

Postigo, Hector (2012) *The Digital Rights Movement: The Role of Technology in Subverting Digital Copyright*, Cambridge: MIT Press.

Postill, John (2011) *Localizing the Internet: An Anthropological Account*, New York: Berghahn.

Postill, John (2018) *The Rise of Nerd Politics: Digital Activism and Social Change*, London: Pluto.

Price, Monroe and Stremlau, Nicole (2018) 'Introduction: Speech and Society in Comparative Perspective', in Monroe Price and Nicole Stremlau (eds) *Speech and Society in Turbulent Times: Freedom of Expression in Comparative Perspective*, Cambridge: Cambridge University Press, pp. 1–16.

Qiu, Jack Linchuan (2009) *Working Class Network Society: Communication Technology and the Information Have-Less in China*, Cambridge: MIT Press.

Qiu, Jack Linchuan (2016) *Goodbye iSlave: A Manifesto for Digital Abolition*, Chicago: University of Illinois Press.

Sandfort, Sandy (1993) 'The Intelligent Island', *Wired*, 1 April. Available: www.wired.com/1993/04/sandfort/.

Sarai (2001) *The Public Domain*, Delhi: Sarai; Amsterdam: Waag.

Sen, Krishna and Lee, Terence (eds.) (2008) *Political Regimes and the Media in Asia: Continuities, Contradictions, and Change*, London and New York: Routledge.

Servaes, Jan (ed.) (2017) *Sustainable Development Goals in the Asian Context*, Singapore: Springer.

Shah, Nishant (2007) 'Subject to Technology: Internet Pornography, Cyber-Terrorism and the Indian State', *Inter-Asia Cultural Studies*, 8(3): 349–366.

Shah, Nishant (2013) *Whose Changes Is It, Anyway? Towards a Future of Digital Technologies and Citizen Action in Emerging Information Societies*, Hivos: The Hague. Available: https://knowledge.hivos.org/sites/default/files/publications/whosechangeisitanyway_nishantshah.pdf, accessed: 2 October 2018.

Shah, Nishant (2017) 'In Access: Digital Video and the User', in Neves, Joshua and Sarkar, Bhaskar (eds) (2017) *Asian Video Cultures: In the Penumbra of the Global*, Durham, NC: Duke University Press, pp. 115–130.

Shi, Anbin (2018) 'China's Role in Remapping Global Communication', in Thussu, Daya, de Burgh, Hugo and Shi, Anbi (eds), *China's Media Go Global*, London and New York: Routledge, pp. 34–51.

Sinpeng, Aim (2013) 'State Repression in Cyberspace: The Case of Thailand', *Asian Politics & Policy*, 5: 421–440.

Stagars, Manuel (2016) *Open Data in Southeast Asia: Towards Economic Prosperity, Government Transparency, and Citizen Participation in ASEAN*, Cham: Springer.

Stecklow, Steve (2018) 'Hatebook: Why Facebook Is Losing the War on Hate Speech in Myanmar', *Reuters*, 15 August. Available: www.reuters.com/investigates/special-report/myanmar-facebook-hate/, accessed: 2 October 2018.

Sundaram, Ravi (2009) *Pirate Modernity: Delhi's Media Urbanism*, London and New York: Routledge.

Sundaram, Ravi (2015a) 'Post-Postcolonial Sensory Infrastructure', *e-Flux Journal*, 64(April): 1–10. Available: www.e-flux.com/journal/64/60858/post-postcolonial-sensory-infrastructure/.

Sundaram, Ravi (2015b) 'Publicity, Transparency, and the Circulation Engine: The Media Sting in India', *Current Anthropology*, 56 (Supplement 12): S297–S305.

Suzor, Nicolas (2018) 'Digital Constitutionalism: Using the Rule of Law to Evaluate the Legitimacy of Governance by Platforms', *Social Media + Society*, 4(3): 1–11.

Suzor, Nicolas, Van Geelen, Tess, and Myers West, Sarah (2018) 'Evaluating the Legitimacy of Platform Governance: A Review of Research and a Shared Research Agenda', *International Communication Gazette*, 80(4): 385–400.

Sydney Ideas (2018) 'Digital Rights and Governance in Asia: The State of the Art', podcast of panel held at University of Sydney, 12 April. Available: https://sydney.edu.au/news-opinion/sydney-ideas/2018/digital-rights-and-governance-in-asia-the-state-of-the-arts.html, accessed: 2 October 2018.

Tapsell, Ross (2013) 'The Media Freedom Movement in Malaysia and the Electoral Authoritarian Regime', *Journal of Contemporary Asia*, 43(4): 613–635.

Thomas, Amos Owen (2005) *Imagi-Nations and Borderless Television: Media, Culture and Politics Across Asia*, New Delhi: Sage.

Thomas, Pradip Ninan (2011) *Negotiating Communication Rights: Case Studies from India*, New Delhi: SAGE.

Thomas, Pradip Ninan (2012) *Digital India: Understanding Information, Communication and Social Change*, New Delhi: SAGE.

Triastuti, Endah (2017) 'Indonesia's Internet Blueprint: Shifting Experience in Media Culture', in Goggin, Gerard and McLelland, Mark (eds) *Routledge Companion to Global Internet Histories*, New York: Routledge, pp. 479–488.

Tusikov, Natasha (2017) *Chokepoints: Global Private Regulation on the Internet*, Oakland: University of California Press.

Velut, Jean-Baptiste, Dalingwater, Louise, Boullet, Vanessa and Peyronel, Valérie (eds.) (2018) *Understanding Mega Free Trade Agreements: The Political and Economic Governance of New Cross-Regionalism*, London and New York: Routledge.

UNESCO (2018a) *Defining Internet Universality Indicators*, 2nd draft, May, Paris: UNESCO. Available: en.unesco.org/internetuniversality/indicators, accessed: 2 October 2018.

UNESCO (2018b) *World Trends in Freedom of Expression and Media Development: 2017/2018 Global Report*, Paris: UNESCO. Available: https://en.unesco.org/world-media-trends-2017, accessed: 2 October 2018.

Vincent, Alice (2017) '*Black Mirror* Is Coming True in China, Where Your 'Rating' Affects Your Home, Transport, and Social Circle', *The Telegraph* (UK), 15 December. Available: www.telegraph.co.uk/on-demand/2017/12/15/black-mirror-coming-true-china-rating-affects-home-transport/.

Visweswaran, Kamala (2010) *Un/common Cultures: Racism and the Rearticulation of Cultural Difference*, Durham, NC: Duke University Press.

Wang, Hui (2007) 'The Politics of Imagining Asia: A Genealogical Analysis', *Inter-Asia Cultural Studies*, 8(1): 1–33.

Wang, Ting-Yan and Liu, Hong (2018) 'An Emerging Asian Model of Governance and Transnational Knowledge Transfer: An Introduction', *Journal of Asian Public Policy*, 11(2): 121–135.

Wolf, Asher (2017) 'Coconet S.E. Asia Digital Rights Camp: Interviews with Nine Digital Rights Activists', *Medium*, 5 November. Available: https://medium.com/@Asher_Wolf/coconet-s-e-asia-digital-rights-camp-d8134dee7782, accessed: 2 October 2018.

Yang, Guobin (ed.) (2015) *China's Contested Internet*, Copenhagen: NIAS Press.

Part 2

Financial, Social and Cultural Transactions

8 Embedding Digital Money amongst Chinese Migrant Factory Workers

Tom McDonald

The United Nations Capital Development Fund situates China's rapid expansion of digital payment systems as an exemplar of its 'Better Than Cash Alliance' initiative, claiming that:

> The growth of digital payments using existing platforms and networks in China has brought with it a much wider range of digital financial services that are both expanding financial inclusion and economic opportunity for individuals, and creating valuable new business models for companies.
>
> (Kapron and Meertens 2017: 8)

On the ground, the rapid proliferation of digital money platforms in China in the last decade has provoked more than simply a change in consumer habits. It has also given rise to predictions that these shifts in monetary practices will engender corresponding social transformations. Hopes have been pinned on the perceived potential of digital money for ameliorating the difficulties and dangers of handling cash, bringing more people into participation in markets, reducing corruption and even addressing the wide inequalities in wealth that exist in the country. While many of the claims made regarding the potential for digital money to foster financial inclusion are not unique to China alone, the Chinese case is arguably exceptional given the sheer scale of both users and transactions implicated in these new processes (for a discussion, see Maurer 2015), along with the distinctive convergence of several popular digital payment services into existing social media platforms such as WeChat and QQ (Economist 2016). While scholars of China have often pointed out that Chinese people's treatment of money means it can be regarded as an unusually social artefact, its new digital form provides an important opportunity for scholars to consider afresh the seemingly social propensities of money, along with the rationalities that guide its usage in everyday life (Bruckermann and Feuchtwang 2016; Martin 2014).

The claims surrounding the perceived socially ameliorative potential of digital money in China clearly connect with the central theoretical underpinnings of money in anthropology and the broader social sciences. Simmel pointed out that money was capable of simultaneously producing 'both a disintegrating and a unifying effect' (Simmel 1978 [1900]: 345). To him, money was integrative in the sense that it represented 'pure interaction in its purest form' (Simmel 1978 [1900]: 129). Money's use, he asserted, was able to increase the personal freedom of individuals, both by liberating them to engage in professions of their own volition and by allowing them to tap into the resources of networks outside their own. However, Simmel likewise claimed that money's disintegrative effects could also be writ large in the moral confusion it caused by virtue of the fact that it potentially enabled everything—even human relationships—to be reduced to a single value. At its worst, Simmel noted, money was capable of fostering intense and damaging greed. Marx (1976 [1867]) also held similarly contradictory views on money, noting its force in severing the producers of goods from that which they produce. But he also saw money's socially constitutive agency, questioning how money could be 'the bond which ties me to human life and society to me, which links me to nature and to man, is money not the bond of all bonds?' (1975: 377). Clearly, the euphoric claims surrounding digital money need grounding within the varied potentialities of money astutely pointed out by both Simmel and Marx.

This chapter presents data from migrant factory workers in Shenzhen, China on their use of and attitudes towards digital money, which suggests that understanding money's potentially social nature provides the opportunity to develop understandings of money that may reach beyond linear continuum of money as 'social' or 'asocial', 'integrative' or 'disintegrative'. Instead, I argue that it is necessary to unpick the multiple and contesting platforms, functions and uses of digital money that are emerging in the region in order to see how money is, to borrow from Polanyi, being shaped by market processes to become embedded and disembedded in social relations during specific moments and to varying degrees (1944). This chapter will demonstrate how the divergent perceptions held by workers regarding the digital money platforms WeChat Wallet (*weixin qianbao*), QQ Wallet (*QQ qianbao*) and Alipay (*zhifubao*) suggest that while the embedding and disembedding of money is defined through market processes, workers' own acute awareness of the distinctive nature of each of these platforms allows them to play a hand in shaping such processes. Most significantly, workers identify Alipay as the platform seen to offer the greatest autonomy from the multiple distinctive spheres of social relationships they otherwise maintain online, leading them to attribute it to be most suited to the storage of larger amounts of money. This points to a need to acknowledge how digital money platforms insert themselves between 'people' and 'markets' in order to mediate such processes of embedding and disembedding.

Market—Society Relations

> Money circulates in Chinese communities in ways premised on an entirely different logic than that of capitalism ... building pure interaction and allowing personal liberty at the same time.
>
> (Martin 2014: 32)

Anthropologist Emily Martin made the above reflections based on her ethnographic fieldwork conducted in rural Taiwan in the early 1970s, while the region was undergoing what appeared to be a rapid capitalisation. Documenting her participants' distinctive economic practices surrounding waged labour, marriage and rotating credit societies, Martin argued that these evidenced a unique set of Chinese cultural logics whereby money facilitated social integration and was conducive to social relationships. Martin was able to take Simmel's account of the divergent nature of money into opposing integrating and disintegrating forces, and use it as the basis for cross-cultural comparison, claiming that 'money in Chinese society works mostly, but not entirely, to create social integration; money in the United States works mostly, but not entirely, to create social disintegration' (2014: 13). Martin's positive assessment of money in China was informed by what she perceived to be the articulation of money in Taiwan 'with forms of exchange based on kinship and community', that, she claimed, 'held the disintegrating potential of money in check' (Martin 2014: 14). While Martin's documentation of the flows of money through rural financial institutions of labour, marriage and rotating credit societies appeared to adhere to familiar profit-oriented forms of investment, she astutely pointed out that 'elements of a capitalist economy can exist without implying that the whole system of capitalism as we know it is present' and argued that distinctive logics were at play to prevent members unduly profiting from their exchanges (2014: 26).

Martin's assertion that money in China carries its own distinctive and integrative nature appears to resonate with the convergence of Chinese digital money services into the country's social media platforms, while also arguably representing an implicit challenge to the idea that the self-regulating market economy of the modern nation state is necessarily one where money has been disembedded from social relations. In Polanyi's magnum opus, *The Great Transformation*, he attacks one of the central assumptions of classical economics, which holds that the self-regulating system of markets represents a reflection of a natural and primitive orientation of man towards profit (1944). Polanyi attempts to debunk this myth by drawing on historical and ethnographic accounts to argue that there was 'no economy prior to our own, even approximately controlled and regulated by markets' (1944: 46) and that 'man's economy, as a rule, is submerged in his social relationships' (1944: 48).

Polanyi's ideas would go on to be central to the development of the substantivist tradition. In mobilising his argument, Polanyi highlights how many so-called 'tribal societies' actually appear to have economic systems which are 'run on non-economic motives' (1944: 48). In such societies, production and distribution are instead ensured through principles of reciprocity, redistribution and householding. Polanyi describes reciprocity as the creation of cycles of obligation, whereby 'today's giving will be recompensed by tomorrow's taking' (1944: 53). Redistribution, by contrast, is typically performed by an intermediary who 'will often attempt to increase their political power by the manner in which they redistribute the goods', with these activities generally 'forming part of the prevailing political regime' (1944: 53, 55). The third principle, householding, can be defined as 'production for one's own use'—whether as an individual or as a group—although Polanyi is keen to assert that these activities are not driven by motives of gain (1944: 55). Polanyi delineates all of these activities as being distinct from a drive for profit, or labouring for remuneration.

Polanyi's argument is relevant in the case of the migrant factory workers who feature in this study because it provides a framework for illuminating the dual imperatives they face between the need to safeguard what little money they can accumulate through their engagement in capitalistic wage labour practices and the need to maintain social connections with friends and family located in both their new urban environment and their (frequently rural) places of origin. Furthermore, by revealing how these imperatives may, at different times, be both in conflict and alignment with each other, I argue that digital money serves to complicate assumptions that such technologies may in-and-of-themselves bring about particular social effects.

Fieldwork on Factory Work: Tracing Exchange Processes through Platforms

The interview and ethnographic data presented below were collected during fieldwork as part of an ongoing project into digital money and migrant labour. The bulk of the data was collected during the summer of 2016, working with migrant factory labourers in an industrial area on the peripheries of the city of Shenzhen, in south-east China. Most participants were male migrant workers in their early 20s, as this group comprised the bulk of factory workers in the area. Migrant factory workers were selected as the object of this study owing to the unique vantage point they offered for observing the uptake of digital payment platforms. It has been well documented that such groups of workers already rely heavily upon digital networks and find particularly inventive uses for them as a means for coping with the dislocation and discrimination they frequently encounter at the hands of their employers and pre-existing urban residents (Qiu 2009; Sun 2014; Wallis 2013; Wang 2016). Furthermore, I felt that the financially precarious social position such workers occupy ought to engender a unique set of perspectives on money, attuned to making the most of the limited financial resources they are able to draw upon. Precedent already exists for highlighting how the economic practices of such groups often defy mainstream economic assumptions.

The remainder of the chapter attempts to address some of these issues by describing three specific characteristics of money observed in digital payment platforms. The first two hinge on a correlation between the strength of social ties existing amongst individuals and the appropriateness of money to feature in such interactions. The third form centres on moments when money is rendered particularly impersonal. I also show how each of these forms of money is viewed by migrant workers to be clustered on one of three digital money platforms: WeChat Wallet, QQ Wallet and Alipay. Although other digital money platforms do exist in China, these three occupy the focus of this analysis simply because migrant participants only discussed these during the interviews.

Many of the initial interview questions focused on migrants' use of particular functions (such as money transfers, deposits and red envelopes) shared across all three platforms. As fieldwork progressed, it gradually became apparent that migrants held distinctive views on each of these platforms, which led me to adjust the questions to try and further tease out such opinions. Participants' names have been altered to conceal their identity.

It should be noted that these platforms have had unique developmental trajectories. While Alipay arguably led internet-based payment services in China, first launching in 2004, before developing a mobile app in 2009 (Kapron and Meertens 2017). Competitors WeChat Wallet and QQ Wallet came later, in both 2013 and 2014, respectively, although the company that owns these two services had been experimenting with digital payments since 2005 (Kapron and Meertens 2017; Niu 2014). Since their introduction, these payment platforms have experienced phenomenal growth, with official statistics showing the number of users of mobile online payment platforms in China growing from 125,480,000 in 2013 to 527,030,000 in 2017 (China Internet Network Information Center 2015; China Internet Network Information Center 2018). Today, these platforms all offer largely similar sets of features, allowing for transfers of funds between individual users and the payment of goods or services in both physical and online stores. All of these platforms also allow (and in fact encourage) users to link their digital wallet to their conventional bank account in order to facilitate the transfer of money to and from the platforms. While infrastructurally similar, a number of specific affordances and norms of use amongst participants have given rise to market processes of embedding and disembedding to occur in different ways across these platforms.

Embedding Exchange in Social Relations

One common theme emerging from discussions with participants pointed towards how the utility of certain digital payment platforms was often viewed as springing from the way that they effectively embedded monetary exchange within social relationships. This was particularly so in the case of WeChat Wallet and QQ Wallet, both of which were new functions that had been integrated into pre-existing popular social media platforms (WeChat and QQ). WeChat in particular has established itself as the main conduit for messaging with friends and family. In 2017, WeChat's 'Moments' social networking feature also claimed the highest usage rate (87.3%) amongst social networking applications in China, exceeding that of QQ's 'QZone' feature (64.4%) (China Internet Network Information Center 2018). WeChat's position as a locus for online interactions amongst one's personal connections thus leant the platform to facilitating a range of monetary exchanges between migrants and others that they knew.

A key instance of embedding could be observed in the case of digital red envelopes. This feature allowed users to send a virtual red envelope, which mimicked the appearance of paper red envelopes traditionally gifted during festivals or events marking major life stages. Although WeChat Wallet, QQ Wallet and Alipay all offered digital red envelope functions, WeChat's centrality to participants' daily online interactions meant that the overwhelming majority of red envelope exchanges were centred on this platform. Polanyi's (1944) description of reciprocity as an economic practice that runs contrary to the logic of markets was especially apparent in migrants' logics and behaviours surrounding the distribution of digital red envelopes into WeChat messaging groups. Sending such envelopes into online groups entailed specifying a total cash value to be distributed to all group members, along with the number of red envelopes that the funds would be randomly distributed between. Once sent into the WeChat group, members had the opportunity to obtain a red envelope by 'grabbing' (*qiang*) it faster than other users, upon which the amounts distributed and recipients would be revealed to all group users. Online red envelope distribution could also be categorised as a reciprocal activity, thanks to the way that it created ongoing cycles of obligation. There was often an expectation that when one individual sent money into a messaging group, other group members would follow suit. One such example comes from Xi, a factory labourer in his early 40s, who described how sending red envelopes within WeChat groups could foster an atmosphere of excitement amongst group members which also avoided the expense or hassle of organising in-person meetings outside.

Male migrant worker, Wu, also discussed such exchanges in similar terms: 'If you send a red envelope into the group, it may only be

5 RMB, but let's say you send it and split it between 30 people who compete for it… I reckon this is enlivening an atmosphere'. The obligation to participate in the creation and maintenance of these episodic, socially vivacious and money-infused flurries of exchange was something reported by numerous participants and which further confirms the reciprocal nature of these activities.

Reciprocity could also be witnessed—albeit in a more overtly codified form—in WeChat 'gambling groups' (*dubo qun*). These groups, which were often comprised of upwards of 100 members, were distinctive in that members generally did not know all of their fellow members, although a personal invitation from an existing member was typically required to join the group. Although rules differed across groups, one of the most common arrangements involved a fixed amount (for instance 5 RMB) being sent into the group, which would be split into random portions across five red envelopes to be grabbed by its members. The group member who managed to win the second largest envelope amount would become responsible for sending the next red envelope into the group. Multiple rounds of red envelope distribution would often occur in a single day. Although members of these gambling groups insisted that conversation rarely took place within the groups, even here it can be argued that the gambling itself constitutes a social act.

Steinmüller's (2011: 268) ethnographic description of gambling in rural China discusses how a distinction is made between 'social gambling' (*wan*, literally 'to play') and 'problem gambling' (*du*, 'to gamble'). In WeChat gambling groups, the low stakes and emphasis on the pleasurable, entertaining atmosphere created through the activity suggest that such practices are located firmly towards the *wan* end of the spectrum.

This tendency towards reciprocation in the exchange of digital red envelopes within WeChat groups was further underlined by workers' insistence that such exchange activities were not motivated by personal gain. Participants maintained that the purpose of sharing envelopes into groups was to deepen 'feeling' (*ganqing*) with one's friends, or simply because it was 'fun'. Workers typically shunned features which allowed them to track their red envelope transaction history, or view the cumulative balance of all such transactions. Likewise, some participants spoke with distaste about news reports they had heard that software engineers had developed code which could automate the 'grabbing' of digital red envelopes, as this was seen to distort the activity into a profit-oriented enterprise.

Beyond sending red envelopes to groups, workers embedded money into social relations in other ways, with WeChat again being a preferred platform for this. For example, many workers explained that even for seemingly simple transfers of money between individual friends (for the settling of small debts, for instance) they would almost always elect to use a WeChat's digital red envelope function rather than the 'transfer' feature. Although both features achieve the same result by transferring funds between users, the latter was felt to be friendlier and somewhat more emotional. In this instance, simple acts of remuneration are arguably being refashioned so they carry affectations of reciprocity. Much like the use of 'uncle' or 'auntie' to address seniors in cases where no biological relatedness exists can constitute a kind of 'fictive kin', digital red envelope exchange between individuals may also be considered a form of 'fictive gifting'.

Even within the realm of transactional exchange for consumptive purposes, migrants tended to view WeChat as being best suited for those moments where the exchange was nonetheless embedded in a broader relational frame. This could be witnessed in the fact that although both WeChat Wallet and Alipay were accepted as a payment method by the majority of shops and traders in the field site, WeChat Wallet was accepted in the widest variety of outlets including convenience stores, hole-in-the-wall eateries and market traders, all of whom sold cheap good and services to low-income migrant labourers. Alipay, by contrast, was more readily accepted (alongside WeChat Wallet) in a smaller comparatively narrower selection of stores such as large supermarkets, department stores and online retailers, all of which tended to be synonymous with more impersonal forms of service. Migrant worker Chen gave one such example of how WeChat Wallet's use by small traders, many of whom were also fellow migrants, fitted into his daily consumptive practices: 'I often go to a particular [food stall] and I've added their WeChat, after I have eaten I will just leave, and on the way back I'll transfer the money, and it's fine'. By choosing to pay for his regular early-morning meal from a small street-side vendor using digital money, one can observe WeChat Wallet's role in mediating such recurring transactions, and how digital money sometimes actually serves to *delay* payment rather than invariably speeding up such processes. This runs contrary to popular discourses surrounding digital money, which Maurer notes generally emphasise the technologies as being faster and more 'efficient' (2015).

Shove's examination of the changing notion of convenience in relation to Euro-American domestic housework practices is useful here, demonstrating the concept's transformation from either denoting ease of use or time-saving, to indicating an enhanced 'capacity to shift, juggle and reorder episodes and events' (Shove 2003: 170). Chen's ability to spatially and temporally separate the consumption of a service (in this case, his rice porridge breakfast) from the act of payment allows him and the vendor to continually reaffirm their mutual trust in one another. Here, money acts as more than just a means of settling dues owed: the repertoires surrounding its exchange possess communicative capacities through which migrant workers seek to add density to their daily social interactions within an otherwise largely anonymous and uncaring city.

The Problems of Embedding Exchange amidst Weak Ties

While factory workers' accounts of their use of WeChat Wallet seemed to centre on economic activities that embedded exchange within broader social relationships, such an arrangement was largely resisted on QQ Wallet, where the involvement of money on the platform was regarded as largely incommensurate with the envisaged sociality seen as inherent to QQ itself. A key reason for this perceived incompatibility came from the fact that many of the contacts which factory workers kept on their QQ accounts were in fact previous classmates from school or other people from their home town. This was partly due to the fact that QQ had been in use as far back as 1999, whereas WeChat had only launched in 2011. While WeChat had successfully established itself as the hub of sustained interaction with an individual's closest family or friends, workers' interactions with contacts on QQ were, by contrast, often spasmodic and comparatively free from obligations (such as the need to maintain sustained interaction, reply promptly or engage in the exchange of gifts or favours). When interactions did occur on QQ, they often took place through the platform's online games, QZone social networking function as well as the instant messaging chat tool.

Granovetter's (1973) discussion of 'weak ties' is useful in making sense of why migrant workers judged the social interactions that took place on QQ to be an altogether less suitable venue for the embedding of various forms of economic exchange. Granovetter argues that far from being inconsequential, weak ties are actually central to interpersonal flows because large networks of such ties create multiple paths along which interpersonal flows (of information, goods, etc.) may travel. Granovetter asserts that 'removal of the average weak tie would do more "damage" to transmission probabilities than would that of the average strong one' (1973: 1366). QQ's emphasis on gaming, the sharing of photos and chatting meant that the platform was considered to be comparatively entertaining and playful. Granovetter's notion of weak ties becomes significant once we consider more specifically what kinds of interpersonal flows QQ was judged to be appropriate for. While personal photos, activities of gaming avatars and informal chatter sustained such loose connections with comparatively little effort, in the case of migrant worker participants, money was considered to be largely improper within such flows. This is not to say that money could not act in impersonal ways (as will be discussed in the final section below, sometimes the impersonal qualities of money were actively exploited by workers).

Qualms regarding the embedding of exchange amidst weak ties became especially acute in the context of strangers, as many workers had previously used the QQ network as a venue for meeting and chatting to strangers, resulting in their contact list on the platform containing numerous individuals whom they had never met offline. Elsewhere, I have written extensively on how online spaces in China have become a key domain through which individuals explore and enact imaginations of the stranger and have explained the various moral anxieties that emerge from such interactions (McDonald 2016; McDonald Forthcoming). However, in the context of the migrant factory workers in this study, doubts surrounding the authenticity of users on QQ often intermingled with concerns around the use of digital money, or the potential risks of accounts owned by friends being hacked into by unknown individuals who then might falsely purport to be their friend. A migrant factory worker named Zhang recounted once receiving multiple messages from a friends' account asking to borrow money through the platform. Wang, a male factory worker, shared his own thoughts on why QQ was particularly prone to such deception:

> In my own opinion I don't think QQ is that safe … WeChat is comparatively safer. For QQ, I only have to know your account number, then it is possible to hack your QQ.
>
> (interview)

Furthermore, many workers reported that their QQ accounts contained many more contacts than was the case for WeChat. While this may have partly been a function of the longer duration that most migrant workers had been using QQ for, many workers saw this as a further indicator of the unsuitability of QQ for handling financial transactions. When delays in processing transactions occurred, this was interpreted as being evidence that the network was overburdened with users. As male migrant worker Xie explained:

> QQ Wallet, normally that network is poor quality. Too many people use it, so I don't use it that much. Sometimes after you use it, at 8 o'clock you get a message saying [the money] is sent, but it won't arrive in the account until 10 pm. That's inconvenient.
>
> (interview)

While the abundance of weak ties and unknown strangers on QQ led to this platform being thought of as ideal for gaming or largely inconsequential chatter, this same characteristic also resulted in migrant participants viewing QQ as being almost *too* social, raising concerns about the safety of keeping money in one's QQ Wallet.

'Economic Connections' and Private Accounting

The final group of transactions detailed in this chapter regards those that migrant workers felt to be more directly shaped by market processes and were therefore understood to be comparatively free from social and emotional interaction. Transactions falling into this category were largely clustered on the Alipay payment platform. Alipay differed from both WeChat Wallet and QQ Wallet in that this platform had not emerged within a pre-existing social media service. Alipay's origins were instead a payment processing tool for online shopping marketplaces such as Taobao and Alibaba. Only later did the platform begin to offer customers the ability to transfer funds between individuals, face-to-face payment in stores and savings accounts. Although Alipay was felt to disembed economic transactions from social relations, this was generally not perceived to be a problem by migrant workers; in fact, participants actually suggested that this feature was central to its appeal. Workers often claimed that Alipay's relative disconnect from online social networks made it ideal for large transactions and the storage of personal savings. One worker explained that he preferred to use the network for expensive purchases 'like travel tickets, plane tickets, hotels' (interview). Similarly, while WeChat Wallet was often accepted in small local shops, Alipay was more often accepted in larger supermarkets and department stores.

Several workers saw the distinctive handling of contacts on Alipay as an additional indicator of the disembedding of transactions from social relations that the platform offered. Alipay's contact list feature differed from that of WeChat and QQ in that users generally only added others to this list for the explicit purpose of transferring funds. Although users could allow Alipay to access their phone's contact list, the dominance of WeChat and QQ as social media platforms meant that it was far more common for individuals to maintain contact by 'friending' each other within WeChat or QQ itself, rather than through exchanging mobile phone numbers. This resulted in the overall number of contacts being made available by allowing Alipay access to one's phone contact list remaining comparatively small. However, rather than viewing the relative absence of one's extended circle of friends and family from one's Alipay contact list as a matter of inconvenience, migrant worker Li instead held the opinion that this afforded him greater control over which of his personal contacts he wished to interact with on the platform: 'In reality [Alipay's contacts] are choice-based, normally you will manually add people, but generally speaking… if you don't have any financial exchange, then you won't add [them]' (interview). Factory workers apparent enthusiasm for this comparatively selective venue for conducting economic exchange thus appears to run contrary to the pattern described in the previous two sections, which asserted that economic transactions tend to be more embedded when they appear within stronger social ties.

This anomaly might in part be explained by considering the degree to which migrant workers perceived those connections occurring on Alipay as being social at all. The testimony of factory labourer Zhao is particularly illuminating in this respect: 'Normally there is no communication with contacts on Alipay, it's normally only an economic connection. Alipay contacts ... they're mainly based on money, apart from this there is not really any other use [for Alipay]' (interview). What is so interesting about Zhao's position is that it suggests that while workers do, in one sense, evaluate digital payment platforms by preferring to use services which allow for the submerging of economic activity within social relations (as seen in the case of WeChat Wallet's selection over QQ Wallet), workers concurrently seek out the utility offered by those platforms, such as Alipay, which facilitate relatively depersonalised market exchanges. Even users themselves appear to play a hand in preserving Alipay's status as a venue for 'purely economic' transactions. Deng, a male migrant worker in a factory, explained how the commonly perceived 'transactional' nature of Alipay meant that those trying to engender social exchanges on the platform would provoke mistrust in the eyes of fellow users: 'Normally, ... if you send out friend requests [on Alipay]... a lot of people will not accept the invitation, they think you are trying to borrow money or something like that'. Similarly, Alipay has at various times tried to implement top-down efforts to introduce new 'social' features onto the platform, which have often been met with resistance from users (He 2016).

Workers' perceptions of a separation of Alipay from their own social networks could be further witnessed in the case of *Yu'e bao*, a special savings account feature that had been introduced onto the platform in 2013. Unlike the main digital storage wallets offered (WeChat, QQ and Alipay), Yu'e bao paid customers interest on funds kept in this special wallet built into the Alipay platform. These interest rates were higher than those offered by conventional accounts from mostly state-owned banks, which were in turn fixed by China's central bank. Yu'e bao appealed thanks to the fact that it awarded customers with daily interest payments which were made visible on the platform, a practice which contrasted sharply with retail banks, where paying interest on an annual or monthly basis remained the norm. Yu'e bao has proved tremendously popular across China, with the amount stored on the platform increasing from 0.2 billion RMB in 2013 to over 810 billion in 2017 (Kapron and Meertens 2017). Almost all migrant worker participants reported using this service. Furthermore, most spoke about it in favourable terms, especially when compared to their experiences of retail banking. Numerous workers described how Yu'e bao was becoming central to their savings strategy, despite the fact that the increasing costs of living in the city (caused by rocketing rental charges, food prices, etc.) and the stalling salaries (owing to increasing lack of availability of overtime work) meant that factory labourers often reported finding it difficult to put away money every month. While some workers expressed interest in starting a business or investing in the stock market, most felt these options too risky in nature.

Saving through Yu'e Bao constituted an altogether safer option, with its guaranteed returns being appreciated by workers favouring more conservative forms of investment. Worker Hu explained that Yu'e Bao was reliable in that 'Every day [interest payments] arrive in my account. It records it every day' (interview). Alipay (along with its Yu'e Bao service) is thus precisely of interest because it seems—at least when compared against other platforms—to best embody formalist economic ideals. By establishing itself as relatively separated from the interpersonal connections of kinship and friendship that typify WeChat and QQ, Alipay has come to be regarded as suited for impersonal transactions with large business or online retailers and for facilitating individual accumulation of wealth. Alipay manages to fulfil workers' own desires to engage in some of the few market processes disembedded from social relations that they regard to be to their advantage given their otherwise precarious economic situation. Although the ability to save some money when purchasing goods online, to avoid having to queue in the bank, or to gain a slightly higher interest rate may seem somewhat paltry rewards given the otherwise extractive nature of the wage labour and rental economy they are the subjects of, their adoption of Alipay services nonetheless points to a willingness for money to be both digitalised and depersonalised when it produces efficacious situations. While Alipay was predominantly viewed by migrant worker participants as best suited for relatively obligation-free economic exchanges, it is worth mentioning that there were certain exceptions to this case.

One such example was the use of Alipay by migrants for the purpose of sending remittances to kin from their place of origin. Although not all migrant workers continued to send money home to their parents, for those who did, Alipay was often preferred because it helped them avoid the bank charges incurred when transferring money between banks in different provinces. Furthermore, Alipay had introduced a feature that, for a small fee, made it possible for users to initiate transfers directly to a traditional bank account. Migrant worker participants described how useful this feature was, given that their own parents and grandparents were often reluctant to use such digital payment platforms themselves. Migrant labourer Wang astutely pointed out why, even if their seniors had access to Alipay accounts, it would likely be of limited use in their rural environs. 'They have no need [for Alipay], because everything on Taobao is young people's things: dresses, clothes, these things… if people from my hometown bought these things to wear at home, it wouldn't quite fit' (interview). Wang's description is significant in a broader sense, in that it serves to demonstrate how various forms of money—both digital and otherwise—are often tied into particular infrastructures which may in turn limit their ability to be exchanged for particular goods, commodities or other monetary forms.

More broadly though, the exceptional issue of remittances sent through Alipay helps frame the above comparison of the three distinctive constellations of embedding and disembedding of market processes within social relations, by making clear the kinds of complexities of practice that might easily be effaced by the generalisations this chapter is attempting to make. The fact that Alipay, the platform which migrants predominantly associated with dispassionate, transactional exchanges, also served to facilitate some migrants' remittances to their parents is significant when one stops to consider what such remittances may mean. Stafford has discussed in some detail the debt of nurturance that underlies parent–child relationships in China, whereby adult children feel a responsibility to return the nurturance their parents bestowed on them when they were young (2000). Thought of these terms, Alipay remittances serve as a reminder that while the affordances of particular exchange platforms often tend to intersect with the sociability of money in distinctive ways, individual acts of exchange are always dependent upon a multitude of idiosyncratic factors and considerations, which can equally give rise to unexpected uses and outcomes.

Embedding and Disembedding Processes

This chapter has documented the existence of a broad spectrum of arrangements of market processes that range from integration within to separation from, social relationships. I have shown how new technologies for the use of digital money in China can be highly embedded in social relations through facilitating everyday practices of reciprocity, redistribution and remuneration. This is particularly the case in instances where strong social ties exist between those carrying out exchange (as seen in WeChat Wallet), whereas the presence of weak ties tends to lead to the exclusion of digital monetary exchange from such relations (QQ Wallet). The propensity of digital money to be employed in such acts of exchange is, however, decidedly more complex than a simple correlation between strength of tie and density of exchange, as demonstrated in the case of Alipay, which has come to be viewed as a platform primarily for the facilitation of depersonalised and 'purely economic' connections. The clustering of these specific ideologies and practices of monetary exchange around particular digital media platforms—along with notable exceptions to such norms—underlines the fact that these patterns are indicative not of sharp cleavages, but rather a general spectrum of uses for new digital monetary forms which tend to be shaped by the affordances of specific digital payment platforms. This finding is of broader significance in two different ways. First, it helps to build a more nuanced picture of the subjectivity of migrant factory workers in China. Often such workers are (for good reason) portrayed as being at the receiving end of global economic processes that are overwhelmingly extractive in nature. This is especially the case for those workers employed in intensive modes of assembly line labour of the kind carried out by the participants in this study, most of whom were involved in the manufacture of consumer electronics goods.

While workers' adoption of the kind of embedded exchanges seen in WeChat might appear to be a logical route for them to counter the depersonalising effects of the global monopoly capital inherent in their labour relations (Pun 2016: 105–133), such an assumption is arguably undermined by their own engagement in the kinds of private accounting activities that are centred within Alipay and which leverage impersonal interactions, wide networks and (through Yu'e Bao) concepts of individual accumulation. My argument here is not so much that factory labourers are being inconsistent in their economic actions, but rather that it is important to find ways to avoid one-dimensional renderings of workers' capacities as financial actors. By acknowledging the fact that factory workers increasingly elect to store leftover money on Alipay, in part because it is understood to be less implicated in the continuing social flows of money between kin and friends, one may also point towards alignment with ongoing processes of individualisation occurring across Chinese society (Yan 2009). Aside from acknowledging the economic agency of Chinese migrant factory workers, the divergent nature of economic practices across digital money platforms is also useful in a second sense, in helping to lay the ground to start to re-examine some of the questions central to economic anthropology in the light of the development of new monetary forms.

The distinct ways that digital money platforms appear (in conjunction with their associated norms of use) to foster different processes of embedding and disembedding challenge both outright substantivist and formalist positions by instead showing individuals' willingness to employ particular ideologies of money at moments when they appear to be beneficial to themselves. In one sense, digital money appears to be not that different from money in its traditional forms, in that it is always both personal and impersonal (Hart 2007). This realisation is of significance, however, on returning to think through the kinds of emancipatory assumptions surrounding digital money that were mentioned in the introduction to this chapter. If one is truly attempting to assess whether novel forms of digital money are really 'both expanding financial inclusion and economic opportunity' in China, as suggested by Kapron and Marteens, then this chapter underlines the limitations of techno-deterministic assumptions that digital payment technologies will necessarily produce specific social effects (2017: 8). Without understanding the degree to which economic action is embedded in, or disembedded from, social relations, and the social contexts and underlying motivations within which such processes occur, there is a risk that our own particularistic notions of what constitutes financial inclusion and economic opportunity may come to overshadow the interpretations of precisely those individuals that our very discussions are intended to be in aid of.

Acknowledgements

I am especially grateful to Adrian Athique, Emma Baulch, Pun Ngai, Joy Lin and Guo Yanan for their comments on earlier drafts of this chapter. The work described in this chapter was supported by a grant from the Research Grants Council of the Hong Kong Special Administrative Region, China (Project No. HKU 27606617) and by The University of Hong Kong.

References

Bruckermann, Charlotte and Feuchtwang, Stephen (2016) *The Anthropology of China: China as Ethnographic and Theoretical Critique*, London: Imperial College Press.

China Internet Network Information Center (2015) *35th Statistical Report on Internet Development in China*. Available: https://cnnic.com.cn/IDR/ReportDownloads/201611/P020161114, accessed: 6 October 2018.

China Internet Network Information Center (2018) *41st Statistical Report on Internet Development in China*. Available: https://cnnic.com.cn/IDR/ReportDownloads/201807/P020180711391, accessed: 6 October 2018.

The Economist (2016) 'WeChat's World: China's WeChat Shows the Way to Social Media's Future', *The Economist*, 6 August 2016. Available: www.economist.com/business/2016/08/06/wechats-world, accessed: 6 October 2018.

Granovetter, Mark (1973) 'The Strength of Weak Ties', *American Journal of Sociology*, 78: 1360–1380.

Hart, Keith (2007) 'Money Is Always Personal and Impersonal', *Anthropology Today*, 23(5): 12–16.

Kapron, Zennon and Meertens, Michelle (2017) 'Social Networks, E-Commerce Platforms, and the Growth of Digital Payment Ecosystems in China: What It Means for Other Countries'. Available: www.betterthancash.org/tools-research/case-studies/social-networks-ecommerce-platforms-and-the-growth-of-digital-payment-ecosystems-in-china, accessed: 30 September 2018.

Martin, Emily (2014) *The Meaning of Money in China and the United States*, Chicago, IL: Hau Books.

Marx, Karl (1976 [1867]) *Capital: Critique of Political Economy*, London: Penguin Books.

Maurer, Bill (2015) *How Would You Like to Pay?: How Technology Is Changing the Future of Money*, Durham, NC: Duke University Press.

McDonald, Tom (2016) *Social Media in Rural China: Social Networks and Moral Frameworks*, London: UCL Press.

McDonald, Tom (Forthcoming) 'Strangership and Social Media: Moral Imaginaries of Gendered Strangers in Rural China', *American Anthropologist*.

Ngai, Pun (2016) *Migrant Labor in China: Post-Socialist Transformations*, Cambridge: Polity.

Niu, Q. (2014) 'iOS banshouji QQ jiaru QQ qianbao gongneng tengxun shou Q he Weixin liangtiao tui zuo yidong zhifu (iOS version of QQ mobile adds QQ Wallet function. Tencent mobile Q and WeChat, doing mobile payments on both fronts)'. Available: https://cn.technode.com/post/2014-03-21/qq-mobile-payment/, accessed: 6 October 2018.

Polanyi, Karl (1944) *The Great Transformation*, Boston, MA: Beacon Press.

Qiu, Jack (2009) *Working-Class Network Society: Communication Technology and the Information Have-Less in Urban China*, Cambridge: The MIT Press.

Shove, Elizabeth (2003) *Comfort, Cleanliness and Convenience: the Social Organization of Normality*, Oxford: Berg.

Simmel, Georg (1978 [1900]) *The Philosophy of Money*, London: Routledge and Kegan Paul.

Stafford, Charles (2000) Chinese Patriliny and the Cycles of Yang and Laiwang', in Carsten Janet (ed) *Cultures of Relatedness: New Approaches to the Study of Kinship*, Cambridge: Cambridge University Press, pp. 37–54.

Steinmüller, Hans (2011) 'The Moving Boundaries of Social Heat: Gambling in Rural China', *Journal of the Royal Anthropological Institute*, 17(2): 263–280.

Sun, Wanning (2014) *Subaltern China: Rural Migrants, Media, and Cultural Practices*, Lanham, MD: Rowman & Littlefield.

Wallis Cara (2013) *Technomobility in China: Young Migrant Women and Mobile Phones*, New York: NYU Press.

Wang Xinyuan (2016) *Social Media in Industrial China*, London: UCL Press.

Yan, Yunxiang (2009) *The Individualization of Chinese Society*, Oxford: Berg.

9 The Digital State

A Tale of Tweets and Foods in Contemporary India

Rajiv K. Mishra

The relationship between state and citizens is no longer confined to the realms of physical space and material media. The state has extended to the digital space, thereby shaping new forms of transactional relationships between citizens and the state. This is reflected with the launch of Digital India programme in 2015 after the Bharatiya Janata Party (BJP) government led by Prime Minister Narendra Modi came to power. This programme has been envisioned with three core areas 'raising digital infrastructures as a core utility', 'governance service on demand' and 'digital empowerment of citizens' (Digital India 2015). In this context, the 'digital state' emerges as both a logistical and discursive force. At one level, the digital state makes its presence in social media domains, where the projection of a Digital India as public engagement exercise works to connect with technologically savvy citizens using Twitter, and glorify the use of technology and 'democratic governance'. However, the digital state also makes its presence strongly felt in the logistics of everyday life by compelling the poor to come under the grip of technology to access food provided by the public distribution system (PDS) that is now ensconced within digital infrastructures centred upon biometric technologies. This chapter attempts to juxtapose the tale of these two faces of the digital state in an illustrative sketch of the 'answerability' of the state in these two digital domains. In the domain of Twitter, I seek to understand the projection of the digital state as technologically savvy, 'democratic' and responsive to citizens. In the domain of PDS, where citizens are compelled to use digital technologies for access, the digital state refuses to be answerable to the suffering caused by malfunction and exclusion. This two-faced sketch of the digital state draws upon mixed methods research using sampled tweets, newspaper archives, in-depth qualitative interviews and qualitative interviews from districts of Delhi and Jharkhand during April and October 2017.

With the vast Digital India programme operating as the flagship of government policy across the breadth of social and economic domains, the centrality of the digital in present times is beyond dispute. These various applications of digital technologies in systemic conglomerations have, by their very design, significant material and political ramifications (Abbate

1999; Winner 1980). At the larger scale, the digital state institutes distinctive connotations of technology and politics that come together to form a ruling regime. As such, we should understand digital applications as sociotechnical systems, which always have historical, social, economic and political underpinnings (Hecht and Allen 2001; Hughes 2000). In practical terms, the development of digital technologies must be analysed through the logics of sociotechnical systems, rather than simply via algorithmic processes and associated claims of neutrality and efficiency. Certainly, the social media and biometric technologies on which I focus here are substantially embedded into the social domain, with the deployment of both these applications illuminating the contrasting realities of contemporary India (Elzen et al. 1996; Shukla 2013). Fundamentally, a 'digitizing' India is characterized by disparities at an extreme level, and this basic reality constitutes a stark setting where competing notions of voluntariness and compulsion in the digital domain determine the dynamics of the technology-driven government-citizen relationship.

The Indian elections of 2014 and the creation of a new political regime ran in parallel with the emergence of new styles of state-to-public relations, especially through new technologies of social media coming to prominence (Coleman 2005). The current Government of India has placed great emphasis upon its intention of using social media as a listening tool for governance and democracy (Financial Times 2014). Much more widely, the drive towards digitalization has been systematized through the umbrella programme of 'Digital India'. At various levels, this programme aims to deploy digital platforms in state functions, to modernize urban environments and financial systems, and to further the development of e-governance and e-democracy, such as initiatives like *'be involved'* where people can contribute through 'Do', 'Discuss', 'Polls' and 'Talk' categories (Government of India 2015). The benefits are supposedly to have greater efficiencies in state services with enhanced digital participation of people by encouraging the use of digital services in the economy. In turn, this is assumed to bring about a drastic reduction of corruption and waste of public expenditure, while creating an interactive system for deepening and widening participation of citizens in the world's largest democracy. Evidently, this participatory dimension of governmental works and policy formulations is dependent upon the ease of use of digital technologies by citizens. In that respect, the vast ambitions of e-governance are subject to material constraints and ideological blind spots within the prevailing 'governmentality' of the Indian state.

Official Twitter accounts are one highly visible component of 'Digital India' as a project of the state, while the other side of this emerging reality is the massive expansion of biometrics technology-enabled food supplies, where citizens are rendered variously invisible or illegible. My contention is that these two faces of the digital state articulate common yet differentiated aspects of the government's transactional approach to its citizens. In the high-visibility domain of social media, the state seeks to project its 'answerableness' to people who are using Twitter as a medium of connecting with the government. On the other front, the compulsory enrolment for Aadhaar and biometrics-enabled PDS for millions to access food grains allows the state to become at once arbitrary and impenetrable. In both instances, the temper of technological governance is best demonstrated where people face exclusions and the 'answerableness' of government is tested. The basic objective of this chapter, therefore, is to highlight the seemingly arbitrary nature of both interactive and distributive governance in India. It attempts to do so by juxtaposing both visible and invisible domains, so that we can make an early test of the promise of the digital state in India.

A Tale of Tweets

The massive use of digital social media platforms like Twitter and Facebook during the 2014 central government elections was unprecedented in India. It reflected the rapid rise of internet users in India from 22.2 million in 2004 to 233.1 million in 2014 (Internet World Stats 2018). The BJP, led by Narendra Modi, made strenuous efforts to capitalize upon its social media presence and to 'target' a large number of Indian voters, with this activity being seen as one of the cardinal factors for success in the 2014 general elections (Ahmed et al. 2016). Narendra Modi was the face of the BJP during elections, and after winning the elections, he tweeted, '*India has won! भारत की वजिय। अच्छे दनि आने वाले हैं।*' (Twitter 2014). With a presence of having 17.3 thousand tweets and 34 million followers as of date, the Prime Minister has invested deeply in social media and digital technologies for connecting to people. These new political uses of social media have become possible due to the rise of Web 2.0 with its interactive and participative features, thereby transforming the business of democratic politics across much of the world in a short space of time (Bargh et al. 2014; Barnett et al. 2017; Blank and Reisdorf 2012; Briendli and Francq 2008; Hague and Loader 1999; Vromen 2017). In conceptual terms, this was presaged by a new discussion of e-democracy, which was itself an extension of the ongoing debate on e-governance (Chadwick 2008; Dunleavy et al. 2011; Loader and Mercea 2012; Madon 2004; Mazzarella 2006). As the participatory public sphere has developed in practice, these policy objectives have tended to be eclipsed by debates emerging from the rise of political 'populism' and the everyday experience of 'government by Twitter', notably in the United States but also elsewhere.

Consequently, Twitter and its role in participatory governance have been discussed and contested by scholars, with obvious connotations for governance and democracy (Ahmed et al. 2016; Jungherr 2014; Murthy

2013; Schwanholz et al. 2018; Sunstein 2018; Tufekci 2017). There are multiple vantage points for understanding the discursive expressions of the state in platforms such as Twitter. The first one incorporates using Twitter to connect to a large number of people for opinion building and influencing their votes during elections which many political parties around the world have done (Jungherr 2014; Small 2011). The second revolves around the use of Twitter to share information related to day-to-day governance, political figures, parties and the works of the regime in power (Boyd et al. 2010; Jason and Kevin 2014; Pang and Ng 2016; Weller et al. 2014). A third articulation emerges from a bidirectional relationship between citizens and governments, where tweets from citizens are used for improving the norms and responsiveness of governance. In the context of populism, a fourth approach could contextualize a hybrid mix of the second and third poles, where Twitter is used primarily for maintaining the popularity of a political leader or party governance. Finally, a fifth pole to the Twitter universe can consider the 'selective answerableness' within a 'tokenistic' democratic space provided to the Twitter audience (Athique 2013; Chadwick 2013; Hindman 2008; Papacharissi 2010; Sunstein 2018). Given the official discourses linking digital technologies with idealistic accounts of efficiency, participation and progress, there is a dearth of literature on issues about the fourth and fifth points in the case of India.

Naturally, the vantage point of analysis determines the topical selection and sampling pattern of Twitter analysis (Burgess et al. 2017; Fuchs 2014). Thus, for our purposes, one face of the digital state is explored here via archival material using *Times of India* online archives and Twitter data (accessed using specific keywords and #hashtags, collated with the help of standard Twitter search). Using these two sources of data, I undertake a litmus test of the democratic channels of e-governance via Twitter. This usefully indicates the contours of the current Government of India's attempt to interact with a new class of technologically savvy Indians and 'speak' to them through the medium of Twitter. For the Twitter data, a small, systematic sample was selected with hashtags and keywords including: #PMOIndia, #FinMinIndia, #RailMinIndia, @ HRDMinistry and @SushmaSwaraj. Given the interpenetration of Twitter as a medium of public interaction and the production and circulation of news in 'mainstream' outlets, I have also analysed archival material from *Times of India* through a random sample of Twitter-related news carried over the three months from 15 August 2017 to 15 November 2017. A further source is the top-right corner of the official web page for 'Digital India', where there are three links to social media platforms: Facebook, Twitter and YouTube (Digital India 2015). Clicking on the Twitter link takes viewers to the official Twitter handle of Digital India, which provides prompts for following other ministries and departments of Government of India.

One thing that seems immediately apparent is use of Twitter by PM and PMO office for extensive information sharing and public relations campaigns. But where citizens are trying to reach the PMO via Twitter, using the hashtag #PMOIndia for their complaints and grievances, there are certainly interesting insights into the temper of participatory democracy in India. One of the tweets mentions: 'Corruption has continued in Gujarat traffic police, they picked up my vehicle and took Rs 200 without slip, and then gave me my bike'. Another tweet says: 'We are indebted to all farmers and answerable to 3 Lakh and more farmers' families who committed suicide'. Further another tweet mentions: 'It's not only about salary, it's about our dignity too. We demand removal of pay anomaly of CIL executives'. Clearly, the citizens who tweeted about the problems in Coal India Limited pay anomalies, intense agrarian crisis and the issue of day–to-day corruption in the Prime minister's home state expected some reply. None was forthcoming. Given the many contentious issues around the implementation of GST at the national level, many citizens also used the PMO tag to highlight anomalies in the GST implementation: 'Govt. has reduced GST by 13% (5% instead of 18%) on Restaurants, But MacDonalds has increased basic rates. The net rates to customer remain same'. Another tweet with a hashtag of #FinMinIndia also mentions the reality of GST implementation, 'Business will find a way to cheat GST or No GST or Reduce GST rate'. None of these tweets received an official reply.

In the predigital era, the reception desk of many public offices supported thick ledgers titled 'Complaint Books'. In the era of digital governance, the offices and ledgers appear to have been replaced by media platforms. Thus, one tweet asks: 'As a common man, where can I complain', with the self-evident answer appearing to be Twitter. However, as much as the official Twitter accounts of #PMOIndia, #FinMinIndia and @HRDMinistry are being used by citizens for lodging their grievances, none of these tweets in my sample received any official response. However, it was also the case that some ministries and respective ministers did selectively reply to tweets directed to them with help of a specific hashtag, as in the case of #RailMinIndia and #SuhmaSwaraj. A traveller tweets,

> Train No. 12873 late by 9 hours, still in train and praying so that at least train reaches by 12, losing patience, dear we are common people may be next time you are in not on driver seat. Be careful.

To this, the official RailMinIndia twitter handle replied with a message saying forwarded to concerned official. Another tweet had a pinch of humour, 'Bhai you Mera failed transaction ka refund dila do, bullet train baad main chalana, 3 mahine ho gaye hain'. This person raises a common issue of failed digital transactions and problems in refund mechanisms, suggesting it is better to resolve current problems then commence a bullet train project. This did not receive a reply. Out the tweets directed to foreign affairs minister (hashtag #SuhmaSwaraj), only one received a reply. This was the case of a non-citizen from Pakistan who wanted to come to India for medical treatment, who tweeted, 'After Allah, you are our last hope: Pakistani to #SushmaSwaraj'. Sushma Swaraj replied to this tweet and assured medical visa would be provided (NDTV 2015).

Another case, reported in the mainstream media, was of a user who tweeted #SushmaSwaraj about her passport-related problem and to whom Sushma Swaraj replied. These rare instances have furnished Sushma Swaraj with the reputation of being an approachable politician and responsive minister, despite their being random anomalies to an overwhelming pattern of non-response. In 100 tweets from five different hashtags, #PMOIndia, #FinMinIndia, #RailMinIndia, #SushmaSwaraj and @HRDMinistry, only three had official replies: two from Railways and one from Sushma Swaraj. Nonetheless, this selective answerableness becomes a source of motivation for many to join Twitter, feeling that they may have some opportunity to petition ministers and ministries. On their part, the state with its functionaries and organizations apparently shows selective choice in answering to people who tag their official Twitter handles with a specific hashtag. It would be cynical, but not perhaps unfair, to suggest that responses are provided in instances where attention to a user's tweet carries the potential of a good media story. The print media now regularly covers the stories of official replies by leaders and functionaries of the government. In my sample of Twitter-related news, three different types of patterns emerged: first, news on acknowledging common peoples' request; second, tweets between political leaders demonstrating praise or discord; and, third, incidences of problematic tweets from government functionaries, their removal and the apologies which followed. This pattern indicates (1) that the ruling regime knows the value of maintaining healthy public relations with people through social media activity, and (2) that the mainstream press recognizes the utility of Twitter as a 'no cost' news feed that conveys the impression of a participatory democracy. This, then, is a new reality being served on the premise of voluntariness, and which caters to the purposes of Twitter by encouraging users on the basis of their desire to be 'heard' by the state. It is obviously not logically feasible to respond equitably to citizens through this medium, which supports my conclusion that this lottery of ministerial patronage is a tokenistic expression of e-democracy.

A Tale of Foods

In contrast to the symbolic domain of 'volunteerness', 'participation' and 'selective answerability' constituted within the domain of Twitter, the second part of this chapter focuses on understanding the fresh compulsions placed upon citizens by the state when it comes to enrolling under biometrics-enabled PDS services. The PDS is a food grain supply system based on socio-economic welfare model of the Indian state. It is a lifeline for poor and especially the below poverty line (BPL) category of people who get food grains in highly subsidized rates from government as they cannot afford to buy food grains at market prices. For this analysis, I draw upon my fieldwork data from one district (South West) of Delhi and two districts (Khunti and Ranchi) of Jharkhand. I have drawn sample from these districts based on the idea of centre (Delhi) and periphery (Jharkhand) to understand how digital practices are being unfolded in the context of geographical and political advantages of locations. Furthermore, having sample from these two states helps to understand the homogenization of accessing digital services in an extremely socioculturally complex country like India. To put this in context: The Indian state is making use of biometrics technologies on a massive scale for identification and authentication of its citizens, ostensibly to ensure the accessibility and delivery of services. This is clearly listed as one of the key objectives of Digital India as per the methodology and approach (Digital India 2015). Among its nine listed points, two of them mention optimal utilization of ICT infrastructure and adoption of unique ID for identification, authentication and delivery of benefits.

Consequently, biometrics and its use for development services have been widely discussed in the Indian context (Aiyar 2017). Some of the challenges coming to the fore with the massive expansion of biometric technologies revolve around numerous aspects of privacy, surveillance and new forms of technological exclusions (Gold 2011; Greenleaf 2010; Krakovsky 2011; Ramanathan 2015). To access food grains via PDS, people have to have an Aadhaar card; if someone does not have an Aadhaar card, then PDS services cannot be availed. Thus, at the most basic level of everyday life, biometrics-enabled PDS is causing severe problems of deniability and exclusion from one of the most important social security programmes of India (Drèze and Khera 2017; Masiero 2015; Shiva 2004). This exclusion is happening due to the compulsory nature of the scheme, the sheer size of the population and the various technological and bureaucratic bugs that afflict the world's largest citizen-registration programme. Although the Supreme Court of India issued a directive in 2015 making Aadhaar card enrolment and its use voluntary and not mandatory, people have effectively been given no voluntary choice of enrolling for Aadhaar in relation to its seeding with PDS (Supreme Court of India 2015a). The recent verdict on Right to Privacy by the Supreme Court has e-emphasized the voluntary choice of people to provide their Aadhaar details or enrol for Aadhaar-based services (Supreme

Court of India 2015b). Nonetheless, along with PDS, the Government of India has pushed for mandatory linking of bank accounts, mobile connections, gas connections, scholarships, pensions and almost all government services with set deadlines. Evidently, this is a tussle between ideas of freedom and control in the day-to-day functions of the digital state, a tussle that reflects competing realities on the dialectic of technological choice and compulsion (Drèze and Khera 2017; Dreze and Sen 2002; Dunleavy et al. 2011; Sreekumar and Rivera-Sánchez 2008). Accordingly, we can readily deduce that while the participation of citizens in the public sphere is voluntary and selective, participation in the digitization of everyday services is constituted as compulsory and universal. This mode of governmentality has significant implications in a vast country afflicted by uneven access to connectivity along with everything else.

The greater reliance of the most marginal and poverty afflicted segments of the population also makes them acutely vulnerable to breakdowns and errors in the mechanisms of these government programmes. With such a vast population, even a small margin of error puts millions of people at risk. While talking to people in one of the urban villages of a Delhi district, residents mentioned that there is simply no assistance available when they face problems in accessing their ration provisions. On the same basis, in a discussion with a group of six to seven women in a remote village of Jharkhand, their distress and displeasure with the state was very apparent and clear. One of the women very vocally said:

> government got this made, but when we face issues with access of our food grains, no one seems to give any attention to it, many times we have to come back since there is no connectivity or the machine does not work.
>
> (interview)

All of the women mentioned that none of the responsible officials were prepared to visit their village to address their grievances and the acute problems caused by technological failures. There was no effective mechanism in place to raise awareness about problems at the point of delivery and provide advice on what people should do. They might, if they were able to, send a tweet perhaps to #PMO. In practice, it is only these face-to-face encounters that reveal the extent to which the ground-level mechanism of biometrics-enabled PDS is a shamble in the places it is needed most.

Furthermore, when asked why they enrolled for Aadhaar, most of them affirmed that they were compelled and were left with no choice if they wished to receive food rations. Most of them mentioned that it was the PDS dealer who compulsorily asked for Aadhaar details and told them that this was the government's directive. One of the villagers said: 'I had some problems with my Aadhaar card, there was a mistake in the name, from the time this has happened, my name was removed from PDS list, I have been facing a lot of problems' (interview). In a similar account, a very old aged person who could only walk with the help of stick had his reality to share. When asked does he have Aadhaar card, he replies: 'I had Aadhaar card, but now there is some problem with it'. He could not articulate the problem, but elaborated by saying:

> I used to get old age pension and use to avail food grains using ration for my wife and me. These were our support since we both are on our own and we don't have anyone to look for us. We don't have any income source, but all of it has stopped now since there is some problem with the card, they have removed us from PDS list and also my pension has stopped.
>
> (interview)

When asked what he has done to resolve the problem or get anyone to help him, he made a sign of helplessness and discomfort, and simply said his problem is unresolved and no one bothers about it. His incomprehension speaks profoundly about the disjunctures inherent in propelling a vulnerable agrarian community into the arbitrary and automated vision of digital governance.

In discussions with other respondents who were PDS beneficiaries under BPL category, a clear pattern of discomfort was apparent. An angry woman, categorized as BPL, was deeply unhappy about the way she and other villagers had to negotiate the reality of the biometrics machines that now govern PDS. Showing her displeasure, she explained:

> For poor people nobody cares, we have to make rounds of the PDS shop due to problems in the machine, sometimes we don't get it for two months and if we go on the third month the PDS dealer denies our rations [....] sometimes there is problem with machine, some time network is not there, what are we supposed to do, should we die of hunger?
>
> (interview)

Adding to this narrative, another woman mentioned: 'I have almost every time faced problems with my fingerprint scans, and I had to call someone from home to provide their biometrics, but there are many families who face the problem in readability of their fingerprints' (interview). When asked whether these problems are being resolved, or had been resolved at any point in time, or whether anyone from the village council or block officials had been able to address these problems, all of them concurred that no one is concerned or willing to provide assistance. The problems which they are facing and frustration of not being heard reflected a sense of feeling that their lives had no value to the state. One of the farmers in a village depicted this stark reality by saying:

> Sir, I am farmer, I work hard to survive, if I don't work in the field my family will not have anything to eat, but the labour which I do these days has no worth and value, if I don't have an Aadhaar card, I have no value.
>
> (interview)

Certainly, peoples' problems at the ground level are going largely unheard, and there is a lot of distress in rural India about the day-to-day problems they are facing as a consequence of compulsory digitization. This hopelessness was also reflected by the words of a tribal woman who narrated her story about three attempts to get her Aadhaar card seeded with her ration card, only to be told each time that there is some unspecified problem with her card. Beyond faulty cards, the frequent problems with readability of fingerprint scans, connectivity issues with PoS (point-of-sale) biometric machines and the frustration of not being able to address such problems are endemic. These fieldwork studies thereby reveal a reality that is irreconcilable with the carefully selected interactions of government officials in social media. The only similarity, perhaps, is that answering and addressing people's appeals in this domain shows comparable signs of non-attention by representatives of the state. These problems can be a matter of life and death. This is reflected in a recent incidence in Jharkhand, where a girl died of hunger as the family was removed from the PDS list and was not able to access food grains. In this setting, the compulsion to become enrolled in Aadhaar becomes a matter of existence for most of the villagers. This compulsion demonstrates how peoples' lives are being impacted by technology-based services which they are forced to depend upon on an everyday basis. Even when they adhere to this compulsion, there is no guarantee that they will not become victims of technological malfunction and bureaucratic malfeasance, the very ills that this system was propounded to address.

Fundamentally, it seems clear that the state is frequently unable or simply unwilling to address the issues of deniability and exclusions which arise from the compulsions that it has enacted. This can be considered as one among the most concerning consequences of state planning and implementation of a biometrics-enabled identification and authentication systems. Based on the premise of efficiency, faster access of services and addressing corruption, biometrics-enabled services are excluding large number of people on daily basis. Ironically, Aadhaar is not a proof of citizenship, and thus even aliens and foreigners can receive an Aadhaar number. In practice, however, Aadhaar is functioning in a manner that citizens are being excluded in their own country, becoming just aliens in effect. Without Aadhaar, it has become increasingly difficult for millions to prove their right to access of social and economic welfare entitlements from the state. With no access to welfare entitlements of food grains the poor, BPL and elderly are faced with technology-induced exclusion and potentially death by starvation. The patterns of exclusion thereby demonstrate the duality of the digital state and how it is transacting at an increasing distance with a diverse population (in terms of race, religion, caste, tribe and linguistic groups but also literacy, agency and means) on an everyday basis.

Transacting the Digital State

These contrasting tales of tweets and foods provide some glimpses of the present realities of Digital India. At one level, the digital has very rapidly become part of our day-to-day life. For someone living in the urban area and using digital devices, social media has become a means to connect to a large number of other citizens, and to petition government, even where this constitutes a lottery of patronage with impossible odds. For people living in rural India, the technological challenges are on a different level. Here, citizens have to grapple with systematic problems which jeopardize their very existence. In one domain, the state operates through discursive modes of selective availability and voluntary usage of a non-essential means of communication. In the other, the state operates through an impersonal and dysfunctional mode of technocratic governance that it is compulsory in nature and effectively a matter of life and death. Some of the dysfunctional aspects of both domains predate the digital, but their systemization on such a large scale amplifies and entrenches these tendencies, while shielding the functionaries of the state behind a virtual wall of convenient distance (Athique 2013; Robinson et al. 2009). The logic of digital transactions suggests that the state wants to be connected with people; however, the virtual wall between the state and people creates distances mediated and negotiated with different actors, institutions and components. The complex infrastructure of technology, players and institutions shapes the characteristics of both 'non-essential' and 'essential' digital transactions.

In the domain of twitter and biometrics-enabled services, different players and institutions mediate the communication between the citizen and the state (Dunleavy et al. 2011). In twitter, the motivation of direct communication with the public for government ministers is enabled by the platform of a multinational company (MNC). It offers a non-essential, yet increasingly popular, way of being 'connected' to the public sphere. The non-essential nature of communication between state and people incorporates discursive exchanges with selective filtering, answering and harvesting of tweet petitions for public relations and media news. In this pattern of communication, there are gains for two key players: the carrier and the government. Twitter gets more users, increases its popularity and amasses more everyday data for further financial gains and expansion. The selective transmission of tweets on public grievances (that is, ones with more emotional and social-cultural appeal) is employed to create a positive image for the ruling regime. For the user whose tweet gets 'selectively heard', there is a sense of elated belief in technology. The amplification of this elated sense of belief in technology as a means of being heard provides the motivation for a large number of people to join twitter. The predominance of twitter as a public medium, and its limited user base, fosters a tokenistic democracy which excludes the frustrations of the larger section of people are not being heard (Chadwick 2013; Hindman 2008). This gain-based tokenistic rendering of democracy incorporates the interplay of technologically mediated political transactions between citizens (petitions) and government (ministries and officials), government and press (public relations), politicians (ruling and opposition parties) and citizens, among politicians (ruling alliance and opposition) and also among citizens as fellow peers (emotional and social-psychological expressions).

In the context of biometrics-enabled PDS, the nature of 'essential' and compulsory communication between the state and citizens incorporates distributive function of the state. This function forms one among the key pillars of India's social welfare model, where large sections of the population living in poverty and below poverty conditions totally depend on it for their survival. With Aadhaar, the 'connection' between the people and the state becomes mediated and negotiated via the technological artefact of biometric machines, PDS dealer, block officials, district food supplies officials, state departments, ministers and third-party biometric service providers. In this case, there is a complex mixture of both government and private players facilitating connectivity. In practice, however, this compulsory techno-bureaucratic infrastructure renders only the biometric machines visible and the dealer who operates them. It effectively conceals the functionaries and officials who manage the system itself. One assumed benefit of biometrics-enabled delivery of food grains is the elimination of illegal, fake and ghost beneficiaries through biometric identification and authentication, thereby delivering savings to the state exchequer. However, to date, the government has signally failed to give a consistent and coherent figure of these purported ghost beneficiaries or the financial savings arising from digitalization. What is more clear is that Government of India has come to believe that the complex issues of privacy, exclusions, individual freedom and rights are necessary 'trade-offs' for providing 'efficient' welfare entitlements. The compulsory nature of this transaction reflects the ardent belief that the developmental problems of India can be addressed with a homogenized technological solution. However, the everyday stories and narratives on biometrics services show a contrary reality. Millions are becoming excluded and denied basic rights and entitlements, rights that are essential for their survival (Ellul 1964; Schumacher 1973).

These 'inefficient' realities not only reveal the glaring differences between state's presumption and actual practices when it comes to digital systems, but also bring to light the deeper implications of Digital India. It appears that the government has elected to blindly follow a particular mode of technology without knowing and understanding the large repercussions and consequences of its usage in a country like India. There is evidently a danger in applying an ungrounded vision of technology without a humane approach attuned to environmental conditions. Certainly, with the use of digital technologies in both cases, the state is seeking to institute pervasive 'connections' between citizens and the state. The premise is increasing and expanding participatory democracy, irrespective of the unequal nature of technical and political processes. The non-essential discursive application of twitter parades tokenistic democracy conceived as a public relations exercise, largely for the benefit of a minority of technologically advantaged users. The massive implementation of biometrics has been rolled out as the part of welfare responsibilities of the state, strengthening its hand in processes of everyday governance. Thus, the distributive function of the state is recast for a large section of population who remain disadvantaged to existing historical, social, cultural and economic barriers. However, compulsory participation and selective provision invariably create an arbitrary democracy where biometric technologies will provide a rationale for exclusion, both wilful and de facto.

For the high priests of the technology and development complex, the problems and trade-offs inherent to Digital India are generally dismissed for the sake of a 'better' future based on an assumed good of development as a national mission. Simply, the state is envisioning and implementing digital technologies in order to overcome the material and bureaucratic challenges of governing the geographical, social and political vastness of India. While the argument is posited that the state's increasing ubiquity due to digital technologies will enhance connectivity and participation in active democracy, the tale of tweets and foods appears to suggest instead the automation of a disembodied and disconnected state. We should be mindful, therefore, of the growing disconnect and increasingly uncaring attitude of the digital state. The tale of tweets and foods at least suggests the possibility of an arbitrary future, where the nature and expression of transactions between citizens and state becomes selective, differentiated, compulsive and exclusive. As the actually existing practices of everyday digital transactions already show instances of such breakdown, there are growing anxieties and mistrust about the imperatives of governance operating behind the two faces of India's digital utopia.

References

Abbate, Janet (1999) *Inventing the Internet*, Cambridge: MIT Press.

Ahmed, Saifuddin, Jaidka, Kokil and Cho, Jaeho (2016) 'The 2014 Indian Elections on Twitter: A Comparison of Campaign Strategies of Political Parties', *Telematics and Informatics*, 33(4): 1071–1087.

Athique, Adrian (2013) *Digital Media and Society: An Introduction*, Cambridge: Polity.

Bargh, John A. and McKenna, Katelyn Y.A. (2004) 'The Internet and Social Life', *Annual Review of Psychology*, 55: 573–590.

Barnett, George A., Ruiz, Jeanette B., Xu, Weiai Wayne, Park, Ji-Young and Park, Han Woo (2017) 'The World Is Not Flat: Evaluating the Inequality in Global Information Gatekeeping through Website Co-mentions', *Technological Forecasting and Social Change*, 117: 38–45.

Blank, Grant and Reisdorf, Bianca C. (2012) 'The Participatory Web: A User Perspective on Web 2.0', *Information, Communication & Society*, 15(4): 537–554.

Boyd, Danah, Golder, Scott and Lotan, Gilad (2010) 'Tweet, Tweet, Retweet: Conversational Aspects of Retweeting on Twitter', *Proceedings of the Annual Hawaii International Conference on System Sciences*. Available: https://ieeexplore.ieee.org/stamp/stamp.jsp?tp=&arnumber=5428313.

Briendli, Yana and Francq, Pascal (2008) 'Can Web 2.0 Applications Save E-Democracy? A Study of How New Internet Applications May Enhance Citizen Participation in the Political Process On-Line', *International Journal of Electronic Democracy*, 1(1): 14–31.

Burgess, Jean, Marwick, Alice and Poell, Thomas (2017) *The SAGE Handbook of Social Media*, London and Thousand Oaks, CA: Sage.

Chadwick, Andrew (2008) 'Web 2.0: New Challenges for the Study of E-Democracy in an Era of Information Exuberance', *Journal of Law and Policy for the Information Society*, 5(9): 9–42.

Chadwick, Andrew (2013) *Hybrid Media Systems*, New York: Oxford University Press.

Coleman, Stephen (2005) 'Blogs and the New Politics of Listening', *The Political Quarterly*, 76(2): 272–280.

Digital India (2015) Available: www.digitalindia.gov.in/content/vision-and-vision-areas, accessed: 8 October 2018.

Drèze, Jean and Khera, Reetika (2017) 'Recent Social Security Initiatives in India', *World Development*, 98: 555–572.

Dreze, Jean and Sen, Amartya (2002) *India: Development and participation*, New York: Oxford University Press.

Dunleavy, Patrick, Margetts, Helen, Bastow, Simon and Tinkler, Jane (2011) *Digital Era Governance: IT Corporations, the State, and e-Government*, Oxford: Oxford University Press.

Ellul, Jacques (1964) *The Technological Society*, New York: Vintage Books.

Elzen, Boelie, Enserink, Bert and Smit, Wim A. (1996) 'Socio-Technical Networks: How a Technology Studies May Help to Solve Problems Related to Technical Change', *Social Studies of Science*, 26(1): 95–141.

Financial Times (2014) 'Narendra Modi to Be India's First Social Media Prime Minister', *Financial Times*, 23 May 2014. Available: www.ft.com/content/e347de5c-e088-11e3-9534-00144feabdc0, accessed: 5 October 2018.

Fuchs, Christian (2014) *Social Media: A Critical Introduction*, London: Sage.
Gold, Steve (2011) 'The Privacy Imperative', *Biometric Technology Today*, 6: 9–11.
Greenleaf, Graham (2010) 'India's National {ID} System: Danger Grows in a Privacy Vacuum', *Computer Law and Security Review*, 26(5): 479–491.
Hague, Barry N. and Loader, Brian D. (1999) *Digital Democracy: Discourse and Decision Making in the Information Age*, London and New York: Routledge.
Hecht, Gabrielle and Allen, Michael Thad (2001) *Technologies of Power: Essays in Honor of Thomas Parke Hughes and Agatha Chipley Hughes*, Cambridge: MIT Press.
Hindman, Matthew (2008) *The Myth of Digital Democracy*, Princeton, NJ and Oxford: Princeton University Press.
Hughes, Thomas P. (2000) *Rescuing Prometheus*, New York: Vintage Books.
Jason, Gainous and Kevin, Wagner (2014) *Tweeting to Power: The Social Media Revolution in American Politics*, Oxford: Oxford University Press.
Jungherr, Andreas (2014) 'Twitter in Politics: A Comprehensive Literature Review', *SSRN Electronic Journal*, 1–90. Available: https://doi.org/10.2139/ssrn.2402443, accessed: 8 October 2018.
Krakovsky, Marina (2011) 'India's Elephantine Effort', *Communications of the ACM*, 54(1): 23–24.
Loader, Brian D. and Mercea, Dan (2012) *Social Media and Democracy: Innovations in Participatory Politics*, Oxon and New York: Routledge.
Madon, Shirin (2004) 'Evaluating the Developmental Impact of E-Governance Initiatives: An Explanatory Framework', *The Electronic Journal on Information Systems in Developing Countries*, 20(5): 1–13.
Masiero, Silvia (2015) 'Redesigning the Indian Food Security System through E-Governance: The Case of Kerala', *World Development*, 67: 126–137.
Mazzarella, William (2006) 'Internet X-Ray: E-Governance, Transparency, and the Politics of Immediation in India', *Public Culture*, 18(3): 473–505.
Murthy, Dhiraj (2013) *Twitter: Social Communication in the Digital Age*, Cambridge: Polity.
NDTV (2015) 'After Allah You Are Our Last Hope'. Available: www.ndtv.com/india-news/after-allah-you-our-last-hope-pakistani-boy-to-sushma-swaraj-1780029, accessed: 8 October 2018.
Pang, Natalie and Ng, Joshua (2016) 'Twittering the Little India Riot: Audience Responses, Information Behavior and the Use of Emotive Cues', *Computers in Human Behavior*, 54: 607–619.
Papacharissi, Zizi (2010) *A Private Sphere: Democracy in a Digital Age*, Cambridge: Polity.
Ramanathan, Usha (2015) 'Considering Social Implications of Biometric Registration', *IEEE Technology and Society Magazine*, 34: 10–16. doi:10.1109/MTS.2015.2396113.
Robinson, David, Yu, Harlan, Zeller, William P. and Felten, Edward W. (2009) 'Government Data and the Invisible Hand', *Yale Journal of Law and Technology*, 11(1). Article 4. Available at: https://digitalcommons.law.yale.edu/yjolt/vol11/iss1/4
Schumacher, Ernst Friedrich (1973) *Small Is Beautiful: A Study of Economics as If People Really Mattered*, London: Blond & Briggs Ltd.

Schwanholz, Julia, Graham, Todd and Stoll, Peter-Tobias (2018) *Managing Democracy in the Digital Age Internet Regulation, Social Media Use, and Online Civic Engagement*, Switzerland: Springer International Publishing.

Shiva, Vandana (2004) 'The Future of Food: Countering Globalisation and Recolonisation of Indian Agriculture', *Futures*, 36(6–7): 715–732.

Shukla, Ravi (2013) 'Technologies in Aadhaar: A Sociotechnical View' *In the Wake of Aadhaar*, 1–30. Available: http://stasis.in/sites/default/files/CSCS-Aadhaar.pdf, accessed: 8 October 2018.

Small, Tamara A. (2011) 'What the Hashtag? A Content Analysis of Canadian Politics on Twitter', *Information Communication and Society*, 14(6): 872–895.

Sreekumar, T.T. and Rivera-Sánchez, Milagros (2008) 'ICTs and Development: Revisiting the Asian Experience', *Science, Technology and Society*, 13(2): 159–174.

Sunstein, Cass R. (2018) *#Republic: Divided Democracy in the Age of Social Media*, Princeton, NJ: Princeton University Press.

Supreme Court of India (2015a) One of the First Directives by Supreme Court to Make Aadhaar Enrolment and Use Optional. Available: http://supremecourtofindia.nic.in/pdf/cir/2015-10-16_1444976434.pdf, accessed: 25 September 2018.

Supreme Court of India (2015b) Verdict on Right to Privacy and other Issues Pertaining to Digital Practices and Data Privacy. Available: http://supremecourtofindia.nic.in/pdf/LU/ALL%20WP(C)%20No.494%20of%202012%20Right%20to%20Privacy.pdf, accessed: 25 September 2018.

Tufekci, Zeynep (2017) *Twitter and Tear Gas: The Power and Fragility of Networked Protest*, New Haven, CT & London: Yale University Press.

Twitter (2014) 'India Has Won'. Available: https://twitter.com/narendramodi, accessed: 8 October 2018.

Vromen, Ariadne (2017) *Digital Citizenship and Political Engagement: The Challenge from Online Campaigning and Advocacy Organisations*, London: Palgrave Macmillan.

Weller, Katrin, Bruns, Axel, Burgess, Jean, Mahrt, Merja and Puschmann, Cornelius (2014) *Twitter and Society*, New York: Peter Lang.

Winner, Langdon (1980) 'Do Artifacts Have Politics?' *Daedalus*, 109(1): 121–136.

10 'Skill-Makers' in the Platform Economy

Transacting Digital Labour

Cheryll Ruth R. Soriano and Joy Hannah C. Panaligan

The increasing global connectivity and the relative affordability of technology heralded the rise of online platform labour or digitally mediated service work. Digital platform workers (also referred to as 'online freelancers' in this chapter) engage in digitally mediated work through online labour platforms and microwork intermediaries such as *Sama-source*, *CrowdFlower*, *Freelancer.com*, and *Upwork*. In contrast to business process outsourcing (BPO) such as call centre work, digital labour platforms represent a new model as they allow business processes to be outsourced without the mediation of formal BPO companies (Graham, Hjorth et al. 2017: 137). In these platforms, clients or buyers of work (mostly located in high-income countries) post jobs in these platforms and aspiring workers (mostly located in low-income countries) bid on them directly (Wood et al. 2016: 1). The Philippines, the site of this study, is second to India in terms of the number of online platform workers actively involved in the market (Graham, Hjorth et al. 2017: 142). This chapter focuses on the rise of 'skill-makers', specialist coaches who attract and train platform workers into this labour market and the 'skill-making economy' which is playing a crucial role in the local popularity and viability of platform labour.

As a lens for analysing digital transactions in the context of labour, the need for skill-makers and the very rise of the skill-making economy embody the monetization of ambiguity underlying digital labour in the global South. Burdened by employment woes such as infrastructural immobility and low wages, countless Filipino professionals and even those who were once deemed as undesirables under local labour standards are found to be migrating to online platform labour in exchange for autonomy, spatial flexibility, the possibility for higher earnings, etc. Government's optimism towards digital labour can be seen in parallel to Richard Florida's notion of the rise of the 'creative class', which was about this new group of socio-economic subjects who had jobs based on creativity and individual talent and who could usher cities into a new era of economic development and prosperity while addressing the unemployment gap (Florida 2006). Valorized under the guise of creativity and flexibility, platform labour is seen as empowerment for Filipino workers:

it provides them with new work opportunities to earn dollars, it gives them entry into the 'global workplace', and it facilitates a flexible work arrangement that allows them to overcome the challenges of daily commute while spending valuable time with their families at home. However, these optimistic narratives are challenged by the pernicious conditions that digital workers face: from exploitation to isolation to the colonization of personal space (for example, Arvidsson et al. 2010; Fuchs and Sevignani 2013; Gandini 2016; Gill and Pratt 2008; Gregg 2011; Hesmondhalgh and Baker 2010; Irani 2013; Peck 2005; Van Doorn 2017).

Digital platform labour may be considered part of the wider category of 'non-standard employment' (Kalleberg 2009). The nature of work would characterize them as among the 'precariat', underscored by 'distinctive *relations of production*' that involve so-called 'flexible' labour contracts, temporary jobs, labour as casuals, 'part-timers...' and 'distinctive *relations of distribution*' characterized by the absence of non-wage benefits such as health coverage, paid leave, or retrenchment benefits (Standing 2014: 969–970). As such, they are less likely to be able to access community support systems or state benefits. Amidst celebrations of flexibility, those in the precariat have 'no secure occupational identity' and 'no occupational narrative they can give to their lives' as a result of constant movement across available jobs that would not allow full use of their educational qualifications (Standing 2014: 969). Recent works on digital labour have also talked about 'flexible exploitation', which pertains to the double-edged nature that affords people new ways of working but also brings with it new kinds of precariousness (Gandini 2016; Graham, Lehdonvirta et al. 2017; Wood et al. 2016). These difficult conditions are not unknown to local platform workers. Yet, although these studies do the important work of training their lens on the problematic realities of digital labour, they at times insufficiently address how local conditions, histories, and dynamics allow workers to rationalize, negotiate, and even challenge these unfavourable work conditions (Hesmondhalgh and Baker 2010; Kennedy 2011).

Skill-makers emerge as an important labour category as they help platform workers reconcile the ambiguous condition of digital platform labour. Skill-makers play a role in ushering aspiring platform workers towards the vision of what they can be in this digital labour environment and train them with 'practical strategies' to achieve 'success'. At the same time, 'skill-makers' are also very well aware of the precarity of platform labour. Most of them current or former digital platform workers too but have achieved some level of success they know the ambiguity of shifting into platform labour from regular full-time employment, the pernicious and unfair conditions yielded by the platforms' design (i.e. labour arbitrage, the platform's socio-technical system of rating workers), and have been exposed to the difficulties of working with foreign clients. In short, they rise as an 'elite group' of workers because they capitalize on their experiences of and exposure to the challenges of digital labour and translate these as positive narratives and skills that they can monetize as training packages. Despite government pronouncements promoting digital labour as a crucial solution to unemployment, mechanisms for supporting workers engaged in labour platforms are absent. For labour migration, several private and public institutions have been set up to help workers aspiring to migrate overseas for jobs in terms of employment seeking, expectation setting, salary identification, taxation, or welfare protection. For BPO-related jobs such as call centre work, foreign companies operating in the country have institutionalized recruitment and employment mechanisms (Kleibert 2015). By contrast, aspiring workers bid for jobs in labour platforms directly and many workers learn the ropes through years of experience and by taking on several gigs from different platforms.

For newcomers, platform labour is confusing: not only is the process of engaging in platform labour fully mediated, but one also needs to discern legitimate platforms and legitimate clients from scams, present oneself and one's skills in a compelling manner and in a foreign language, and manage client's demands. For those transitioning from full-time employment (usually from call centres), to full-time freelancing through platform labour, workers are often wary about security or seasonality of work, the availability of non-salary benefits, or whether there are mechanisms for redress if clients end up not willing to pay for completed tasks. Some workers entering the digital platform economy may not have educational or professional training for jobs that they are eyeing but believe that getting employment is possible if they can get the right 'recipe' for success – again as marketed by skill-makers. Some aspiring workers, situated across the archipelago, but without university degrees, seek new skills or ways to package what they know in order to realize the promises of digital platforms. Strategic pricing is also a common source of ambiguity given the nature of bidding for jobs embedded in the digital labour platform design. With many workers also ending up being victimized by scammers and abusive clients, some of the workers aiming to tap into the rose-tinted promises of this industry require the guidance of people for navigating its complex environment. This chapter will show that it is in presenting their capacity to bridge the difficult realities of platform labour with the aspirational narratives that these 'skill-makers' create value for themselves and their work. As such, monetizing ambiguity as embedded within a specific context of Philippine labour, economy, and society and digital platform labour is at the heart of the transactional nature of this emerging labour category.

Arvidsson claims that in the digital economy, value is increasingly crystallized around the 'progressive mediatization of the social' and 'accompanying new forms of social organization' (2009: 13–14, 27). Arvidsson terms this as *philia*, a form of social capital which arises from one's ability to form affective bonds (ibid: 20). As 'the aggregate of the actual or potential resources which are linked to possession of a durable network of more or less institutionalized relationships of mutual acquaintance and recognition', social capital can be enacted in groups or communities which provides each of its members with the backing of the collectivity-owned capital, or a 'credential' (Bourdieu 1986: 51). In the Philippines, skill-makers have initiated 'online communities' of support (i.e. Facebook groups) that serve as active sites for skill-making while playing an important function for geographically dispersed workers who need to grapple with the ambiguous condition of digital platform labour. These Facebook communities for online Filipino freelancers seek to host expressions of belonging, support, and mutual kindness, as well as sharing of skills, tips, and opportunities among Filipino digital platform workers – abstracted social formations imagined through the shared experience of mediation and communication. However, also following the more recent critiques of online communities as sites of commercial culture that serve as an 'audience base' for various marketing purposes, we explore the role of these communities through shared experiences of platform work while at the same time serving the purpose for skill-making and maintaining an audience of subscribers or potential clients. Skill-makers take advantage of these sites for enacting multiple kinds of transactions – transactions between skill-makers and platform workers, hosting transactions among platform workers, and transactions between skill-makers and digital labour platforms (Athique 2013: 62). In this chapter, we ask: how do skill-makers monetize 'philia' or the formation of social bonds and relationships by helping workers reconcile the ambiguities of digital platform labour? What are the communicative strategies enacted by skill-makers in these 'communities' that allow them to enact multiple transactions and sustain their value in this digital economy?

Systematic Production of Filipinos as 'World-Class Service Workers'

The Philippine government champions digital labour as a way to overcome the various employment woes faced by countless Filipino professionals across age groups and educational background. The 'globalization' of business services propelled by the development of information and communication technology (ICT) allowed for the relocation of voice-based call centres and other back-office processes from the Global North to the Global South. Ranked as having the worst unemployment rates in Asia but with a large English-proficient population, the Philippines has become one of the prime sites of BPO work (Abara and Heo 2013; Errighi et al. 2016). However, the precarious conditions of BPO work, such as constant night shifts and sleep deprivation, highly stressful work environment, working in cramped cubicles for hours, lack of professional advancement, along with the difficulties of daily commute, has compelled some workers to explore alternatives (Errighi et al. 2016; Fabros 2016). The government sees platform labour as a complement to other forms of BPO work, an alternative to overseas labour migration, a catalyst for urban and rural development, and an attractive option for young graduates. The Philippine government has used labour brokerage as one of its neoliberal strategies to bring in much-needed foreign currency inflows (Rodriguez 2010). In the last decades, it has continually touted the mantra of Filipinos being 'world-class service workers and 'modern heroes', helping drive labour export despite the precariousness associated with such work (Parreñas 2001). From foreign domestic labour to call centre labour and now to digital platform labour, Filipinos aim for work that match their distinct traits as the top service workers of the world despite the many exploitative conditions accompanying this distinction (Soriano and Cabanes, forthcoming).

The notion of the Philippines as a nation systematically training and exporting service workers for the global market has been predominantly constructed as a 'natural global order of things' that Filipinos ought to take advantage of (Fabros 2016). Platform labour is envisioned to address rural development and unemployment in the country, but also as an alternative to foreign labour migration. The labels of 'modern heroes' and 'world-class workers' that have been previously attributed to overseas Filipino workers are being gradually conferred on online freelance workers too. They are now labelled as the OFW 2.0, no longer the 'Overseas Filipino Worker' but the 'Online Freelance Worker'. Through digital labour, one still earns dollars and performs as a 'global worker', only this time without having to be away from home. Providing a boost to the Philippine economy, this, however, constructs the Filipino as a global commodity and a colonized subject. In economic terms, the salaries of digital workers place them within the country's middle classes whose monthly income ranges from PHP 15,780.00 (approx. USD 308.00) to PHP 157,350.00 (approx. USD 3,071.00) (Hau 2017; Soriano and Cabanes, forthcoming), with most earnings exceeding the local minimum wage of P512/day or P15,360/month (approx. USD288). Further, local news occasionally highlights 'success' stories of online freelance workers earning millions of pesos in a year, serving as encouragement to workers on the viability of platform labour (see, for example, Garcia 2014). However, if compared to the so-called 'new middle class', who are 'professional and technical workers on the one hand, and wage- and salary-earning administrators, executives, and managers on the other hand', platform workers may be seen less favourably. As the labour is primarily comprised of off-shored low-skilled occupations being taken up by the country's highly educated and young workforce, platform labour in the Philippines is distinctly ambiguous because of the jobs mismatch that predominate this kind of work, which is often characterized as 'less prestigious' in the Global North (Bolton 2010; Kimura 2003: 265; Magtibay-Ramos et al. 2007; Roberts 2016; Rodolfo 2005; Soriano and Cabanes, forthcoming).

Similar to other jobs in the country's BPO industry such as call centres, transcription, or content moderation, most of the jobs under platform labour are believed to involve 'a narrow job description and offer only limited opportunities for acquisition of knowledge and skills replicable in other professions' and, crucially, often have poor 'longer-term employment prospects' (Beerepoot and Hendriks 2013: 824). Yet, the earnings obtained by workers from these jobs allow them significant purchasing power in the Philippine context and maintain 'attractive lifestyles' such as buying a car, paying for a condominium unit, sending children to school, or visiting cafes (Fabros 2016; Soriano and Cabanes, forthcoming; Tadiar 2004). Further, Filipino professionals are also migrating to online platform labour in exchange for autonomy and spatial flexibility. Digital labour, although understood to be facilitating a precarious form of labour, is actually fulfilling for workers in comparison to previous work conditions that tied them to experiences of constraint and control (Soriano and Cabanes, forthcoming). These include the lack of secure employment opportunities and the growing difficulties of commuting from one's home to the workplace due to worsening traffic conditions. At the core of flexibility are the neoliberal ideologies of 'individual entrepreneurial initiative' or 'individual self-realization' that compel the workers to get around the controls of corporate institutions and the inefficiencies of public institutions (Gandini 2016; Van Doorn 2017: 900). Skill-makers promote aspirations of a flexible working environment and 'unlimited opportunities', while training workers for the 'discipline' needed in order to succeed. In doing so, however, it is possible, as Peck has argued, that skill-makers promote the dangers of a narrative which 'glorifies and naturalizes the contracted-out, 'free-agent' economy without regard for the exploitative tendencies of a highly flexible working environment that arise from this economic system (2005: 756).

Micro-celebrities and Communicative Strategies for Influence Building

Rapid advancements in technology-facilitated contemporary shifts on who can become 'celebrities' and obtain a following or influence (Hearn 2008). The concept 'micro-celebrity' pertains to how people used online tools in 'amping up their popularity over the web using technologies like videos, blogs and social networking sites', earning them fame and prominence just like mass media celebrities (Senft 2013: 25). These practices are pursued in light of the so-called 'attention economy' where value is attributed based on the capacity to attract attention in a media-saturated and information-rich world. These include niche-like celebrities thriving in multiple environments such as fashion, food, entertainment, and eventually earning followers by engaging a set of practices to boost popularity and maintain influence (Marwick 2015). But how do micro-celebrities develop influence? Marwick suggests they do so through 'self-presentation techniques': micro-celebrities create a brand, 'use a public persona to be consumed by others' and engage 'strategic intimacy' to attract followers (Marwick 2015: 1–2). While micro-celebrities may be actively engaged in 'self-expression', this also simultaneously works as an economic activity and serves as a way to monetize the self in the digital world.

Micro-celebrities may amass a smaller scale of followers compared to celebrities, but the 'strategies of micro-celebrity can forge a loyal following' on any social media platform (Khamis et al. 2016: 12). As Hearn and Schoenhoff explain, social media works to generate 'a form of "celebrity capital" by cultivating as much attention as possible and crafting an authentic and relatable "personal brand" via social networks, which can subsequently be used by companies and advertisers for consumer outreach' (2016: 194). The notion of self-branding further implies that a micro-celebrity needs to differentiate oneself from the rest by creating a *persona,* a character or role created to project one's image in the content or product they create, and eventually display influence over people (Abidin 2017). They must also specialize the self, since their persona must pertain to the area of expertise the online influencer would like to be associated or known for. This labour specialization of a persona illustrates how advertising shifts from mass media to marketing 'personal sensations' through the use of a personal touch to establish a connection with the audience and target emotions (Malefyt and Morais 2012: 62).

The concept of communicative intimacy is crucial in the reputation-building process of micro-celebrities because it emphasizes the relationship between influencers and followers – or how influencers 'intentionally used digital media to craft, convey, (and) sustain intimacies with their followers' (Abidin 2015: 8). By enacting communicative intimacy, followers can easily relate to influencers because the interactions they have with them seem 'personal' or 'direct' through the recreation of 'intimate exchanges' (Abidin 2015). Abidin identified four types of intimacies appropriated by influencers: commercial, interactive, reciprocal, and disclosive. For instance, commercial intimacies describe the recreation of an 'intimate exchange' between the influencer and followers for commercial interest (ibid: 5). This illusion of intimacy works 'as long as followers (who "may or may not be critically aware of these") feel familiar, close, and emotionally attached to influencers' (ibid: 5). Commercial intimacy includes how an influencer can earn views and hits from emotional posts and personal stories. Interactive intimacy, on the other hand, is an 'extensive integration of face-to-face meet-ups with followers' which can range from informal events organized by influencers or brand sponsorships (ibid: 6). The third is reciprocal intimacy, which refers to forms of facilitating mutual acknowledgement and appreciation between influencers and their followers in the form of shout-outs, retweets, comments, and likes (ibid: 7).

Finally, developed in the context of lifestyle influencers, disclosive intimacies include 'behind-the-scenes' portrayals that allow followers to gain access 'to the private, usually inaccessible aspects of influencers' (ibid: 8). Such personal posts have the capacity to boost attention and craft a notion of authenticity and relatability for their audiences. The enactment of communicative intimacies is strategic, allowing micro-celebrities to increase influence and maintain a 'perception of interconnectedness' between them and their followers (Abidin 2015: 1). Thus, the concept of micro-celebrity and social media influencers is largely understood to operate in niche-like environments such as fashion, entertainment, blog, travel, and the like, and often in the context of affluent societies. There is a research gap in understanding the influence-building process wielded by skill-makers despite their growing influence as major drivers of digital labour in the locale and their role in crafting the imaginaries of workers embracing this form of work.

Skill-Making in the Platform Economy

Through an ethnographic inquiry of online freelance work in the Philippines, we examined the conditions that allowed digital workers to rise as skill-makers, examined the function of 'skill-making' in the digital platform economy, and looked into communicative strategies that they engage. Programmes and services offered by the skill-makers range from 'how to begin as an online freelancer', 'how to sell one's skills', coaching on specific skills (i.e. website development, social media management, web design, or virtual assistance), or advise on how to make successful investments of their earnings. Some of these are shared for free via their websites or Facebook communities but most of the materials are packaged as training programmes or as books for purchase. The cost of a course can range from P3,000 (US$55) to P15,000 (US$300). Based on an interview with a coach/influencer, a beginner course on how to become a freelancer costs P5,000 (US$100). Although prohibitive for a regular platform worker, some of them took such courses with the promise of success, made visible through a constant display of association, which students of whose coach have become 'successful' as well as evidence of material success shared in online communities.

We hypothesized that skill-makers cascade imaginaries of success and mobility to their subscribers while also establishing 'norms of success' for platform workers. In presenting our findings, this section discusses the role of skill-makers and the communicative strategies that they engage: (a) articulating expertise and persona, (b) community building, (c) relatability and authentic communication, (d) responsiveness and reciprocity, (e) calibrated visibility and algorithmic influence, and (f) selective disclosure and aspirational emulation – all of which allow them to maintain online communities of subscribers where they create aspirational emulation and form affective bonds (philia) for enacting multiple transactions.

Articulating Expertise and Persona

Skill-makers curate their 'brand' by articulating expertise and the capacity to build skills in a specific field. As articulated by one skill-maker, 'In freelancing, it's the knowledge and expertise that the audience look for... one becomes an influencer if they look up to you because of the expertise that you have that can help them build the skills they need to succeed' (interview, Ginnie, 37, female). Digital workers seek for ways to improve their skills and how they can market these and skill-makers make sure that they highlight the specific value that they can contribute. To do this, skill-makers assert their expertise – whether in social media management, podcasting, video production, or virtual assistance. This expertise also needs to be articulated consistently. An SEO coach explains:

> If you want to be known for something, you have to be able to always deliver content on a topic. It should be on a regular, consistent basis so people will get to know you like that person, 'that video guy' or that SEO coach and then they will start to like you because you give value. Over time they will start to trust you because they can hear that you're helping people with this and doing something for that. There is nothing that you can get instantly...you have to be consistent with your content, that's the thing that people will look for. If you want to grow your influence because once they see that you are regularly posting something, they will be able to look forward to a specific thing that you serve... It's your fault if you're not consistent you're not giving your audience a chance to follow you properly if you're not consistent.
>
> (interview, Andrew, male)

As explained by one skill-maker, one can establish authority by 'start(ing) with the problem and issue and then provide solutions' (interview, Richard, male). One example is coaching about 'working from home'. In the context of online freelancing, most are attracted to 'working from home' but often unfamiliar about the complexity of managing the overlapping environments of home/family and work. Although seemingly trivial, there are apparently a multitude of issues encountered by online freelance workers who work from home: establishing a quiet and conducive work environment, managing time and work hours, managing client expectations, or being able to address client expectations while caring for the family. All these are provided in targeted coaching programmes and strategies, such as the 'Work from Home Roadmap', which essentially prescribe norms and protocols of managing the work-from-home environment. Another strategy is the curation of a 'persona' by which to establish one's authority and expertise. An online influencer usually takes into consideration the persona they want to project to differentiate one's content from other similar content offered by other skill-makers. The choice of persona is attached to a specific approach that influencers employ to craft an impression of relatability among their followers. As a blogger/mom/entrepreneur and brand ambassador shared (interview, Ginnie, 37):

> In my blog ______, I basically know the customer that I want to talk to...All of the topics that I create (are) aligned with the particular persona I have in mind. I created (this) in my mind as a mom/entrepreneur persona. There are a lot of mommy bloggers but you have to think what makes you stand out. I think my site is known for business related or entrepreneurship topics. I want to communicate that even if you're already a mom you can still set up a business. For the Manila workshop it's a similar strategy we have different personas we have in mind. We split it into different series, so in each (part of the) series there is a persona that the audience needs and we (already) have someone in mind if the topic is about freelance, entrepreneurial and professional.

In the above, Ginnie explains that when she creates content, she has a persona in mind and it also serves as a guide for programming future posts or coaching sessions. This persona can also describe the area of expertise a skill-maker would like to be associated or known for, for example,

> My whole thing is I want people to see, understand and know that I'm always for marketing, like that's the one I want people to know. I'm an expert at social media marketing, expert in branding, personal branding and that I always give value. Marketing, (how to) hustle, personal branding, and entrepreneurship.
>
> (interview, Emmanuel, 25, male)

Community Building

Community building serves as an important anchor for the communicative strategies enacted by skill-makers. Once a brand of expertise or persona is established, a skill-maker begins to accumulate a following.

Williams identified the concept of a 'micro-community', an initial community within the influencer economy that skill-makers develop once they accumulate followers (2016: 169). Most commonly, skill-makers attract a following through face-to-face coaching sessions (this may be given for free while some require payment), beginning with as small as 10–15 aspiring freelancers. As they start earning a name, skill-makers would be invited to speak during online freelancing events, and there would be one or two in different locations in the country every month. These allow the skill-maker to develop a network of trainees, a micro-community (some call this 'tribe,' 'team,' or 'family'), yet even when the trainees have achieved some form of independence or success, they still lovingly label themselves as 'coached by' a particular skill-maker. All our skill-maker informants emphasized the importance of online communities to maintain their network of trainees with possibilities of growing their number:

> For freelancing it's very important for us to build a community like this. Even if its virtual, even if you can only see them online, you still get to be with them. And also it's very hard because there is no pattern, you don't know when you will encounter scammer clients. Sometimes (we have experience that) the client would run away, there are no traces and, they could not pay the freelancer. So if you are just someone and no one gets to help you, it's very easy to be scammed, so that's the reason why the community is really important so we can also guide the newbies… We can help them in their career.
>
> (interview, Clara, female)

Moreover, the influencers also recognize the community as the fastest way to grow one's brand organically because it allows the audience to join in the conversation and share content.

> (The online community) it's important, it's one of the fastest ways to grow your personal brand as an online businessman or as an entrepreneur. I mean it's important 'cause people naturally want to be part of the communities and people gravitate towards that sense of togetherness, they want to belong to a certain group. They also post things that matter to other freelancers, such as a photo of their work space or scammer clients they encounter. They resonate with the value of stuff that we talk about and then share their own experiences
>
> (interview, Emmanuel, male)

The community enables the recognition of the skill-maker's brand or prominence. Once the recognition is earned, this would further develop into richer connections in casual meetups, organized team-building events, and online interactions. The community has a particular value for freelancers who often work from home, mostly in isolation, and therefore functions as a support group for skill-makers and freelancers and which the skill-makers knowingly capitalize on:

> I meet with freelancers face to face, and I couldn't find a group who was doing it at that time so, that's why I started *Meetup.com*, and then I was surprised that the first (event) we had 30 attendees so I started doing more meetups. I've been doing it for the past 4 years and that's how I really wanted to meet freelancers face to face knowing that they are also online most of the time. I know that they also want a break from time to time and to be part of a community and that's what I'm going after-- to build the community slowly both online and through the meetups.
>
> (interview, Melvin, 37, male)

Skill-makers organize events such as informal meetups, workshops, courses, conferences, talks, webinars, and even promotions. Online interactions also work as documentation of offline meetups. Skill-makers thus play the role of a bridge for freelancers to convene online and offline.

Relatability and Authentic Communication

Community building is mobilized by communicating authenticity and relatability. Authenticity as a construct is quite hard to pin down: 'authenticity can be described the same way - you know it when you see it, and you can't fake it' (Williams 2016: 136). Two lessons identified by Williams served as a guide to examine the construct of authenticity in the online freelance community: the first is about finding an authentic self, and the second is to divorce oneself from an agenda and find one's authentic voice (2016: 127). The first lesson illustrates how the audience or readers within the online freelance community gravitate to the message that is rooted from personal experience and struggles. Skill-makers value authentic communication because it is linked to the position they earned in their community. For example, in one of the interviews, Clara, a skill-maker, notes that it is not always necessary to have a content plan or predefined structure; 'random posts' and 'posts from the heart' are more valued because these appear 'more authentic'. Furthermore, authentic communication implies an attempt to balance the potential of monetary gains and conveying one's genuine intent to help, as Emmanuel explains,

> What people love about me is being genuine and being authentic, I'm not trying to make money every single time like some people say that I could monetize my audience so much and that I could make so much money from the people who follow me.
>
> (interview, Emmanuel, male)

Of course, Emmanuel has also gained financially from the courses he offers, and the availability of free courses serves an important purpose of attracting workers and showing a proof of concept.

According to our informants, people eventually know if a skill-maker's posts are driven by personal agenda and the workers get turned off by this. For instance, although an influencer can earn from advertisements in their web pages, engaging too much in sponsored posts can backfire and drive followers away:

> What brings about engagement is mostly authenticity. I noticed that when I post something personal, emotional or like share about my daily struggles, it would typically earn more reactions and engagements compared to a sponsored post. I made a mistake last year because my engagement decreased and I noticed that there are a lot of sponsored posts. Sometimes it's not about getting brands to back you up but mostly you still have to post something from the heart, something that you created and it reflects what you believe and think.
>
> (interview, Ginnie, 37, female)

One would see from the above quote that beyond the transaction of offering skills to aspiring workers, skill-makers are also able to monetize these transactions, including exchanges among the followers in these communities, through sponsored posts and advertisements. However, this particular transaction is less overt and needs to be managed by the skill-maker well to maintain an appearance of authenticity. Authenticity supports and creates credibility in the content they produce and brings them closer to their communities while helping attract new followers. It appears that skill-makers would often provide value first before they seek to monetize this value.

Responsiveness and Reciprocity

Skill-makers engage responsiveness and reciprocity once they build a community. They acknowledge and appreciate their audience's response to their content and, knowing their position as experts, they aim to address inquiries attentively. Some coaches run several accounts to maintain contact to their followers: 'Well, they reach me on Facebook sometimes they would comment on my blog, YouTube channel, and Instagram. I regularly answer them in the channels that they message me in' (interview, Ginnie). Here, a coach offers some examples of how skill-makers mobilize responsiveness and reciprocal intimacy:

> Directly, they message me, and I message back. If they comment I do my best to reply to everyone, every single one. I mean it's hard

> and I try, I don't get to do this all the time, though I do my best. I randomly reach out to people also. The thing that I do sometimes I sent voice notes to people they appreciate it a lot. It's an extra effort, extra layer for me to send voice notes sometimes video, video replies and they appreciate that kind of thing... I just want to give people something of course they have to show that they earned it right.
>
> (interview, Emmanuel, male)

Responsiveness and reciprocity also manifest in terms of how a skill-maker gives back to their followers as a way to acknowledge their support. This can range from featuring mentees who have achieved some success (usually done through video interviews published through Facebook Live in their micro-communities) and posting comments of encouragement, to giving out access to training, free books, or free show tickets. As a transaction, it would appear that when a platform worker subscribes to a training programme or coaching session, they also benefit from a multitude of other 'gifts'.

Calibrated Visibility and Algorithmic Influence

The expectation of being present all the time and obtaining a substantial following through online communities emerged as recurring themes throughout our interviews. These allow influencers to build their brand, earn credibility and serve as a way to earn their subscribers' trust but it also implies that influencers pay close attention to the accumulation of support and the quantification of their influence. The relationship between skill-makers and followers cannot be built on impressions alone; people establish trust through constant visibility. Yet, our interviews support the idea that being consistent and visible in the community should be calibrated, it does not paint a good picture when a skill-maker is only visible at times that they need to promote or sell products and services. Here, 'calibrated visibility' is a construct inspired by Abidin's notion of 'constancy', or the appearance of online availability 24/7 as a strategy micro-celebrities enact to achieve interconnectedness (2013: 4). In the digital platform labour community, however, calibrated visibility implies the constant production of valuable content, while simultaneously allowing community members to engage organically such that skill-makers do not dominate the conversation and avoid the impression of merely taking advantage of the community. To know what works, digital labour influencers also carefully study the pattern of interaction of their community members:

> I've been focusing on sending at 4 pm. It's just so happened (that) I saw a good consistent interaction during that time. It's like piggy-banking on the habits of people. It creates the habit for people

> to anticipate your content… So, I think it's good if you can integrate yourself in their habits because it's hard to gain attention now. It's the currency of the digital age. If you can be there consistently, I noticed some other marketers, they would only email if there is a promotion, if there is a launch, so sometimes people will have an idea that they will only see content if there is promotion. But if you're there, day in and day out, even after promoting something. There is a sense of reliability that you will not just be visible when you (need to) promote.
>
> (interview, Mark, male)

Calibrated visibility is vital because it is construed by the online freelancing community as a reflection of commitment. It is evident that there are common communication strategies that online influencers share such as having a Facebook page, email list, courses, webinars, blog articles, and the like that allow them to convey an active relationship with their followers.

Selective Disclosure and Aspirational Emulation

> Recently I came from Bacolod for a friend's wedding… I shared a picture of me there, and it's like a personal look in my life. And also, since I sent that email on Valentine's day, in the PS part, I included the message I gave to my friend. So it's more about marriage tips, it's mixing up some personal details and the actual marketing tip, so there is a bonus like a personal (insight about), love since it's Valentine's day.
>
> (interview, Mark, male)

Considered as figures of authority, workers are used to seeing professional advice from skill-makers. Inserting a personal story in between professional coaching appears to be a powerful attention grabber, as this creates an imaginary of intimacy between the influencers and their followers, akin to the concept of 'disclosive intimacy' (Abidin 2015). This communicative strategy is suitable to the nature of social media as a space for candid interaction while enacting a sense of 'relatability'. As one worker shared in a focus group discussion: 'His posts makes me think, 'oh he is just like us' (interview, freelance worker, female, 26). Yet, although a slice of the personal is revealed, the focus is on the value of content they provide, looped within personal stories of hardship and success that followers would find relatable. Skill-makers engage 'winning stories', where they share their work history and story of success. In turn, freelancers also post what they have achieved, again presenting an image of possibility, an achievable success for aspiring freelancers that can be emulated:

> They love the inspirational stuff, if you create or share a story about your struggles and how you overcame it, that works a lot especially if it's portrayed in story form, a long story form, text type. They love that stuff, that is how you engage. If you can show them, there is a way to achieve things despite all the odds, that works the best. Again it's either you can educate and inspire. If you can educate them in such a way that it's not boring and in an entertaining way that's also good. If you can educate, entertain, and inspire them that's perfect.
> (interview, Arvin, male)

Inspirational posts also attract others in the community to share their own experience and reveal their success stories to inspire beginners, thereby creating a greater sense of authenticity as these become a collaboration between the skill-maker and their followers – a picture of real-life stories of success and overcoming difficulty. This works to establish the skill-maker's authority and believability within a growing network of followers and community members.

Transacting the Ambiguities of Digital Labour

Digital labour in the Philippines has created opportunities for skill-makers: a labour elite that has become successful and transitioned into becoming online freelancing coaches. These skill-makers cascade imaginaries of success and mobility to their subscribers that also create aspirations for the workers who now have to compete with thousands of new aspirants. By building their respective communities, skill-makers establish their brand of expertise and authority and at the same time enact a range of communicative strategies underscored by authentic communication, calibrated visibility, reciprocity, algorithmic influence, and selective disclosure that all create aspirational emulation among their followers. In turn, digital workers also establish skills and social capital by being attached to the skill-maker and gaining a community of support crucial in an ambiguous labour environment. Invested with the expectation of future returns that are appropriable and convertible, skill-makers establish communities with which they offer a diverse range of training and coaching resources that allow them to build reputation and trust. In turn, digital workers also capitalize on their being coached. This brings to the surface the transactions underlying the relationship between the skill-maker and digital platform workers: skill-makers monetize the value of helping workers solve the ambiguity of the digital platform environment, and in turn, workers see the need for skill-makers due to the perceived value that they can offer for helping them advance in the digital labour economy.

Yet it appears that skill-making is not really just about training platform workers to develop new skills needed to thrive in the digital platform economy, although much of the work falls into this. To maintain influence in this environment, skill-makers also perform multiple kinds of work: creating and sustaining communities, producing and exchanging content in these communities, being continually responsive to queries, negotiating visibility and sharing aspects of one's personal life, among others. Skill-makers also perform unpaid labour for digital platforms. As key movers inspiring local workers to take up platform labour to training them as entrants to this industry, skill-makers essentially function as recruiters for digital platforms by making the ambiguous digital platform environment less complex for local workers – a total gain for digital labour platforms. Indirectly, they also serve as promoters of the government's vision of promoting Filipinos as 'world-class workers' and, in some way, support its goal of reducing unemployment. Recently, we found that government has begun to partner with a prominent skill-maker for promoting online freelancing and delivering training programmes for aspiring digital workers in rural communities under government's 'Rural Impact Sourcing Program'. This is a new development that may further expand the role of skill-makers, the reach of digital platform labour, and the transactions that may be embedded within. One of the challenges is to build collective representation for those espousing the values of work outside the norms of labour, and which can help workers manage some of the underlying ambiguities (ibid: 978). With little tangible support, skill-makers work to manage the ambiguities of digital platform labour through the creation of protocols and guidelines to help workers bargain for better rates, negotiate job scope, avoid scammers, or find labour platforms that provide better deals.

The very idea of having to invest in 'skill-making' programmes in order to become successful creates norms and lofty standards that further create asymmetries that disadvantage certain workers while benefiting others. A skill-maker takes the position of one who has obtained success, as one who has expertise but continually expands skills, one who has the capacity to discern good clients, one who can navigate a global workplace, one who invests earnings in the right places, one who can successfully navigate a 'work-at-home' environment, and one who presents an appearance of sincerity while being able to monetize this influence – all of which allow them to gain the trust of their followers. Nonetheless, skill-makers are digital workers too. Although they are admired and obtain a significant following, they take the stance of being 'one of them'. Skill-makers, a growing league of influencers in the local digital labour economy, strategize their narratives of success and promote recipes for success in digital platform labour. They create the notion that anyone can be like them, successful, entrepreneurial, well-networked, and 'contributing to bigger social good'. However, the reality is that the skills and assets that allow them to flexibly navigate across digital labour spaces and opportunities to negotiate with clients may not be as easy to come by for others, who will remain in the general labour pool. Nonetheless, the relationships between skill-makers, as mentors and advocates, and the flexible pool of precarious labour create a series of critical transactions around opportunity in the platform economy, thereby establishing norms and protocols that both mitigate and perpetuate the precarity of digital platform workers. These transactions between different categories of labour deserve further research if we are to properly understand the consolidation of the platform economy.

References

Abara, Anna Charmaine and Heo, Yoon (2013) 'Resilience and Recovery: The Philippine IT-BPO Industry during the Global Crisis', *International Area Studies Review*, 16(2): 160–183.

Abidin, Crystal (2013) 'Cyber-Bffs*: Assessing Women's 'Perceived Interconnectedness' in Singapore's Commercial Lifestyle Blog Industry *Best Friends Forever', *Global Media Journal: Australian Edition*, 7(1): 1–20.

Abidin, Crystal (2015) 'Communicative Intimacies: Influencers and Perceived Connectedness', *Ada: A Journal of Gender, New Media, and Technology*, 8: 1–16.

Abidin, Crystal (2017) '*Influencer Extravaganza: A Decade of Commercial 'Lifestyle' Microcelebrities in Singapore*', in Hjorth, Larissa, Horst, Heather, Bell, Genevieve, Galloway, Anne (eds) *Routledge Companion to Digital Ethnography*, London: Routledge, pp. 158–168.

Athique, Adrian (2013) *Digital Media and Society: An Introduction*, Cambridge: Polity Press.

Arvidsson, Adam (2009) 'The Ethical Economy: Towards a Post-Capitalist Theory of Value', *Capital and Class*, 33(1): 13–29.

Arvidsson, Adam, Malossi, Giannino and Naro, Serpica (2010) 'Passionate Work? Labour Conditions in the Milan Fashion Industry', *Journal for Cultural Research*, 14(3): 295–309.

Bolton, Kingsley (2010) 'Thank You for Calling: Asian Englishes and 'Native-like' Performance in Asian Call Centres', in Kirkpatrick, Andy (ed) *The Routledge Handbook of World Englishes*, London: Routledge, pp. 550–564.

Bourdieu, Pierre (1986) 'The forms of capital', in Richardson, John G. (ed), *Handbook of Theory and Research for the Sociology of Education*, New York: Greenwood, pp. 46–58.

Errighi, Lorenza, Khatiwada, Sameer and Bodwell, Charles (2016) 'Business Process Outsourcing in the Philippines: Challenges for Decent Work', *ILO Asia-Pacific Working Paper Series*. Available: www.ilo.org/wcmsp5/groups/public/---asia/---ro-bangkok/---sro-bangkok/documents/publication/wcms_538193.pdf, accessed: 15 July 2018.

Fabros, Alinaya (2016) *Outsourceable Selves: An Ethnography of Call Center Work in a Global Economy of Signs and Selves*, Quezon City: Ateneo de Manila University Press.

Florida, Richard (2006) *The Rise of the Creative Class: And How It's Transforming Work, Leisure, Community and Everyday Life*, New York: Basic Books.

Fuchs, Christian and Sebastian, Sevignani (2013) 'What Is Digital Labour? What Is Digital Work? What's Their Difference? And Why Do These Questions Matter for Understanding Social Media?', *Triple C*, 11(2): 237–293.

Gandini, Alessandro (2016) 'The Reputation Economy', in *The Reputation Economy: Understanding Knowledge Work in the Digital Society*, London: Palgrave Macmillan, pp. 1–12.

Garcia, Cathy Rose (2014) 'How Pinoy Earned P7.5-M from Freelance Work in Just 1 year', *ABS-CBN News*. Available: http://news.abs-cbn.com/business/07/27/14/how-pinoy-earned-p75-m-freelance-work-just-1-year, accessed: 1 August 2018.

Gill, Rosalind and Pratt, Andy (2008) 'In the Social Factory? Immaterial Labour, Precariousness and Cultural Work', *Theory, Culture and Society*, 25 (7–8): 1–30.

Graham, Fiona (2010) 'Crowdsourcing Work: Labour on Demand or Digital Sweatshop?', *BBC News*. Available: www.bbc.com/news/business-11600902, accessed: 1 May 2018.

Graham, Mark, Hjorth, Isis and Lehdonvirta, Vili (2017) 'Digital Labour and Development: Impacts of Global Digital Labour Platforms and the Gig Economy on Worker Livelihoods', *Transfer: European Review of Labour and Research*, 23(2): 135–162.

Graham, Mark, Lehdonvirta, Vili, Wood, Alex, Barnard, Helena Hjorth, I. and Simon, D. Peter (2017) *The Risks and Rewards of Online Gig Work at the Global Margins*, Oxford: Oxford Internet Institute, Available: www.oii.ox.ac.uk/publications/gigwork.pdf, accessed 21 May 2018.

Gregg, Melissa (2011) *Work's Intimacy*, Cambridge: Polity Press.

Hau, Caroline S. (2017) *Elites and Ilustrados in Philippine Culture*, Quezon City: Ateneo de Manila University Press.

Hearn, Allison (2008) 'Insecure: Narratives and Economies of the Branded Self in Transformation Television', *Continuum: Journal of Media and Cultural Studies*, 22(4): 495–504.

Hearn, Alisson and Schoenhoff, Stephanie (2016) 'From Celebrity to Influencer: Tracing the Diffusion of Celebrity Value Across the Data Stream', in Marshall, P. David, and Redmond, Sean (eds) *A Companion to Celebrity*. Chichester: John Wiley and Sons, pp. 194–212.

Hesmondhalgh, David and Baker, Sarah (2010) 'A Very Complicated Version of Freedom: Conditions and Experiences of Creative Labour in Three Cultural Industries', *Poetics*, 38(1): 4–20.

Irani, Lilly (2013) 'The Cultural Work of Microwork', *New Media and Society*, 17(5): 720–739.

Kalleberg, Anne (2009) 'Precarious Work, Insecure Workers: Employment Relations in Transition', *American Sociological Review*, 74(1): 1–22.

Kennedy, Hellen (2011) *Net Work: Ethics and Values in Web Design*, Basingstoke: Palgrave Macmillan.

Khamis, Susie, Ang, Lawrence and Welling, Raymond (2016) 'Self-branding, 'Micro-celebrity' and the Rise of Social Media Influencers', *Celebrity Studies*, 8(2): 1–17.

Kimura, Masataka (2003) 'The Emergence of the Middle Classes and Political Change in the Philippines', *The Developing Economies*, 41(2): 264–284.

Kleibert, Jana Maria (2015) 'Services-Led Economic Development: Comparing the Emergence of the Offshore Service Sector in India and the Philippines', in Lambregts, Bart, Beerepoot, Niels and Kloosterman, Robert C. (eds) *The Local Impact of Globalization in South and Southeast Asia: Offshore Business Process Outsourcing in Services Industries*, London and New York: Routledge, pp. 29–45.

Magtibay-Ramos, Nedelyn, Estrada, Gemma Esther and Felipe, Jesus (2007) 'An Analysis of the Philippine Business Process Outsourcing Industry', *Asian Development Bank*, Available: www.adb.org/sites/default/files/publication/28359/wp093.pdf, accessed: 15 July 2018.

Malefyt, Timothy and Morais, Robert (2012) *Advertising and Anthropology: Ethnographic Practice and Cultural Perspectives*. London: Berg.

Marwick, Alice (2015) 'You May Know Me from YouTube: (Micro)-Celebrity in Social Media' in Marshall, P. David and Redmond, Sean. (eds) *A Companion to Celebrity*, Hoboken, NJ: John Wiley and Sons Inc., pp. 333–350.

Parreñas, Rhacel S. (2015) *Servants of Global Migration: Women, Migration, and Domestic Work*. Stanford, CA: Stanford University Press.

Peck, Jaime (2005) 'Struggling with the Creative Class', *International Journal of Urban and Regional Research*, 29(24): 740–770.

Roberts, Sarah (2016) 'Commercial Content Moderation: Digital Labourer's Dirty Work', in Noble Safiya Umoja and Tynes, Brendesha M. (eds) *The Intersectional Internet: Race, Sex, Class and Culture Online*. New York: Peter Lang, pp. 147–159.

Rodolfo, Ceferino (2005) 'Sustaining Philippine Advantage in Business Process Outsourcing,' *Philippine Institute for Development Studies*, 28. Available: https://serp-p.pids.gov.ph/serp-p/download.php?d=4101ands=1, accessed: 1 June 2018.

Rodriguez, Robyn Magalit (2010) *Migrants for Export: How the Philippine State Brokers Labour to the World*. Minneapolis: University of Minnesota Press.

Senft, Theresa (2013) 'Microcelebrity and the Branded Self', in Harley, John, Burgess, Jean and Bruns, Axel. (eds) *A Companion to New Media Dynamics*, Wiley-Blackwell, pp. 346–354.

Soriano, Cheryll Ruth and Cabanes, Jason Vincent (forthcoming) 'Digital Labour Imaginaries in the Global South' in Schofield-Clark, L., Gajjala, R. Polson, E. (eds) *Routledge Companion to Media and Class*. London and New York: Routledge.

Standing, Guy (2014) 'Understanding the Precariat through Labour and Work', *Development and Change*, 45(5): 963–980.

Van Doorn, Niels (2017) 'Platform Labour: On the Gendered and Racialized Exploitation of Low-Income Service Work in the 'On-Demand' Economy'', *Information, Communication and Society*, 20(6): 898–914.

Wood, Alex, Graham, Mark. Lehdonvirta, Vili., Barnard, Helena. and Hjorth, Isis (2016) 'Virtual Production Networks: Fixing Commodification and Disembeddedness', *The Internet, Policy, and Politics Conferences*, 1(33). Available: https://ora.ox.ac.uk/objects/uuid:b17c46f0-8cb5-4e9f-bb08-18223146c23d, accessed: 13 July 2017.

Williams, Ryan (2016) *The Influencer Economy: How to Launch Your Idea, Share It with the World, and Thrive in the Digital Age*, Los Angeles, CA:Ryno Lab.

11 The Enterprising Self

Disability and Digital Entrepreneurship in China

Haiqing Yu

In 2015, a video of a televised speech by a stammering and staggering man called Cui Wanzhi went viral on the Chinese Internet and YouTube. It was broadcast by Anhui Satellite TV in its program 'Super Public Speakers' on 27 April 2015. The show featured Cui as an exemplary e-commerce entrepreneur with disabilities. He rose above this to become named as one of the 'Global Top 10 e-Entrepreneurs' by Alibaba, China's e-commerce giant. Cui was born with physical disability due to a breech birth and lack of medical facilities in a rural village in Anhui province. He managed to get a university degree and upon graduation he became a street vendor and a petit businessman. In 2007, he became an e-entrepreneur on Taobao (a customer-to-customer retail platform owned by Alibaba) selling female apparel, and since 2013 onward he has been specializing in the qipao dress (the cheongsam). He has provided more than 500 job opportunities, employed dozens of disabled people, offered training to people with disability in e-commerce business, and supported more than 20 disabled people to run their own online stores. Cui said during his speech:

> I was born different… Although I stagger when walking and stammer when speaking, I own my company whose annual sales exceed 10 million yuan ($1.5 million) … [As my father told me,] *don't complain: rely on yourself.* If I cannot change the reality, I'll change myself… If one chooses complaints, one's heart will be filled with pain, darkness and despair' if one chooses gratitude, one's world will be full of sunshine, hope and love.

His catch phrase 'Don't complain: rely on yourself' has become viral in Chinese social media, as have his speeches at numerous functions and on local and national TV. Cui has become known as the 'Mr. Cheongsam' (qipao xiansheng) and one of Alibaba's poster boys to promote its e-solutions to disability employment and its social inclusion agenda. This agenda sits squarely with the Chinese government's goal of poverty elimination and achieving 'overall moderate prosperity' through e-solutions and a collaborative approach. Such an agenda has significant implications for groups of people who have traditionally been disadvantaged, especially people with disabilities. They are now the focus of attention in China's new campaign to achieve a balanced, network-based, and inclusive digital economy.

Mr. Cheongsam Cui is one of a small number of successful e-entrepreneurs with disabilities advocated by Alibaba, the major industry collaborator of Chinese Disabled Persons' Federation (CDPF)—the key intergovernmental and supra-governmental organization that represents, provides key service supports, and advocates for disabled people in China. In response to the Chinese government's call for harnessing digital technologies for economic restructuring and poverty alleviation, CDPF has teamed up with Alibaba and other private and nongovernmental sectors to increase employment training and opportunities for people with disabilities in China (Fisher et al. 2018). Disability employment and entrepreneurship has been advocated as key to the national inclusive development policies. Digital economy has been promoted as central to China's industry upgrading and economic restructuring. Under such a context, CDPF and its industry partners have taken measures to encourage people with disabilities to explore innovative solutions to economic participation as a way to improve their income, life quality, and social inclusion.

Alibaba is one of China's digital companies that have responded to such a disability inclusion strategy via digital technologies. It has collaborated with local CDPF branches to train disabled people to shop online, run e-stores, and/or work as custom service personnel through cloud computing on its platforms (Taobao.com and Tmal.com). It is reported that in 2017 there were 160,000 e-stores run by e-sellers with disabilities on the Taobao retail platform, with a total annual transaction volume of CNY12.4 billion (USD 1.8 billion). I addition, 2.46 million buyers with disabilities spend an annual expenditure of CNY 22.1 billion (USD 3.2 billion) in online transactions (Aliresearch 2017). Even though these numbers are small compared to the total number of e-stores and consumers on Chinese e-commerce platforms, they are indicative of new opportunities for employment and poverty alleviation of people previously excluded from the traditional labor market (Goggin et al. 2018). This is confirmed by a recent report in *People's Daily*, the key Party mouthpiece, on the improved situation of disability employment in China (Pan 2018).

Successful individuals like Mr. Cheongsam Cui have been promoted in the mainstream media as examples of disabled entrepreneurs who ride on the wave of digital economy to make a successful and fulfilled life. Cui himself has also participated in such a media offensive through a self-promotion campaign: he has refashioned himself as an Internet celebrity, an e-commerce celebrity, and a disability celebrity through highly publicized public talks, media presence on TV programs, and packaged digital media presence on WeChat and other social media platforms. His book entitled *Don't Complain Rely on Yourself*, which is part autobiography and part self-help 'chicken soup for the soul', was published in 2016. He even managed to have a film made in 2017 about his life through crowdfunding. Not only the 'rely on yourself' discourse but also that of 'if he (a disabled person) can do it, so can you (disabled or not)' has underlined such choreographed media framing of e-entrepreneurship with disability from both the top-down (by the government, DPF, their industry partners, and mainstream media) and the bottom-up (by disabled entrepreneurs and disabled people's organizations).

This kind of 'triumph over tragedy' stories about people with disabilities has underscored the mainstream discourse about disability in China for decades. The recent emphasis on disability entrepreneurship, particularly digital entrepreneurship, adds a new dimension to our understanding on how population is managed and governed in postsocialist digital China. This chapter examines the rise of the digital economy and its impact on disability entrepreneurship in China. In particular, it analyzes the neoliberal logic that underscores the promotion of disability e-entrepreneurship in the mainstream media. Mr. Cheongsam is among many other individuals with disabilities from rural China whom I encountered and had opportunities to interview during my fieldwork in 2016 and 2017 on projects related to rural informationization and e-commerce. Cui represents the opportunities and paradoxes of Chinese digital economy of disability. Following Aihwa Ong and Hentle Yapp's elaboration of exceptionalism (Ong 2006; Yapp 2017), I argue that disability has been treated as exception in China's postsocialist trajectories of development both within and without. It has recently emerged as a new form of exceptionality in digital transactions among the Chinese state, China's digital champions, individual digital entrepreneurs, and average citizens. The framework of disability as exception and exceptionality therefore opens up our critical enquiries about the invisible human infrastructure that underpins digital transactions in China.

Disability as Exception

Yapp develops an account of disability as exception, following Aihwa Ong's liminal work *Neoliberalism as Exception* (Ong 2006; Yapp 2017). Yapp seeks to illustrate how disability as an identity category becomes a key neoliberal technology of difference both within and without: within China, disability as exception functions as a master narrative of individual perseverance and eventual triumph over all odds; outside China, disability as exception is used to humanize a racialized China as authoritarian and developmentally behind. He points out that 'disability as an identity category becomes a key neoliberal technology that produces populations and modes of subjectivation' (Yapp 2017: 635).

As a neoliberal technology, disability policies and discourses emphasize individual agency and materialistic individualism. This is not entirely new. It is known that there has been a lack of disability welfare, education, medical provision, and social support for people with disabilities in China, particularly in rural areas (Shang et al. 2009). People with disabilities have to primarily rely on their families and themselves for a living. The narratives of individual triumph over difficulties, perseverance over forms of inequality, and eventual independence from family support and state welfare have permeated the mainstream media.

The emphasis on individual choice, autonomy, and agency is central to new governmentality in late- and postsocialist China (Bray and Jeffreys 2016; Hoffman 2006). Young people are asked to improve their *suzhi* (human quality) through education and volunteering and charitable activities, and to be responsible and patriotic in a competitive job market (Hoffman 2006; Yu 2017). People with disabilities, particularly successful individuals like Mr. Cheongsam Cui, are included in such as a political discourse. Cui has portrayed himself as an average person of a humble origin (from a rural Anhui village) who aspires for social mobility through education. Cui has recounted many occasions of discrimination that he encountered during education and job-seeking processes. But more importantly he has emphasized again and again the importance of self-reliance and entrepreneurship to his success. He is a master in turning setbacks into motivations for success, from a rural boy with disabilities to a university graduate and from a street vendor to an e-entrepreneur.

After being rejected by an elite high school in his hometown, Cui managed to get into a local high school. From there he went to a university in the northwestern province of Xinjiang, so he could prove his independence in a faraway land. Being a poor village boy, he had to earn his own living expenses through business activities such as trading CD and cassette players. His university degree and street vending experience did not help him in seeking formal employment due to discrimination at the job market. After being rejected many times at job fairs and interviews due to his disability, Cui joined millions of the floating population of rural-to-urban migrant workers as a sojourning petty trader in the capital city of Anhui Province, a small business owner (bookstore, gift store, Internet cafe), and finally e-commerce poster boy for Alibaba. Cui's early experience as a petty trader resonates with millions of sojourning laborers from rural origins who are treated by urban residents as second-class citizens without basic rights and access to social welfare, health, education, and insurance and who are treated as subhumans by exploitive employers (Solinger 1999).

Unlike the rural-to-urban migrant workers, Cui has actively accumulated *suzhi* capital through education and entrepreneurship. His identity as a university graduate and later entrepreneur with disabilities separates him from the vast majority of sojourning laborers in cities. The same identity also marks him apart from individuals who fail in managing their own health, wealth, and life, such as HIV/AIDS carriers and sufferers or sufferers of occupational disease such as pneumoconiosis (Ho 2014; Yu 2016). The latter are subject to policing through various forms of formal and informal mechanism of exclusion and are blamed for their failure to be self-enterprising and self-governing subjects (and therefore they are doomed for contracting the chronic and incurable diseases). As discussed later in the chapter, emphasis on *suzhi* and affirmative identity is central to the concept of the enterprising self, with disability as no exception. Such an affirmative approach to disability is championed by individuals with disabilities, as well as CDPF (Dauncey 2012).

While at the individual level disability is no exception to the neoliberal technology of population governance, at the international level disability as exception has underlined China's rise. Many scholars have pointed out how disability was brought to the political agenda and chosen as a forerunner in reforming China's welfare system in the 1980s by Deng Pufang (disabled son of China's paramount leader Deng Xiaoping) and CDPF (Kohrman 2005). Disability became visible in the public discourse in the post-Mao era (from its relative invisibility in the Mao era), with the establishment of the CDPF in 1988 and the passage of the Law on the Protection of Disabled Persons in 1990 under Deng Pufang's leadership. Deng's political connection and influence obviously played a role in raising the profile of disability in China. But what is more significant is how disability as exception is used in improving China's reputation as (known in the West) a socially regressive, political repressive, and developmentally behind country, and in its intention to join the international community, particularly after the 1989 Tiananmen incident (Kohrman 2005; Yapp 2017).

China has strived to be an active advocate and champion for global disability rights since the 1980s. Contrary to its international image as an authoritarian state with a poor human rights record, China has taken a progressive stance in promoting disability rights: utilizing state-controlled media and screen outlets to facilitate disability awareness and publicize the state's role in promoting disability rights, particularly in education, rehabilitation, employment and job creation, and poverty alleviation; sponsoring and participating in disability sporting events such as Paralympics; supporting disability-related organizations and treaties, such as convening the first World NGO Summit on Disability in Beijing in 2000 and rectifying the Conference on the Rights of Persons with Disabilities (CRPD) in 2007 (Aliresearch 2017; Dauncey 2007; Stein 2010; Sun et al. 2011). Its humanitarian approach to the most vulnerable population and its valorization of people with disabilities as national heroes (such as champions of Paralympics or exemplar e-entrepreneurs) work to impress both its citizens at home and audiences on the world's stage.

Sports diplomacy, starting from the ping-pong table, has marked China's reemergence and acceptance into eventual leadership in the international community (Murray 2013). Disability sports have been incorporated into such a public diplomacy strategy. Even before the establishment of CFPF, the Chinese Disabled Sports Association was set up in 1983 and China participated in the 1984 Paralympics (New York). It only took China 20 years to top the medal tally at the Athens Summer Paralympics in 2004. Contrary to the Mao era when a 'healthy' and abled body was equated to a physically, mentally, and more importantly politically healthy nation, the incorporation of disability sports and increasing visibility of disabled people on screens and in the mainstream media in the post-Mao era are underlined by the imperative of 'looking good' on the international stage (Brownell 1995; Dauncey 2007). Now as China becomes the world's second largest economy and biggest digital economy, disability again becomes incorporated into the politics of looking good in public diplomacy, as illustrated in the next section.

Digital Entrepreneurship with Disabilities

Mr. Cheongsam Cui and many other celebrity e-entrepreneurs with disabilities celebrated by Alibaba and CDPF have all held the promise of the Internet, information and communication technologies (ICT), and e-commerce as the new route toward self-efficiency, self-advocacy, and self-fulfillment. In our interview with Cui, he recounted how the Internet opened a barrier-free and bias-free brand-new world for him to explore his options and test his potential as a self-made man. He has held a strong faith in the role of the Internet in creating new opportunities for people with disabilities since he opened an Internet café in 2001. By 2007 Cui's fixed assets had increased from the initial RMB50,000 (USD 7,300) to RMB200,000 (USD 29,000) from the Internet café business. In 2007, Cui decided to invest all his money in running an online store selling female clothes on Alibaba's e-commerce platform Taobao.com and later Tmall.com. He made one million yuan in profit in 2008.

In 2013 Cui added custom-made qipao/cheongsam to his product line, under the patented brand 'Peacock Love' after his profit margin in fashion clothing shrank in an increasingly competitive e-commerce market. He soon made 'Peacock Love' the No. 1 cheongsam brand on Tmall.com, with an RMB50 million profit in 2014. He was subsequently chosen by Alibaba as one of its best ten e-entrepreneurs, and his legendary story as 'Mr. Cheongsam' has been featured in numerous media. Cui has intuitively ridden on the high wave of China's boom in e-commerce and the government's disability employment strategy through digital economy. The role of Internet and ICT in general in disability enablement and empowerment has been recognized in scholarly writings and government reports. It is pointed out that the Internet has enabled people with disabilities to increase social interaction, seek information and mutual support, overcome barriers of prejudice and stereotypes, increase employment opportunities, and promote social inclusion (e.g. Goggin and Newell 2003; MacDonald and Clayton 2013).

In the Chinese context, research has found a positive relation between online activities, network building, and generation of social capital for people with disabilities (Huang and Guo 2005). It is found that access to the Internet and participation in disability communities online can build and extend one's sociality, gain support from peers and the government, and facilitate self-expression and self-advocacy (Huang and Guo 2005; Guo et al. 2005; Zhang 2017). Such a networked digital life generates an affirmative and socialized identity and can also enable one to become an online entrepreneur, such as selling one's writings or running e-stores on Chinese e-commerce platforms (Dauncey 2012). There have been scholarly debates on the paradoxes of digital enablement for people with disabilities, either from the design perspective, user experience, or public policy analysis. They are concerned about issues related to access, online vulnerabilities and risks, the possibilities of new forms of social isolation, and hence further digital exclusion of people with disabilities (e.g. Chadwick and Wesson 2016; Dobransky and Hargittai 2016; Ellis and Kent 2011). People with disabilities in China also experience the promise and peril of digital technology and connectivity in the form of digital inclusion but social exclusion (Lin et al. 2018).

In the mainstream discourse, however, digital technologies and economy are held as the new panacea in promoting disability employment and entrepreneurship in the context of China's leadership call for upgrading its economy and achieving overall moderate prosperity by 2020. The digital economy is seen by Chinese business and political leaders as a new frontier in the creative and collaborative approach to digital inclusion, with e-commerce as a key indicator. In China the digital economy has surged since 2015, with a 30.61% share of the nation's 2016 GDP (China Daily 2017). The fast expansion of ICT and the digital economy in China seems to offer new solutions to perennial problems in disability employment services, particularly for rural residents. Two policy frameworks have influenced the emphasis on e-solutions to disability employment. One is put forward by former Chinese Premier Wen Jiabao in 2015 to upgrade China's economy and innovative capacity through 'Internet+' and 'mass entrepreneurship and mass innovation'. ICT has been central to Chinese digital capitalism and a communications-led economic restructuring (Hong 2017).

The second policy framework comes from Chinese President Xi Jinping's call to take targeted measures for poverty alleviation (also in 2015 for local governments to follow local characteristics in poverty alleviation so as to reach his goal of eradicating absolute poverty), and achieving 'overall moderate prosperity' by 2020 (China Today 2017). This policy framework highlights the priority of the 'moderate prosperity' process for people with disabilities, with emphasis on poverty alleviation and employment/income increase for people with disabilities through concerted efforts by the government, corporates, social organizations, and entrepreneurial individuals with disabilities. E-solutions to disability employment have hence shifted from the accessibility of ICT and digital networks to 'Internet + disability' and 'e-commerce + disability' issued by CDPF in 2016 and 2017 respectively (Fisher et al. 2018).

While not abandoning concentrative employment units (i.e. welfare workshops and enterprises), CDPF has enforced the disability employment quota system under which a 1.5% quota for disability employment is imposed on all employers with over 30 staff or a penalty levy must be paid to the Disabled Persons Employment Security Fund. The fund is managed by the CDPF at all levels of government to provide employment support for people with disability and employers, such as vocational training and job placement. This policy has been abused by private companies who falsify disability employment figures by providing 'shadow' employment positions to people with disabilities in order to avoid paying the disability employment levy, without actually providing employment opportunities to these people. The challenges of providing employment opportunities for people with disabilities in the formal economy are not unique to China. Barriers, discrimination, and constraints that people with disabilities experience have forced many of them to seek self-employment and micro-entrepreneurship in the informal and digital economy, similar to other national contexts (Hwang and Roulstone 2015; Namatovu et al. 2012). Such *push*—discrimination from the mainstream job market and necessity for survival—and *pull*—opportunities of e-commerce and digital technologies as well as government's policy and financial support for disability self-employment—factors have contributed to an increasing number of people with disabilities engaging in small businesses from offline to online (O2O).

The informal sector consists of production or service units that are not registered formally with the government. In the Chinese context, it includes self-employment in small family and courtyard economy. The 'courtyard economy' appeared in the 1980s and 1990s when women and people with disabilities in rural villages were encouraged to engage in income-earning economic activities such as handicrafts, livestock breeding, and small-scale trade (Judd 2002). E-commerce has revived the courtyard economy by expanding its impact and benefit through the O2O model. Quite often people with disabilities are employed in such household- or courtyard-based e-businesses as casual or seasonal workers doing packaging, sorting, and categorizing online orders, or doing custom services on the computer or with their phones.

Self-employment by people with disabilities in the cities is not new either. Even in the pre-Internet era, disabled *getihu* (self-employed individuals) were given tax exemption on their income. They were few in number compared to those employed in welfare enterprises. Most were engaged in the 'traditional trades' associated with disability, such as running tailor shops, shoe repair shops, barber shops, newspaper booths, three-wheelers, massage clinics, and engaging in other low-skill and low-end manufacturing jobs. In the 21st century China has witnessed a paradigm shift in disability welfare and services. Its disability employment policies have moved: (1) from concentration to dispersion (Guo and Bricout 2009), (2) from the state-led-and-dominated approach to a socially concerted and market integration approach (Qu and Zhou 2016), (3) from offering preferential employment opportunities to encouraging individual agency, upskilling, and self-empowerment in disability employment and entrepreneurship (Deng, Yao, Hui, He, Lu, and Tang 2017; Gao 2017), (4) from a focus on traditional industries (including manufacturing) to the digital and social economy and entrepreneurship (Hsu 2017; Leach 2013). Disability entrepreneurship or start-up has become the new buzzword in the official documents of CDPF, and the Chinese government often plays a leadership role in encouraging and supporting disability digital entrepreneurship or employment (Fisher et al. 2018).

Self-employment as e-entrepreneurs has been promoted as the most decent and viable avenue for disability employment in digital China. Disabled entrepreneurs like Mr. Cheongsam Cui have been made celebrity entrepreneurs and exemplary individuals with disabilities. Their stories of 'triumph over tragedy and all odds' have shaped a non-tragic view of disability and a particular version of disability entrepreneurship, that is, the enterprising self. The emphasis on self-reliance and self-fashioning, as in Cui's motto 'Don't complain: rely on yourself', works to reshape the image of disability in an affirming manner. It helps to portray a positive image of disability and of a materialist individualism.

The Enterprising Self

The affirmative approach to disability and the emphasis on self-management and individual choice and agency are central to the neoliberal technology of governmentality in postsocialist China. The enterprising self is an identity, subjectivity, project, and enterprise in the making. As Lois McNay puts it, following Foucault's framework about the self as enterprise, the dynamics of control in neoliberal regimes 'operate not through the imposition of social conformity but through the organized proliferation of individual difference in an economized matrix' (McNay 2009: 56). China is not recognized as a neoliberal state but characterized by a mix of some elements of the neoliberal logic and its cultural and socialist traditions (Yu 2011). Nonetheless, McNay's points about the indirect style of social control and population management through activities of enterprise, such as consumption, entrepreneurship, and commodification of subjective and social experience, are relevant to the discussion about disability and digital entrepreneurship in China. The ideas of active differentiation (rather than standardization or homogenization), individual autonomy and self-responsibility (rather than dependency), and entrepreneurial self-regulation and governance all constitute the self as a form of project and human capital. Disability is no exception to this logic.

In the Chinese mainstream discourse, although the role of CDPF and government in supporting disability welfare and employment is emphasized, individual persons with disabilities who 'have made it' are celebrated as exemplars of the national policy of 'mass entrepreneurship and mass innovation'. They have been used as affirming examples of disability who can turn individual misfortune, disability, or impairment into a positive experience and entrepreneurial identity. E-entrepreneurs with disabilities are often portrayed as self-reliant and self-fashioning individuals who take control of their own fate despite setbacks; they are willing to take risks and be responsible for their own success or failure. Cui's route toward success and celebrity e-entrepreneurship is not without setbacks. But he bounced back after each failure and found new meanings of conducting himself (*zuoren*).

Conducting oneself is enterprising. It is not the external qualifications, 'advantages or limitations of opportunity, education, relationships or social class', that define the enterprising self, but the inner 'qualities within the individuals, such as perseverance, determination, endurance and hard-work' (Davies 2010: 194). This new discourse of entrepreneurial identity emphasizes self-cultivation and self-making as the fabric of the postsocialist moral economy. As David J. Davies demonstrates, successful and entrepreneurial individuals like Jack Ma of Alibaba have been celebrated as the new business models for success (2010). This new discourse of success emphasizes the capacity for persistent endurance despite being an underdog at the start and for modeling the correct self in a competitive market economy. In fact, Jack Ma is the most celebrated poster boy of China's digital economy, and revered by millions of young entrepreneurs and wannabe entrepreneurs. Mr. Cheongsam has referred to Ma from time to time in his semi-biography, public speeches, and interviews.

Like Ma, Cui portrays himself as an underdog who becomes successful with persistent endurance of physical, financial, and psychological difficulties. He is a relentless self-promoter, a social media celebrity, and a classic example of somebody who turns disability into a marketing advantage and self-brand. Cui commented in our interview that it was his disability and his suffering that had become the selling point of his celebrity status, which in turn helps boost sales of his online business. Cui is now a celebrity public speaker with regular appearance on local and national television and interviewed by celebrity TV personalities. His media fame increases his number of fans and followers on social media who in turn increase the sales of his e-stores on Taobao, Tmall, and WeChat. He has opened China's first Qipao-themed restaurant through crowdsourcing via WeChat—he raised RMB6 million in 15 days—to enable more integration of online sales with offline experience for customers (Cui 2016: 154).

E-commerce has enabled the success of some disabled people who previously would have been excluded from economic productivities, by relying on themselves and ICT. They have internalized the discourse of the enterprising self as a form of neoliberal governmentality, just like that of *suzhi* from the 1980s onward that has been used in Chinese official and popular discourse to classify individuals based on an abstract set of differences in physical, educational, intellectual, financial, ideological, and moral qualities. The *suzhi* discourse is closely tied with China's capitalist transformation and the need to set up subjects attuned to the competitive market and ready for rational choice making (Anagnost 2004; Yan 2003). It is used to justify the extraction of surplus value from people of low *suzhi* (such as migrant workers and peasants) to support the economic and social production by the high-*suzhi* people (often educated and skilled, middle class, and urban) (Anagnost 2004). It 'justifies social and political hierarchies of all sorts with those of "high" quality gaining more income, power and status than the "low"' (Kipnis 2006: 295).

The digital economy and entrepreneurship, however, have challenged the conventional assumption about *suzhi*, which is no longer measured by one's physical, material and educational attainments alone. In the current political environment that calls for mass entrepreneurship, high *suzhi* is marked by an entrepreneurial spirit and subjectivity, through which each person becomes responsible for their own physical and economic wellbeing. Individuals are no longer treated as employees or job seekers, but entrepreneurs or 'entreployees' equipped with a 'readiness to self-responsibly bring one's own abilities and emotional resources to bear in the service of the individualized projects' (Hartmann and Honneth 2006: 45). Underlying individual autonomy and difference is a profoundly normalizing process. Virtually everybody in China has become enmeshed in this new discourse of entrepreneurial and self-fashioning identity.

This normalizing process of self-making as the enterprising self fails to interrogate the neoliberal strategies of co-option and exception. As Aihwa Ong points out, we need to explore and interrogate 'the interplay among technologies of governing and of disciplining, of inclusion and exclusion, of giving value or denying value to human conduct' (2006: 5). The increased inclusion of disability in China's digital economy should not come at the expense of active exclusion of people with disabilities, rural women, ethnic minorities, and those on the margins in the sociopolitical structure as *social* beings. Individuals like Cui have arisen from the bottom of the society through education (with a university degree and hence achieving social mobility), opportunity (during China's e-commerce boom), and entrepreneurship. Not all people with disabilities benefit from the e-commerce and e-entrepreneurship approach. The preferential policies on inclusive growth through e-commerce have greater impact for people with physical disability, and hearing or vision impairment. Other people remain excluded from e-commerce because of access barriers such as location, poverty, or literacy. Many people with disabilities are either not registered with their local CDPF as having a disability, or their local CDPF is not able to support them.

Support for people with intellectual disabilities is still concentrated in traditional welfare enterprises. For less Internet-savvy people with disabilities, self-employment is still confined to the traditional trades as mentioned previously. Furthermore, opening an e-store does not automatically generate income. In fact, many e-retailers do not make much profit. The majority of people with disabilities live in poor rural areas or are among the urban poor. The lack of respect for disabled people and of access to quality and inclusive education and unbiased employment opportunities are common problems faced by people with disabilities in China. Middle-class, well-educated, and well-connected men with disabilities are more likely to rise up the social ladder and succeed as entrepreneurs than their rural and female counterparts (Hsu 2017). As Rosalind Gill points out, 'the new forms of work and new laboring subjectivities' have posed new challenges to forms of inequality, and the preference of entrepreneurial individual subjectivities disavows structural power relations that produce the myth of egalitarianism and equality (2014).

Disability and Digital Entrepreneurship

The discourse of digital and disability entrepreneurship is based on the promise that the digital economy is empowering people with disabilities and other marginal groups, as they can participate in economic activities without having to face physical, financial, and social barriers. E-commerce and digital economy can remove some of the traditional physical, educational, and age barriers to disability employment and entrepreneurship. Many people with disabilities and other disadvantaged groups have new opportunities to seek jobs and become micro-entrepreneurs. This is a positive sign of the up-skill and up-stream trend in disability employment, particularly among the younger and educated generation who are fluent in the language of blogs, social networking, and e-commerce. However, it must also be recognized that the celebration of disability entrepreneurship and the discourse of enterprising self are undermined by the structural inequality that face people with disabilities, such as the prevalence of non-regular employment in the labor market and casualization of employment in the informal economy. Disabled people and women are often exploited as the reserve army of flexible and cheap labor. Their participation in the digital labor force is characterized by casualization and flexibilization, and hence low-skilled and low-paid jobs.

The culture of enterprise and the discourse of enterprising self have encouraged a confident, thrusting, and responsible citizenship. Successful e-entrepreneurs like Mr. Cheongsam Cui are portrayed as a new type of role models to inculcate an enterprising subjectivity for the purpose of national image: to look good and legitimate. He has devoted his time to giving public speeches on disability e-entrepreneurship and offering advice to young people on e-commerce start-ups. Apart from employing disabled people in his business, he has opened the 'Peacock Love Business School' to train disabled people to run e-stores on Taobao and Tmall, often as his subcontractors. It is politically, socially, and economically looking good for Mr. Cheongsam. Such an ethic of enterprising self can maximize its own power and quality of life while helping others, without the burden of Maoist self-sacrifice and altruism. Nonetheless, the Maoist role model, Lei Feng, was revived in the early 2000s to encourage young people to volunteer and help others while helping oneself at the same time through the moral sense of 'feeling good' and practical sense of 'self-entrepreneurialism' (gaining experience and skills to enhance career opportunities in a competitive job market) (Jeffreys and Su 2016).

Lei Feng has inspired a growing number of idealistic and resourceful youths to volunteer in social services or take handy philanthropy such as donating steps on WeRun as a 'technology of self' in order to transform themselves into moral, entrepreneurial, responsible, and functional subjects (Fleischer 2011; Yu 2017). This enterprising citizenship is inward-looking in that it requires self-examination, self-improvement, and self-cultivation. It asks people to turn critical eyes inward toward themselves, rather than outward toward the state, the government, and broader politico-economic structure. The ethics of the enterprising self and the politics of looking good are thus intertwined in the exceptional discourses of disability and e-entrepreneurship in digital China. Both are technologies of self-governance at the individual and social level as well as national branding at the international level. The construction of disability discourse and disability entrepreneurship is intertwined with China's attempts to upgrade and restructure its economy, to achieve balanced and overall moderate prosperity, and to take a leadership role as a game changer and rule setter in the new international order.

Disability is taken as exception in these ambitious endeavors, as exemplified first in its proactive attempts to conform to the international standards on disability rights (in the 1980s and 1990s), soften the image of the Chinese authoritarian state (after the 1989 Tiananmen incident), challenge the West of its misconception of China as lacking in human rights (in the first decade of the 21st century), and now project itself as a leader not a follower of the new world order (Stein 2010). The framework of disability as exception and exceptionality therefore opens up critical enquiries about the invisible human infrastructure that underpins digital transactions in China. The rise of China as the world's largest digital economy is built upon myriad forms of digital transactions among the Chinese state (represented here by CDPF), its national digital champions (represented here by Alibaba), grassroots digital entrepreneurs (such as Mr. Cheongsam), and individual citizens. These digital transactions are manifested significantly in the capital, material, symbolic, cultural, and ideological domains. With this in mind, this chapter has taken to task the discourse of disability as exception as a starting point, allowing us to interrogate the implicit logic of the enterprising self that is embedded in discourses of digital entrepreneurship in China.

References

Aliresearch (2017) 'Wangluoshidaizhucan: puhuiyuchuangfu (E-era Assists Disability: Inclusive Development and Wealth Creation)', 18 May 2017. Available: http://i.aliresearch.com/img/20170518/20170518103747.pdf, accessed: 16 May 2018.

Anagnost, Ann (2004) 'The Corporeal Politics of Quality (Suzhi)', *Public Culture*, 16: 189–208.

Bray, David and Jeffreys, Elaine (eds.) (2016) *New Mentalities of Government in China: Emerging Professions, Vocations and Associations*, London and New York: Routledge.

Brownell, Susan (1995) *Training the Body for China: Sports in the Moral Order of the People's Republic of China*, Chicago, IL: University of Chicago Press.

Chadwick, Darren and Wesson, Caroline (2016) 'Digital Inclusion and Disability', in Attrill, A. and Fullwood, C. (eds) *Applied Cyberpsychology: Practical Applications of Cyberpsychological Theory and Research*, Nottingham: Palgrave Macmillan, pp. 1–23.

China Daily (2017) 'Top 10 Provincial Regions in Digital Economy', 8 May 2017. Available: www.chinadaily.com.cn/bizchina/2017top10/2017-05/08/content_29241255.htm, accessed: 10 January 2018.

China Today (2017) 'Jingzhunpupin: Zhongguofupinzhanluo de zhongdazhuanbian (Targeted Poverty Alleviation: Significant Changes in China's Poverty Alleviation Strategies)', 24 February 2017. Available: www.chinatoday.com.cn/spc/2017-02/24/content_735968.htm, accessed: 10 January 2018.

Cui, Wanzhi (2016) *Bu baoyuankaoziji* [*Don't complain' rely on yourself*], Xiamen: The Straits Publishing and Distributing Group.

Dauncey, Sarah (2012) 'Three Days to Walk: A Personal Story of Life Writing and Disability Consciousness in China', *Disability and Society*, 27(3): 311–323.

Dauncey, Sarah (2007) 'Screening Disability in the PRC: The Politics of Looking Good', *China Information*, 21(3): 481–506.

Davies, David J. (2010) 'China's Celebrity Entrepreneurs: Business Models for 'Success'', in Edwards, L. and Jeffreys, E. (eds) *Celebrity in China*, Hong Kong: Hong Kong University Press, pp. 193–216.

Dong, Zhifeng, Yao, Jiani, Hui, Xia, He, Jing, Lu, Qi, and Tang, Yunyu (2017) 'Zizhuyutazhu: woguocanjirenjiuye de lujingxuanze (Self-Help vs Being Helped: A Choice for Chinese Disabled People in Employment)', *Baijiazhengming* (*Contending Views*), 4: 65–68.

Dobransky, Kerry and Hargittai, Eszter (2016) 'Unrealized Potential: Exploring the Digital Disability Divide', *Poetics*, 58: 18–28.

Ellis, Katie and Kent, Mike (2011) *Disability and New Media*, New York: Routledge.

Fisher, Karen, Yu, Haiqing, Li, Bingqin and Goggin, Goggin (2018) 'Impact of the Digital Economy Disability Employment Support in China', in Stepan, M., Duckett, J. (eds) *Expanding Public Services under Xi Jinping: The Role of e-Solutions and New Organisational Arrangements for Providing Better Services*, MERICS Papers on China.

Fleischer, Friederike (2011) 'Technology of Self, Technology of Power: Volunteering as Encounter in Guangzhou, China', *Ethnos*, 76: 300–325.

Gao, Yuanyuan (2017) 'Cong fuchianzhidaonenglikaifa: Canjirenjiuyebaozhangzhuanxingyanjiu (From Job Allocation to Capacity Enhancement: The Transformation of Disability Employment Security Services)', *Xibuluntan* (*The Western Region Forum*), 27(3): 88–95.

Gill, Rosalind (2014) 'Unspeakable Inequalities: Post Feminism, Entrepreneurial Subjectivity, and the Repudiation of Sexism among Cultural Workers', *Social Politics*, 21(4): 509–528.

Goggin, Gerard, Yu, Haiqing, Fisher, Karen and Li, Binqing (2018) 'Disability, Technology Innovation and Social Development in China and Australia', *Journal of Asian Public Policy*, doi:10.1080/17516234.2018.1492067.

Goggin, Gerard and Newell, Christopher (2003) *Digital Disability: The Social Construction of Disability in New Media*, Lanham MD: Rowman & Littlefield.

Guo, Baorong, Bricout, John C. and Huang, Jin (2005) 'A Common Open Space or a Digital Divide? A Social Model Perspective on the Online Disability Community in China', *Disability and Society*, 20(1): 49–66.

Hartmann, Martin and Axel, Honneth (2006) 'Paradoxes of Capitalism', *Constellations*, 13(1): 41–58.

Ho, Wing-Chung (2014) 'Biopolitics, Occupational Health and State Power: The Marginalization of Sick Workers in China', *The China Quarterly*, 219: 808–826.

Hoffman, Lisa (2006) 'Autonomous Choices and Patriotic Professionalism: On Governmentality in Late-Socialist China', *Economy and Society*, 35(4): 550–570.

Hong, Yu (2017) *Networking China: The Digital Transformation of the Chinese Economy*, Urbana, Chicago and Springfield: University of Illinois Press.

Hsu, Carolyn (2017) *Social Entrepreneurship and Citizenship in China: The Rise of NGOs in the PRC*, London and New York: Routledge.

Huang, Jin and Guo, Baorong (2005) 'Building Social Capital: A Study of the Online Disability Community', *Disability Studies Quarterly*, 25(2). Available: www.dsq-sds.org/chapter/view/554/731, accessed: 05 August 2018.

Hwang, Se Kwang and Roulstone, Alan (2015) 'Enterprising? Disabled? The Status and Potential for Disabled People's Microenterprise in South Korea', *Disability and Society*, 30(1): 114–129.

Jeffreys, Elaine and Su, Xuezhong (2016) 'Governing through Lei Feng: A Mao-era Model in Reform-Era China', in Bray, David and Jeffreys, Elaine (eds) *New Mentalities of Government in China*, London: Routledge, pp. 30–55.

Judd, Emily (2002) *The Chinese Women's Movement between State and Market*, Stanford, CA: Stanford University Press.

Kipnis, Andrew (2006) 'Suzhi: A Keyword Approach', *The China Quarterly*, 186: 295–313.

Kohrman, Matthew (2005) *Bodies of Difference: Experiences of Disability and Institutional Advocacy in the Making of Modern China*, Berkeley, CA: University of California Press.

Leach, Anna Veronica (2013) 'China's Landscape Is Fertile for Social Enterprises', *The Guardian*, 6 December 2013. Available: www.theguardian.com/social-enterprise-network/2013/dec/06/china-landscape-fertile-social-enterprise, accessed: 10 May 2017.

Lin, Zhongxuan, Yang, Lui and Zhang, Zhi'an (2018) 'To include, or Not to Include, that Is the Question: Disability Digital Inclusion and Exclusion in China', New Media and Society, doi:10.1177/1461444818774866

MacDonald, Stephen J and Clayton, John (2013) 'Back to the Future, Disability and the Digital Divide', *Disability and Society*, 28(5): 702–718.

McNay, Lois (2009) 'Self as Enterprise: Dilemmas of Control and Resistance in Foucault's the Birth of Biopolitics', *Theory, Culture and Society*, 26: 55–77.

Murray, Stuart (2013) 'Moving Beyond the Ping-Pong Table: Sports Diplomacy in the Modern Diplomatic Environment', *PD Magazine*, Winter, pp. 11–16. Available: http://publicdiplomacymagazine.com/wp-content/uploads/2013/02/30008_PDMAG_2013-31.pdf#page=11, accessed: 05 August 2018.

Namatovu, Rebecca, Dawa, Samuel, Mulira, Fiona and Katongle, Celestine (2012) 'Entrepreneurs with Disabilities in Uganda', Research Report. Available: http://trustafrica.org/en/publications-trust/icbe-research-reports?download=62:entrepreneurs-with-disability-in-uganda&start=40, accessed: 05 August 2018.

Ong, Aihwa (2006) *Neoliberalism as Exception*, Durham, NC: Duke University Press.

Pan, Yue (2018) 'How Is 9.4 Million Disability Employment Achieved [940 wan canjirenjiuyeshizenyangshixian de]', *People's Daily*, 6 August. Available: http://finance.people.com.cn/n1/2018/0806/c1004-30210777.html, accessed: 07 August 2018.

Shang, Xiaoyuan, Fisher, Karen R. and Xie, Jiawen (2009) 'Discrimination against Children with Disability in China', *International Journal of Social Welfare*, 18: 1–11.

Stein, Michael Ashley (2010) 'China and Disability Rights', *Loyola of Los Angeles International and Comparative Law Review*, 33(7): 7–26.

Solinger, Dorothy (1999) *Contesting Citizenship in Urban China: Peasant Migrants, the State, and the Logic of the Market*, Oakland: University of California Press.

Sun, Shuhan, et al. (2011) 'China and the Development of Sport for Persons with a Disability, 1978–2008: A Review', *Sport in Society*, 14(9): 1192–1210.

Qu, Shaoxu and Pei, Zhou (2016) 'Xietongshijiaoxiacanjirenjiuyefuwumoshi de chuangxinyanjiu (Concerted Perspective on Disability Employment Models)', *Guihailuncong (Guihai Tribune)*, 32(5): 54–59.

Yan, Hairong (2003) 'Neoliberal Governmentality and Neohumanism: Organizing Suzhi/Value Flow through Labor Recruitment Networks', *Cultural Anthropology*, 18(4): 493–523.

Yapp, Hentyle (2017) 'Disability as Exception: China, Race, and Human Rights', *American Quarterly*, 69(3): 633–652.

Yu, Haiqing (2011) 'Dwelling Narrowness: Chinese Media and Its Disingenuous Neoliberal Logic', *Continuum: Journal of Media and Cultural Studies*, 12(1): 33–46.

Yu, Haiqing (2016) 'The Biopolitics of China's HIV Governance', in Bray, D. and Jeffreys, E. (eds) *New Mentalities of Government in China: Emerging Professions, Vocations and Associations*, London and New York: Routledge, pp. 182–203.

Yu, Haiqing (2017) 'Philanthropy on the Move: Mobile Communication and Neoliberal Citizenship in China', *Communication and the Public*, 2(1): 35–49.

Zhang, Chao (2017) ''Nothing about Us without Us': The Emerging Disability Movement and Advocacy in China', *Disability and Society*, 32(7): 1096–1101.

Zhao, Xintong and Zhang, Chao (2018). 'From Isolated Fence to Inclusive Society: The Transformational Disability Policy in China', *Disability and Society*, 33(1): 132–137.

12 Resilient Love

Intimacy, Social Media Surveillance and (Dis)Trust in Metro Manila

Jozon A. Lorenzana

Mediated Intimacy

When people use communication technologies to initiate, maintain or end intimate relations, new relationship practices and norms influenced by the capacities and affordances of technology consequently emerge. In turn, these emergent relationship expectations constitute intimacy. This chapter dwells on mediated intimacy, the personal connections made through digital platforms in the context of romantic and conjugal relationships (Baym 2010). Recent accounts suggest that mediated intimacy is characterised by constant connection, partner surveillance and wider access to potential romantic partners (Gershon 2010; Gregg 2013; Hobbs et al. 2017; Su 2016). These aspects generate paradoxes, tensions and emotions that define contemporary experiences of intimacy. In her study of distant Chinese lovers, Hua Su (2016) finds that messaging applications such as QQ enable partners to stay connected. However, being always technologically accessible generates a relationship expectation of constant connection that comes into conflict with lovers' need for privacy or desire for autonomy (Su 2016: 239, 242). With social media's capacity to visibly document interactions and activities in a networked social space, lovers also are able to monitor each other in both private and public domains of social media platforms (Gershon 2011).

Illana Gershon observes how young Americans conduct surveillance even in their partner's private Facebook accounts as evidenced by the practice of sharing passwords (2010: 192). While allowing access to private communication signifies trust and intimacy among couples, it also becomes a source of tension that leads to break-up (Gershon 2010: 195). As partners conduct mutual surveillance on social media, they become prone to feelings of jealousy, uncertainty and dissatisfaction (Elphinston and Noller 2011; Fox and Warber 2014). The anxiety (and temptation) of lovers increases with the possibility of mobile dating applications to immediately access potential romantic or sexual partners, further complicating and destabilising intimate relations (Hobbs et al. 2017). Bauman's claim that intimacy has become unstable and fragile resonates with the dynamics of digitally mediated intimate relations (Bauman 2003). Using a political economy approach, anthropologists and sociologists argue that transformations in social and economic arrangements alter, shape or constitute experiences, practices and ideologies of intimacy (Illouz 2012; Padilla et al. 2007; Rebhun 1999). Hence, the current instability of intimate relations derives from the way market logics and neo-liberal values (e.g. competition, efficiency) are shaping expectations of being intimate (Gershon 2011; Illouz 2012).

Furthermore, changing notions of self and personhood based on physicality, emotional satisfaction and individual autonomy also feed into how people choose partners and relate to one another (Giddens 1992; Illouz 2012). As a result of these transformations lovers become more strategic and calculative; intimacy assumes a transactional and momentary character (e.g. Hobbs et al. 2017; Hoefinger 2013). Indeed, the experience of intimacy is accompanied by tensions such as the importance of self-interest versus ideals of love that include 'authentic sentiment, loyalty and social obligation' (Hoefinger 2013: 4; Rebhun 1999: 59, 172).

The integration of new media into the intimate realm exacerbates the transactional, commercial or neo-liberal tendencies of relationships. For example, Gershon finds that Facebook predisposes US college students to competitive self-presentations and constant surveillance that transform them into neo-liberal selves and, consequently, strain their relationships (Gershon 2011). Dating sites and applications facilitate various types of transactional arrangements that range from one-off sexual encounters to engagements which involve physical and/or emotional intimacy that varies in intensity and duration (Bernstein 2007; Hobbs et al. 2017). While critiques of contemporary intimacy lament its commodification and fragility, ethnographies of love in different societies complicate such understanding by presenting possibilities of being intimate that embraces its economic logic (Constable 2009; Padilla et al. 2007; Zelizer 2005). Nicole Constable argues that transactional or commodified forms of intimacy coexist and transform with countervailing discourses of reciprocity, gift-giving, assertions of love and claims to altruism and bounded authenticity (Constable 2009: 58). Linda Anne Rebhun proposes the term 'economic intimacy' as a form of conjugal love in Northeast Brazil (1999).

Despite transgressions committed by partners, sharing the burden and labour of the household bonds them together as they survive the uncertainty of a modernising economy (Rebhun 1999). In other words, norms and moral ideals about love change with social and economic transformations that define tensions in intimate relations. As digital media become part of peoples' experiences and practices of love, moral tensions arise from contradictions between existing and emergent norms and practices of intimacy. In this chapter, I look at moral tensions arising from the practice of digital media surveillance in romantic and conjugal relations. Using the case of working-class Filipinos in Metro Manila, the study examines the practice of sharing passwords in the Philippine context where it is seen less as a gesture of intimacy but more as a sign of distrust. I aim to identify the moral tensions generated by digital media surveillance and explain how they affect trust in intimate relations. Based on ethnographic data, I find that sharing passwords indicates the transactional nature of trust in a digital media environment where intimate relations become uncertain. Building trust through partner surveillance or transparency comes in conflict with moral expectations of autonomy and privacy among working-class Filipinos. However, ethnographic examples also reveal that intimacy can be sustained under watchful eyes of lovers. I discuss these themes in the following pages, beginning with some assumptions on how uses of communication technologies generate norms and moral tensions.

Moral Tensions and Digital Media

Current approaches on the moral dimension and ethical implications of digital media practices generally proceed by examining the affordances of the communication technology and its social consequences and/or how people regard the technology and its uses. Both orientations consider the materiality and affordances of digital media as the bases for practices and norms but they differ in emphasising the role of technology and social agents in explaining moral tensions. I briefly discuss two ethnographic studies to demonstrate how these two approaches operate and complement each other.

Gershon's work on Facebook use among American teenage couples analyses how moral dilemmas emerging from usage of social media can be explained by the structure of technology (2010, 2011). She suggests that the means and design of communication shape the communicative expectations of media users and subsequent norms that guide them. When digital media users face ethical dilemmas, according to Gershon, technology plays a part by altering the range of information communicated as well as the publics involved (Gershon 2010: 201). Facebook, for example, predisposes self-disclosure beyond the private domain. Gershon goes further on to acknowledge that as a communication technology is used beyond the sociocultural context that produced it, the assumptions built into the technology become more visible and problematic (Gershon 2011: 869). Again, how the private and public are demarcated and managed on one's Facebook page illustrates the value placed by its American creators on drawing a boundary between those two domains. As I will show in the following sections, such feature of digital media platforms becomes a source of anxiety among Filipino users who value transparency in intimate relations. Finally, drawing on historical analysis of new media, Gershon critiques the nature of disembodied communication as morally suspect because it transforms how people determine each other's social status and trustworthiness (Gershon 2010: 201). Clearly, implicit in her analysis is the role of the medium in affecting how both communicators and their actions are perceived (cf. McLuhan 1964). Indeed, for Gershon, moral tensions are also rooted in both communicative distortions via the medium and how digital media users perceive or misconstrue such communicative acts and practices.

While Gershon emphasises the means of communication in generating moral tensions, Assa Doron looks at the social meanings of communication technologies (2012). He suggests that the mobile phone is not just a technology that enables action but also a symbol and manifestation of relations and personhood (Doron 2012: 418). Crucial to Doron's understanding is the manner in which the mobile phone becomes integral to social processes and how the object eventually acquires its social meanings. Thus, objects or technologies assume moral labels and their uses create tensions. Gershon and Doron's modes of analysis complement each other as the former is oriented towards understanding how the medium of communication transforms moral frameworks and the latter is focused on specifying the moral status of the technology of communication in relation to its societal context. Integrating the two approaches allows us to make connections between the emergent norms based on the structure and cultural assumptions of a medium and the status of a technology within a moral economy. From this perspective, a vital component in analysing moral tensions is to specify the sources of morality or moral frameworks that people use to evaluate practices and technologies. Jarret Zigon argues that sources of morality range from institutions to popular discourses (2008: 163–164). These include moralities based on shared socio-economic positions, i.e. class and gender (Rebhun 1999: 109–111). Crucial to Zigon's conceptualisation of morality is the notion of being ethical, which involves:

> …stepping-away from…morality as embodied dispositions…[It] is a conscious acting on oneself either in isolation or with others so as to make oneself into a more morally appropriate and acceptable social person not only in the eyes of others but also for oneself.
>
> (Zigon 2008: 165)

In other words, when people face moral dilemmas they may act in socially acceptable ways that also allow them to be authentic moral agents. Current ethnographic studies on mediated intimate relations tend to focus on heteronormative relationships among young middle-class subjects in Western contexts (e.g. Gershon 2010; Hobbs et al. 2017). As such, there is a need to investigate other socio-economic groupings and cultures, in order to ascertain a wider range of moralities that frame digital media practices and experiences. Thus, the present chapter examines mediated intimacy among working-class Filipinos, whether heterosexual or queer, focusing on the consequences of surveillance in their relationships. When I conducted depth interviews among research participants, a recurring theme was monitoring partner's on- and offline activities. Regardless of gender, the practice of exchanging passwords or checking their partner's mobile phone was a topic that sparked intense discussion. Hence I ask the following questions: what do digital media practices of surveillance mean for working-class Filipino couples? What are the moral entanglements of partner surveillance? And, what does the practice of surveillance and its attendant moral tensions tell us about the nature and experience of intimacy?

Working-Class Couples in Metro Manila

Philippine cities such as Metro Manila provide an appropriate setting to investigate working-class practices and experiences of mediated intimacy. Not only is digital connectivity readily accessible but also opportunities to develop intimacy are common in the city. The Philippine capital attracts workers from around the country and their situation of physical isolation from kinship networks predisposes them to develop friendship or intimate relations among strangers or co-workers. Raul Pertierra reveals how using SMS (short messaging service) creates discursive spaces of intimacy among strangers (2014). He describes how closeness develops through mutual self-disclosure between strangers but it does not cover the maintenance stage of relationships where tensions and conflicts occur (Pertierra 2014: 46). Extending Pertierra's work, the present study focuses on mediated intimacy in the context of people who are already in relationships, wherein digital surveillance has become a practice. It is more concerned with the moral tensions in relation to the practice and its consequences on intimacy in general. Thus, the study hopes to uncover the different moralities at play in surveillance in intimate relations among workers with different backgrounds, including gender identity and sexual orientation. The Philippine context also provides a case to study the interplay of moralities because of the diverse sources of morality that include religious institutions (Roman Catholic, Protestant, Islam), popular culture, global media, schools and even the workplace. In other words, alongside the circulation of modern notions of intimacy is still the lingering influence of institutional moralities promoted by both the state and church as well as underlying local practices.

My research participants come from a barangay (smallest political/territorial unit) in Quezon City where they work as wage earners in retail and food establishments and security agencies. Their ages range from 21 to 33. Two queer/gay participants have steady partners while eight other participants have heterosexual relationships (married or dating). In examining practices of mediated intimacy, I conducted depth interviews to elicit narratives and limited observations to contextualise the claims of research participants. I asked about their life trajectories (from where they come from and how they found work), their relationships (how they met their current partners and their experiences together) and the ways digital media figure into their relationships. Even without preselecting on this basis, my respondents' experiences and practices of relating to their partners already incorporated digital devices and social media platforms, particularly Facebook. Interviews lasted for an hour. I transcribed the interviews and identified themes and tensions in their responses and narratives in which partner surveillance was a salient theme. Interview excerpts were translated from Filipino to English. In the following ethnographic sections, I describe my research participants' experiences of mediated intimacy and discuss the tension between moralities emerging from the structure of media platforms and moral expectations relating to surveillance.

Surveillance, Concealment and Revelation among Lovers

Consistent with experiences elsewhere mediated intimacy among Filipino working-class couples, who are in committed or non-committed relationships, is characterised by feelings of insecurity and paranoia (e.g. Su 2016). The affordance of social media to enable contact with strangers or pre-existing networks threatens relationships. Most of them cited the threat of third parties and being witness to break-ups and betrayals in their social network. Crucially, they mentioned how mobile phones and Facebook enabled and facilitated infidelity. Bella, 33, and a mother of two, confided that her feelings for an old male friend were rekindled when they found each other on Facebook. She admitted being at fault, especially in reference to her husband, who cooked well and looked after their children despite working shifts as a security staff. Bella's story was what my other informants feared might happen to them. But the possibility was not remote because Bella's workmate, Gloria, had confronted her husband over a Facebook friend. Even among queer participants, interactions with other people, including friends, generated suspicions. Thus, partners resort to gaining access to one's mobile phone and social media account to provide each other some assurance.

A common surveillance practice that I noticed is for a suspicious party to take her partner's digital device when they are together. As a matter of routine, partners check the messages and conduct interrogations, especially when they suspect their partner's motives for interacting with a friend or stranger. For instance, the constant beeping of the phone as new messages come in generates suspicions. Confrontations happen when a partner sees evidence of infidelity or flirting with another party in the form of text exchanges. One queer participant even shared: 'When my friend's (also a research participant) partner suspected that he was flirting with other men, he called them up and told them to back off'. From there, the relationship deteriorates or the guilty party becomes subject to more surveillance by a partner. In a context where monitoring a partner through digital media becomes a matter of practice, certain ways of evading surveillance emerge. Alice Marwick finds that people strategically conceal and reveal personal information in a social media environment characterised by interpersonal surveillance (2012).

Jestoni, 28, described how the dynamic of concealment and revelation worked. His story shows how he hid his liaisons with other women. When I met him in 2017, he worked as a supervisor in a supermarket and had a steady live-in relationship. Two years ago he was a sales clerk in one of the city's large malls. Jestoni revealed that he would entertain proposals from other women. A typical mall employs hundreds of contractual employees and provides opportunities to meet new co-workers as employers constantly hire (and fire) every five months. However, they are not allowed to form and show romantic relationships at work. Tall, fit and good-looking, Jestoni attracted the attention of women at his workplace. When he fancied a co-worker, he asked discreetly for her mobile number. They would exchange text messages. At the outset, Jestoni would let her know that he had a girlfriend. I asked him what happened after they exchanged messages. Jestoni revealed that interactions became more intimate during drinking sessions. Conscious about being seen as taking advantage of the situation, he would wait for women to signal interest in him: 'They stay close to you, pretend they are drunk but they're not, and then they ask you to accompany them on their way home. When it's just the two of us, you know what happens'.

According to Jestoni, such encounters lasted only for a night. However, he had liaisons that continued for a couple of months. In such situations, he would tell the girl to wait for his text message or request her to send him messages only during certain times of the day when his girlfriend was away. He did not also add them on Facebook because his girlfriend knew his password. The temporal structuring of interaction is one strategy of concealment that parties who transgress use to evade surveillance. Jestoni's girlfriend caught him once meeting up with a co-worker, and from then onwards his girlfriend would take and check his mobile phone every time they were together. In this situation, the act of controlling a partner's mobile phone, supposedly a private entity, signifies distrust in a relationship. I shall discuss the theme of distrust and the moral tensions generated by practices (e.g. sharing passwords, checking a partner's mobile phone) tied to concealment and revelation among lovers in the next section.

Passwords and the Morality of Trust, Transparency and Authenticity

Gershon suggests that sharing passwords has become a sign of trust and intimacy but such notion is also debated among young romantic couples in the USA (2010: 195). However, among my research participants, it connotes distrust in a partner. Similar to the practice of inspecting a partner's message inbox or call list, sharing passwords has more to do with social control. This interpretation is consistent with Doron's argument about how the mobile phone has become an object of distrust that facilitates transgressions in North India (2012: 429). The mobile phone affords its users to expand relationships and share information that consequently blurs the boundary between the public and private domains and disrupts traditional power relations in the family (Doron 2012: 428–429). For example, Doron describes how a daughter-in-law may ruin a family's reputation by sharing her ordeals with her natal family. Thus, in a traditional Banares family that Doron observed, a daughter-in-law's access to a mobile phone was restricted. In this sense, communication technologies facilitate threats to the established moral order in relationships. Hence, they need to be controlled. In an analogous fashion, the mobile phone and social media platforms facilitate transgressions in monogamous intimate relationships.

However, addressing such threats by monitoring a partner's messages, calls and social media activities generates moral tensions among romantic and married couples. In the case of my queer and heterosexual research participants, surveillance in monogamous arrangements becomes entangled with the tension between privacy/autonomy and transparency. Citing Laura Kipnis, Gregg characterises modern relationships as one in which lovers 'must know everything there is to know about one another' (Kipnis 2003; Gregg 2013: 302). Thus, on one hand, partners operate under the assumption that they can demand openness in the relationship, but, on the other, they are also conscious of the need for privacy and autonomy. This tension is exacerbated by the dynamic of concealment and revelation: partners hide or show aspects of themselves from each other for particular reasons. Experiences of digital surveillance among Filipino working-class couples also tell us that concealing and showing aspects of one's self relate to the morality of authenticity and trust in relationships. Hence, trust among partners depends on how they become authentic in their relationship. Despite the moral tensions digital surveillance brings into relationships, it becomes a way of (re)establishing trust and ascertaining authenticity.

The stories of Elena and Bobby illustrate the moral tensions generated by digital surveillance: between transparency/authenticity, on one hand, and privacy/autonomy, on the other. Elena, 28, worked as a security staff and is married to a tricycle driver. One day she found out that her husband changed his Facebook password. She was angry:

> I was like a fool guessing. Why does he have to change it? You know why? He is hiding something. Sometimes we are using it not to lie, hide [something]. I cannot tell if he is lying, maybe he doesn't want anyone to interfere in his life. Even if we're married, there are things he does not know about me and I don't want him to meddle. There is a boundary that he must not [cross]...
>
> (interview)

Elena implied that hiding or the refusal to reveal passwords also had to do with respecting the privacy and autonomy of partners. But this came in tension with the trustworthiness of her partner:

> I was offended by his changing passwords on Facebook...He told me it is for security because others borrow his phone. He wants to avoid being hacked...He willingly gave his password. If he didn't, I would have suspicions. First of all, I would lose trust in him. Second, what is he hiding from me? Why does he have to change it? If he does not give [his password], he is hiding something.
>
> (interview)

Elena's suspicion had a basis. Previously her husband changed passwords when he had an affair with a neighbour right across their street. She described how her partner concealed his interactions with their neighbour by exploiting the privacy features of social media and the design of his mobile phone:

> On FB [Facebook] he would hide their chat window. Even when his FB page is open you won't see them chatting. He would remove the page history. The cell phone has a password. Messaging is on a private box. It has a code. You won't see a notification because it is hidden. Then he hides the phone itself. Or he would drain the batteries. He removes the battery. Then he borrows somebody else's phone to text. So he would show us nothing. They would really try to hide so they won't get caught. You would anticipate everything. All that's possible including removing the SIM card. His phone has dual SIM. One is turned off. I opened his phone and found two SIM cards, the other is turned off. Messages won't get through. That's what dual SIM can do. They communicate exclusively on the other SIM. Like they have dual personalities. If you want to hide [something], you create your own world, you create another persona.
>
> (interview)

Elena reveals practices of concealing illicit interactions on digital media that translate to compartmentalisation of spaces of intimacy, thereby creating new 'personas' or selves. 'Hiding' in the sense that my informants use the term resonates with Goffman's performative self that does not sit well with the demands of trust in a monogamous relationship. Trust, according to Giddens, is 'built upon mutuality of response and involvement...faith in the integrity of another is a prime source of feeling of integrity and authenticity of the self' (1990: 114). Concealing one's affairs or illicit interactions through digital media diminishes one's authenticity because, as Elena explains: 'one becomes "dual"'. In other words, one does not show a consistent self.

While queer participants have varying attitudes towards monogamy, they pointed out the same moral issues of privacy, autonomy and authenticity surrounding digital surveillance. The next story presents not only a queer perspective but also that of being a partner that is constantly being monitored. It also shows how less expectation of fidelity among queer couples predisposes them to value personal autonomy in the relationship compared to heterosexual couples (Heaphy et al. 2014).

Since coming to Manila five years ago from the Visayan island of Negros Oriental, Bobby, 25, has been employed as a staff in retail establishments. At the time of the study, he served at the take-away food counter of a supermarket. He had a steady relationship with a bisexual guy, Randy, who was a supervisor at a shopping mall. Unlike a common pattern of paid intimacy between Filipino queer/gay people and straight/bisexual men in which the former provides monetary and material support in exchange for sex and company (Canoy 2015), Bobby and Randy's relationship was anchored on emotional and physical intimacy. Bobby admitted that he entertained other men but loved Randy most. They lived apart but regularly met once a week. One day, when I came by to say hello and pick up some food, Bobby was not his usual cheerful self. He was bothered because a boyfriend, who worked overseas but also comes from Negros Oriental, wanted to visit him. Bobby was anxious that Randy might know. For days he agonised over the possibility of being caught. He admitted that he loved his partner but the other guy was better-looking and had made an offer to live with him in Negros. The visit did not push through, but Randy discovered the planned rendezvous when he checked Bobby's phone.

Every time they met, Randy monitored his messages and calls. Bobby shared that despite deleting messages on Facebook, his partner always found a way to see traces of them. Randy went as far as calling up Bobby's boyfriend from Negros. He said that he would end the relationship should Bobby continued seeing other men. Randy refused to talk to Bobby for days but the latter wasted no time in wooing back his lover by sending him messages and making up for his indiscretion. I asked Bobby if he also checked his partner's phone. He did not because 'it's up to Randy if he is real or not'. Bobby's remark echoes the same importance given by Elena to authenticity. He also explained that his mobile phone and social media account are 'personal stuff', thus implying his respect for personal boundaries. In this sense, Bobby valued his partner's privacy and autonomy over the practice of reciprocating partner surveillance.

The two examples show that trusting in a digital media environment creates moral tensions. There is a trade-off between trust and privacy. Revealing, sharing or asking for passwords suggests how gaining trust involves surveillance that allows partners to exercise control in relationships and maintain exclusivity. However, experiences of research participants also reveal that digital surveillance is not always mutual, particularly when partners see more value in other aspects of their relationship such as privacy and autonomy of the partner. In the next section, I further discuss how other aspects in intimate relations override issues of trust.

Trust, Affective Labour and Being Ethical

When partners decide to renew their relationship, they engage in affective labour to regain trust. Compared to dating and queer couples in this study, married ones tend to make an effort to stay in the relationship. Reasons for staying together include their commitment to provide for their children and economic security. Based on my participants' accounts, the more committed partner exerted effort to empathise and to show care. I find that this form of affective labour is not just a consequence of the social pressure induced by the institution of the family in Philippine society but also an attempt by partners to be ethical in their relations (Miralao 1997: 193). They figure out socially appropriate courses of action (Zigon 2008). In the case of my research participants, they maintain their integrity while giving their partner an opportunity to rebuild trust in their relationship. In this situation, they become calculative and consider what would be at stake should they end the relationship.

The story of Jenny, 29, and Robert, 32, who are in a long-distance relationship, illustrates how partners take an ethical approach when transgressions happen. They have two daughters of preschool age and both needed work to make ends meet. Jenny was a bartender in a café while Robert worked overseas in Saudi Arabia and recently in Palau. Like other families with distant partners, Jenny and Robert constantly communicated through text and Skype. The couple would schedule regular interactions on Skype so Robert could talk to their children. Jenny shared that her husband's situation in Saudi Arabia as a migrant is lonely. Apparently Robert developed a close friendship with a female overseas worker. She found out her husband's affair when he came back to visit and noticed that he would use his laptop late at night and chat with someone.

> He met her in Saudi [Arabia]. I can understand. It is a very strict country. Maybe that's his happiness. He has Internet and they communicated there. But when he was already here in the Philippines and he was still communicating with her, that's when I reacted. What is the reason why you are still communicating? 'She is just a friend'.
>
> (interview)

Jenny knew his password on Facebook but respected his privacy.

> I know his password but I haven't opened his FB [Facebook] account for almost a year. At least he also has his own privacy. Also I have trust in him. Even while he was in Saudi Arabia and Palau I didn't open his account. He let me know...Others catch their partners. I don't want to do it. He has his own decision. He's older than me.
>
> (interview)

Despite the setback in their relationship, Jenny empathised with her husband's situation:

> You are apart from each other, there is a temptation. You become attached to the person. There is difference between here and there... I'm broad minded...But I was also hurt. I'm not numb. I didn't do anything but work, manage the home, take care of the kids. Just doing everything is stressful. I don't even go out. I don't want to give him a reason. Because I try to understand that he is far away. ...The communication is different when you are distant from each other... He is alone there. Though he has friends but it's different when he is with family. I try to understand his feelings because he is far from us. And I make more time to update him.
>
> (interview)

Jenny understood the risks of being apart from her husband and remained committed to the relationship. Aware of the demands of communication in a long-distance relationship, she showed care by engaging in more frequent phatic communication through messaging applications. However, trust in the relationship became conditional. Jenny told Robert: 'If you want my trust, I will give it to you but do not waste it. I will not give it to you forever as is' (interview). In this sense, Jenny acted ethically by showing empathy that is also consistent with her authentic self that is both broad-minded and conscientious. Given the conditional nature of trust in mediated intimacy, it requires surveillance. In the case of partners who tend to be jealous, monitoring is part of the process of trusting. For example, Bobby was constantly monitored by his partner after he was caught planning a tryst. However, five months after the incident, I learned that communication between two became less frequent.

'*Hindi na siya nagpaparamdam* (he is not making his presence felt anymore)', reported Bobby. Respecting his partner's autonomy, Bobby said that he will not pursue him. He also suspected that he might have a new lover because his workplace, one of the city's shopping malls, provided opportunities to meet potential partners. Bobby quipped: 'I have many options, anyway' (interview).

Resilient Love?

In this chapter, I examined what digital media practices of surveillance mean for queer and heterosexual working-class Filipino couples and their moral entanglements. By analysing the moral tensions generated by digital surveillance, the study also aims to characterise the current configuration of intimacy. Experiences of research participants suggest that digital surveillance, such as sharing passwords and checking a partner's phone, is seen less as a form of intimacy than as a sign of distrust. Such practice is bound up with the tension between transparency and privacy/autonomy and the dynamic of concealment and revelation that calls attention to a person's authenticity in a relationship. In a context where monogamous relationships are threatened by changing notions of intimacy based on autonomous individuals and the capacity of digital media to provide spaces to meet potential partners, surveillance becomes part of maintaining trust. Intimate relationships are under intense scrutiny. Despite the moral tensions generated by practices of surveillance and the deterioration of trust, working-class lovers who find value in the relationship become ethical and find ways to stay together. Such pattern is common especially among those who come from the provinces and rely on each other's resources to survive in the city.

Whether or not they remain committed to the relationship is a gendered situation. Married heterosexual couples consider the welfare of their children and their economic security. Queer and dating (heterosexual) couples, however, have more freedom to end a relationship and start anew. That working-class couples stay together for economic reasons is a finding that resonates with Rebhun's notion of economic intimacy (1999). Love is also about 'maintaining the household, sharing the burden of work, overcoming hardships, and accepting shortcomings, irritating habits and failures in one's partner' (Rebhun 1999: 211). Indeed, while digital surveillance subject relationships to moral tensions and scrutiny, the case of Filipino working-class couples shows that love has become resilient. Depending on partners' commitment and investment in the relationship, intimacy in the age of social media can withstand the stress of transgressions. However, experiences of research participants also suggest that trust is not necessarily re-established. One can stay in a relationship even with little trust in which digital surveillance provides a sense of security. So while current literature characterise intimacy as fragile, the present study suggests the possibility of its resilience as partners stay together to survive or as they find another chance to love.

References

Bauman, Zygmunt (2003) *Liquid Love: On the Frailty of Human Bonds*, Cambridge: Polity Press.

Baym, Nancy (2010) *Personal Connections in the Digital Age*, Cambridge: Polity Press.

Bernstein, Elizabeth (2007) 'Buying and Selling the 'Girlfriend Experience'': The Social and Subjective Contours of Market Intimacy', in Padilla et al. (eds) *Love and Globalization: Transformations of Intimacy in the Contemporary World*, Nashville, TN: Vanderbilt University Press.

Canoy, Nico (2015) 'Intimacy Is Not Free of Charge': An Intersectional Analysis of Cultural and Classed Discourses of Intimacy among Gay and Transgender Identities', *Sexualities*, 18(8): 921–940.

Constable, Nicole (2009) 'The Commodification of Intimacy: Marriage, Sex and Reproductive Labor', *Annual Review of Anthropology*, 38(1): 49–64.

Doron, Assa (2012) 'Mobile Persons: Cell Phones, Gender and the Self in North India', *The Asia Pacific Journal of Anthropology*, 13(5): 414–433.

Elphinston, Rachelle and Noller, Patricia (2011) 'Time to Face It! Facebook Intrusion and the Implications for Romantic Jealousy and Relationship Satisfaction', *Cyberpsychology, Behavior, and Social Networking*, 14(11): 631–635.

Fox, Jesse and Warber, Katie (2014) 'Social Networking Sites in Romantic Relationships: Attachment, Uncertainty, and Partner Surveillance on Facebook', *Cyberpsychology, Behavior, and Social Networking*, 17(1): 3–7.

Gershon, Illana (2010) *The Breakup 2.0: Disconnecting Over New Media*, New York: Cornell University Press.

Gershon, Illana (2011) 'Un-Friend My Heart: Facebook, Promiscuity, and Heartbreak in a Neoliberal Age', *Anthropological Quarterly*, 84(4): 865–894.

Giddens, Anthony (1990) *The Consequences of Modernity*, Stanford, CA: Stanford University Press.

Giddens, Anthony (1992) *The Transformation of Intimacy: Sexuality, Love and Eroticism in Modern Societies*, Stanford, CA: Stanford University Press.

Gregg, Melissa (2013) 'Spouse Busting: Intimacy, Adultery, and Surveillance Technology', *Surveillance and Society*, 11(3): 301–310.

Heaphy, Brian, Donovan, Catherine and Weeks, Jefferey (2014) 'A Different Affair?: Openness and Non-monogamy in Same-Sex Relationships', in Duncombe, J., Harrison, K., Allan, G. and Marsden, D. (eds) *The State of Affairs: Explorations in Infidelity and Commitment*, Abingdon: Routledge, pp. 167–186.

Hobbs, Mitchell, Owen, Stephen and Gerber, Livia (2017) 'Liquid Love? Dating Apps, Sex, Relationships and the Digital Transformation of Intimacy', *Journal of Sociology*, 53(2): 271–284.

Hoefinger, Heidi (2013) *Sex, Love and Money in Cambodia: Professional Girlfriends and Transactional Relationships*, London: Routledge.

Illouz, Eva (2012) *Why Love Hurts: A Sociological Explanation*, Cambridge: Polity.

Kipnis, Laura (2003) *Against Love: A Polemic*, New York: Pantheon Books.

Marwick, Alice (2012) 'The Public Domain: Social Surveillance in Everyday Life', *Surveillance and Society*, 9(4): 378–393.

McLuhan, Marshall (1964) *Understanding Media: The Extensions of Man*, New York: McGraw Hill.

Miralao, Virginia (1997) 'The Family, Traditional Values and the Socio-Cultural Transformation of Philippine Society', *Philippine Sociological Review*, 45(1/4): 189–215.

Padilla, Mark, Hirsch, Jennifer, Muñoz-Laboy, Miguel, Sember, Robert and Parker, Richard (eds.) (2007) *Love and Globalization: Transformations of Intimacy in the Contemporary World*, Nashville, TN: Vanderbilt University Press.

Pertierra, Raul (2014) 'Localizing Mobile Media: A Philippine Perspective', in Goggin, Gerard and Hjorth, Larissa (eds) *The Routledge Companion to Mobile Media*, New York: Routledge, pp. 42–52.

Rebhun, Linda (1999) *The Heart Is Unknown Country: Love in the Changing Economy of Northeast Brazil*, Stanford, CA: Stanford University Press.

Su, Hua (2016) 'Constant Connection as the Media Condition of Love: Where Bonds Become Bondage', *Media, Culture & Society*, 38(2): 232–247.

Zelizer, Viviana (2005) *The Purchase of Intimacy*, Princeton, NJ: Princeton University Press.

Zigon, Jarrett (2008) *Morality: An Anthropological Perspective*, Oxford: Berg.

13 Chinese Transcreators, Webtoons and the Korean Digital Wave

Brian Yecies, Aegyung Shim and Jack Yang

Webtoons are fast becoming an important part of the expanding digital media industries, with interest in this niche comic form increasing on a monthly basis across a range of mobile apps and online websites (i.e. platforms). The major South Korean (hereafter Korean) web service provider Naver (aka Korea's Google) has developed a global webtoon platform called 'Line Webtoon', which is accessible across multiple markets and in multiple languages. Given this reach and its impact on cultural transactions, this chapter argues that one of Naver's significant, yet overlooked, contributions to the thriving digital environment across Asia is made by the volunteer amateur user-translators, or transcreators, who localize webtoon content across 32 different languages. Put simply, transcreation is a dual exercise of 'translating' and 'recreating' a media text in a new language, while attempting to preserve the text's original meaning. Accordingly, 'co-creation' is a cultural transactional process that can be explained by the marketing, distribution and localization of Korean- and English-language webtoons across many parts of the globe. As a concept appropriated from the fields of management and manufacturing, co-creation seeks to enhance the value of products, that is, audiovisual content in the present investigation, as well as services and user experiences by facilitating the involvement of intermediaries through networks and thus raising the overall competencies of organizations (Romero and Molina 2011).

Seeking to explain how this transnational cultural practice is undergoing notable transformation, this chapter examines how a coterie of volunteer translators are generating value-co-creation for Naver, the webtoon industry and the global media industry more broadly through their digital transcreation activities. The authors focus in detail on the Chinese cultural intermediaries who are relaying a variety of Korean webtoon genres and series for fans spread throughout the Chinese diaspora. This study demonstrates how developments in the webtoon industry are contributing symbiotically to both the expansion of the Korean digital wave and its revitalized links with China, while also providing a previously unrecognized transactional account of the soft power phenomenon. In so doing, the chapter engages with the concept of cultural transactions and the critical role of intermediaries in furnishing exchange across cultures.

The Platformization of Webtoons

A cursory inspection of headlines in the trade papers and popular press reveals that the global distribution of online comics in the 2010s has gradually evolved into a mature creative industry linked to the rise of blockbuster films, as well as online and mobile games, and other media. For the USA, with the success of popular superhero movie series such as *Spider-Man*, *X-Men*, *Avengers*, *Wonder Woman* and *Batman*, etc., the comics industry has been enjoying a period of unparalleled growth, reaching out to a greatly enlarged readership, including more and more female fans. According to *ICv2*, an online trade magazine for the comics industry, the combined total sales of print and digital downloads of comics and graphic novels in the USA and Canada exceeded the US billion dollar threshold in 2015 through to 2017 (Biggs 2018). While digital comics sales are not as strong as print comics sales, the innovation of alternative payment models means that digital comics can be sold in various ways, including all-you-can-view subscriptions offering thousands of comics for a flat monthly or annual payment. Webtoons – a portmanteau term merging 'web' and 'cartoons', coined in Korea in the early 2000s – are the latest platform to energize the comic and entertainment industry, as well as Korea's creative industries and the nation's soft-power digital wave. Webtoons differ from most webcomics (referring to the practice of uploading comic strips to websites for free and then monetizing them), which are digitized versions of paper comics published online (e.g. Comixology, Marvel.com).

In 2000, webtoons were first published by Korean telecom carrier Dacom's web service provider Chollian, but it was not until 2003 and 2004 that Daum (Daum.net) and then Naver (Naver.com) platformized webtoons in the vertical scrolling format with which we are now familiar. Artist Kang Full's *Love Story* first appeared on Daum in October 2003 as one of the earliest serialized webtoons. A slowly unfolding taboo romance involving a white-collar worker and a high-school girl, *Love Story* was published as a serial over 43 weeks rather than as an episodic comic strip. It attracted over 60 million page views (Lynn 2016: 5), and the industry has steadily grown since then. Today, Naver and Daum (now known as Daum-Kakao) are Korea's first and second largest web service provider, respectively, and the development of the current webtoon business environment has largely been a result of their early efforts. By the end of 2014, Korea's webtoon industry had reportedly reached 450 billion won (approx. $410 million USD), and it was expected to double by 2018 (Chinese Culture News 2015). Due to its expanded language offerings, globalization strategies and international offices, Naver has forged a dominant leadership position in the global industry. In Korea, Naver and Daum have established a distinctive online comics viewing platform and model (initially for free), expanded the market, discovered various ways of using IP (intellectual property) and devised a micropayment transactional model for viewing both current and archived weekly episodes and series.

While there are some obvious differences between various webtoon companies, the basic webtoon platform enables creators to own their own mobile-optimized comics, readers to scroll and binge-watch entire series and fans to comment on individual episodes. Here, the term 'platform' connotes the type of conventional online and mobile Web 2.0 participatory environment that has become driven by user-generated content, streaming media, blogging and social computing (Gillespie 2010). According to Line Webtoon's English site this 'global digital comics service platform' offers over 200 daily updated online comic series for free – accessible on computer desktops, mobile web, and Apple iOS and Android portable devices (Line Webtoon 2018a). Similar to Korea, Chinese platforms have innovated comparable models for circulating and producing digital comic strips. China's comic platforms Manhuaren and Tencent Comic, for instance, are major e-comic digital sites, and their comics are also available through mobile apps. These Chinese platforms have emulated the successful business models emerging from Korea, and it is clear from our industry interviews that Korean webtoon firms and practitioners have their eyes on the rising Chinese market, and also co-producing with or licensing to partners in China. However, scholarship on this topic has yet to imagine the role of webtoons in the expansion of the Korean digital wave, and its global impacts on Korean and Chinese popular culture more broadly. This chapter takes a small step in that direction.

In July 2014, Naver launched its global webtoon servicing platform Line Webtoon site, as its mobile app, utilizing its vast store of previously published webtoons. Specifically, for both the PRC and Greater China markets, Naver built a simplified and separate traditional Chinese version of its webtoon platform. Already having popular Korean titles such as *Noblesse* by Son Jae-ho and Lee Kwang-su, and *The God of High School* by Park Yong-je (with official translations) in its stable was helpful in attracting traffic to the platform. Soon, Naver began using a number of local overseas offices in Japan, Indonesia, Thailand and the USA, to recruit new local comic artists to create local stories, while also offering readers a steadily increasing number of Korean webtoons with translation. Chinese readers have had access to popular Korean titles and other international webtoon series via one of the official sites, or via an Apple or Android mobile phone with the Line Webtoon app (downloaded outside of China and used in conjunction with a VPN because the Line Webtoon app was officially banned in China). Users also have had access to Naver's partnering Chinese-language platform *Dong Man* comic and animation apps, where all Korean webtoons are subtitled in Chinese. According to Line China in late 2016, there were nearly a billion page visits (982,332,000 to be exact) of webtoons accessed on android devices in China from 24 individual platforms via seven different app stores (including 360 Apps, Baidu Apps, Ying Yong Bao, Wandoujia, PP Helper, Huawei Apps and Oppo Apps) (Line China 2018).

As these statistics suggest, the webtoon ecosystem is expanding exponentially, especially in China where the numbers and scale of both industry players and readers have been growing at unprecedented rates. For these reasons, there is much to gain from working in China or with a Chinese partner. As Chua points out, China has an obvious trump card in this large domain: '… its massive audience/consumer market. The desire to profit from this market has driven regional producers to co-produce in China' (Chua 2012: 8). Line Webtoon's simplified and traditional Chinese webtoon sites are designed to do exactly that: to build a substantial resource for conducting cultural transactions and facilitating exchanges across cultures and industries. In doing so, this can enable local and global content creators, as well as international readers to come together under the Line Webtoons umbrella platform banner. The increasing presence of webtoons on online and mobile platforms and apps, and the fundamental changes in distribution channels and user interface, has transformed traditional market structures and industry value chains at home and across many parts of the world (Jin 2015; Lynn 2016). More specifically, according to the 40-page industry booklet distributed to potential creator-owned comic artists/writers at the 2018 Comic-Con International: San Diego in 2017, Line Webtoon recorded over 10 million daily unique readers and over 40 million monthly unique readers, and, to date, over 35 billion webtoon episodes have been read (Line Webtoon 2018b: 5). These figures alone tell an interesting story about the Korean digital wave.

The Digital Wave and Soft Power Success Story

Significant audiences and innovations in the digital world continue to contribute to Korea's 'soft power success story', which has long been known to academics, policymakers, practitioners, and media and popular culture fans alike. A succinct definition for the concept of 'soft power' can be drawn from the heavily cited international relations work of Joseph Nye, who highlights three key elements required for a nation-state to develop soft power or attractiveness: its culture, its political values and its foreign policies (Nye 1990). Advances across these core components establish soft power as an allure to a country and its popular culture, encouraging positive engagement. Korea's creative industries, with some assistance from the various Korean governments (notably after censorship was deemed illegal by the courts in 1996), have been both feeding off and assisting the expansion of Korea's 'soft power' through the export of Korean media and cultural products, simply known as the 'Korean Wave' (Kim 2013; Kuwahara 2014; Lee and Nornes 2015). Since the end of the 1997 Asian financial crisis, the term 'Korean Wave' has encapsulated the global charismatic appeal of Korean cinema, television dramas, popular music, online games, fashion and food. This cultural success story has benefitted from the rapid development of the country's advanced information and communication technology (ICT environment, which continues to place Korea at the top of various ICT country indices (i.e. ITU 2017; OECD 2017).

Digitization – the amalgamation of digital technologies, techniques and practices, as well as the opportunities they provide – has thus been an essential feature of Korea's cultural and social transformation. South Korea has leapfrogged conventional development stages to move from a traditional agrarian society to a paradigmatic information society in only a few decades (Goldsmith et al. 2011). As the newest contributor to the Korean Wave in this digital setting, the webtoon industry takes full advantage of online publishing platforms, not only for distribution and consumption, but also for delivering feedback on aesthetic issues and two-way communication among professional and amateur artists, as well as readers. Unlike digital comic sites such as Marvel Unlimited and DC Comics, which primarily offer previously published content, Korean webtoon platforms offer a dynamic content model. Each episode of a comic series is uploaded on a weekly cycle and reader feedback is instantaneous, allowing artists to modify story details as they unfold. Both famous and unknown artists can publish work on these open platforms, and Line Webtoon in particular allows readers to upload and thus share fan-subbed versions of webtoon episodes. By comparison, this practice is generally illegal in China. Hence, webtoons are unique from other types of digital comics. The way of viewing a webtoon, that is, scrolling down a vertical strip – allows the reader to take in a single episode in a couple of minutes, catering especially to readers using a mobile phone or tablet.

In spite of their distinctiveness, online and mobile webtoons have now become part of a maturing ecosystem, that is – to extend James F. Moore's cornerstone study – a co-evolving digital environment, economic community and web of industry activity that springs from the intersections of 'capital, customer interest, and talent generated by a new innovation…' (Moore 1993: 76). The webtoon and larger digital comics industry is rapidly expanding via new online and mobile immersive virtual reality, augmented reality and mixed reality environments, technologies and platforms, and Naver is one of the major organizations contributing to this transformation. According to the online tracking service *similarweb.com* (as of January 2019), Naver's Line Webtoon

English-language site is the 6th most visited arts/entertainment-animation/comics site, and the 634th most popular site worldwide (up from 12th and 956th, respectively, since February 2018), recording over 54.3 million visits per month (SimilarWeb 2019). According to our discussions with US-based webtoon creators who have their eyes on the digital comics market, this is an astoundingly high number compared to the potential sales and readership of an illustrator's more traditional print and online comics. However, differing from other webcomics that are well known internationally, webtoons use a vertical comics format that is optimized for mobile devices and enhanced by a content delivery method that works on both slower and high-speed Internet infrastructure. Against the background of this globalization of culture, we will go on to consider a close inspection of the popular *Winter Woods* (2014–2017) webtoon series and argue that some of the most dynamic developments in Korea's creative industries are taking shape in cartoon sector.

Transcreators and Cultural Transactions

The success of the global distribution and circulation of webtoons owes a debt of gratitude to the translators who, through their volunteer labor, have begun to reduce language barriers. At once, these intermediaries facilitate a better understanding of Korean comics for people of other nations, languages and cultures. As a vital component of the mediation process by which webtoons circulate, a cohort of translators with a wide range of professional and non-professional skills have emerged. Some rely on machine-translation assistance afforded by readily accessible online and mobile tools such as Traduwiki, Wikitranslate and Google Translate. According to our interviews with a number of leading webtoon platform executives in South Korea, China and the USA, many translators are fervent fans who learned or have been learning Korean, thus pursuing such translation activities as a hobby. Korean webtoon translators are thus part of a larger media culture that includes unpaid fan translators and fansubbers of Japanese manga and other foreign animated films and television programs, which is a distinctive subcultural phenomenon addressed by Lee (2011). Although manga is mentioned only in passing in another study, this type of voluntary 'collective translation' is part of a larger 'crowdsourcing' initiative whereby a semi-anonymous band of user-participants works to localize software, websites, articles, reports, literary texts and interviews (Gambier 2016: 393). The reliance by Naver on – and apparent exploitation of – webtoon translators fits squarely within this definition.

Considering this, the increasing activity of volunteer webtoon text translators and their crucial role in the webtoon localization processes, as well as the function of these artist and reader 'go-betweens', certainly warrant further investigation. Localization is defined generally as a 'process of adapting a product or service to a particular language, culture, and desired local "look-and-feel"' (O'Hagan and Ashworth 2012: xix). This involves the 'comprehensive adaptation of the message into the receiver's environment in terms of both language and cultural context' (Ibid: 17). From this viewpoint, translators have joined the ranks of the 'new wave of intermediaries operating between platforms, creators, advertisers, and traditional media' (Cunningham and Craig 2016: 5420). Put simply, the transnational and transactional affordances of Web 2.0 enhanced platforms such as Line Webtoon are enabling these intermediaries to play a significant role in the facilitation of cultural exchanges, as well as audience gratification. While the current processes under investigation are intertwined with conventional translation, that is, converting a text from one language into another and maintaining the salient meaning of the original text, translating webtoons involves a nuanced and deliberative process. That is, webtoon translators engage in a structured process across cultural zones that is both self-managed and shaped by the guidelines and basic infrastructure offered on the Line Webtoon site – accessible via the contributor's space.

Prospective and active translators can register to become a translator, and also learn which webtoon series and titles are in need of translation. Meanwhile, interested viewers can consume the latest translations by 'worldwide webtoon fans'. Of the various industry stakeholders, Line Webtoon has developed the most advanced interface for translated content across its main English-language site, featuring the voluntary work of user-translators in 32 different languages. Here, the application of Moore's pioneering work on business ecosystems is highly pertinent. These 'unofficial fan translators' (so labeled by Line Webtoon) or transcreators (labeled by the authors) are playing a key role in maintaining Naver's dominant industry position, as well as the general expansion of the webtoon industry. Specifically, they are enabling both Line Webtoon and Naver to 'coevolve capabilities around a new innovation: they work cooperatively and competitively to support new products [i.e., new webtoon series], satisfy customer needs, and eventually incorporate the next round of innovations' (Moore 1993: 76). In this sense, webtoon translators and consumers are actively engaging with one another simultaneously via participatory culture and the localization of content. That is, fans simultaneously consume webtoons while producing user-generated cultural content of their own that multiplies the exchanges across cultural zones, primarily in the form of translation and commentary.

The Research Method

Two methods are employed in our preliminary study: (1) conducting a number of informal industry interviews, and (2) collecting, analyzing and visualizing a big data set. First, our observations, ideas and conclusions are informed by knowledge gained through conversations that the lead author has held between 2017 and 2018 with 26 industry representatives. In South Korea, interviews were organized with agencies, producers, practitioners, policymakers and platform executives from: ComixVR Webtoons, Korea Creative Content Agency, KOMACON (Korea Manhwa Contents Agency), Lezhin Entertainment, Mr. Blue, Nulook Media (Yoon Tae-ho), Realies Pictures (Won Dong-Yeon), Sejong University – Department of Cartoon Animation, Seoul Business Agency (SBA) – Contents Industry Division, TappyToon and Wagit Webtoon Contents Agency (SBA). In China, consultations were held with representatives from the Beijing Film Academy's Advanced Innovation Centre for Future Visual Entertainment and major media companies U17 and Perfect World, as well as transmedia producers from Stanley Tong's Li Xiang Jing Jie Co. Finally, in the USA, coauthors Yecies and Shim spoke with a range of artists who are contributing to the English-language Line Webtoon site, such as Ryan Benjamin (*Brothers Bond*), Karl Altstaetter (*Mirror*), Ryan Pagelow (*Hapi Buni*) and Sung Kang (of *The Fast and the Furious* fame). The authors are grateful to these industry representatives who have shared invaluable insights on the rise and transformation of the webtoon industry; limited space prevents a more thorough analysis and discussion of their diverse views and experiences.

Second, the present study of cultural transactions in the realm of webtoons employs a simple machine processing system and a publically available API used to harvest specific types of data from the Line Webtoon website. In some of our previous work (Yang and Yecies 2016; Yecies 2016; Yecies and Shim 2016; Yecies et al. 2016), we have shown different important ways for understanding this type of localized digital cultural exchange and transnational communication across the Asian region. In effect, and with the computing tools available at The SMART Infrastructure Facility at the University of Wollongong, the authors are applying basic big data research methods, such as supervised machine learning – with a human assisting in data classification, unsupervised machine learning – to assist with classification, clustering and prediction, and graph analysis to understand social connections between translators, translated texts and readers/users. The specific data in this study include webtoon metadata, user profile and contribution lists. Webtoon metadata consist of four raw attributes including ID, author, number of likes and genre. Among them, the 'number of likes' indicates the conspicuous popularity of a particular webtoon. For the user profile, we have recorded a user's unique ID, initial registration date, geo-location, name of translation team (if any) and primary language. The contribution list identifies the particular series and episodes that a translator has completed partially (a percentage) or completely.

Through this basic data collection process, the authors have begun to analyze some of the global translation activities on this platform in more depth than meets the eye. By our count, in January 2018 there were a total of 27,710 foreign-language translators localizing 32 different language versions of serialized content on the Line Webtoon site. Among these are 17,041 translators working specifically with Asian languages, categorized by geolocation of ID registration: China, Indonesia, Japan, Malaysia, Mongolia, Philippines, Thailand and Vietnam. Included in this subset of active Asian language translators on Line Webtoon are 1,136 translators (roughly 4% of the total) who are working on both simplified and traditional Chinese-language versions of a large number of popular titles such as *Winter Woods, Yumi's Cells, Girls of the Wild's* [sic], *All That We Hope To Be, unTouchable, I Don't Want This Kind of Hero, Salty Studio, My Kitty and Old Dog, Gepetto, Super Secret* and *Eggnoid.*

The basic statistics in Figures 13.1 and 13.2 illustrate the different genres upon which some of Line Webtoon's volunteer transcreators have focused. More attention to the possible links between these genre choices and the reception of genres of other popular Korean Wave contents, such as K-dramas and films in these markets, is needed elsewhere. Suffice it to say that we've begun to notice interesting connections between the most prevalent webtoon genres and the genres of other Korean contents in China, Philippines and Indonesia, for example, that are analyzed in previous

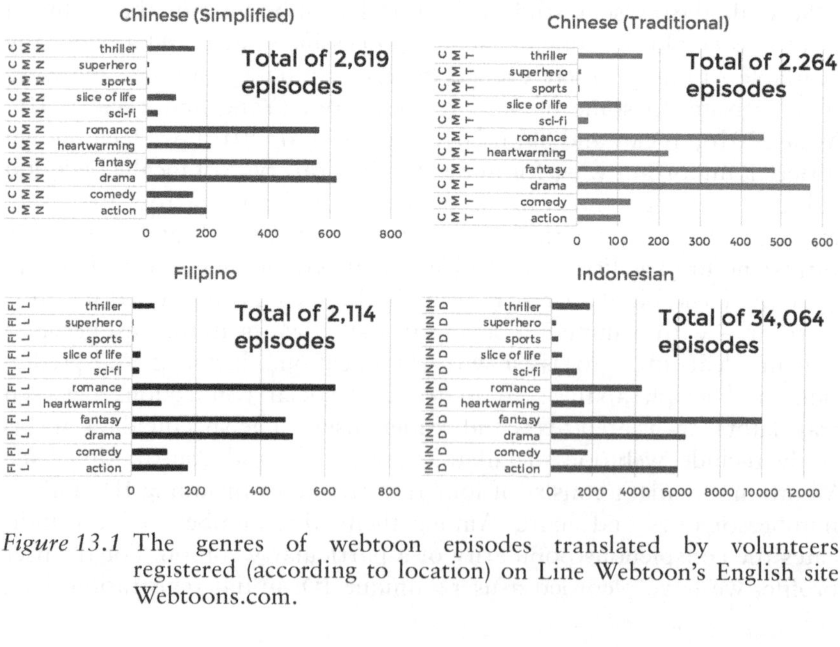

Figure 13.1 The genres of webtoon episodes translated by volunteers registered (according to location) on Line Webtoon's English site Webtoons.com.

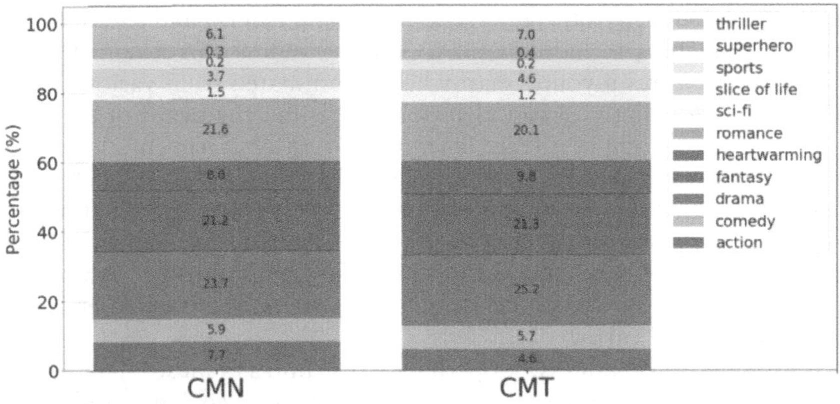

Figure 13.2 Visual comparison of webtoon genres translated into simplified Chinese (CMN) and traditional Chinese (CMT).

studies (Shim and In 2011; Yang 2012). Furthermore, recent industry reports on TV dramas also reveal that both webtoon and K-drama fans in China are attracted to similar romance, fantasy and drama genres. For instance, according to the Response About Content on the Internet website run by Korea Broadcast Advertising Corporation, the top five Korean dramas aired in China in April 2018 include the romantic drama *Something in the Rain*, human drama *My Mister*, legal drama *Suits* (remake of the US show), melodrama *Tempted* and police drama *Live*. In short, the relatively inconspicuous volunteers on Line Webtoon are doing a significant amount of the heavy lifting for this particular platform, which is playing a key role in the global spread of Korean and other country's webtoons, while expanding the larger webtoon production, distribution and consumption ecosystem.

A Big Kiss across Cultures

In the next part of this chapter, we single out *Winter Woods* as a possible example of transcreation. *Winter Woods* stands out for its very high fan ratings (9.79 out of 10), and it is the series presently most favored by Chinese translators. In fact, every episode published has been fully translated – often through the joint efforts of up to six different translators working independently of each other – while series such as *Yumi's Cells* and *Super Secret*, by comparison, have yet to be fully translated. *Winter Woods*, a romantic noir-fantasy produced in a two-season, 129-episode format, is a top webtoon series among Chinese fans. Launched in November 2014 by writer Cosmos and artist Van Ji (with assistance from Lee Hyenseo), this creative adaptation of Mary Shelley's

Frankenstein, or, The Modern Prometheus (1818) features four protagonists (Jane Reina, Winter Woods, Zoe Lev and Adora) and a handful of minor characters, including a portly talking yellow parrot named Roy. The story features a young man who is reanimated from various body parts by a grieving German alchemist following the death of his wife and their unborn child. As the alchemist's 1000th experiment, the young man outlives his creator, and is eventually brought to the USA after World War II. Flash forward to present-day America, and we discover that the *Frankenstein*-like character has been named 'Winter' by Jane, a struggling writer, who invites this child-like person into her apartment (and life) – on a dare from a colleague who encourages Jane to embrace life's unexpected turns.

Through sheer kindness – or perhaps to use him as a muse – Jane tutors Winter in what it means to be human (e.g. how to sleep, bathe and interact with others) and helps him develop a range of feelings and emotions. The vagaries of their relatively shallow romantic relationship – as well as encounters with mysterious characters and some comic relief involving Winter's reanimated pet bird – drive the narrative's episodic twists and turns. As for the other two main characters, Zoe Lev is a violent sadist who is (inexplicably) loved by a blind girl with an acute sense of smell named Adora. Zoe often tortures Adora, whom he keeps in seclusion, and frequently kills people 'to save them' from their terminal illnesses. A number of other peripheral characters and unexplained subplots in this genre-bending noir webtoon series contribute to its intrigue. At the time of writing, the final episode (#52) of season one, which we have dubbed 'the Big Kiss', is one of the highest-ranked *Winter Woods* episodes in terms of reader likes. Despite Winter and Jane's relationship experiencing some tension, the season ends by showing the couple embraced in a passionate kiss. While the visual content remains a constant between all of the translated editions, the English-language and Chinese versions are differentiated by a few but consistent minor grammatical and stylistic changes, particularly regarding the terms used as sound cues (i.e. rattle, smack, step, slam, etc.). While this is to be expected – especially while viewing them on side-by-side screens, given that each translator creates nuances based on their individual skills, experience and tastes – there is at least one major error where Zoe is mistakenly called 'Roy' in the simplified Chinese version.

The greatest point of difference in the final episode is the omission of the kiss in both Chinese versions. Could this be a one-off technical error? More likely, the Chinese translators edited this motif out of the original text but, if they did so, for what purpose? Someone using the name Cher122134 provided the simplified Chinese translation in this episode, while four people using the handles LoNgTaKsWiFtIe, ㄚㄚ, Bella and 葉妮 jointly contributed to the traditional Chinese version. We have noticed other instances in which portions of an episode were missing in the

Chinese translation. In the English version of episode 5 in season 1, for example, Jane tells Winter to bathe because he smells bad. Entering the bathroom, Jane slips on a bar of soap and falls on top of his naked body. This comical scene was cut from both the simplified and traditional Chinese versions, presumably because it contained 'mature content'. But again, more investigation is needed to assess the true intent behind these and similar omissions. Such instances illustrate the imperfections of amateur translation, and the uneven contributions that a wide variety of volunteers with greatly varying backgrounds are making – albeit with the best of intentions – to the webtoon platform.

Cultural Intermediaries and Value Co-Creation Communities

The unique feature of the *Winter Woods* series – and the larger webtoon environment, for that matter – as we argue above, is value co-creation. This is a process that can be explained by the marketing, distribution and localization of *Winter Woods* and other webtoons in China. Value co-creation is actively pursued in the service-based industries to which webtoons belong. It seeks to enhance the value of products, services and user experiences by facilitating the involvement of individual customers through networks and thus raising the overall competencies of organizations (Romero and Molina 2011). In this way of thinking, consumers are considered to be 'active' business partners who work with companies to co-create the values associated with their products and services (Waldner et al. 2012). The strong participatory culture found in the webtoon industry's user base suits this concept. Unlike traditional/print comics companies that have limited opportunities to actively seek feedback from readers and incorporate their requests, suggestions and compliments, webtoon translators are able to respond to user-generated feedback, typically in the form of likes (votes) and comments from readers. Those who participate in this process are true co-creators; they are neither paid employers of the webtoon industry nor passive consumers merely satisfied to be fed preprepared cultural products. In the digital era, borrowing a term from Bourdieu (1984), co-creators such as the ones discussed herein can be understood as 'cultural intermediaries'.

Webtoon translators clearly mediate between different national industries and cultures, thereby facilitating the cross-cultural production and adoption of webtoons in China and elsewhere. In that respect, translators of Korean webtoons are invaluable contributors to the re-production and distribution processes, and thus active facilitators of cross-cultural flows. They remain inconspicuous for the most part, unless a reader makes the effort to cast a like for the translation and/or follows the translator's other work, in which case the translator's ID and work can be noted and traced. The work done by cultural intermediaries is a key part of the political economy of webtoons as a cultural industry. Specifically in China, webtoons are attracting increasing attention from Chinese firms and their platforms for the ways in which they exploit the cutting-edge affordances of the digital era, helping to build a new media ecosystem across all aspects of licensing, production, distribution and consumption. In our view, cultural intermediaries serve as inconspicuous drivers behind this type of bilateral collaboration, proving equal to if not more effective than partners working through official channels that depend on the heavy guidance of the authorities. As long as the window for webtoons is open in countries like China, consumers and fans can view them, form their own communities and drive ever-increasing cross-cultural flows.

In our view, the surge in webtoons in China – and the rapid development of the online and mobile environments in which they operate – fits well with the 13th Five-Year Plan of the People's Republic of China (2016–2020) with its emphasis on developing the nation's advanced information and communication technology infrastructure and its digital creative industries. The policy was adopted in March of 2016, the same year that PRC officials began to rethink the relationship between the Chinese and South Korean creative industries. Because of the popularity of Korean films in Asia over the past decade, Korean cultural industries have been viewed as natural partners for cooperative projects (Yecies 2016). Nonetheless, we remain aware that cultural intermediaries also feed into a degree of 'soft-power competition'. Similar to the study of 'game localizers' in Mangiron and O'Hagan (2006), we see webtoon translators as part of a new breed of 'transcreators', who have certain, albeit restricted, liberties when producing different language versions. Herein lies the cultural power of such intermediary figures, many of whom are becoming celebrities in their own right. Not only are they welcomed by site administrators such as the ones interviewed for this study, but users vouch for their skills by 'liking' their work, adding yet another layer of peer evaluation and value co-creation across various webtoon platforms.

Negotiating Cultural Barriers

Nowadays, when mobile phones and apps are making webcomics readily available, the volume of traffic in series such as *Winter Woods* depends entirely on the taste of users – that is, after censorship of political and culturally sensitive content is taken into consideration. In 2019, the webtoon culture being fostered in China is much more than a simple linear reading culture, on the same level as other manifestations of Korean popular culture. The Chinese fansubbers such as Cher122134, LoNgTaKsWiFtIe, 丫丫, Bella and 茱妮, who between them translated all of *Winter Woods* episode #52 in season 1, are serving as transcreators of this Korean webtoon and its original creators. They are operating in the absence of any direct marketing input from the Korean side, or formal censorship interference on the China side. However, it is worth mentioning the damaging embargo on Korean popular culture in China that occurred between 2016 and 2017 resulting from China's disapproval of the US's installation of the Terminal High Altitude Area Defense (THAAD) missile system on the southern part of the Korean peninsula. As a result of the THAAD 'crisis', Korean creative producers and practitioners across the Korean Wave spectrum experienced a near-total ban on Korean popular culture. Despite years of fruitful Korea-China film and digital media collaborations, the 'THAAD missile crisis' led to unexpected barriers to entry in the Chinese market for K-pop performances, product advertising, the use of Korean stars in Chinese films and television series, film coproductions and remakes, and official translations of Korean webtoons. It also caused a noticeable public backlash toward many Korean-brand white goods and consumer products.

Despite this setback, the webtoon phenomenon shows no signs of coming to an end – it is essentially a grassroots movement that functions partly outside the political system and operates behind the scenes. It is these online communities – which regularly break the law and bypass China's Internet firewall – that are perpetuating webtoon culture in China. Thus, although the official crackdown on Korean cultural contents once posed a threat to joint webtoon ventures in mainland China, these efforts have so far failed to curb what we might call a microculture grassroots intermediating activity. Through these user-led activities we can understand the importance of the webtoon platform as a space where cultural intermediaries are driving both the circulation and consumption of webtoons, as well as the larger flows of Korean popular culture. It is clear that Chinese interests have a major stake in the extended cultural forms afforded by the webtoon industry. Although the industry has been developed by a wide variety of Korean artists, agencies, policymakers and vertically integrated media companies, China has become a key territory and Chinese readers have become collaborative partners in the creation of the webtoon ecosystem, as both fans and translators. Moreover, since the election of Korean President Moon Jae-in in mid-2017, webtoon companies, agents and artists in Korea are again turning to China now that the freeze on bilateral relations has begun slowly to thaw in the post-THAAD missile crisis era.

As far as the authors can see, and from what their interviews with industry representatives have revealed, both Korean and Chinese webtoon players and platforms dream of extending their reach into the global market. The dream focuses on the economic opportunities available there, as well as upon potential solutions for the domestic market to overcome limitations created by the censorship apparatus. At the same time, the relatively small Korean market is becoming oversaturated with webtoons and forcing artists, agencies and firms to look farther afield – just as the limitations of the domestic film industry forced some of Korea's most talented postproduction practitioners to seek new opportunities in China in the late 2000s. However, while platforms such as Naver, Daum-Kakao, Lezhin Entertainment, Topco, Comico and Da'on Creative would prefer to launch their own platforms in China, they continue to face legal restrictions and cultural barriers there. Hence, a viable financial model for profitable Korea-Chinese webtoon co-ventures has yet to be developed. According to the authors' conversations with KOMACON in Korea, and U17 and Perfect World in China, few if any remakes of Korean webtoons for the Chinese market have involved profit sharing through co-investment. For Korean firms such as Naver, localizing webtoons, or at least facilitating the crowdsourced creation of multi-language versions, has become a key localization strategy, primarily achieved by adapting user-translations. This simple but time-consuming process avoids the costs of translating original Korean elements into Chinese cultural content – an important consideration when funding is short and a mature economic model for the industry is yet to be developed. At the same time, this volunteer work elides the need for formal co-planning, coproduction and co-investment strategies that are commonly utilized in the film industry. For Korean firms and practitioners, participating in the Chinese cultural market is one of the most conspicuous and effective ways to expand Korea's cultural industries. As part of this expanding webtoon ecosystem, Chinese translators have begun to contribute to new and significant localization activities that in turn are likely to inspire continued growth in this sector.

Transactions across Cultures and the New Era of Platformization

This chapter has explored how a small army of Chinese translators is generating value-co-creation for Naver and its Line Webtoon platform, the webtoon industry and the global media industry more broadly by playing a significant role in the transcreation of digital culture. As we have seen, a group of translators working on simplified and traditional Chinese-language versions of *Winter Woods* and hundreds of other titles are contributing to the diffusion of Korean webtoons among audiences across the Chinese diaspora and beyond. These cultural intermediaries are contributing symbiotically to both the expansion of the Korean Wave and China's potential soft power ambitions abroad by encouraging Chinese producers in the digital creative industries and the creative economy. Further research on Line Webtoon's volunteer transcreators is needed, for instance, by extending the questions about user-translators raised by translation studies scholars, such as Gambier (2016): where do volunteer webtoon translators sit on the professional spectrum? How are they remunerated (if at all) by Line Webtoon and other firms for their contributions? What are the economic and industry implications of this freely provided work for profit-orientated webtoon companies? What has been the reception of volunteer translations among target language groups? Furthermore, how are Korean webtoons inspiring the production of Chinese and other country's digital comics, and how are these platforms and practitioners boosting the international appeal of foreign media by integrating lessons learned from Line Webtoon and other webtoon platforms and their content? These and other key questions await further inquiry.

To conclude, we return briefly to the concept of soft power to emphasize the importance of grassroots work such as discussed above, and the negotiated nature of cultural transaction across geographic and digital spaces such as the ones inhabited by webtoon firms and platforms. From this viewpoint, and from what we have learned by speaking to some highly active industry representatives, the nature of cultural transactions stemming from webtoon transcreation opens up the broader negotiated nature of cultural exchange and begins to shed light on larger formations within human culture. Clearly, Korea's expanding cultural industries across these physical and digital zones, as well as the focused recruitment of individual intermediaries such as webtoon translators are playing a vital role in the evolving digital economy in Asia and beyond. The Line Webtoon platform and its transcreators are drawing global audiences closer together via charismatic content, while stimulating interest in creating, sharing and engaging with new digital media. As such, and as Athique observes about the television medium elsewhere, the webtoon industry is benefitting from: 'the ongoing mitigation of technological and regulatory barriers, the cultural proximities of audiences seem likely to become a more readily observable factor in delineating the zones within which media content is commonly circulated' (Athique 2016: 130). Indeed, webtoon platforms and apps feature examples of collaborative consumption, and the range of observable webtoon practices gives us an insight into the everyday transactions that underpin the larger transmutations of the media industries. Platforms such as Line Webtoon and its multi-language sites, as well as the global practitioners who inhabit these platforms, are emerging as new media power players, challenging the older print and competing digital comic industries and disrupting multiple media and entertainment ecosystems. As we have seen, Line Webtoon is driving both the 'participatory society' and the so-called shared economy, and volunteer transcreators are central to this development. Support for this study was provided by the Australian Research Council Discovery Project "Mobile Webtoons: Creative Innovation in a New Digital Economy" (DP180101841).

References

Athique, Adrian (2016) *Transnational Audiences: Media Reception on a Global Scale*, Cambridge: Polity Press.

Biggs, John (2018) 'Comic Sales Are Down as Readers Abandon Print', *Techcrunch.com*, 19 July 2018. Available: https://techcrunch.com/2018/07/18/comic-sales-are-down-as-readers-abandon-print/, accessed: 19 July 2018.

Bourdieu, Pierre (1984) *Distinction: A Social Critique of the Judgement of Taste*, London and New York: Routledge.

Chinese Culture News (2015) 'South Korea's Online Comics Market Has Grown in Size', *China Economic Net*, 15 January 2015. Available: www.ce.cn/culture/gd/201501/15/t20150115_4344376.shtml, accessed: 15 January 2015.

Chua, Beng-Huat (2012) *Structure, Audience and Soft Power in East Asian Pop Culture*, Hong Kong: HKU Press.

Cunningham, Sand Craig D (2016) 'Online Entertainment: A New Wave of Media Globalization?' *International Journal of Communication*, 10: 5409–5425.

Gambier, Yves (2016) 'Rapid and Radical Changes in Translation and Translation Studies', *International Journal of Communication*, 10: 887–906.

Gillespie, Tarleton (2010) 'The Politics of 'Platforms', *New Media & Society*, 12(3): 347–364.

Goldsmith, Ben, Lee, Kwang-Suk and Yecies, Brian (2011) 'In Search of the Korean Digital Wave', *Media International Australia*, 141: 70–77.

ITU (2017) *Measuring the Information Society Report 2017*, Geneva: ITU.

Jin, Dal Yong (2015) 'Digital Convergence of Korea's Webtoons: Transmedia Storytelling', *Communication Research and Practice*, 1(3): 193–209.

Kim, Youna (2013) *The Korean Wave: Korean Media Go Global*, Oxon: Routledge.

Kuwahara, Yasue (2014) *The Korean Wave: Korean Popular Culture in Global Context*, New York: Palgrave Macmillan.

Lee, Hye-Kyung (2011) 'Participatory Media Fandom: A Case Study of Anime Fansubbing', *Media Culture and Society*, 33(8): 1131–1147.

Lee, Sangjoon J. and Nornes, Abé Markus (2015) *Hallyu 2.0: The Korean Wave in the Age of Social Media*, Ann Arbor: University of Michigan Press.

Line Webtoon (2018a) Available: www.webtoons.com/en/, accessed: 8 October 2018.

Line Webtoon (2018b) 'Creators Wanted', 2018 Comic-Con International: San Diego booklet, Los Angeles, CA: Line Corp.

Lynn, Hyung-Gu (2016) 'Korean Webtoons: Explaining Growth', *Institute of Korean Studies Annual*, 16: 1–13.

Mangiron, Carmen and O'Hagan, Minako (2006) 'Game Localisation: Unleashing Imagination with 'Restricted' Translation', *The Journal of Specialised Translation*, 6: 10–21.

Moore, James (1993) 'Predators and Prey: A New Ecology of Competition', *Harvard Business Review*, 71: 75–86.

Nye, Joseph (1990) *Bound to Lead: The Changing Nature of American Power*, New York: Basic Books.

O'Hagan, Minako and Ashworth, David (2012) *Translation-Mediated Communication in a Digital World: Facing the Challenges of Globalization and Localization*, Clevedon: Multilingual Matters.

OECD (2017) *OECD Digital Economy Outlook 2017*, Paris: OECD Publishing. doi:10.1787/9789264276284-en, accessed: 8 October 2018.

Romero, David and Molina, Arturo (2011) 'Collaborative Networked Organisations and Customer Communities: Value Co-Creation and Co-Innovation in the Networking Era', *Production Planning & Control*, 22(5–6): 447–472.

Shim, Doo Bo and In, Cheol Min (2011) 'Popular Culture Formations in Asia and the Context of Taiwanese Drama Consumption in South Korea', *The Journal of Asiatic Studies*, 144: 155–183.

SimilarWeb (2019) Available: www.similarweb.com/website/webtoons.com, accessed: 8 February 2019.

Waldner, Florian, Zsifkovits, Martin and Heidenberger, Kurt (2012) 'Emerging Service-Based Business Models in the Music Industry: An Exploratory Survey', Paper presented at *the International Conference on Exploring Service Science*, Geneva, Switzerland.

Winter Woods (2018) Available: www.webtoons.com/en/romance/winter-woods/ep-0/viewer?title_no=344&episode_no=1, accessed: 8 August 2018.

Yang, Jonghoe (2012) 'The Korean Wave (Hallyu) in East Asia: A Comparison of Chinese, Japanese, and Taiwanese Audiences Who Watch Korean TV Dramas', *Development and Society*, 41(1): 103–147.

Yang, Jie and Yecies, Brian (2016) 'Mining Chinese Social Media UGC: A Big-Data Framework for Analyzing Douban Movie Reviews', *Journal of Big Data*, 3(3): 1–23.

Yecies, Brian (2016) 'The Chinese–Korean Co-Production Pact: Collaborative Encounters and the Accelerating Expansion of Chinese Cinema', *The International Journal of Cultural Policy*, 22(5): 770–786.

Yecies, Brian and Shim, Aegyung (2016) *The Changing Face of Korean Cinema: 1960 to 2015*, Abingdon: Taylor and Francis.

Yecies, Brian, Yang, Jie, Shim, Aegyung and Berryman, Matthew J. (2016) 'The Douban Online Social Media Barometer and the Chinese Reception of Korean Popular Culture Flows', *Participations: Journal of Audience and Reception Studies*, 13(1): 114–138.

14 Insurrectionary Tendencies

The Viral Fever Comedies and Indian Media

Akshaya Kumar

Over the last five years, a YouTube channel, The Viral Fever (TVF), has gained enormous popularity across urban India. In the first episode of one of their recently launched shows entitled *Barely Speaking with Arnub*, the host Biswapati Sarkar – one of the most popular faces of the channel – interviewed Shahrukh Khan – one of Hindi cinema's most popular stars. Sarkar was mimicking the loud and outrageous self-projection of Arnab Goswami, a popular television news anchor for the channel Times Now. The interview predictably satirized Khan himself as well as his associates in the film industry, but also lampooned Rahul Gandhi – a prominent politician – and Yousuf Pathan – an Indian Premier League (IPL) cricketer. There was a seamless movement across films, television, social media and journalism in this brief discussion, which actually brought TVF and Khan together via their promotional campaigns. As was evident in the brief segment at the end of the video, Khan was promoting his upcoming film *Happy New Year* (2014) while TVF was promoting their channel and its new show. Incidentally, Khan also owns an IPL team, which itself is a promotional cocktail of cricket, Bollywood and the ancillary media industries. IPL itself is a rather curious cocktail:

> Since 2010, the Board of Control for Cricket in India has been fighting to prove that the Indian Premier League is comparable to a soap opera. The board has been attempting to show the Competition Commission of India that the IPL is not primarily a 'unique format of cricket,' but rather an entertainment programme. The BCCI contends that the IPL is just another sporting event 'designed for commercial purposes and to attract television broadcasters.' In fact, the cricketing body has argued that the IPL is an entertainment programme that competes with, among other shows, the talent show 'India's Got Talent' and the drama 'Yeh Rishta Kya Kehlata Hai'.
>
> (Sagar 2018)

Designed by the BCCI (Board of Control for Cricket in India) as an 'action-packed reality show', IPL is a television extravaganza, only much better integrated and amplified in scale than the emerging web-based clusters, like TVF. Just as IPL does not aspire to be a unique form of cricket, TVF does not aspire to be a unique form of audiovisual storytelling. As a part of the shared force field of cross-promotional media franchises, they take modular forms – cricket and comedy, for example – and wrap them in what I shall term as the membrane of the popular. The reason behind TVF launching the cross-promotional series with the Arnub character was one of their most popular videos – *Bollywood Aam Aadmi Party: Arnub Qtiyapa*. In the show, Sarkar mimicked Goswami as 'Arnub with a u' and invited on his show panelists impersonating prominent political personalities, while literally speaking about Bollywood. It is entirely possible that this strange alchemy across various tiers of the media, cricket and politics seems utterly absurd to an outside observer. But at the same time, to Indian viewers increasingly familiarized with mixed codes, TVF shows only appear as a creative hybrid of news television, cinema, cricket, reality television, etc. Instead of addressing a privileged inner circle, the mixing of codes drawn from the top layer of media references – heavily regurgitated across social media platforms, television channels and web-based forums – builds solidarity with the celebrity circuit and an entire world of interpenetrating promotional frenzy that is mounted upon them.

Instead of presenting TVF as a unique or representative case, I invite us to think of the modalities it pioneered which are now widely distributed across numerous web-based channels, platforms and series – a witty rehashing of the disassembled constellations drawn from the promotional design of various media platforms. In this new rendering of digital transactions, references are drawn from celebrity news and an increasingly contiguous lifeworld of cross-advertising, including reality television and web series. Some of these web-based platforms are hosted on YouTube as channels, while some have also developed their own platforms while retaining a presence on YouTube. Let us first engage with this predominantly digital domain of the popular. One might indeed argue that there is nothing new or unique about celebrity gossip, blended with news, opinions and commentary under a witty sign – often disparagingly termed page 3 material. Entertainment magazines for a long time, and certain entertainment television channels too, have been serving this cocktail for a while. How do we distinguish the digital moment?

Scholars across the world grip the digital variously, never quite agreeing on one privileged way of seeing. For Jonathan Beller, the digital is marked by computational capital which is particularly invested in systems of computation propelled by the capacity to treat the image as a data source, which could then be fed into sophisticated algorithms (2016). For Pasquale, the corporate ownership of these computational systems by large capital renders the contemporary world as a black box society in which information and its processing, which crucially determine our lives, remain opaque to the people (2015). Neves and Sarkar situate the digital within ad hoc practices of video making, suggesting that the 'medium's advantages have multiplied with chroma keying and nonlinear editing suites, networked publics and platforms for rapid duplication and sharing, cheaper equipment and simplified do-it-yourself operations' (2017: 17). For them, the penumbra of the global describes

> the global itself as a penumbral formation. This sense of a continually evolving global is markedly different from the gradual dialectical incorporation of various locals within a homogeneous and universal structure: penumbral globality would, of necessity, remain partial and contingent, as an emergence.
>
> (5)

The penumbral also, however, 'gestures toward the irrepressibility of local media practices in the face of dominant global norms' (2). Athique, Parthasarathi and Srinivas, on the other hand, explore Indian media in the times of the privatization of state media monopolies, new inflows of investment capital and remediation via digital technologies as an interlocking domain (2018a, 2018b). In two volumes on industrial and market dynamics, they take a comprehensive and long-term view of Indian media situated within the journey from media development towards media economy. The digital media is therefore situated as a formalization drive for corporate capital within this comprehensive frame, updating a similarly elaborate discussion by Athique (2012).

Without pretending to offer anything comparable, I focus on a particular constellation of digital media, which however remains tethered to a vast domain of popular media. A crucial move, therefore, remains the identification, consolidation and narration of this domain of the popular as an intelligible and contiguous realm. For this, I coin a phrase – the membrane of the popular. A membrane is a pliable sheet acting as a partition lining. It is a thin elastic boundary which *lines* the popular in such a way that it *prohibits* an attempt to directly access the constituents of the popular. I use the metaphor of the membrane without discounting its materiality. Its thinness ensures an approximate feel while also holding the shape of the popular. The digital is the materiality of this membrane refusing the popular to remain segmented across platforms. What Henry Jenkins calls 'convergence culture' therefore is a reference to the interpenetrations which render a contiguity to the realm of the media (Jenkins 2006). But, in the case of Indian media, the ions that are mobilized to enable this interpenetration are those of celebrity, who constitute the alphabet of the popular (see Kumar, Forthcoming). These celebrity-ions need to be unhinged from their 'native' platforms so as to serve the mandate of the digital popular. We are therefore confronted by a shift from relatively autonomous media ecosystems of film, television, sports, politics and news to an increasingly contiguous ecosystem characterized by rapid exchanges. The membrane of the popular – a digital layer of media activity where constituents are casually referenced without actually being dealt with – holds the shape of this ecosystem.

More importantly though, it is not only that certain media platforms prefer to hold the popular via this membrane. Instead, the bulk of digital media activity participates in this multimodal traffic to reconstitute the popular, for all practical purposes. As I shall later argue via TVF, this reconstitution primarily serves the interests of the advertising industry. Only in the advertising universe does celebrity serve a flat purpose, and to that extent, there appears to be a 'natural' parity between a film actor and a cricketer or politician. When this advertorial imperative is expanded and knit into a media constellation, politicians, cricketers, actors, models, journalists or anyone sufficiently famous sit upon a similarly flat bench of *celebrity function* – which I call the membrane of the popular – from where they can be picked, briefly mocked at and sat right back down (Kumar, Forthcoming). The instrumentality of the celebrity-function for media is thus significant. The membrane is where they are stacked up and rearranged. On this membrane an increasing variety of new media platforms have germinated in the last decade. As one of the most prominent and popular of these, TVF deserves closer attention. I argue in the following pages that the life cycle of TVF content can be broadly divided into three segments. Even as they graduated from short commentary or parody videos to more sophisticated ones, and then to full-fledged web series, most of the tendencies consolidated in the first phase continued to flourish.

The Qtiyapa Videos

The web-based channel was started in 2010 with a series of 'Qtiyapa' videos. Qtiyapa itself is a parody coinage of a common low-intensity slur implying fooling around. In this entire series, TVF videos would comment on popular media content, such as Hindi films and songs. Two of the more appreciated videos out of these would be: (i) *Gaana wala song* making fun of *Ishq wala love* from a big-budget film, *Student of the Year* (2012), and (ii) a two-part running commentary over the visuals of *Gangs of Wasseypur* I & II (2012), blending together the trends on social media and IPL. Various other Qtiyapa videos were a riot of parody: *Rowdies* against MTV Roadies, one of the most popular reality television series showcasing aggressive masculinity of young men through various physical routines; *Lagey Raho Shetty Bhai* against the action films of Rohit Shetty, one of the most successful producer-directors of the time, *Breaking Good* against the American television series Breaking Bad; *Order Your Siddhu Now* against Navjot Singh Siddhu, a well-known Indian cricketer turned commentator; *Qissa Missing Dimaag Ka* against one of the longest running crime series CID and many more. In each of these videos, meticulously identified tendencies were identified and exaggerated for a parody effect. The Qtiyapa series was thus heavily invested in and dependent upon the media content it was mocking at. In fact, it was feeding off some of the most popular media commodities produced in India.

In its introductory graphic of the Qtiyapa videos, however, a TVF hoarding would slam down a television set, implying the end of TV and the rise of a new platform, a different set of attitudes, and certainly an alternative engagement with consumer choice and time. Uploaded on YouTube, these videos garnered much attention not merely on account of their extraordinary wit, but because they lampooned something widely known, even if often unloved. To that extent, TVF was inaugurating an urban youth specific content – particularly targeting the single men – steering them away from television as a familial platform. Several of these videos featured a melodramatic mother, often played by Nidhi Bisht, parodying the overtly melodramatic tendencies of general entertainment channels of Indian television. In one of these videos – *The Life of Aai* (mother in Marathi) – this hopelessly melodramatic mother who refuses to listen to reason is idolized for Mother's Day. *Suron ka Sasur*, on the other hand, lampoons the absurdly melodramatic styling of the most popular reality show, Indian Idol, by highlighting the occasional bursts of emotion displayed by the judges. The three judges mimic their celebrity counterparts, leaving the auditioning candidate flummoxed. Indeed, this baffled candidate is a stand-in for TVF's imagined audience, who fails to appreciate the inexplicable popularity of *Indian Idol* and what Anna McCarthy calls a 'neoliberal theatre of suffering' in reality television (McCarthy 2011).

Therein lies the double-edged allure of neo-liberal media – if it promotes, on one hand, a theatre of suffering in reality television, from its inner folds emerges the theatre of wit that questions the absurdity of its counterpart. As much as TVF stylizes itself in opposition to TV, it also maintains an abiding relation to it, even if in mimicry and laughter. The gulf between the two is constituted by generational shifts, or familial versus individualist consumption of media content. What McCarthy argues about American reality television holds true for much of the content on Indian television, whether it is soaps, crime series or a whole bunch of reality programmes:

> The television courtroom, both a simulation of the justice system and a source of binding juridical decisions, is a space where governance and entertainment blend together...As a form of governance, these programs are notable in their disciplinary reliance not on the inculcation of virtue but rather on shame and scolding.
>
> (2011: 18)

This neo-liberal theatre of suffering, to the extent that it upholds a disciplinary constellation of public shaming, paves the way for an alternative constellation where the attendant moral outrage is scoffed at, ridiculed and parodied for its hollowness. In the TVF imaginary, there's an invocation of the rebellious tendencies which stand outside the moral stranglehold of Indian media. The Internet and its apparent association with the 'free' world are instrumental in the advertisement for a media constellation aspiring to break the shackles. Qtiyapa videos, therefore, marked the beginning of what could be called a post-censorious media imaginary. Marked by informality, commentary, occasional abuse and a commitment to breaking the familial rules, the TVF videos evidently address the small town north Indian migrant men working in the information technology (IT) hubs of peninsular India. The embedded idea of the north Indian small towns is relatively consistent with the rise of small town nostalgia in Hindi cinema since mid-2000s, which I have discussed at length elsewhere (Kumar 2013). TVF videos shifted this nostalgia industry from the multiplex to the web, targeting an overlapping demographic, while offering quirky comic sketches of the small towners. In terms of maturation on this axis, one could cite *Munna Jazbaati* as an early frivolous portrait, and Jitendra Maheshwari in *Pitchers* (2015) as a rather sophisticated one, both featuring Jitendra Kumar, TVF's best-known actor.

The sustained clarity about the target demographic was instrumental in the rise of TVF, and was vitally supported by the digital feedback loop of likes, comments, shares and subscriptions. They also pioneered creative routines of addressing their target demographic directly, asking them to *participate* in the TVF campaign for a web-based platform. The consistency of the TVF team and their increasingly familiar actors also upheld this growing intimacy with their participant-audiences. Indeed, all these efforts were also encouraged by the demographic overlap between the TVF team and their audiences, who shared a journey from various provincial locations to an apparently cosmopolitan world. This would show up in a variety of their videos where parents make surprise visits into the TVF world. On all such occasions, the viewers are treated to the allegorical *intrusion* of Indian television into the TVF space – the conservative morality of provincial north Indian parents thus sits uncomfortably alongside the flat-sharing children's growing ease with a liberal outlook.

The overlapping conflicts within a cross-generational divide also pitched as the conflict between a provincial imaginary and a newfound liberal one have been TVF videos' bread and butter. While one of the more creative examples of the above would come from their first web series *Permanent Roommates* (2015–), a key series woven around this overlapping tension is *Tech Conversations with Dad* (2014–). The episodes of the series are designed as a single conversation between a father and his son, who lives away from the family in a bigger city down south. The son is haunted and frustrated by his over-inquisitive father who is only beginning to learn the ways of the World Wide Web. The episodes range from discussions on Twitter, Facebook, online ticket bookings and mobile applications. Almost invariably, we witness Jeetu, the son, interrupted by his persistent father's endless queries, to the extent that he regrets any mention of a technical word, anticipating further queries. However, the gulf staged is not merely confined to the older generation's delayed familiarity with the Internet, but more so about the apparent irrelevance of the technological platforms for a provincial imaginary, based on a close-knit sense of the social. The parents' repurposing of social media for reinforcing familial ties, or their cluelessness about the millennial language, distances them further away from the world inhabited by the offspring, who have already naturalized the Internet as their everyday habitat.

We thus witness the father fail to understand why he would be interested in the everyday life of Amitabh Bachchan – a veteran Indian star rather active on Twitter – who he is interested in as an actor. In the episode on data breach, on learning that Cambridge Analytica can help win elections, he wants to fix a deal with them to contest for the general secretary of a neighbourhood committee. We also witness a stark difference in their surroundings – the father may be sprawled in a large balcony under a mosquito net, or have a gramophone behind him while the son sleeps on a couch in a suburban flat, or is out on a date to an Italian restaurant. Yet the series also offers an opportunity to embed advertising for Airtel data packs, Flipkart online sale, Ola cabs or Mi Smart TVs. The series thus aggregates the usage of Internet education to showcase the cleavages across differential social vantages with the addition of web-based convenience to the provincial lifeworld. The humour that emerged out of the encounter between two contrary social imaginaries is creatively manoeuvred towards advertising the algorithmic economy to those not yet 'connected'. Out of these additions for brand placement emerged the more thoroughly promotional and professional face of TVF, enabling it to be a player in its own right within the cross-promotional economy of celebrity traffic.

The Insurrectionary Youth: Promotional Insertions, Hinglish and Informality

The groundwork for the membrane of the popular was done by Qtiyapa videos, which drew heavily upon the media content from television, cinema, cricket and social media. Incisions were made thereafter to insert the celebrities within this membrane, to knit them into the promotional artifice so that they could benefit from the impressive consumer traffic and attention being harvested by TVF. The metadata on

YouTube provided a reliable feedback loop to establish a quantitative basis of their popularity. The above-mentioned series – *Barely Speaking with Arnub* – was a resultant effect of this quantifiable popularity upon which the celebrity insertions were mounted to enable an enthusiastic cross-promotional vocabulary. Unlike earlier videos where the promotions were understated – slipped through without direct emphasis – the celebrity insertions made the promotions increasingly emphatic and direct. Together with All India Bakchod (AIB), TVF began to lead the web-based platforms featuring film promotions, a staple diet of reality television for a long time. Once again, if one needed any proof against TVF's posturing of being antagonistic to television, this was one. With celebrity insertions, the divide between television and TVF was increasingly artificial and platform specific. With an increasing penetration of mobile phones and more affordable Internet data packs, the target demographic of urban youth was expanding and was made directly accessible on their portable devices, as opposed to the privileged platform of nuclear families – television.

While TVF has meticulously developed content specifically for the urban youth, television has not necessarily remained far behind or let go of the demographic. Historically speaking, the television has been central to the collapse of walls between autonomous horizons of media activity. The expanding bouquet of satellite television since the late 1990s compelled television channels safely ensconced within their generic profile to compete with other channels (Kumar, Forthcoming). In this supremely competitive media climate, at least three tendencies hold particular value as agents which consolidate and converge the genres and segmentations spread across media platforms and typologies. First, the celebrities came to represent the pre-eminent cross-promotional commodity which could easily traverse the divide between news, drama, reality television and sports telecast, but remains invaluable due to the scarcity attendant within stardom. Second, an equally important resource for traversing the formal functional imperative of a particular channel and its wider appeal for 'general entertainment' would be the language tailor-made towards conflicting yet encompassing imaginaries. For most of the Hindi language media, this meant leaning towards Hinglish, to attract the urban youth. For example, Channel V underwent a makeover from a music channel to one invested in youth-oriented shows, particularly inhabiting a climate saturated in social media.

Among the popular serials on the channel are (i) *Sadda Haq*: *My Life My Choice* – the story of a girl who wants to be a mechanical engineer, but her family thinks that a girl's main objective should be to get married and have kids, (ii) reality show *Confession* that caters to small town teenagers' day-to-day problems. The choice of language on these and many other shows is Hinglish – forging new intimacies across disjointed orders of urbanity and youth in contemporary India. Channel V programming gradually pushes Hinglish into smaller towns. On these shows, Hinglish is the language spoken on campuses, but also at home to communicate with elders who also talk back in the same language. Mobile or online chatting and SMSes also shape the use of Hinglish (Parmar 2014). Hinglish is therefore an invitation to break down the walls of formal distinctions and celebrate the rise of a multimodal informality. It is the symbol of a new social imaginary consolidating with the help of identities saturated in references drawn out of the expanding media ecosystem, of which all the platforms are beneficiaries. Hinglish therefore represents a temperament of informal reaggregations, in a relentless process of reconciling with bearing witness to the present. It is this present and the act of bearing witness that enjoins various media platforms.

Even as TVF championed this cause to influence a rupture and consolidate its own identity, the tendencies cut across a wide variety of content. As Prakash (2014) informs us, *Navbharat Times*, a prominent Hindi newspaper, operates in a 'mission mode' to style itself in an alternative language imaginary. With a variety of new experiments, the newspaper has styled itself as the avant-garde of informal code-mixing, the leader in replacing the formality of the printed world with the informality of the spoken one. Similar tendencies could be witnessed across various news channels, pulp fiction, FM radio, weblogs, social media, online music channels and entertainment magazines – all of them deploy an informal and multimodal language imaginary invested in the vagaries of speech mixed eclectically. In her co-edited book *Chutnefying English*, Rita Kothari traces the shift from English to Hinglish in Hindi cinema, from a language situated outside the sphere of everyday Indianness to the simultaneity between Indian and global, *des* and *pardes*, nation and diaspora (Kothari 2011). Trisha Gupta, in an article on the expanding role of English in Hindi film production among cast and crew members uncomfortable with spoken Hindi, shows how Hindi is increasingly accessed via English, or at least the Roman script (Gupta 2011).

The two authors grapple with an ideological flattening, yet marked by a pragmatic discomfort of fully reconciling, across what used to be two distinct planes of articulation. While Kothari concludes that the reconciliation is undergoing a celebratory spell, Gupta suggests that alienation and discomfort linger over the voice of Hindi cinema. The key reorientation at work in the post-liberalization period, however, was towards a transitory community to be addressed anew. The Hindi film industry sought to reorient the contours of capital, desire and travel within emergent genres to address this new community in perpetual transit (Athique and Hill 2010; Kumar 2017). Madhava Prasad also writes that 'the speakers of certain languages have begun to discern the limits of their language as their worlds become embedded in other encompassing worlds. *The experience of the pressure of these limits is arguably one of the defining experiences of modernity* (Prasad 2011: 71, emphasis in original). The Hinglish moment of postcolonial history is forged together by the embedding of an urban middle-class world within encompassing diasporic imaginaries and the concurrent transformations in the industrial-political reconfigurations of urban India.

Third, the foregrounding of a deep irreverence for the referents is drawn from the popular corpus. The idea of youth-specific content across the spectrum is built around the freedom to mock, ridicule and insult. In the resultant scenario, both the digital media and celebrities thus mocked at appear to be winners, having a hearty laugh about the hollowness of popular culture, as a construct in which they merely play their respective roles as predetermined. The participants are redeemed of their stakes while the membrane of the popular is successfully lampooned as well as reinforced. I would argue that irreverence in digital media upholds an *insurrectionary* ritual, as opposed to the dominant *cathartic* mode of suffering on television. This insurrection, however loud and witty its declaration of independence and aversion against catharsis, remains deeply tied to it. By co-opting the celebrities within this insurrection, the ritual allows them to restore and re-present their 'real' selves by celebrating the insurrection within. Consider, for example, Khan being asked about him buying film awards at the ceremonies in the Arnub show, where he jokingly admits that in the first half of his career he was buying the awards which they now pay him to accept, further adding that his account is now in balance.

Perhaps the most well-known instance of such an insurrection would however be the *AIB Knockout* – a roast comedy show held in Mumbai, 2015 featuring actors Ranveer Singh and Arjun Kapoor as the roast and producer-director Karan Johar as the host (roast master). With many of the most famous Bollywood families in attendance, the AIB Knockout deployed what is now a standard insult comedy form of American humour. While it riled up many people, including celebrities, with the outrageous insults handed out to even those not in attendance, the roast became an occasion for the 'online community' – led by TVF who put out a video in favour of the Knockout – to argue their right to freedom of speech. The most vociferous members of this community invariably comprised of stand-up comedians and artists engaged in web-based content creation. Their stirring defence of the digital platform notwithstanding much of the attention accorded to the show was because of the plethora of celebrities involved and the unprecedented abusive nature of the language. The Knockout tore apart the wall of public decency that celebrities are often hidden behind. Instead, the insurrectionary ritual saw them own up to the insults privately hurled at them – particularly, Johar's relentless insults upon his own sexuality. The Knockout stretched the irreverent tendencies of online humour to their absolute extremity, and in multiplication with scores of celebrities in simultaneous attendance, it became the ultimate dream – with decisively nightmarish incisions upon it – of digital media. It went viral, and was taken down due to court cases slapped against it, only to re-emerge online weeks later.

The Knockout was a fatal wound to the cathartic imaginary, but it also decisively set apart AIB and TVF. The former was a bunch of metropolitan 'boys' with direct connections with film celebrities, engaged in importing them into borrowed American idioms. Whereas the latter, engineers having migrated from small towns of north India, brought up on a heavy dose of cathartic storytelling, leading an insurrectionary charge against it. Unlike AIB, hidden behind TVF's insurrectionary charge, however, was some reasonable empathy for the cathartic routines.

Upscaling: Blending the Cathartic into the Insurrection

A few months before the Knockout, TVF released its first web series – *Permanent Roommates*. The series marked an ambitious expansion of the Qtiyapa form, not so much marking an end to the witty stand-alone videos, as an entry into the multichannel network environment of YouTube. Vonderau describes them as intermediary companies that sell advertising, cross-promote affiliated YouTube channels and develop video brands (2016). They have often been criticized as driving YouTube's commercialization, a seemingly recent phenomenon that sees hithertho informal practices of video making and sharing being increasingly formalized. YouTube, no longer a platform built on singular viral videos, is therefore driven by an algorithmic preference for aggregation, which Vonderau explains thus:

> While the current surge of YouTube Spaces, affiliated film school programs, online help centers, or creator playbooks ('What do you want to learn today?') have been explained (and promoted) as a form of professionalization, it de facto works as a means to streamline and standardize production input. Although benefitting franchisees that lack personality, talent, and a business plan, a franchise relationship is always weighted in favor of the franchisor. For YouTube, it enables an informal vertical integration that allows to spread the risk involved in company expansion while maintaining the benefits of economies of scale... As a speculative activity, aggregation thus has consequently moved the value of video away from the very video itself.
>
> (2016: 370)

However, YouTube was not the only franchisor in TVF's expansion. TVF itself began to host other channels, mainly Girliyapa, The Timeliners and The Screen Patti. The more insurrectionary, experimental and loud content was offshored to the lesser brands while TVF itself graduated a more 'mature' blend of the cathartic and the insurrectionary. *Permanent Roommates* marked the beginning of this tendency to distinguish itself from the 'online community' – while sharing the web as a resource and platform, TVF began to work towards long-form content with embedded brand promotions. In June, 2015 with *Pitchers*, TVF also launched its own video streaming platform – TVFPlay. The series continues to be available on YouTube, with nearly a week of delay after the release on the application. The expansion on YouTube as well as TVFPlay, into a significant variety of web series, and hosting a broad range of collaborators on its platforms, has led to the emergence of a formidable TVF portfolio, showcased at various media events by the team as creative artists and entrepreneurs. In this new architecture, TVF has gone from being a small mockumentary company to an elaborate promotional platform – it promotes new creative media enterprises and actors apart from various web-based applications by hosting them on its platform, while also collaborating with celebrities for cross-promotion. But even as it does so, TVF's highly successful attempts at web series reground the cathartic melodramas within the neo-liberal settings of IT hubs. The protagonists of the TVF series still emerge from north Indian small towns within the technology companies of peninsular India. Meeting in chic cafes, ordering food online, having long-distance love affairs and having Skype conversations for formal and informal purposes does not diminish their melodramatic imaginaries, it only regrounds the old afflictions within a new order, and stages a creative confrontation between the two.

Let us consider *Permanent Roommates*, for example. The series features a long-distance relationship of three years between Tanya and Mikesh, which is given a jolt by Mikesh's surprise proposal for marriage on his trip back home from the USA. While Tanya thinks it is too early for commitment, Mikesh's persistence, and his chemistry with her peculiarly liberal father, makes her relent. The entire first season explores the commitment phobia of young couples in the middle of ambitious urban lives. A live-in relationship thus emerges as a compromise, the spell of partial commitment. Tanya's premarital pregnancy in the next season, however, turns things upside down. The entry of Mikesh's parents gives the series its foundational conflict – the liberal and adventurous lives of the small-town parents, who otherwise represent the conservative standpoint, in a comic tension with the conservative moorings of the lead couple, who otherwise represent the liberal cosmopolitan order. As discussed above, the generational interplay allows the series to explore the conflicts attendant within the social indices of urbanity, gender, age and morality. Mikesh's parents, for example, are far more adventurous than the looming threat of parental censorship suggests. Not only do they accommodate the live-in relationship or Tanya's pregnancy, they are quick to empathize with the couple's misadventures and also share their own. The adults therefore come across as just as vulnerable, adventurous and confused as their young counterparts. Even in the relationship, Mikesh comes across as less mature and dependable than Tanya does. And some of the key sequences which articulate the deepest subjective anxieties and desires are staged with the in-laws – between Mikesh and Tanya's father, Brijmohan, and between Tanya and her mother-in-law.

In this way, the series stages firm, clever but delicate insurrectionary incisions upon the cathartic templates of Indian television. It ruptures an entire range of stereotypes instead of reinforcing them. *Permanent Roommates* is a fascinating attempt not because it stands far apart in its temperament and staging, but because it takes the familiar template of romantic comedies but rearranges the units of their representation. One could indeed argue that it does not campaign for the disruption of the conservative imaginary; instead, it stages a somewhat nuanced, progressive route towards the conservative destination – the reinforcement of the familial order, which it upholds, albeit with qualifications. The lead couple may not be situated within the conservative fold of uninterrupted romance, marriage and childbearing, but while *acknowledging* the interruptions of contemporary urban life – long-distance relationships, premarital sex, independence from familial control and the vagaries of desire – they are gradually brought within the fold. They come to learn that they are not necessarily as different from their previous generation as they might think. The 'traditional' order may appear static, but its resilience should not be underestimated – it accommodates the new generation to perpetuate itself, while also making key allowances. What the series achieves with inserting compassion and caution into the insurrectionary mix, it also enables us to read allegorically. The case made by *Permanent Roommates* also illustrates a powerful argument regarding the relationship between web-based and television series. The cathartic tendencies of television need not be seen as fundamentally antagonistic – they could be just as resilient as the parental control in the series.

As Roy illustrates, Indian television already went through a thorough makeover to accommodate a massive cross-promotional transactional economy, without making any fundamental changes to the catharsis as its essential value (2011). With the insurrectionary posturing of the Qtiyapa videos behind them, TVF stages a possible reconciliation by partly returning to the familial fold of the 'mainstream' publics. It concedes the insurrectionary ground to the other channels within the portfolio so as to focus on its own preferred destination – addressing the masses. Herein lies a key aspect of what is often overlooked in the public discourse on digital media. Just because it takes the web route to slip outside the control of distribution in media industries – whether films or television – the digital media may not necessarily demand and claim permanent autonomy. The digital platforms allow experimentation to the extent that they are propelled by the promise of cross-promotions. Having reached the limits of attention via the insurrectionary predicament, the cathartic mainstream offers an unenviably vast horizon. TVF videos, as exceptional as they may have seemed in relation to television soaps, comfortably share that horizon eventually. Also, *Permanent Roommates* was primarily endorsed by Ola cabs, an app-based taxi hailing service in direct and fierce competition with Uber. The omnipresence of Ola cabs in the series, with its logo frequently and carefully advertised, is a direct acknowledgement of the series' dependence on the capital raised for advertising. TVF's later series *Pitchers* was similarly endorsed by Kingfisher, an Indian beer brand, and *Tripling* (2016) by Tiago, a car then recently launched by Tata Motors. On a film or television screen, anything equivalent would be considered jarring and distasteful. For numerous web series in circulation on a variety of platforms now, such belligerent advertising appears to be normative. Thus digital transactions in India media are indeed already marked by a particular tendency, reflected in the trade-off of censorship and advertising – an exchange of values that needs some careful elaboration.

The Advertorial Afflictions of the Post-Censorious Imaginary

The metropolitan youth, the privileged addressee of an expanding variety of digital media, is the most easily quantifiable, and therefore predictable, of audience demographics. But even more importantly, it is the same demographic that is increasingly leading the charge of digital media production, thereby enabling them to best address 'people like us'. The TVF team remains relatively exceptional in this category mainly because their strength has been to address the youth residing in the *gulf between* the small towns of north India and metropolitan cities – a gulf that is also occupied by the TVF team. Also, on television, to rate and predict the growth of particular shows, the advertisers have to depend on television rating points, which are known to be a deeply flawed metric, on account of incomplete formalization of the economy. The streaming websites and applications, on the other hand, have a perfectly measurable data footprint. As most of the production enterprises raise capital from advertisers and venture capitalists, a 'reliable' measure of popularity goes a long way in establishing the credentials. As per Ivan Ascher's conceptualization of *portfolio society*, a new division is introduced which 'separates those who are free to run the race from those who are free to bet on its outcome', those *whose credibility must be calculable*, from those with the power to calculate (2016: 124).

The digital media frenzy to target metropolitan youth is closely tied to the reliable statistics of credit worth which can be sold to big brands and celebrity portfolio managers. Digital streaming platforms allow them to diversify their risk by plugging into youth specific narratives. But at the same time, TVF's own growth over the past few years has allowed it to diversify its portfolio, steering away from urban youth specific content. However, to the extent that the TVF content remains free of subscription charges, they remain heavily dependent on the capital raised via advertising, whether through brands' promotions or celebrities. Herein lies an inescapable reality of web-based content – their reliance on advertising ties them to the advertisers' preferred target demographic. An obvious example of the same would be TVF's *Tripling* which is a series conceptualized as a road trip because Tata Motors offered capital to promote its new car, Tiago. While the series showcased most of the key features TVF is known for, it is quite unmistakeably a very long advertisement for the car. Various episodes end up quite unfunny and the grip over the narrative is compromised in order to keep the road trip going.

On one hand, the digital media showcase a relentless celebration of the post-censorious freedoms. Unlike films and television, there is no censorship on the web, which has led to a whole range of content – whether freely available on YouTube or independent streaming websites, or even the new series commissioned for Netflix and Amazon Prime – in pursuit of unclaimed freedoms. *Sacred Games* (2018) and *Inside Edge* (2016) are therefore marked by a curious interest in abusive language, nudity and visual or verbal references to sexual intercourse. Several other videos or series on the web, particularly those by AIB, are delimited only by the policies of YouTube, and often go overboard in the usage of abusive language. I argue that these tendencies are constitutive of a post-censorious imaginary because they are precipitated by the burning desire to break free from the censorious orders of Indian media, even if not necessarily tethered to a narration which requires the freedoms available outside of censorship. This imaginary is therefore propelled by an unstable desire, as if to undo media censorship retroactively. On the other hand, the advertorial afflictions are the lifeblood of web-based videos and series; TVF may yet be at the bottom rung of the ladder. Various content creators advertise brands and products in such a way that they appear to be driven not so much by the imperatives of narration as by the advertorial ones.

How should we make sense of a reconciliation in which censorship appears to have been replaced by advertising? What does this tell us about the privileged locus of digital media? Censorship, as a regime of permissibility, often marks its presence in absences – as in the refusal to allow nudity or coitus on screen. It therefore allows the emergence of creative possibilities which sit *beside* the impermissible, exploring the neighbourhood around, finding indirect means of articulation. Advertising, on the other hand, is traditionally marked by the multiplication of direct address and brevity. When inserted into audiovisual storytelling of longer forms, advertorials have to creatively negotiate attention and address. If the advertorial layer is foregrounded, the narrative autonomy of storytelling is conceded to the market, in much the same way as censorship reveals the grip of the state over the narration. The freedom of the web as a resource and platform is predicated upon the loosening grip of the traditional systems of control over media. However, merely shifting to the web does not reclaim the freedoms, unless the creative practitioners only demand the freedom to advertise. The loud frenzy of post-censorious celebrations is therefore a way of *distracting* the audience from the fact that the freedoms earlier tethered to the state are increasingly shifted to the advertisers.

Insurrection to Transaction

The digital is often couched within a euphoric celebration of a landmark rupture. Away from this euphoria, my focus in this chapter has been the web-based creative media channels, particularly the TVF comedies. By disassembling their less than a decade-old corpus, I highlight the development of key tendencies. Marked by irreverence, informality and witty commentary, the early TVF videos made their mark by establishing a witty reappropriation of the membrane of the popular. They drew upon a vast variety of popular content to repurpose it – as an insurrection upon the cathartic mainstream of Indian media content, as a youthful outside to the familial domesticity addressed by television. They projected a humorous dissent and celebrated the freedoms of World Wide Web, rapidly building an intimate bond with their target demographic. In the following years, however, the upscaling mandated by the search for a revenue model witnessed TVF being rehabilitated within a cross-promotional ecosystem. Apart from endorsing brands and celebrities, they also moved to an independent streaming platform and released a romantic comedy web series – *Permanent Roommates*.

I have argued here that the insurrectionary challenge of TVF posed to television reached its limits and was eventually reconciled with the cathartic 'mainstream' through a series of transactions between advertisers, platforms and content producers. We are thus offered a drama that creatively manoeuvres stereotypes reinforced by television, and makes space for the insurrection within the cathartic, setting aside the promised direct assault upon television. By arguing that the insurrection had its affective basis in a post-censorious imaginary, I also establish that the advertorial imperatives of the 'free' realm of the digital sit heavily upon the shoulders of this insurrection. Regardless of the noisy tendencies of the digital, it remains tethered to a well-identified target demographic of metropolitan youth, with a particular focus on single men. To escape the clutches of this often self-imposed identification and reimagine the mass audience, the symbolic value created by the traditional media – whether cinema or television – remains inescapable. As the most successful of online streaming platforms, TVF's journey thereby illustrates the *limits* of digital media disruption. To unsubscribe itself from a narrow target demographic and its attendant advertorial compulsions, the digital must engage in critical transactions, both economic and discursive, with older media cultures, notably television.

References

Ascher, Ivan (2016) *Portfolio Society: On the Capitalist Mode of Prediction*, Cambridge: MIT Press.

Athique, Adrian (2012) *Indian Media: Global Approaches*, Cambridge: Polity Press.

Athique, Adrian and Hill, Douglas (2010) *The Multiplex in India: A Cultural Economy of Urban Leisure*, Abingdon: Routledge.

Athique, Adrian, Parthasarathi, Vibodh and Srinivas, S.V. (2018a) *Indian Media Economy Volume I: Industrial Dynamics and Cultural Adaptation*, New Delhi: Oxford University Press.

Athique, Adrian, Parthasarathi, Vibodh and Srinivas, S.V. (2018b) *Indian Media Economy Volume II: Market Dynamics and Social Transactions*, New Delhi: Oxford University Press.

Beller, Jonathan (2016) 'Informatic Labor in the Age of Computational Capital', *Lateral: Journal of the Cultural Studies Association*, 5(1). doi:10.25158/L5.1.4.

Gupta, Trisha (2011) 'Death by Dialogue', *Caravan*, 1 May 2011. Available: www.caravanmagazine.in/reviews-and-essays/death-dialogue, accessed: 27 July 2018.

Jenkins, Henry (2006) *Convergence Culture: Where Old and New Media Collide*, New York: NYU Press.

Kothari, Rita (2011) 'English *Aajkal*: Hinglish in Hindi Cinema', in Kothari, Rita and Snell, Rupert (eds) *Chutnefying English: The Phenomenon of Hinglish*, New Delhi: Penguin Books, pp. 112–127.

Kumar, Akshaya (Forthcoming) 'Media Portfolios After Credit-Scoring: Attention, Prediction and Advertising in Indian Media Networks', *Postmodern Culture*, 28(1).

Kumar, Akshaya (2013) 'Provincialising Bollywood? Cultural Economy of North-Indian Small-Town Nostalgia in the Indian Multiplex', *South Asian Popular Culture*, 11(1): 61–74.

Kumar, Akshaya (2017) 'Animated Visualities and Competing Sovereignties: The Formal Dwellings of Hindi Cinema', *Social Text*, 35(3): 41–70.

McCarthy, Anna (2011) 'Reality Television: a Neoliberal Theater of Suffering', *Social Text*, 25(4): 17–41.

Neves, Joshua and Sarkar, Bhaskar (2017) *Asian Video Cultures: In the Penumbra of the Global*, Durham, NC: Duke UP.

Parmar, Suman (2014) 'Hinglish of/for the Young: Channel V', *Hinglish Workshop*, 18–19 August, Sarai, New Delhi. Available: sarai.net/hinglish-workshop-18-19-august-2014-recordings, accessed: 3 August 2018.

Pasquale, Frank (2015) *The Black Box Society: The Secret Algorithms That Control Money and Information*, Cambridge, MA: Harvard University Press.

Prakash, Rohit (2014) 'Remix ke daur ki Hindi: 'Hinglish' aur Navbharat Times', *Hinglish Workshop*, 18–19 August, Sarai, New Delhi. Available: sarai.net/hinglish-workshop-18-19-august-2014-recordings, accessed: 3 August 2018.

Prasad, M. Madhava (2011) 'The Republic of Babel: Language and Political Subjectivity in Free India', in Ghosh, Anjan, Nair, Janaki and Guha-Thakurta, Tapati (eds) *Theorizing the Present: Essays for Partha Chatterjee*, Delhi: Oxford University Press, pp. 65–81.

Roy, Abhjit (2011) '*Jassi Jaissi Koi Nahin* and the Makeover of Indian Soaps', in Basu, Partha Pratim and Chanda, Ipshita (eds) *Locating Cultural Change: Theory, Method, Process*, New Delhi: Sage, pp. 19–53.

Sagar (2018) 'The BCCI's Fight to Prove That the IPL Is Entertainment Comparable to a Soap Opera, Not a Distinct Form of Cricket', *Caravan*, 22 June 2018. Available: www.caravanmagazine.in/society/sports/bcci-fight-ipl-entertainment-soap-opera, accessed: 3 August 2018.

Vonderau, Patrick (2016) 'The Video Bubble: Multichannel Networks and the Transformation of Youtube', *Convergence*, 22(4): 361–375.

15 *Hijabers* on Instagram

Visualising the Ideal Muslim Woman

Emma Baulch and Alila Pramiyanti

The chapter explores a distinct set of social transactions around gender, consumption and performance within the domain of Islamic communication; that is, digital spaces where participatory practices multiply discursive interchanges within the global Islamic community. For its case study, the chapter undertakes a semiological analysis by studying the 'enframement' (Spyer and Steedly 2013) of hijaberness in Instagram by members of Indonesia's Hijabers Community (HC). HC was established on Facebook by four 'modest fashion' designers – Dian Pelangi, Jenahara, Ria Miranda and Ghaida Tsuraya – in 2011. Since that time, HC's activities migrated to Twitter and again, more recently, to Instagram. The designers employed strategies common to the cultivation of microcelebrity – a global phenomenon in which ordinary people use online affordances to develop popular following among niche audiences, typically using performative strategies that evince an authentic self well within reach of their fans (Abidin 2016, 2016b; Marwick 2015; Senft 2008).

The chapter extends cross-cultural work on the influencer phenomenon on Instagram, which connects to debates seeking to considering whether and how women exert control over their bodies in post-feminist performances of female entrepreneurship and consumer choice on social media. Our study supports the argument that consumer-led female empowerment championed on social media sites like Instagram is exclusionary of large sections of female populations, because it infers that the less one's capacity to consume, the less worthy one is of being free (Beta 2014; Duffy and Hund 2015). However, we also find that other impulses related to Muslimah (Muslim women's) empowerment, but not directly to consumption, find expression in this predominantly consumption-oriented phenomenon. First, hijabers use Instagram to model ideal husband-wife relations that echo the Indonesian Muslim feminist agenda to reform the institution of marriage. They post images and captions to present evidence of their monogamous marriages in which husband and wife stand on an equal footing. Second, the hijabers use captions on Instagram to 'anchor' their images in interpretations of scripture (Barthes 1977: 38). This shows how they are using the platform as a stage for dakwah ('the call, invitation or challenge to Islam', Millie 2017: 38).

On the one hand, this anchoring may be seen to sanitise the consuming middle-class Muslimah by identifying her as pious (not hedonistic). But on the other, it could also be seen to reveal how hijabers are adopting the tactics of microcelebrity culture to posit their consuming bodies as those capable of authoritatively guiding Muslimah in the interpretation of scripture.

In a substantive sense, these power dynamics play out on the ground can only be revealed by ethnographic research, not by semiological analysis of the performance alone. Nevertheless, we argue that it is significant that the hijabers use of Instagram for *dakwah* coincides with a broader fragmentation of Islamic authority, as digital uptake and the commoditisation of global Islam prompt the proliferation of knowledge-sharing activities outside the mosque (Echchaibi 2011, Scholz et al. 2008). Some scholars argue, this re-spatialising of knowledge sharing not only prompts new contests among male religious authorities, but also affords women greater power in shaping the ways preacher address audiences at preaching events (Millie 2017; Slama 2017). Thus, we consider how the hijabers' Instagram posts could be seen as efforts to advance such feminisation. Ultimately, we argue that a textual analysis of the hijabers' Instagram posts is complicated by their historical positioning at the intersection of digital uptake and rising consumerism, democratisation and Islamicisation in Indonesia. This positioning requires acknowledging the multiple lineages globalising digital cultures in order to grasp the qualities and effects of the operation of social capital in HC. Indeed, as we will see below, such lineages bear their trace in the hijabers' Instagram posts, and prompt us to conceptualise hijaberness as constituted by a 'composite habitus' – bodily comportments that betray the acute sensibilities both structured by and necessary to the successful navigation of the various distinct social environments that become available to people through their use of smartphones. (Waltorp 2015: 50). 'Composite habitus' is useful not only because it can afford access to the complex social implications of the hijaber phenomenon, but also because it can open space for acknowledging both the powerfully homogenising effects of platforms' cultures of use, and their important variations. We aver, more innovative understandings of such variations are needed; they cannot always be accounted for through reference to 'local specificities'. 'Composite habitus' advances the agenda for internationalising digital media studies by retrieving digital cultures evolving in the Global South from conceptual frames that relegate them to the derivation and particularity.

Hijabers in Indonesia

One of the most striking developments of the late-20th- and early 21st-century Indonesia has been the rapid increase in the number of Muslim women who wear the veil – a development with its roots in the growth of political and public Islam beginning during the 1990s. In the 1980s, veiling served as a sign of opposition to the authoritarian New Order regime, which was determined to quash the growth of political Islam (Ingham and Dirgantoro 2006, Jones 2010). But after the Suharto regime relaxed restrictions on political Islam in the 1990s, and as the consumer economy began to expand, notions of consumer choice began to infuse veiling practices, rendering veiling also a sign of the individual transformation consumerism makes possible. In the Indonesian context, then, hijab-wearing can be understood as a socially progressive move linked to women's increasing visibility with the expansion of consumer culture, rather than a socially conservative move aimed at preserving long-standing notions of Muslim femininity. As Slama and Barendregt point out, many young Southeast Asians are opting 'to live "the modern life" religiously and often in ways more orthodox than their parents or grandparents would have done only one or two generations before them' (2018: 4). Indeed, when Pramiyanti asked the research participants to qualify what constitutes a modern Muslim woman, they invoked a sense of veiling as something modern, and also a sense of dwelling in a marketplace for Muslim commodities, which presented them with an expanding array of choices.

IMA: Oh, a modern Muslimah (Muslim woman) is veiled but free to do as she wishes because now there are no limitations on veiled women. It used to be the case that it was difficult for veiled women to find a job – you had to unveil if you wanted to work. But now with the rise of Muslim fashion on Instagram, it's considered fine for veiled women to work (interview 13 October 2016).

SHAFIRA: I decided to don the veil when I started to see all the different styles on Instagram, and on television. From 2014 on hijab fashion has been growing, with more and more designers emerging. All the fun different styles on Instagram are so inspiring. There are so many online shops, too – all selling fun designs and some are really weird (interview, 13 October 2016).

The decision to don the veil presents women with a number of style choices, including the *jilbab* (a simple piece of cloth pinned under the chin), the *kerudung* (short veil loosely draped over the head leaving the hair partially visible), the *cadar* (a long, knee-length veil covering the face) and the *hijab* (colourful fabrics wrapped closely around the head, often associated with high-end fashion trends). Part of an increasingly crowded Islamic popular cultural field, these various styles of veiling are often tethered to established class positions, signalling various degrees of proximity to the modern and the global. Therefore, they exist in varying degrees of antipathy and affinity to one another. Islamic intellectuals, for example, look down upon tele-preachers, and the hijabers are keen to distance their style of veil from the simpler *jilbab*. For example, the hijabers adopted the term 'hijab' to distinguish their style of veiling from practices associated with the *jilbab* and deemed 'improper'. The so-called '*jilbab gaul*' (trendy veil), and later '*jilboobs*', phenomenon – by which women combined *jilbab*-wearing with tight-fitting jeans and tops showing their curves and sometimes their skin – was criticised by Islamic scholars, who deemed it failed to qualify as Islamic dress (Beta 2016: 26). The hijabers' use of the term 'hijab' worked to differentiate the style from *jilbab gaul*, but it also worked to mark it with global nuances.

The term 'hijabers' is specific to Indonesia, but its appearance in Indonesian lexicons coincided with that of resonant terms, like hijabistas (hijab and fashionista) or hijabsters (hijab and hipster) in Malaysia, Singapore, Middle East, the UK and North America (Lewis 2015; Tarlo 2010; Tarlo and Moors 2013). Use of the term 'gestures' towards the global – being a hijaber marks one as part of a global community of transnationally mobile Muslimah keen to present themselves as at once fashion conscious, tech-savvy, transnationally mobile career women in possession of considerable buying power. The Indonesian hijabers aspire to be global, but the cultural contexts they inhabit shape the meanings of their dress styles in ways that distinguish them from the hijabis in Muslim-minority contexts (Lewis 2015; Tarlo 2010; Tarlo and Moors 2013). Tarlo and Moors, for example, aver that Muslim women use Islamic fashion to 'disrupt and challenge public stereotypes about Islam, women, social integration and the veil, even if their voices are often drowned out in political and legal debates in these issues' (2013: 3). But the picture of hijabis as those who defy or resist a prevailing Islamophobia does not apply to the Indonesian hijabers, and our study of them shows how global Islamic fashion is unfolding in distinct ways at various conjunctures, Islamophobic and otherwise. Indeed, in her study of the HC on Instagram, Beta notes its discursive construction as a sign of middle classness and consumer power. She contends that the hijabers proffer a tame alternative to both the vulgar style of 'jilbab gaul' and the 'gloomy Arabic veils'; they flaunt 'their ability to adjust to a level of colorfulness—the fun, safe Muslims—that requires respectable financial means and in turn accretes as cultural capital: an ability to be accepted as global and cosmopolitan' (Beta 2014: 385).

Our research affirms this finding, but we propose an extended interpretation of it. In Beta's analysis, the taming of the veil is presented as a consequence of the expansion of Islamic consumer culture *in Indonesia*, whereas we contend that hijabers' rendering as 'fun, safe' Muslims may also be seen as a function of a *transnational* culture of Instagram's use (Duguay 2016; Marwick 2015), which sanctions performances of middle classness as an acceptable mode of bodily comportment on the platform, and reinforces the Hijabers' inherent elitism. At the same time, it is precisely this culture of use that enables the hijabers to take up positions as reformers within a broader field of Islamic communication. Armed with the cultural capital their hijabs afford them, hijabers use captions to interpret their photos through references to the al-Qu'uran and Hadith, thereby employing Instagram as a stage for dakwah, and both implicating themselves in and extending the fragmentation of Muslim authority that broadly manifests (Echchaibi 2011; Millie 2017; Slama 2017).

Keeping Cool, Staying Virtuous

In 'Keeping cool, staying virtuous', a study of young Danish Muslim women, Karen Waltorp discusses how their uses of social media both structure and are structured by norms governing acceptable comportment for young Muslim women. On the one hand, the women 'use smartphones and social media to reproduce moral norms, since they do not publicly question or challenge what should be considered private and what can be considered public, what is acceptable and not'. On the other hand, social media use opens up strategies 'through which they can conceive of possible ways to challenge… [such] norms'. Waltorp presents (one of her informants) Bita's social media use as exemplary of both the possibilities and limitations of smartphones for young Muslim women in Denmark. Bita wears the veil in Denmark but only sends photos to her boyfriend in Iran with her veil off, for fear that he will consider her 'boring and old-fashioned, wearing the veil in a European city where nobody forced her to' (Waltorp 2015: 50). She deleted her Facebook account on his request, but then established a new one using a pseudonym. Unbeknownst to her boyfriend, she and he share 300 friends on Facebook.

> She is monitoring him close, all the while he (thinks he) is controlling her visibility. Officially she complied, but through the smartphone and social media she has made her own rules in the relationship. She is keeping cool and staying virtuous.
>
> (Waltorp 2015: 50–52)

This kind of practice, which involves the concurrent performance of multiple identities in distinct fields, is evidence of what Waltorp, drawing on Bourdieu, calls a 'composite habitus' – bodily comportments that betray the acute sensibilities both structured by and necessary to the successful navigation of distinct social environments that become available through smartphone use (Bourdieu 1984: 169–208; Waltorp 2015: 50). Smartphones serve as extensions of the body, and enable people to straddle distinct 'fields' (realms of practice with unique sets of rules and forms of cultural capital), both concurrently and in the course of their everyday – for example, while walking to the shop, cooking or watching television at home, or hanging out in the mall. One may imagine, for example, that a veiled Bita could be hanging out with her friends downtown while sharing photos of her unveiled self with her boyfriend in Iran, and also while secretly surveilling him from her pseudonymous Facebook account.

Composite habitus is usefully applied to the hijabers, but here it manifests in a different way. The women Waltorp studies use social media to augment the spaces available to them for identity experimentation – online and offline they play with various subject positions in various fields, thereby revealing their agency in donning and removing the veil. The hijabers maintain a coherent identity, donning the veil both online and offline. However, their apparently coherent habitus is concurrently structured by and oriented to two distinct fields: on the one hand, a culture of Instagram use which posits the ideal woman as the consuming woman, and links female empowerment closely to her capacity to consume (high-end luxury goods) (Marwick 2015); on the other hand, developments in Islamic communication – specifically, the increasingly influential role women are playing in shaping public Islam. Such feminisation can be seen as a feature of a broader fragmentation of Muslim authority arising from the commodification of Islamic signs and the digitisation of Islamic communication.

Influencers and Microcelebrity

A number of writers contend that that the internet expands opportunities for what Goffman (1959) refers to as front-stage self-making, and what Jenny Sundén refers to as 'writing oneself into being' (2003: 13; Mendelson and Papacharissi 2011). With the advent and popularisation of web-based image sharing, such self-making increasingly proceeds through strategic manipulation and posting of photographs. Alluding to the rise of Instagram as evidence of the increasing importance of visual texts in contemporary culture, Highfield and Leaver point to the need for greater attention to images in the study of online identity performances, and Marwick argues that images offer qualitatively different resources for identity construction, and calls for new frameworks for understanding identity construction online. This chapter is specifically concerned with literature examining women's image making and image sharing on social media, especially the microcelebrity phenomenon and its key resource the selfie. Microcelebrity is a subset of celebrity defined by its relationship to particular media forms (the use of social media to gain celebrity status) and media practices (new branding and marketing strategies that take advantage of the affordances and cultures of social media platforms), and works on microcelebrity centre largely on debates concerning the extent to which women's work using social media to visibilise the empowered, consuming woman is in fact empowering

(Abidin 2016; Duffy and Hund 2015; Kavakci and Kraeplin 2017; Marwick 2013; Senft 2008).

Duffy and Hund lament microcelebrities' embodying of post-feminist ideas, in which female power is entangled with consumer power and 'individual choice, independence and modes of expression rooted in the consumer marketplace' are celebrated (Duffy and Hund 2015: 3). For example, positing the fictional Bridget Jones as a post-feminist icon (single working woman who lives at home yet hankers for a white wedding), McRobbie argues that 'elements of popular culture are perniciously effective in regard to this undoing of feminism, while simultaneously appearing to be engaging in a well-informed and even well-intended response to feminism' (2007: 255). Duffy and Hund contend that digital culture entrenches rather than challenges post-feminism by positing the consuming woman as the ideal woman: 'What is especially problematic about digital expressions of post-feminist self-brands is the extent to which visibility gets articulated through normative feminine discourses and practices, including those anchored in the consumer marketplace' (Duffy and Hund 2015: 3).

In a similar vein, both Marwick and Duguay argue that, aesthetically speaking, the kind of femininity being celebrated on Instagram rarely diverges from conventional standards of feminine beauty. In Marwick's study, Instagrammers display an affinity for emulating 'the tropes and symbols of traditional celebrity culture, such as glamourous self-portraits, designer goods and luxury cars' (Marwick 2013: 139). Duguay's comparative study of queer influencer Ruby Rose's accounts on Vine and Instagram highlights how the platform tames marginalised identities by presenting them as a subset of mainstream culture. On Vine, Rose appears in a full-throated embrace with her girlfriend but on Instagram the couple pose in shots depicting their coupledom as a variant of bourgeois, sex-evacuated bliss. But for Abidin, by using Instagram to stage disintermediated relationships between their performances of femininity labour and those who gaze upon it, microcelebrities capitalise on post-feminist ideology and extend ownership over the means of production (Abidin 2016a). Their image making endeavours are subversive, because they reframe selfies – constructed in the dominant discourse as frivolously vain – as a 'prized asset' the production of which makes visible women's tacit 'femininity labour' and reveals their intimate knowledge of how to manipulate, arrange and adorn their bodies to extend/augment its commodity value, enacting 'subversive frivolity' (Abidin 2016: 15–16).

Digitisation of Islamic Communication

In some respects the case of the hijabers supports Abidin's argument for the agency inherent in microcelebrity performances. The hijabers are certainly agents in the moulding of Islamic pop culture, possessing not only consumer power as individuals, but also the ability to generate new networked publics, involving the production, circulation and consumption of images by women and for women. These women use their cell phones and social media affordances to produce themselves, and design paths for circulating their self-productions, sparking dialogues across distant sites among female strangers commonly engaged in crafting the ideal look of the modern Muslimah. They enhance the visibility of women who lay claim to empowerment, and they develop technological prowess to forge trans-local connections among Muslim women who commonly idealise such values. Therefore, in Castellian terms, they possess 'network making power', that is 'power wielded by actors and networks of actors with the capacity to set up and program a network'. However, by virtue of their socio-economic position and capacity to consume, they also possess 'networking power': 'the power that actors in global networks exert over those excluded from the network' (Castells 2011: 773 470). Indeed, as we will see, the performance of hijaberness rests on exhibitions of such networking power; the hijabers are at pains to construct the hijaber habitus as a distinctly middle-class one, to which only the wealthy may belong. Such efforts work to link women's power exclusively to their identities as consumers, and validate the idea that the ideal woman is a consuming woman – an idea that suggests the less consuming power a woman has, the less worthy she is of being free.

It is this exclusionary dimension that renders the term 'subversive' a poor descriptor of the hijabers' frivolity, which serves to shore up rather than undermine existing class and gender divides. If the hijabers are to be deemed agentive, it is not for the way they capitalise on post-feminist ideology to extend ownership of the means of producing 'femininity labour', but for their role in advancing a broader feminisation of Islamic communication, entailing the increasingly influential role of women in the articulation of Islamic knowledge. Against this background, the hijabers can be seen to queer gender distinctions prevailing in the field of Islamic communication, by which the role of authoritative addresser is commonly constituted as male, and the role of listening, consuming addressee as female. On Instagram, hijabers adopt the tactics of microcelebrity culture to posit their consuming bodies as those capable of authoritatively addressing Muslimah in the interpretation of scripture. By doing so, they contribute to a phenomenon scholars have referred to as the fragmentation of Muslim authority in recent years.

Current scholarship on contemporary developments in Islamic communication has focused on such fragmentation, a function of digital uptake and the broader commoditisation of global Islam, both of which result in increased opportunities for undertaking and participating in preaching activities outside of the mosque. Echchaibi chronicles the rise of Baba Ali, a US-based preacher who uses humour and everyday language to deliver sermons on YouTube. Echchaibi sees Baba Ali as exemplary of a new clutch of Muslim preachers who are using digital media to reach transnational audiences, thereby delocalising sources of Muslim authority, 'generating new producers and locales of religious meaning in Dubai, London, Paris and Los Angeles' (Echchaibi 2011: 25, for other examples see Alatas 2017; Scholz et al. 2008). In Alatas', Echchaibi's and Scholz et al.'s studies, males employ new media to renegotiate existing authority structures. But scholars focusing on Indonesian Islam show how gender binaries are also being dismantled as preaching events increasingly extend beyond the mosque. Millie and Slama also both note the marked feminisation of Muslim audiences, and the new roles women are playing in shaping the articulation of authority.

In Millie's study of preaching events in West Java, for example, women commonly constitute 70% of the audience. Therefore, they play a pivotal role in sustaining the viability of preaching as a vocation, and preachers take care to orient themselves to the women attendees. They craft their oratory in ways designed to grab the women's attention, by telling jokes, singing songs and proffering interpretations of scripture that are sensitive to women's realities (Millie 2016: 132). Slama shows how mobile digital devices and digital social media endow the Muslimah with consumer agency in their dealings with preachers. Discussing the use of Whatsapp and Blackberry Messenger by middle-class women in Yogyakarta to seek affective connections and emotional support from *ustadz* (preachers) – a practice they refer to as 'charging their hearts', he writes: 'Put simply, ustadzs cannot risk ignoring the emotional needs of their female followers. If they cannot find the right words at the right time, their followers will choose to charge their hearts elsewhere' (Slama 2017: np).

Studying Visual Social Media

While images make up an increasingly large part of digital culture, available studies of visual social media offer few methods for qualitatively reading images – that is, for analysing their contents but also for understanding how their particular social efficacies might be distinct from those of text-based forms of identity construction. Abidin, for example, relies heavily on interviews and observational methods to understand the tacit labour involved in making and engaging with microcelebrity images (2016a, 2016b). In their chapter exploring 'methodological and ethical considerations' for studying visual social media, Highfield and Leaver also rely on hashtags rather than visual analysis methods to understand what Instagram images mean (2016: 47). Marwick uses Instagram images as hooks to discuss microcelebrity practice rather than to analyse their special potency as images (2015). Frosh alludes to this gap when he positions selfies in a historical trajectory of the evolution of photography as a media form, noting how 'non-representations and technological changes are made analytically pre-eminent in work on visual social media' (Frosh 2015: 1607).

In this chapter, we use Spyer and Steedly's notion of 'enframement' to hone in on images in a qualitative reading of the hijabers' Instagram posts. They write: '[b]y "enframement" we mean the various ways the image is foregrounded or separated from its general environment in order to be apprehended as an image', and lay out a range of devices for enframing images (Spyer and Steedly 2013: 19). These include border effects enclosing an image; depth of field and camera angles, which present the viewer with a framework by which to understand an image, bringing certain objects to the fore and relegating others to the background; frames of reference, or 'sets of ideas that direct how the image should be evaluated, viewed or comprehended'; and finally, language, including captions, but also the time stamps that appear on digital photographs, or thought balloons. We contend that a focus on enframement allows us to read the connotative dimensions of a form (photography) that purports to be merely denotative, as Barthes has argued (1977).

Many studies of microcelebrities focus on particular influencers (Kavakci and Kraeplin 2017; Marwick 2015). By contrast, our study applies the same treatment to elite and non-elite (founders and ordinary members), all included in the cohort of 26 hijabers interviewed by Pramiyanti between May and October 2016. This treatment is apt because our interest here is in the discursive fields structuring hijabers rather than the tactics used by individual microcelebrities to self-brand. Participants were recruited by targeting key elites (founders and social media administrators) and then snowball sampling ordinary members in Jakarta, Bandung and Yogyakarta. In order to understand how members of HC use Instagram to construct hijaberness, we analysed interviewees' accounts. Posts were coded manually by looking for core and common patterns. We discuss these patterns below, drawing attention to how multiple tactics are used to enframe hijaberness on Instagram. The analysis shows that any one post undergoes multiple enframements, and it is this enframing, we argue, that tugs the HC in two directions; like guy ropes, it tethers the hijabers to divergent fields, revealing the 'composite habitus' that constitutes hijaberness (Waltorp 2015).

Enframing Hijabers

Existing studies show how Muslim women use Instagram to link veiling to prevailing notions of feminine beauty (Jones 2017; Kavakci and Kraeplin 2017). They do so by presenting images of the hijabi body situated in non-places or culturally evacuated backgrounds that work to focus the viewer's gaze on the hijab-enframed face, suggesting its inherent beauty across space and time. In such images, the hijabi self appears evacuated of context (the background is blacked out or the portrait is taken at such close range that the background is unidentifiable), inviting an exclusive focus on the body and face, and allowing the hijabis to demonstrate that their veiled selves are well able to conform to conventional notions of beauty. This practice is also discernible in some of the hijabers' posts. For example, in one post, Syifa Fauziah, Chairwoman of HC Jakarta, appears as little more than a hijab-enframed face. Seated in the back of a car – a taxi perhaps – in an unidentifiable location, Fauziah looks away from the camera towards the light falling on her cheeks, her hand held delicately under her chin, as if to gesture to her averted gaze. Fauziah's face is heavily made up – lipstick, foundation and rouge all clearly visible on her fair skin and pert smile (Figure 15.1).

But images depicting the hijaber as a passive beauty are not common in the corpus of posts we collected. What distinguishes the Indonesian hijabers from those Kvakci and Kraeplin (2017) and Jones (2017) study is their interest in presenting as not only 'beautiful' but also especially empowered and independent Muslimah, and this requires a certain kind of enframement – setting her in a broader social world featuring performances of bodily and intellectual strength. Such strength is communicated in the posts in several ways. Some post images of themselves engaged in vigorous physical activity, others include posts that show them to be intrepid travellers (and, thus, that devout Muslim women are publicly present and active) and others still that highlight their roles as equal partners in marriage.

For example, contrasting the above-described post, in which Fauziah's veiled face occupies the entire frame of the photograph, a travel snap pans well back from her face, and shows her modestly dressed body engulfed by the well-recognisable rugged landscape of the Grand Canyon. This reframing directs the viewers gaze away from her beautifully veiled face, and towards her emplacement in iconic exotic settings.

Figure 15.1 @syifaf. Screengrabbed, July 2017.

This image is exemplary of how depth of field is being used to evince a sense of the hijaber as empowered for her mobility. What is being signified here is an agentive, active Muslimah publicness: not a publicness limited to inviting a gaze, but one that gazes back, if not into the camera, then at the 'other', the dry, rough-hewn American landscape (Figures 15.2–15.4).

The image of the hijabers as Muslimah in possession of agency is further reinforced by their posts showing them engaged in sporting activities. In Figure 15.5 Irina confidently rides a horse, and Figure 15.6 shows Ghina at an archery range. These posts, too, contrast those focusing on the veiled Muslimahs' physical beauty – rather than resting on her face, the camera pans back to enframe the hijaber in social settings attesting to her independence and physical vigour. In both images, too, the hijabers appear alone – unaccompanied by a man – and in both they also wear practical, sporty outfits – pants, mid-length hijabs and runners.

When hijabers appear side by side their husbands, it is in posts that posit the ideal marriage as one in which husband and wife enjoy equal status. In the posts below, Udhe and Fitri sit or stand at the same height as their husbands. Fitri and her husband are shown looking at an unknown object out of frame, suggesting a common purpose, and Udhe and her husband gaze into each others' eyes, suggesting reciprocity. Udhe captions her post thus:

> It becomes difficult if both parties don't make an effort. If one person has already tried to be romantic but the other person doesn't

Figure 15.2 @syifaf. Screengrabbed, July 2017.

Figure 15.3 @irineorene. Screengrabbed, January 2017.

Figure 15.4 @ghinaafaa. Screengrabbed, January 2017.

Figure 15.5 @ulydarojah. Screengrabbed, April 2017.

Figure 15.6 @fitriaulia. Screengrabbed, April 2017.

> even try, everything starts to fall away. Try to make habit of doing little things for each other, like opening the car door, eating from the same plate, feeding each other, being gentle with each other, giving each other presents, or going out once in a while.... From the simple to the complex things, the important thing is that both put in equal effort to keep the relationship happy and romantic until old age, noting the importance of keeping the harmony and intimacy between husband and wife.

This orienting of the HC towards the ideal of the independent Muslimah, and especially the way the hijabers use the trope of the empowered Muslimah wife, is significant in light of a Muslim feminist agenda, which for some time has been focused on agitating for the reform of the institution of marriage. In a chapter exploring how Islamicisation and democratisation co-constituted one another in early 21st-century Indonesia, Suzan Brenner reviews a number of Muslim initiatives that dedicated themselves in the 2000s to legislative reform on polygamy, domestic violence, marital rape and child brides (Brenner 2011: 478). Lobbying and campaigning by such groups resulted in the passing of a bill criminalising domestic violence in 2004, although their efforts to outlaw polygamy in the same year failed.

Notably, more recently the call for reforming the institution of marriage emerged again, after the world's first congress of Muslim scholars in Cirebon, West Java in 2017, which resulted in a fatwa denouncing these practices. Reporting on the Congress, Kathy Robinson writes: 'Violence against women and women's rights within the family were key issues.... The congress ended with ... fatwa reinforcing the value of female religious authority. The first fatwa argued for a minimum age of marriage of 18, the second, that sexual violence against women, including within marriage, is *haram* (forbidden)' (Robinson 2017, np). The hijabers do not explicitly reference the feminists' arguments, but their orientation towards transnational mobility, physical activity and, most notably, equality in marriage provides a soft popular cultural scaffolding for the Muslim feminist agenda, and implicitly challenges discourse of Muslimah femininity sanctioning the idea of God-given male superiority. Brenner discusses how such a discourse was invoked in a debate taking place in the late-1990s at a workshop organised by women's organisation Rifka Annisa:

> At [the seminar] some women in the audience voiced their skepticism toward the organization's methods and goals. One middle-aged woman accused Rifka Annisa of advocating divorce as the answer to domestic violence, even though Islam urges people to avoid it. Others in the audience saw Rifka Annisa as interfering with the God-given hierarchy that places husbands above their wives.

> In support of one attendee's remark that 'men's nature/destiny is to be above women' *(kodratnya pria ada di atas perempuan),* another woman in the audience reminded those present that, during the obligatory daily prayers, 'women are always behind men'—in other words, that men have a divine right to be leaders over women. A number of people in the mostly female audience applauded in response.
>
> (Brenner 2011: 482)

At the same time, however, the social settings that enframe the hijabers as mobile and independent women also identify them as those with access to sites and spaces restricted to people of considerable economic means. Consistently, these settings depict a world of high-end consumption featuring luxury sports, fancy restaurants, foreign foods and international tourism. Such consistency reveals the high-end setting as a key piece of visual vocabulary employed by the hijabers as they write themselves into Instagram, and works to limit the hijabers' empowerment to those who inhabit a middle-class subject positioning. Interestingly too, these spaces often reflect a decidedly Occidentalist orientation. For example, the hijabers' posts about their holidays depict them as independent and intrepid explorers, but also as those whose affinities for travel orient to the West rather than Muslim-majority countries, identifying them as a subset of a global, cosmopolitan elite, Muslim and otherwise. Food posts similarly work to identify the hijabers as members of a middle class. By posting an image of ramen, Wanda is able to register her presence at a Japanese restaurant – a setting well beyond the reach of any ordinary Indonesian. Indeed, Wanda suggests as much on the caption she pens to accompany the post:

> I am so grateful that Allah has blessed me with the ability to eat delicious food. I can buy anything I want. All my cravings can be satisfied. When I got home I felt so full I could barely stand. This turned my mind to people who live on the street – do they forget what it feels like to have a full stomach? Thank you Allah, please allow me to pass on your blessings to others.

Posts calling on Muslimah to enact acts of kindness during the fasting month, organised around the hashtag 'ibadah jangan kendor' (Don't let your worship slack off), also provide opportunities to showcase this middle-class habitus. The two images below were posted during this Ramadhan challenge programme organised around the hashtag. Figure 15.7 depicts an image of a pair of thongs (flip-flops), adorned with the words #ibadahjangankendor across the toe-line, which dafinamaalina donated to her office musholla (prayer room), and identifies her as a white-collar worker in a clean, carpeted office. Figure 15.8 depicts an image of prayer

Figure 15.7 @pratiwanda. Screengrabbed, July 2017.

Figure 15.8 @hijaberscommunity. Screengrabbed, July 2017.

mats atop a washing machine – in the comments, meiswari explains that these are the prayer mats she has taken home from the office to wash, in her expensive front-loader washing machine – an item that marks her as socioeconomically privileged: most Indonesians hand-wash their clothes in a bucket (Figure 15.9).

Next, we move to a consideration of the posts' captions, which affords a different interpretation again. Diverging from microcelebrity practice chronicled by other scholars, entailing the use of captions for product promotion (Abidin 2016), captions promoting products are not entirely absent from the posts, but they usually appear as 'parasitic' comments that take advantage of key hijaber' fame on Instagram to advertise hijab-related wares. The hijabers, by contrast, use captions to interpret their posts through reference to scripture – the Qur'an and Hadith. This enables them to claim their activities on Instagram as forms of dakwah, thereby framing hijaberness as something more than a subset of microcelebrity culture – it is also a mode of Islamic communication, analysis of which requires an engagement with work on contemporary developments in the mediation of Islamic knowledge. By claiming the sharing of images of their consuming bodies as forms of dakwah, the hijabers attest to the fragmentation of Muslim authority, a phenomenon linked variously to electronic mediation (Echchaibi 2011; Scholz et al 2008), and the increasingly important role female consumers are playing in shaping interpretations of scripture (Millie 2017; Slama 2017).

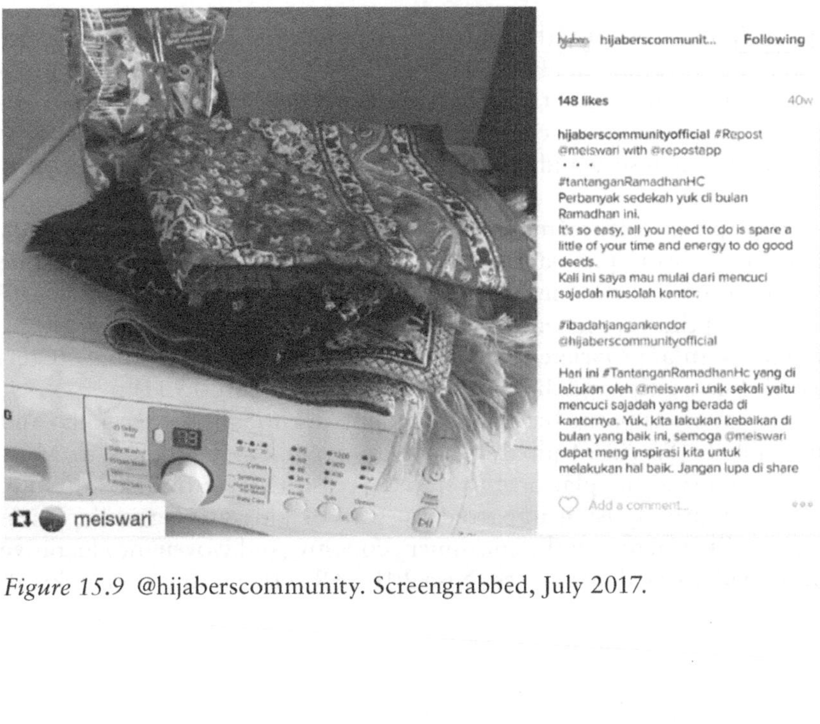

Figure 15.9 @hijaberscommunity. Screengrabbed, July 2017.

Captions allow the hijabers to present themselves as pious subjects, aware of their good fortune, au fait with scripture and confident in its interpretation, observant of the daily rhythm of prayer and always eager to do good deeds. In the posts we collected, hijabers' dakwah efforts are abundantly evident. For example, Syifa Fauziah interprets the above-discussed image of herself at the Grand Canyon by way of a flowery citation from the Qur'an which reads:

> Who has created the seven heavens layering one upon the other, you can see no fault in the creations of the Most Beneficent. Then look again: Can you see any rifts? Then look again and yet again, your sight will return to you in a state of humiliation.
>
> (Surat Al-Mulk verse 3–4).

Similarly, Wanda to a post depicting sites featured in her tour of Europe, Wanda appends a caption expressing her humility as a subject of Allah:

> Allah, please allow me to add other stars as many as possible on Your blessed earth. It is not only about taking pictures to feed my Instagram, but it is more to feed my soul. Because little that I knew, a tinie-tiny human like me needs to learn more from other creatures in other places. I go somewhere as no-one, then I come him still as no-ne but with many stories to tell. May this map always (leeds) to you. #alhamdullilah #travelgram #traveling #solotravel #backpacking #tourist #europetrip #map #lessonlearned #terimakasihlpdp

The included hashtags also enframe the caption, providing the reader with more information about her trip. By way of the hashtags, we learn that she undertook the trip as a solo backpacker, and that it was related to a government scholarship to study overseas ('lpdp'). Leeds is mentioned because Wanda undertook her master's degree in Leeds, UK (Figure 15.10).

Other posts feature more flippant or humorous captions. Ghaida Tsuraya, for example, captions an image of herself outside a mosque in Turkey with a passing reference to the 'Keep Calm and Carry On' dictum – in this case amended to refer to dzikir (remembrance of Allah), offered as an appropriate remedy for a state of anxiety: 'Galau? (Confused?) Keep Calm and dzikir on', she advises (Figure 15.11).

In her analysis of the Instagram accounts UkhtiSally (Sister Sally) and Duniajilbab (World of jilbab), Eva Nisa argues that Indonesian Muslimah are using the platform to develop a 'soft' form of dakwah – i.e. a form of proselytising imparted by way of glossy images, depicting women as key actors in the consumer economy, and woven into lucrative social media-based businesses (Nisa 2018: 68–71). The hijabers' dakwah

Figure 15.10 @pratiwanda. Screengrabbed, July 2017.

Figure 15.11 @gdaghaida. Screengrabbed, June 2017.

efforts may be similarly described as 'soft' (as opposed to 'hard' sermons at preaching events) for their reliance on images and discourses of consumption, and both cases – the hijaber case and Nisa's study – extend discussion of the feminisation of Muslim publics proceeding as part of the fragmentation of Muslim authority (Echchaibi 2011; Scholz et al. 2008). As touched on earlier, Milllie's and Slama's studies show how the fragmentation of Muslim authority affords new roles for women in public Islam. As audience members and consumers, women are positioned to shape preaching practices.

The hijaber case extends this work attending to women's expanded role in public Islam, because it shows how they exert power not only as consumers of religious authority. They, like the Instagrammers of which Nisa writes, style *themselves* as religious authorities, interpreting images of their consumerist selves through reference to the Quran and Hadith to offer Islamically flavoured style and lifestyle advice for a young Muslimah middle-class public on Instagram. This use of Instagram positions the hijabers as not only a subset of post-feminist microcelebrity culture on Instagram, but also a feature of the fragmentation of Muslim authority, entailing the proliferation of Muslim authority figures whose power rests on their ability to command audiences outside of mosque contexts. Advanced concurrently by consumerist ideology and digital uptake, this fragmenting transforms the gender politics of Muslim public-ness. It feminises Muslim audiences, Muslim address and even (in the case of the hijabers) the notion of Muslim authority.

The Virtues and Limits of Consumer Sovereignty

In Indonesia, the hijab has evolved, in contradistinction to other forms of veiling such as the jilbab and the kerudung, as a sign of consumer sovereignty: the ability to mix and match, devise a unique style, transform yourself, be yourself. Indeed, the hijbers use their Instagram posts to present visual evidence of the hijab as a sign of consumer sovereignty. Much of this evidence takes the form of documents of the hijabers' middle-class lifestyles – the expensive clothes they wear, the expensive places they go. On Instagram, the way the hijabs put their sovereignty on display is to repeatedly and overtly tie it to wealth: a capacity to choose is being linked to a capacity to consume. This is not a phenomenon brought about by the spread of online social media. Since the expansion of commercial television and the advertising industry in the 1990s has commonly settled down on middle-class bodies. But a transnational culture of Instagram's use reinforces the link between the hijab's function as a sign of consumer sovereignty and a middle-class positioning and therefore rearticulates a middle-class cultural ascendance. The hijabers rely on this ascendance to invest their particular style of veiling with cultural capital.

However, these documents of the hijabers' wealth and middle class lifestyles also provide evidence of other things. Not only is the hijaber a sovereign consumer who mixes and matches items in her wardrobe to come up with a unique look. She is also one who is sovereign in other ways: fit, active and publicly present, and engaged in monogamous marriages in which husband and wife are considered equal. Therefore, the hijabers cash in on the cultural capital their middle classness affords them into order to buy into the myth of consumer sovereignty, but also into other kinds of sovereignty, linked to mobility and equal marriage partnerships. They echo a Muslim feminist agenda but wrap it in a discourse of consumer sovereignty.

In this chapter, we have drawn on Spyer and Steedly to study the enframement of hijab-wearing in the hijabers' posts, thereby undertaking a visual analysis to understand how meanings of hijaberness are communicated via combinations of images and captions (2013: 19). The analysis shows that any one post undergoes multiple enframements (even prior to its circulation – a process that entails the ongoing re-enframement of the image through reposts, the addition of hashtags and @mentions), rendering the posts polysemic. Hijabers enframe their Instagram images largely by playing with borders, depth of field, frames of reference and captions.

Other hijabi celebrity accounts feature self-portraits taken at a close range, often with a non-identifiable or out-of-focus background (Jones 2017; Kavakci and Kraeplin 2017). In such portraits, the hijab borders the face, accentuating its Muslim-ness, offering the hijabers opportunities to demonstrate that hijab-wearing conforms to conventional notions of feminine beauty, denoted by the youthful, made-up, fair-skinned face. Some such portraits appear in the corpus we collected, but the hijabers favour self-portraits that emplace them in a deeper field: broader 'everyday' settings revealing of her bodily and mental agency, and identify her as more than just an object of a gaze. Consistently, such everyday settings enhance the hijabers' performance of empowerment on Instagram by identifying her as a certain kind of social subject – one who enjoys free access to spaces limited to the well-to-do. Frames of reference work to naturalise a claim to empowerment that is contingent on class privilege, a culture of Instagram's use deems the performance of advanced consumer power a fit and proper bodily comportment on the platform. Finally, the hijabers also enframe their images through use of captions to interpret the visual evidence of their bodily agency, independence and consumer power as key elements of Islamic practice. These multiple enframings reveal HC's locatedness in two distinct fields, each of which holds distinct implications for analysing the HC.

The first is a global consumer culture, Muslim and otherwise, accessible only to the well-to-do, constructed from a visual grammar alluding to holidays in Europe and the USA (at least in the case of Asians), fine dining and white-collar careers. In this, the hijabers reflect broader culture of Instagram use favouring representations of femininity in keeping with a mainstream (Duguay 2016; Marwick 2015). Arguably, this limits women's power to their consumer power, affirming Duffy and Hund's assertion that microcelebrity culture reproduces dominant gender norms (2015). In their glossy, thoughtfully composed images of their middle-class everyday, the hijabers both emulate corporate media (they make hijaberness look like a tv ad or a glossy magazine) and bring threatening identities in to a mainstream fold (i.e. they retrieve veiling from the threat of *jilboobs* and *jilbab gaul*). In light of Marwick's and Duguay's arguments, we may surmise that this taming is a function of a transnational culture of Instagram use – it is linked to how Instagram is discursively constituted as a media form, and demonstrates the operation of what Spyer and Steedly refer to as frames of reference: 'sets of ideas that direct how the image should be evaluation, viewed or comprehended' (2013: 19). Nevertheless, with a nod to Abidin's 'subversive frivolity', we posit that cloaking themselves in middle-class consumer culture enables the hijabers to present controversial female subjectivities (for example, the Muslimah wife who stands on an equal footing with her husband) in a palatable format (2016a). In this way, they shape Muslimah pop culture consumers' aspirations in a way synchronous with a Muslim feminist agenda to reform the institution of marriage.

The second is a field of specifically Islamic communication, rapidly changing as new technologies and new practices for imparting and consuming Islamic knowledge emerge in context of changes to the way Islam is being practised in Indonesia. This latter field harbours a more nuanced gender politics than the former, partly because of a context of flux in Islamic communication, rendering dominant gender norms somewhat up for grabs. Therefore, works such as Duffy and Hund's, which presume a settled consensus on what constitutes 'normative feminine discourses and practices', are inapplicable to this context (Duffy and Hund 2015: 3). If the hijabers are to be considered agentive in the shaping of Islamic communication, it is not for the way they capitalise on post-feminist ideology to extend ownership of the means of producing femininity. Rather, it is for the way they interpret images of their consuming selves through reference to the Qur'an or Hadith, thereby positioning themselves as holders and imparters of Islamic knowledge. On Instagram, hijabers adopt the tactics of microcelebrity culture to posit their consuming bodies as those capable of authoritatively addressing Muslimah in the interpretation of scripture.

Acknowledgement

This article was produced with funding from the Australia Research Council ('Mobile Indonesians: social differentiation and digital literacies in the 21st century' DP130102990) and the Indonesian Directorate General of Higher Education.

References

Abidin, Crystal. (2016) 'Aren't These Just Young, Rich Women Doing Vain Things Online? Influencer Selfies as Subversive Frivolity', *Social Media and Society*, 1(2), 1–17.

Alatas, Farie. (2017) 'Sufi Sociality in Social Media. In 'Piety, Celebrity, Sociality: A Forum on Islam and Social Media in Southeast Asia', in Slama, Martin and Jones, Carla (eds), *American Ethnologist*. Available: http://americanethnologist.org/features/collections/sufi-socilaity-in-social media, accessed: 8 November 2017.

Barthes, Roland. (1977) *Image, Music, Text*, New York: Hill and Wang.

Beta, Annisa. (2014) 'Hijabers: How Young Urban Muslim Women Redefine Themselves in Indonesia', *International Communication Gazette*, 74(4–5): 377–389.

Beta, Annisa. (2016) 'Socially Mediated Publicness in Networked Society for Indonesian Muslim Women', *Jurnal Ilmu Komunikasi*, 13(1): 19–30.

Bourdieu, Pierre. (1984) *Distinction: A Social Critique of the Judgement of Taste*, Cambridge, MA: Harvard University Press.

Brenner, Susan. (1996) 'Reconstructing Self and Society: Javanese Muslim Women and 'The Veil', *American Ethnologist*, 23(4): 673–697.

Brenner, Susan. (2011) 'Private Moralities in the Public Sphere: Democratization, Islam, and Gender in Indonesia', *American Anthropologist*, 113(3): 478–490.

Castells, Manuel. (2011) 'A Network Theory of Power', *International Journal of Communication*, 5: 773–787.

Duffy, Brooke Erin and Hund, Emily. (2015) 'Having It All' on Social Media: Entrepreneurial Femininity and Self-Branding Among Fashion Bloggers', *Social Media and Society*, 1(2): 1–11.

Duguay, Stefanie. (2016) 'Lesbian, Gay, Bisexual, Trans, and Queer Visibility Through Selfies: Comparing Platform Mediators Across Ruby Rose's Instagram and Vine Presence. *Social Media + Society*, 2(2), 1–12.

Echchaibi, Nabil. (2011) 'From Audio Tapes to Video Blogs: The Delocalisation of Authority in Islam'. *Nations and Nationalism*, 17, 25–44.

Frosh, Paul. (2015) 'The Gestural Image: The Selfie, Photography Theory, and Kinesthetic Sociability', *International Journal of Communication*, 9: 1607–1628.

Goffman, Erving. (1959) *The Presentation of Self in Everyday Life*. Garden City, AT: Doubleday.

Highfield, Tim and Leaver, Tama. (2016) 'Instagrammatics and Digital Methods: Studying Visual Social Media, From Selfies and Gifs to Memes and Emoji', *Communication Research and Practice*, 2(1): 47–62.

Ingham, Sue and Dirgantoro, Wulandani. (2006) 'Identity, Religion, Repression, or Fashion ? The Indonesian Jilbab', *Broadsheet*, 36(1), 25–29.

Jones, Carla. (2010) 'Materializing Piety: Gendered Anxieties about Faithful Consumption in Contemporary Urban Indonesia', *American Ethnologist*, 37(4): 617–637.

Jones, Carla. (2017) 'Circulating Modesty: The Gendered Afterlives of Networked Images in 'Piety, Celebrity, Sociality: A Forum on Islam and Social Media in Southeast Asia', in Slama, Martin and Jones, Carla (eds) *American Ethnologist*. Available: http://americanethnologist.org/features/collections/piety-celebrity-sociality/circulating-modesty, accessed: 8 November 2017.

Kavakci, Elif and Kraeplin, Camille.(2017) 'Religious Beings in Fashionable Bodies: The Online Identity Construction of *Hijabi* Social Media Personalities', *Media, Culture and Society*, 39(6): 850–868.

Lewis, Reina. (2015) *Muslim Fashion: Contemporary Style Cultures*, Durham, NC: Duke University Press.

Marwick, Alice. (2015) 'Instafame: Luxury Selfies in the Attention Economy', *Public Culture*, 27: 137–160.

McRobbie, Angela. (2007) 'Postfeminism and Popular Culture', *Feminist Media Studies*, 43: 255–264.

Mendelson, Andrew and Papacharissi, Zizi. (2011) 'Look at us collective narcissism in college student Facebook photo galleries. In Z. Papacharissi (ed.), A networked self: Identity, community and culture on social network sites (pp. 251–273). New York, NY: Routledge.

Millie, Julian. (2017) *Hearing Allah's Call: Preaching and Performance in Indonesian Islam*, Ithaca, NY: Cornell University Press.

Nisa, Eva. (2018) 'Creative and Lucrative Da'wa: The Visual Culture of Instagram amongst Female Muslim Youth in Indonesia', *Asiascape: Digital Asia*, 5: 68–99.

Robinson, Kathryn. (2017) 'Female Ulama Voice a Vision for Indonesia's future', *New Mandala*, 30 May 2017. Available: www.newmandala.org/female-ulama-voice-vision-indonesias-future/, accessed: 30 May 2017.

Scholz, J., Selge T., Stille, M. and Zimmermann, J. (2008) 'Listening Communities? Some Remarks on the Construction of Religious Authority in Islamic Podcasts', *Die Welt des Islams*, 48(3): 457–509.

Senft, Teresa. (2008) *Camgirls: Celebrity and Community in the Age of Social Networks. Digital Formations*, New York: Peter Lang.

Slama, Martin. (2017) 'Heart to Heart on Social Media: Affective Aspects of Islamic Practice in 'Piety, Celebrity, Sociality: A Forum on Islam and Social Media in Southeast Asia', in Slama, Martin and Jones, Carla (eds) *American Ethnologist*, 8 November 2017. Available: http://americanethnologist.org/features/collections/piety-celebrity-sociality/heart-to-heart-on-social-media, accessed: 8 November 2017.

Slama, Martin and Barendregt, Bart. (2018) 'Introduction: Online Publics in Muslim Southeast Asia: In Between Religious Politics and Popular Pious Practices', *Asiascape: Digital Asia*, 5: 3–31.

Spyer, Patricia and Steedly, Mary Margaret (eds.) (2013) *Images that Move*, Santa Fe, NM: School for Advanced Research Press.

Sundén, Jenny. (2003) *Material Virtualities*, New York: Peter Lang Publishing.

Tarlo, Emma (2010) 'Hijab Online', *Interventions* 12(2): 209–225.

Tarlo, Emma and Moors, Annelies (eds.) (2013) *Islamic Fashion and Anti-Fashion: New Perspectives from Europe and North America*, New York: Bloomsbury.

Waltorp, Karen. (2015) 'Keeping Cool, Staying Virtuous: Social Media and the Composite Habitus of Young Muslim Women in Copenhagen', *Medie Kultur*, 58: 49–67.

List of Contributors

Adrian Athique is an Associate Professor in cultural studies in the Institute for Advanced Studies in the Humanities, University of Queensland. He was previously Chair of the School of Arts at the University of Waikato. Adrian has published extensively on Asian media and digital sociology, including the books: *The Multiplex in India: A Cultural Economy of Urban Leisure* (with Douglas Hill, Routledge 2010), *Indian Media: Global Approaches* (Polity 2012), *Digital Media and Society: An Introduction* (Polity 2013), *Transnational Audiences: Media Reception on a Global Scale* (Polity 2016) and *The Indian Media Economy* (two volumes, edited with Vibodh Parthasarathi and SV Srinivas, Oxford University Press, 2018).

Emma Baulch is an Associate Professor of media and communications at Monash University Malaysia. Her research examines Indonesian media and popular culture from the perspective of everyday life, with a specific focus on how media technologies shape social life. Her PhD was a study of the role electric guitars played in shaping communities of amateur musicians in Bali in the late-1990s, published by Duke University Press in 2007 as *Making Scenes: Death metal, Punk and Reggae in 1990s' Bali*. Her postdoctoral work examined how television and digital technologies influence the formation of pop music genres, and is forthcoming as a book, titled *Genre Publics: Pop, Technologies and Class in Indonesia* with Wesleyan University Press. Baulch's current research examines digital infrastructures and everyday life in South East Asia. In 2017, with Jerry Watkins and Amina Tariq, she co-edited *mHealth innovation in Asia: Grassroots Challenges and Practical Interventions* (Springer).

Angela Daly is an Assistant Professor in the Chinese University of Hong Kong Faculty of Law, and holds adjunct positions at Queensland University of Technology (Australia) and the Tilburg Institute of Law, Technology and Society (Netherlands). She is a socio-legal scholar of the regulation of new technologies. She is the author of *Private Power, Online Information Flows and EU* Law (Hart 2016) and *Socio-Legal Aspects of the 3D Printing Revolution* (Palgrave 2016), and is the co-editor of *Good Data* (Institute of Network Cultures 2019). She was lead Chief Investigator on the UK Intellectual Property Office-funded '3D Printing and IP Law Futures' project (2016–2018).

Michele Ford is a Professor of Southeast Asian studies and the Director of the Sydney Southeast Asia Centre at the University of Sydney, Australia. Michele's research interests focus on labour movements, labour migration and trade union aid. Michele is the author of *From Migrant to Worker: The Global Union Federations and Labor Migration in Asia* (Cornell ILR Press 2019) and *Workers and Intellectuals: NGOs, Unions and the Indonesian Labour Movement* (NUS/Hawaii/KITLV 2009). She is the editor *of Social Activism in Southeast Asia* (Routledge 2013) and a co-editor of several volumes including *Activists in Transition: Progressive Politics in Democratic Indonesia* (Cornell in press), *Beyond Oligarchy: Wealth, Power, and Contemporary Indonesian Politics* (Cornell SEAP 2014) and *Women and Labour Organizing in Asia: Diversity, Autonomy and* Activism (Routledge 2008).

Gerard Goggin is Professor of Media and Communications at the University of Sydney. He has a longstanding interest in social, cultural, political, and human rights dynamics of Internet, mobile media, and other digital technologies. Key publications include *Location Technology in International Context* (2019), *Routledge Companion to Global Internet Histories* (2017), *Disability and the Media* (2015), *Global Mobile Media (2011), Cell Phone Culture* (2006), *Virtual Nation: The Internet in Australia* (2004), and *Digital Disability* (2003).

Luke Heemsbergen is a Lecturer in communication at Deakin University. His research and teaching seek to light fires and build bridges at the intersection of digital communication and political life. His core research stream engages how radical decentralisations of communication technologies and practices afford shifts in democratic governance. This includes considering new formations and functions of publics through radical transparency and the social-political implications of distributed 3D printing.

Michael Keane is a Professor of Chinese media and cultural studies at Curtin University, Perth. He is an author or editor of 15 books on China's media. Michael's most recent book is *The Chinese Television Industry* (BFI Palgrave 2015). He is a program leader of the Digital China Lab at Curtin University. Michael's expertise includes China's cultural and media policy, creative industries in China and East Asia, Chinese and East Asian media, TV formats in Asia and East Asian cultural exports.

Akshaya Kumar received his PhD degree in film and television studies from the University of Glasgow, UK. He joined IIT Indore in December 2017 as an Assistant Professor in the School of Humanities and Social Sciences. He is currently finishing a manuscript provisionally titled *Provincializing Bollywood: Bhojpuri Cinema in a Comparative Media Crucible*, and his essays have appeared in *Social Text, Television and New Media, South Asia: Journal of South Asian Studies* and other leading journals in media and cultural studies.

Luzhou Nina Li is a Lecturer in Communications and Media Studies in the School of Media, Film and Journalism at Monash University, Australia. Her research focuses on digital culture, global media and cultural industries, media history, Chinese media, among others. Her work has appeared in *Television & New Media*, *International Journal of Cultural Studies*, and *Media, Culture & Society*.

Jozon A. Lorenzana is an Assistant Professor in the Department of Communication, School of Social Sciences, Ateneo de Manila University. Dr Lorenzana's research interests include skilled migration in the Global South, cultures of the Filipino middle classes, the social consequences of new media and the anthropology of moralities. His recent papers are published in journals such as *Bandung: Journal of the Global South* and *New Media and Society*.

Jiajie Lu completed his PhD with the Digital Media Research Centre, Queensland University of Technology, in 2017 and is now a lecturer of media and communication in the College of Literature and Media at Dongguan University of Technology in Dongguan, China. His research and teaching attempt to develop a multicultural approach to understand how media technologies influence human society in various cultural contexts.

Fiona Martin researches digital journalism and dialogic technologies, as well as the uses, politics and regulation of online media. She is the co-author of *Sharing News Online* (Routledge, 2018) and has contributed to *Internet Research Ethics for the Social Media Age* (Peter Lang, 2017) and *Ethics for Digital Journalists: Emerging Best* Practices (Routledge, 2014). She is a co-author and editor of *The Value of Public Service Media* (Nordicom, 2013) with Gregory F. Lowe.

Tom McDonald is an Assistant Professor at the University of Hong Kong. He obtained his PhD in anthropology from University College London in 2013, where he also worked on the *Why We Post* project, a European Research Council-funded global comparative ethnographic study exploring the impact of social media use across a range of different societies. His monograph, *Social Media in Rural China: Social*

Networks and Moral Frameworks (UCL Press), was published in 2016. He also co-authored the volume *How the World Changed Social Media* (UCL Press, 2016). McDonald is currently working on a new Hong Kong Research Grants Council-funded project investigating the use of digital money by migrant workers in China.

Rajiv Mishra is currently completing his PhD at Jawaharlal Nehru University, New Delhi. His research interests include the social-technical interfaces arising from the conceptualisation, design and implementation of digital systems in the social domain.

Tom O'Regan is a Professor of media and cultural studies at the University of Queensland. His research interests are in production studies of film, television and new media; audience measurement of broadcasting and cultural institutions. Tom has been a key figure in the development of cultural and media studies in Australia and is a co-author of *Rating the Audience: The Business of Media* (2011) with M. Balnaves and B. Goldsmith, *Local Hollywood: Global Film Production and the Gold Coast* (2010) with B. Goldsmith and S. Ward, *The Film Studio: Film Production in the Global Economy* (2005) and *Cinema Cities/Media Cities* (2003) with B. Goldsmith; and *The Future for Local Content* (2001) with Goldsmith, Cunningham and Thomas. He is also the author of *Australian National Cinema* (1996) and *Australian Television Culture* (1992). He also co-edited *Mobilising the Audience* (UQP, 2002) on audience development strategies in the arts and media sectors.

Joy Hannah Panaligan is part of the digital labour research team under the Newton Tech4Dev network, a collaboration between De La Salle University and University of Leicester and funded by the British Council. Joy has a Master of Arts degree in applied media studies from De La Salle University.

Alila Pramiyanti is a PhD candidate at the Digital Media Research Centre, Queensland University of Technology, Australia, and a lecturer at Telkom University, Indonesia.

Aegyung Shim received her PhD in film studies, arts and media from the University of New South Wales, and she presently researches transnational aspects of Asia's film, digital media and entertainment industries. She was a Korea Foundation Research Fellow and visiting scholar in the Institute for Social Transformation Research at the University of Wollongong, and is the co-author of *Korea's Occupied Cinemas, 1893–1948* (2011, Routledge), *The Changing Face of Korean Cinema, 1960–2015* (2016, Routledge) and *South Korea's Immersive Webtooniverse and the New Media Revolution* (forthcoming, Rowman and Littlefield International) – all with Brian Yecies.

Cheryll Ruth R. Soriano is an Associate Professor in the Department of Communication at De La Salle University in Manila. Broadly, her research focuses on the intersections of digital cultures and social inequality. From end December of 2016 until April 2017, she was an Australia-APEC Women in Research Fellow hosted by the Centre for Communication, Politics and Culture of the School of Media and Communication of the Royal Melbourne Institute of Technology. Her co-edited book, *Asian Perspectives on Digital Culture: Emerging Phenomena, Enduring Concepts* (with Sun Sun Lim), was published under Routledge's Internationalizing Media Studies series.

Pradip Thomas is an Associate Professor in the School of Communication and Arts, University of Queensland. His research focuses on communication and social change, communication rights, political economy of communications, religion and media. He has served as Vice President of the International Association of Media and Communications Research and is the author and editor of several books on the media in India including *Strong Religion, Zealous Media: Christian Fundamentalism and Communication in India* (2008, Sage), *Political Economy Of Communications in India: The Good, The Bad and The Ugly* (2010, Sage), *Negotiating Communication Rights: Case Studies from India. New Delhi, India* (2011, Sage) and *Digital India: Understanding Information, Communication and Social Change* (Sage, 2012).

Ariadne Vromen is a Professor of political sociology at the University of Sydney, and her research interests include political participation, social movements, advocacy organisations, digital politics, and young people and politics. Ariadne has completed extensive research on young people's political engagement. She has recently published her book: *Digital Citizenship and Political Engagement: The Challenge from Online Campaigning and Advocacy Organisations* (2017, Palgrave Macmillan).

Kimberlee Weatherall is a Professor of law at the University of Sydney Law School, teaching and researching across intellectual property law and the IP-trade nexus. She is the editor, with Dr Rebecca Giblin, of *What if We Could Reimagine Copyright* (2017, ANU Press). She was a member of the Australian Government's Advisory Council on IP and the Advisory Committee Member to the Australian Law Reform Commission Inquiry, *Copyright and the Digital Economy.* Kimberlee is also a board member of the Australian Digital Alliance. She is a member of the Australian Computer Society's Technical Advisory Board on Artificial Intelligence Ethics.

Adele Webb is a PhD researcher at the University of Sydney, studying democratic theory and its application to political histories and contemporary political dynamics in Asia.

Huan Wu is a Research Associate working at Digital China Lab in Curtin University. She received her doctoral degree from the Chinese University of Hong Kong and has worked in Shanghai Jiao Tong University. Her research interests include the development of creative industries in China and the interaction between new media and disadvantaged groups.

Jie 'Jack' Yang is a Lecturer in Big Data and Database Programming in the School of Computing and Information Technology at the University of Wollongong. He completed his MA from Huazhong University of Science and Technology, China, and he received his PhD in spatial modelling from the University of Wollongong, Australia. His research involves translating conceptual models into implementation programs and code prototyping for machine learning algorithms, and he brings together different aspects of computing methodology, such as deep learning, clustering, and Hadoop/Spark-based technique for massive data processing. Dr. Yang has contributed to numerous cross-discipline projects, and he is currently a chief investigator on the 2018–2020 ARC Discovery Project, 'Mobile Webtoons: Creative Innovation in a New Digital Economy' – with Associate Professor Brian Yecies.

Brian Yecies is an Associate Professor in Communications and Media at the University of Wollongong. He researches on film and digital media, creative industries, cultural policy, Big Data and digital humanities research methods. He is a chief investigator on two Australian Research Council Discovery Projects: Digital China: From Cultural Presence to Innovative Nation (2017–19), and Mobile Korean Webtoons: Creative Innovation in a New Digital Economy (2018–20). His books include *Korea's Occupied Cinemas, 1893–1948* (Routledge, 2011), *The Changing Face of Korean Cinema, 1960–2015* (Routledge, 2016), and *South Korea's Immersive Webtooniverse and the New Media Revolution* (Rowman and Littlefield, forthcoming) – co-authored with Aegyung Shim, as well as *Willing Collaborators: Foreign Partners in Chinese Media* (Rowman and Littlefield, 2018) – co-edited with Michael Keane and Terry Flew.

Haiqing Yu is an Associate Professor and Vice Chancellor's Principal Research Fellow in the Digital Ethnography Research Centre, School of Media and Communication, RMIT University, Australia. She researches the sociopolitical and economic impact of China's digital media, communication and culture on China, Australia and the Asia Pacific; and is currently working on projects related to China's digital expansion in Asia, Chinese-language digital/social media in Australia and digital economies of disability.

Index

For Product Safety Concerns and Information please contact our EU
representative GPSR@taylorandfrancis.com Taylor & Francis Verlag
GmbH, Kaufingerstraße 24, 80331 München, Germany